With the gospel accounts under more scrutiny than ever, J. Warner Wallace crafts an original defense for the claims of Christ. In *Person of Interest*, he wields not only his investigative wit but also his narrative expertise. You'll be glad you came along for this case!

Greg Laurie, senior pastor of Harvest Christian Fellowship,
author of *Billy Graham: The Man I Knew*

J. Warner Wallace is the most creative and intrepid detective I've ever met. Having worked with him on several episodes of NBC's *Dateline*, I've seen firsthand his uncanny ability to discover clues where no one else sees them. Wallace's unique capacity to piece together a case has resulted in several complex crimes being solved. Now Wallace tackles perhaps his toughest case: solving a deeply personal mystery involving his own religious faith. In *Person of Interest*, he cleverly intertwines the story of a highly challenging crime he cracked as a parallel to his own personal quest. Skillfully uncovering clues, connecting the dots, Wallace makes the case that being a believer is his true calling.

Robert Dean, producer of NBC News *Dateline*

Jim shows readers how Jesus is the only person able to fulfill every Old Testament prophecy of the coming Messiah and what systems needed to be in place for the Savior's message to spread throughout the known world. It's the fine-tuning argument filtered across history.

Hillary Morgan Ferrer, president of Mama Bear Apologetics

In this innovative new book, America's foremost cold-case detective uses his astute mind and sharp investigative skills to explore the evidence for Jesus outside the Bible and why he remains relevant even in our increasingly skeptical culture. Just as criminals can't escape Jim's pursuit, truth can't hide from his investigative acumen. Follow the clues and emerge encouraged!

Lee Strobel, bestselling author, founder of the Strobel Center for
Evangelism and Applied Apologetics at Colorado Christian University

What explosive event split world history in two? The stunning conclusion of this master cold-case homicide detective's meticulous research, analysis, and deliberation will leave Christians delighted and skeptics devastated.

Gregory Koukl, president of Stand to Reason (str.org),
author of *Tactics* and *The Story of Reality*

In *Person of Interest*, J. Warner Wallace has combined an impressive depth of research with his sharp detective skills. If you read this book, you will have to reckon with Jesus, not just as a historical person but as Lord and Savior.

Alisa Childers, author of *Another Gospel*, host of the *Alisa Childers Podcast*

Tired of the dreary academic apologist writing in a hard-to-comprehend English dialect? Then this is the book for you. Wallace makes an engaging and compelling case for Jesus and his deity. If you want sheer enjoyment with routine punches of power-filled Jesus facts, your pleasurable evenings are before you with this book in hand.

James Tour, chemist, nanotechnologist, and professor of chemistry,
materials science, nanoengineering, and computer science at Rice University

J. Warner's writing style pulls you into the narrative; you can't help but join his exploration as a detective. And J. Warner also provides a fresh angle. With its panoramic perspective, this book offers a fascinating journey into some lines of evidence most of us hadn't even considered!

Craig S. Keener, F. M. and Ada Thompson Professor of Biblical Studies at Asbury Theological Seminary, author of *The Historical Jesus of the Gospels*

Detective Wallace sifts through thousands of years of history looking for clues, explaining his findings like Sherlock Holmes recounting his reasoning to Watson. The events that prepared the way for Jesus and the impact of his life and teachings bear all the marks of a divine story line. Jesus is the ultimate person of interest.

David Wood, founder of the Acts 17 Apologetics ministry, host of the *Acts17Apologetics* YouTube channel

Either the foundational details of Jesus life, death, and resurrection happened within history and must be reckoned with, or they did not happen, and Christianity falls apart. J. Warner Wallace demonstrates, by using standard and reliable methods of investigation, that Jesus Christ is who he claimed to be.

John Stonestreet, president of the Colson Center, host of *BreakPoint*

In *Person of Interest*, J. Warner does something new and remarkable. He shows why history was divided into two eras by the person of Jesus. This book is comprehensive, the argumentation is convincing, and the delivery compelling. If a skeptic wants to know whether the story of Jesus makes sense, give them this book and they'll discover that Jesus makes sense of history itself.

Justin Brierley, host of the *Unbelievable?* radio show and podcast, author of *Unbelievable?*

J. Warner Wallace invites his reader to much more than a mental exercise, but rather engages their questions with insight, careful process, personal testimony, and creative visuals that ultimately lead those who believe to a richer faith and those who don't, to wonder and welcome.

Ruth Chou Simons, *Wall Street Journal* bestselling author of *Beholding and Becoming* and *GraceLaced*, artist, and founder of gracelaced.com

J. Warner Wallace turns his vast investigative skills on history's all-time number-one person of interest. Bring your doubts, bring your skepticism—but if you bring them in open-minded honesty . . . be prepared to render a shocking verdict.

Scott Hanson, host of *NFL RedZone*

I've been studying the historical Jesus for decades, and Detective Wallace made some fresh insights I had not thought of before. *Person of Interest* is perfect for a skeptic open to considering the evidence for Jesus or for a believer who wants to go deeper in his or her faith.

Sean McDowell, professor at Biola University, speaker, and author of *Chasing Love*

Person of Interest offers unique insights you won't find anywhere else. This approach to the investigation of Jesus's identity is novel, the amount of research is breathtaking, the narrative is compelling, and the visuals are incredible. What a gift to the church!

Natasha Crain, speaker, blogger, podcaster, and author of
Talking with Your Kids about Jesus and *Faithfully Different*

Person of Interest is a fast-paced investigation that leads to a crystal clear conclusion. Drawing on his years as a police detective, J. Warner probes the experiences of the arts, humanities, sciences, and even all the major religious traditions of the past two millennia! Wallace gathers the evidence that will leave you beyond a reasonable doubt.

Michael J. Behe, biochemist, professor at Lehigh University,
and author of *Darwin's Black Box*

J. Warner Wallace demonstrates the reality and relevance of Jesus to a skeptical post-Christian world. He shows it is possible to piece together highlights of the life of Christ wholly apart from Scripture. *Person of Interest* is a masterpiece of intrigue, identifying Jesus as the quintessential person of history.

Hank Hanegraaff, president of the Christian Research Institute,
host of the *Bible Answer Man* broadcast and the *Hank Unplugged* podcast

J. Warner Wallace takes a unique approach by investigating Jesus's existence as a "missing person" case and shows how—*without relying on the New Testament manuscript evidence*—we have sufficient evidence in human history to testify to the truth about Jesus.

Josh D. McDowell, author of *Evidence That Demands a Verdict*

J. Warner Wallace makes a convincing case for the historicity and deity of Jesus without relying on the New Testament manuscripts. With over two hundred illustrations, *Person of Interest* helps us understand why Jesus still matters today, even for those who are skeptical of the Christian Scriptures.

Kevin Sorbo, actor, author of *True Faith*

Several years ago Jim Wallace burst onto the scene and applied his years of highly successful police detective work, using these techniques to inquire about the truth of Christianity. Add to this that Jim previously had been a card-carrying atheist well into his adult life, and what emerged was a new angle that has excited the world of apologetics ever since. I am more than pleased to endorse fully the excellent research that has resulted, including *Person of Interest*. What a boost to the field of Christian evidences!

Gary R. Habermas, Distinguished Research Professor at
Liberty University, author of *The Historical Jesus*

Person of Interest is an instant classic about the most influential human being in history: Jesus of Nazareth. J. Warner has done an unbelievable job collecting evidence and communicating the enormous impact Jesus has had on the world. You will not want to put this book down. And you shouldn't. J. Warner shows you why Jesus should be the central person of interest in your life now and for eternity.

Frank Turek, president of CrossExamined.org, author of *I Don't Have Enough Faith to Be an Atheist* and *Stealing from God*

Jesus changed my life forever, but I'm not the only one he has transformed. In *Person of Interest*, J. Warner Wallace explains how Jesus changed the world in a way that confirmed his existence and demonstrated his deity. This book will help you understand why Jesus can change your life just as he changed mine—and just as he changed all of human history.

Darryl Strawberry, legendary baseball player, author of *Turn Your Season Around*

Because of my background—the many arrests and trials I experienced—evidence is of major interest to me in proving anything to be real and believable. J. Warner provides clear and convincing evidence to prove the deity of Jesus from nothing more than Jesus's unparalleled impact on human history. Read *Person of Interest* and allow Jesus to change your life the way he changed mine.

Michael Franzese, former New York mobster and caporegime
of the Colombo crime family, author of *Blood Covenant*

J. Warner explores the evidence for Jesus, both circumstantial and factual. His fuses and fallouts analogy provides the most logical explanation for historical events from his well-reasoned inferences. In a way that's as methodical as his homicide investigations, J. Warner builds a compelling case for why Jesus's significant place and contribution matter.

Mark E. Safarik, criminal profiler, Behavioral Analysis
Unit, Federal Bureau of Investigation (Ret.)

Person of Interest is exquisitely detailed in showing how prophecies about Jesus match up with the unique time in history in which Jesus appeared, setting in motion stunning changes in the world that continue to benefit us today in everything from education to science to the arts. Even the case notes at the end of the book are a gold mine.

Jeff Myers, president of Summit Ministries, author of *Unquestioned Answers*

Without Jesus, there is no way, there is no truth, and there is no life. That's why I was delighted to find that J. Warner Wallace had written *Person of Interest*. I pray God uses it to reach millions with the glorious gospel.

Ray Comfort, evangelist, president of Living Waters,
and author of *Faith Is for Weak People*

In *Person of Interest*, the imagery and unique delivery that Wallace uses make the book feel like you're reading an intriguing mystery, while also being educated on lesser-known facts surrounding the Christian faith. I would recommend this book for all those who are new to investigating the Christian faith, as well as seasoned readers who would like to hear the evidence presented from a fresh, unique perspective.

Jon McCray, creator and host of the *Whaddo You Meme??* YouTube channel

J. Warner Wallace's ability to take heavy content and break it down for others is second to none. His illustrative genius bleeds through the pages of his work, arresting readers with a special ability to connect the head and the heart. If you're looking for a read that is both investigative and illustrative in nature, look no further! In *Person of Interest*, Wallace takes you on a journey you'll never forget.

Bobby Conway, founder of OneMinuteApologist.com, author of *Doubting toward Faith*

PERSON
OF
INTEREST

PERSON OF INTEREST

WHY JESUS STILL MATTERS IN A WORLD
THAT REJECTS THE BIBLE

J. WARNER WALLACE

"AMERICA'S FOREMOST COLD-CASE DETECTIVE"

ZONDERVAN
REFLECTIVE

CONTENTS

SPECIAL THANKS

As always, I am indebted to my primary editor, first reader, appendix creator, and inspiration for everything I write, my wife, Susie Wallace. Thanks also to Caleb Nelson for his critical research on universities (chapter 8) and Christian scientists (chapter 9) and Samuel Bodnar for his research on the impact of Jesus on other religious systems (chapter 10). I am also grateful for the friendship and input of Gary Habermas, David Wood, Richard Howe, Stephen Ross, and Hank Hanegraaff, who helped me think more clearly about issues related to literary evidence, Islam, the relationship between Christianity and science, and the prophecies of Daniel. Finally, many thanks to my dear friends and partners Frank Turek and the incomparable, indispensable Amy Hall, whose input made this book immeasurably better.

PREFACE

No-Body Homicides

"You can have a seat if you'd like," offered my sergeant as he guided me into his office.

Instead, I stood next to the chair, hoping to shorten the meeting.

"Jim, I need you to carry the Hayes case across the finish line," he said, pointing to the chair. "Can you do that for me?" Kyle was more than my supervisor; he was also my friend. We had worked together for years as part of our undercover team and then on SWAT. Now we were both assigned to the homicide unit. I was the lead investigator in our cold-case detail; Kyle supervised my team along with the other homicide detectives.

"I was afraid you were going to ask for that," I said as I resigned myself to sitting in the chair beside his desk. "You know how I feel about that case."

"I also know you can solve it," he replied with an all-too-familiar smile. Kyle barely attempted to disguise his order as a request, and I knew I would eventually have to acquiesce.

"I really want this case solved, and I'll do all I can to help you," he said.

"That's because the case *matters* to you. I'm up to my neck in two others right now, and they're much stronger. How can I possibly add a third case with so little evidence?"

"That's why I said I would *help* you," he replied.

I knew Kyle was an outstanding investigator in his own right, but since he was a sergeant supervising an entire team of detectives burdened with "fresh" homicides, I feared he would be too distracted to help much with an old unsolved murder.

"I'm not even sure it's true her husband killed her," I said, hoping to demonstrate how much work still needed to be done in the case. Steve Hayes had been the primary person of interest in his wife Tammy's disappearance for nearly ten years, but no one had been able to collect enough evidence to prove she had been murdered. I read the case but had prioritized it behind several other cold homicides that were stronger evidentially.

"Look, Jim, I'm going to retire next year, and you're not far behind me. I remember when this crime occurred. I was a brand-new patrol sergeant, and it was the first homicide I had to work as a supervisor. It *does* matter to me. I'd really like to see it solved before we're retirees."

"NO-BODY HOMICIDE"

"No-body homicide" cases are incredibly difficult to investigate and prosecute. Few of these cases are ever filed with the district attorney because prosecutors must (1) prove the victim was murdered (and isn't simply missing) and (2) prove that the defendant committed the crime. These types of murders require a special approach to solve and communicate to a jury. This unique approach can also be used to investigate the case for Jesus.

I walked back to my office and looked at the stack of notebooks and reports on my desk. How was I going to add Tammy Hayes to my caseload? Not a single piece of physical evidence had been booked under her case number. Worse yet, we didn't even have her body.

Tammy's disappearance appeared to be a "no-body homicide" case: she and her husband, Steve, moved to our city in April 2000. A month later, Steve reported her missing (three days after having an argument). He claimed Tammy drove off in anger and still hadn't returned. The initial officer took the report as a missing person case because that's all he believed it to be. Tammy's husband seemed certain that she would return, and Tammy—raised in the county foster care system—didn't have any other close relatives to interview. As a result, the officers trusted Steve's version of the story. No one photographed Tammy's home, and CSI wasn't called to collect any evidence. The detective later assigned to the case interviewed Steve and set the case aside with the expectation Tammy would return once she "cooled down."

And that's the way the case remained for *years*.

By the time another generation of detectives decided to follow up on Tammy's disappearance (to close the case for recording purposes), Steve had completely remodeled their home. A new detective contacted Steve, expecting to find that Tammy had returned. She hadn't. She never came home, never tried to call Steve, never wrote to ask him for a divorce. Instead, Tammy had *vanished*. No contact. No credit history. No sightings. It was clear *something* happened to Tammy, but detectives were unable to determine the truth about her disappearance. The case went cold. Steve remained a person of interest, but detectives were frustrated by the lack of evidence.

That was about a *decade* before my conversation with Kyle.

 WHAT'S TRUE AND WHAT MATTERS

"I'd like to go tomorrow," Susie said one Saturday afternoon. "Ben and Arlene promised to meet us in the parking lot and sit with us during the service."

For three years I'd successfully postponed this day. Susie had wanted to go to church for years, but when we moved to a new town, I tried to extend the delay. I wasn't raised in a Christian home, and I didn't have any Christian friends during my high school or college years. Most of the outspoken believers I met at work were people I had occasion to *arrest*. I wasn't impressed, and I often mocked Christians in front of my friends and coworkers.

God didn't matter to me because I didn't think he existed, and the Bible didn't matter to me because I didn't think it reported anything true.

I was similarly disinterested in the Loch Ness Monster, Bigfoot, and *Grimm's Fairy Tales*. There's a relationship between what's true and what matters. Few of us order our lives around, spend time thinking about, or make decisions based on our belief in Bigfoot. As a thoughtful nonbeliever, I considered Jesus and the Bible equally fictional and irrelevant.

But I loved my wife, so I told her I would be willing to go to church, at least *occasionally*. She wasn't a Christian, but she believed in God and wanted to raise our kids with a similar belief. I didn't like the idea, but I agreed to visit our friends' church.

As we entered the huge sanctuary, I could see Ben was watching me. We had been friends for years, and I recognized the mischievous expression on his face.

"You're making me nervous," I said. "Stop staring at me."

"I'm just watching to see if you're going to spontaneously burst into flames," he joked. He knew it was my first time in an evangelical church for anything other than a wedding or a funeral.

"Very funny. Will the holy water burn?" I replied.

"You're safe. We don't use holy water here."

The assembly space resembled a large open warehouse, the music was loud, and the atmosphere was *very* informal. Susie, who attended Catholic masses as a child, leaned over and whispered, "It doesn't seem very reverent, does it?"

Eventually the pastor appeared on the stage and started preaching from a Bible. He was surprisingly . . . normal. He talked with charm and confidence, referencing New Testament passages as though they were true. None of this impressed me, however, until he said something that grabbed my attention:

COLD CASES

Most crimes have a shelf life. Thefts, assaults, burglaries, and robberies must be solved in a limited amount of time, depending on the statute of limitations governing a jurisdiction. But not murders. Murders stay open until they are solved; they have no "statute of limitations." Cold cases are, therefore, simply unsolved murders. As a new investigator of Christianity, I applied my expertise as a cold-case detective to the execution— and resurrection—of Jesus.

"Jesus was the smartest man who ever lived."

Really? That's a bold claim, I thought. But he didn't stop there.

"The teaching of Jesus transformed the world because Jesus is God incarnate."

What? God incarnate?

"What does that mean?" I asked Ben.

"It means Jesus, who is God, became a man," he whispered.

I thought about it all the way home. This pastor acted like Jesus mattered, like Jesus was something more than an ancient fairy tale told by uneducated, unscientific people in an uninspiring era. At one point he said Jesus even claimed he was God. If that were true, why would anyone think Jesus was the smartest man who ever lived? I was more inclined to think Jesus was crazy.

Maybe that's why Susie looked surprised when I told her I wanted to buy a Bible. The pastor's words piqued my curiosity. How could he—or anyone else—think Jesus was the smartest man in human history?[1] Why did he believe Jesus was God? Why would someone foolish enough to claim this about himself matter to anyone, let alone me?

I purchased a small pew Bible to find out. I spent less than seven dollars; I saw no point in wasting money to answer these simple questions. I began to read through the Gospels and found Jesus's teachings admirable in several ways. He preached a high, counterintuitive moral standard. His concern for the disadvantaged was extraordinary. His love of the disaffected was remarkable. He called his followers to live a life of love, sacrifice, and service. The New Testament recorded the life and teaching of Jesus, along with his miracles, death, and resurrection.

I didn't think any of it was true.

Why would someone trust this ancient collection of carefully crafted myths?

This tale of a miracle-working Jesus who thought he was God might have been impressive to ancient sheepherders and farmers, but why would anyone raised in the twentieth century (or beyond) believe it? Why would anyone think this ancient, fictional character matters?

I spent the next six to eight months trying to determine if the Gospels were anything more than irrelevant fiction. I investigated the claims of the Gospels using every tool I possessed as a detective. I tested the Gospels as eyewitness accounts, investigated the history of early Christianity, evaluated the nuanced differences among the New Testament texts, and applied forensic statement analysis to the writings of Matthew, Mark, Luke, and John. I've written about this analysis in *Cold-Case Christianity*, but there was another important aspect of my investigation I've never written about, until now:

I also investigated Jesus as if he were a person of interest in a no-body homicide case.

The Hayes case lacked a crime scene. No scene was ever photographed or recorded in any way. Not a single piece of physical evidence existed when I reopened the case at Kyle's request. To make matters worse, we didn't even have Tammy's body. Yet five years later, we successfully prosecuted Steve for his wife's murder. It wasn't easy, but I took a unique approach tailored to cases that lack a body and a crime scene.

The case for Jesus can be investigated in a similar way. As in the Hayes case, we don't have Jesus's body, and we don't have a "crime scene" to provide us with physical evidence. Despite these limitations, we can still make a case for the historicity and deity of Jesus. We can do it without a body—*and without any evidence from the New Testament.*

You read that correctly.

The more I investigated the existence and deity of Jesus, the more I realized the Bible *wasn't* the only available source of information. *I didn't need the evidence provided by the Gospels to know the truth about Jesus.* If some evil regime had destroyed every Christian Bible before I was born—if there hadn't been a single New Testament manuscript to testify about the life or deity of Jesus—I would *still* have been able to determine the truth about him. If I had investigated the case for Jesus like a no-body homicide cold case, I would have discovered everything I needed to know.

Join me as I employ the simple investigative strategy I used to solve the Hayes no-body homicide case. Once I've revealed it to you, we'll apply this approach to the case for Jesus. If you're someone who rejects the New Testament as I did, you may be shocked at how much you can still learn about Jesus. If you're already a believer, this book will help you understand why Jesus *still matters*.

As in my other books, I'll teach you how to be a good detective. You'll learn some of the techniques I've used to solve our agency's most difficult cases. Many of my investigations have received national attention. I've been told by network producers that I've appeared on NBC's *Dateline* more than any other detective in the country. For this reason, I've changed several names and swapped details of my criminal cases to protect the identity of victims (and suspects) and to safeguard the progress of cases still under investigation. Despite this, you'll discover the truth about what happened to Tammy, and you'll also discover the truth about Jesus.

If Jesus was truly the smartest, most interesting, and most transformative man who ever lived—if he was truly *God*—we ought to be able to make a case for his existence and impact, even *without* a body or any evidence from the New Testament. When our investigation is complete, we'll determine if Jesus matters. We'll discover if he was a work of fiction, just another ancient sage, or history's uniquely divine person of interest.

Chapter 1

THE FUSE AND THE FALLOUT

Jesus without the New Testament

Truth will come to sight; murder cannot be hid long.
—WILLIAM SHAKESPEARE

It's like all those quiet people, when they do lose their
tempers they lose them with a vengeance.
—AGATHA CHRISTIE

I stepped back from the whiteboard and stared at the diagram.

"Admiring your own work?" asked Kyle as he entered the conference room.

"Not much to admire . . . yet," I replied.

Kyle stood with his hands on his hips and an incredulous look on his face. "Yeah, no kidding! What does this have to do with the Hayes case?" Kyle was a general contractor before becoming a police officer, and his diligent, workman-like, "I can fix anything" attitude was incredibly helpful in a team investigation.

My background, on the other hand, was in the arts. I earned a degree in design and another in architecture before shifting careers and adopting the profession of my father. When I was a young man, literature, the visual arts, music, education, and science were what mattered most to me. Homicide investigations allowed me to exercise some of these interests as I tried to find creative ways to solve our most difficult cases. So while my diagram may have looked confusing to Kyle, I knew it was the key to solving the case and presenting it to a jury.

In the center of the drawing was a bomb illustrated as a cluster of dynamite sticks. Concentric rings radiated from the bomb, delineating the blast radius. A long bomb fuse draped to the left of the dynamite.

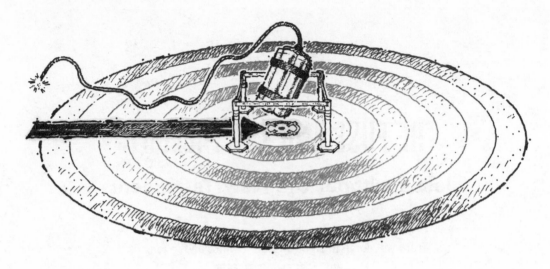

"I'm taking an approach that will help us solve the crime and prosecute the killer," I explained. "This diagram is the key."

"Okay, I'm waiting . . ." he replied.

"Look, we don't have any evidence from a crime scene, and we don't even know where Tammy's body is. But here's what we suspect: something terrible happened to Tammy the day she vanished. If she was killed, an explosion of anger occurred in that moment." I pointed to the bomb. "It was as though a bomb was detonated."

Kyle leaned in. He seemed a bit more interested in my diagram now.

"That didn't happen out of the blue," I continued. "There's a reason Tammy disappeared *when* she did." I pointed to the fuse. "These kinds of crimes are typically the result of an increasingly hostile sequence of events that preceded them, right? If Steve killed Tammy, a fuse was burning in their relationship leading up to the explosion. Our investigation of the fuse will reveal any growing anger between them. It'll also reveal any planning or preparatory steps Steve took. If he's responsible, the evidence from the fuse will point to him."

"It'll also explain why he did it *when* he did," interjected Kyle.

"Exactly," I replied. I pointed to the concentric rings of the blast radius. "And just as every bomb begins with a fuse,

"PERSON OF INTEREST"

The term *person of interest* typically refers to someone who has been identified and is involved in a criminal investigation but has not yet been arrested or formally charged with a crime. In criminal terms, it has no legal standing and can refer to either a potential suspect or someone who is cooperating with the investigation and may have helpful information. Steve was our person of interest because he had been suspected of killing Tammy. Jesus became my person of interest because the pastor believed he was something more than a man.

the blast results in fallout, the debris that bombs inevitably cause. I'll bet Steve's life was different after the explosion. If he killed her, we should find evidence of his involvement in the debris."

"Then let's get started," said Kyle. "I'll help you do some interviews if we can identify the people in Steve's life who might have known him in those days."

"Thanks, I could use the help." I labeled the fuse and fallout areas of my diagram. "This case will be solved once we are able to explain the events *leading up to* Tammy's disappearance and the response *after* her disappearance. The fuse and the fallout will tell us if Steve is a felon."

The **FUSE** and the **FALLOUT** will identify the **FELON**

Over the next year, our cold case team identified and interviewed people who knew Tammy and Steve at the time of Tammy's disappearance. This painstaking process revealed a series of fuse events and fallout responses. With each revelation, the questions surrounding Tammy's disappearance were replaced with answers.

FUSE LENGTH AND BLAST RADIUS

Less significant crimes can be committed successfully with a smaller degree of preparation. Shoplifting, for example, takes little time to plan, while committing a burglary after the store is closed requires more planning. Planning a successful murder is even harder. It takes time for the evil desire to mature. And it takes effort to plot out the manner of death, obtain the right weapon, and formulate a successful alibi.

The more consequential the crime, the *longer* the fuse.

Lesser crimes are also easier to overlook and involve less fallout. If someone steals five dollars from the center console of your unlocked car tonight while it's parked in your driveway, you may not even notice the money is missing for several days. When you do, you might mistakenly conclude it's been *misplaced* rather than *stolen*. But if the same thief steals your *car*, you'll probably notice and file a police report.

When a high-impact event (like a homicide) occurs, it leaves a mark. It takes a while for the fuse to burn, and the debris is difficult to miss.

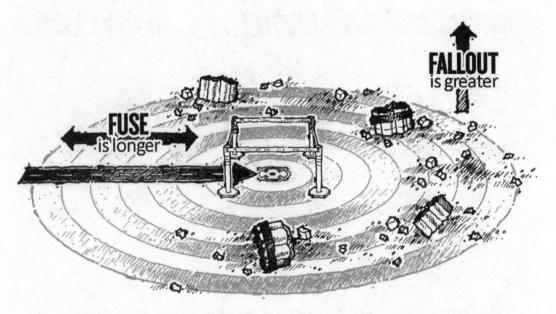

As we investigated Tammy's disappearance, I expected to find a long fuse and significant fallout, but I was looking for more. If someone killed Tammy, I expected the fuse to reveal *why* the killer chose that night in May 2000. Why didn't they kill Tammy in January or June or September? Why 2000 instead of 1999? Was there a deadline unique to the killer? If Steve, our person of interest, was responsible for Tammy's disappearance, the nature and timing of the fuse should match the growing anger, the intensifying pressure Steve may have experienced, and the unique deadline he may have faced.[1]

In a crime as tragic as murder, the fallout is significant. A killer who seeks to hide their victim's body is particularly active *after* the murder has occurred. But beyond that, it's often difficult for a killer to carry on as if they didn't just murder their significant other. They tend to misspeak, behave unusually, or inadvertently reveal their involvement. All these behaviors are important aspects of the fallout.[2]

If investigated thoroughly, the fallout should also reveal the killer *uniquely*. Unless more than one person was involved in Tammy's disappearance, the evidence in the fallout should point uniquely to one suspect. If Steve committed this crime, the debris in the fallout should implicate him, and *no one else*, as our person of interest.

Finally, I've learned to be open-minded and watchful when investigating evidence in the fallout. Some fallout evidence occurs immediately after the crime occurs; other forms of evidence take years to develop. If Steve killed Tammy, virtually every aspect of his world may eventually have been affected. His future romantic relationships, the way he parents his kids, the topics he discusses with friends, the kinds of movies he prefers, where he lives, how much alcohol he drinks—all these areas of Steve's life can provide us with data and help us to determine if Steve was responsible for Tammy's disappearance.

 ## THE EXPLOSION KNOWN AS "JESUS"

I stood in the history section of the Books-A-Million store in Longview, Texas, scanning the shelves and growing more frustrated. The bookshop employee must have noticed the expression on my face.

"Can I help you find something?" she asked.

"I'm not really sure if you have what I'm looking for," I replied. "Do you have any books about ancient history, right before or after the life of Jesus?" I was on vacation with my father in Northeast Texas, and I spotted this bookstore while eating at a restaurant across the street. Only a few weeks had passed since the pastor's statement, and I had just finished my second reading of the Gospels.

The employee took a few steps and pointed to the bottom shelf. "There are some good books here, but they are rather expensive." She was right on both counts. "There's more about early church history in the Roman Empire in our section on Christianity," she said as she gestured toward the next row.

 OBJECTION: THERE IS NO "REAL" EVIDENCE FOR GOD OR JESUS

In legal terms, *evidence* is any type of material item, statement, or assertion of fact (if allowed by a judge) that is used to convince a judge and/or jury of facts or claims related to a case. This definition is intentionally broad because *anything* can be used as evidence to prove a case. That's why we must be open-minded and creative when collecting evidence in the fuse and the fallout. *Everything* we collect has the *potential* to be used as evidence.

On the way out, my dad recognized an important oversight on my part: "How are you planning on getting all those books home in your luggage?"

Thus began my first extraordinary collection of investigative materials related to the existence, life, and activity of Jesus of Nazareth. Every two or three years since, I've donated books to libraries, ministries, students, and bookstores to make room in my office for my next investigation. Although I no longer have the books I bought in Longview, they helped me examine the case for Jesus as though I was investigating a no-body homicide.

If that pastor was correct, Jesus's explosive appearance would demark the pivotal point of history. Even as an atheist, I recognized that the birth of Jesus divided BCE ("Before the Common Era") from CE (the "Common Era"). Something about Jesus initiated a new historical epoch. His appearance was the explosion that broke the human timeline into two "eras."[3]

This explosion, like the explosive event in the Hayes case, was preceded by a fuse and created its own fallout. And just as in the Hayes case, I knew I could determine if Jesus was history's unique person of interest if I examined both sides of the timeline—*even without referencing the New Testament documents.*

FUSE   FALLOUT

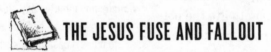

THE JESUS FUSE AND FALLOUT

If Jesus was who Christians claim, I would expect the fuse to be long. Impactful events, after all, typically have longer fuses. The events building toward the appearance of Jesus should span *centuries* if he was the person the pastor described.

I also expected the fuse to act as a timer. If Jesus was something *more* than human, was the timing of his appearance significant? Was there a reason why he didn't arrive centuries earlier or decades later? Was there a historic "deadline" he had to meet? The fuse would reveal the answer.

If the pastor was right about Jesus, I would also expect significant fallout after the life and teaching of Jesus. He clearly affected our calendar, but if he's the divine person of interest the pastor described, I would expect a considerable "ripple effect" beyond the demarking of time.

In addition, the evidence in the fallout would point *uniquely* to Jesus as the cause of the transformation. In fact, I would expect to identify Jesus *specifically* and reconstruct the details of his life *robustly* from nothing more than the debris, even without the descriptions offered on the pages of Christian Scripture. The debris on this side of the explosion would describe Jesus in an unmistakable way.

Finally, if Jesus was truly the smartest, most transformative, and most influential man in history, I would expect the fallout to affect diverse aspects of our world. If Jesus was more than a mere human, I would expect the appearance and teaching of Jesus to change nearly every aspect of the world, and I should find evidence of this impact in unexpected places.

 ## OVERWHELMED

"Are you still at it?"

I had been studying and taking notes for hours, and Susie noticed the sunrise before I did. Prior to that first day in church, I had a very different morning routine, but everything changed when I started investigating the fuse and the fallout related to Jesus. Now I poured nearly as many hours into investigating Jesus off duty as I spent investigating Steve on duty.

Over the next several months, I developed the timeline for Jesus in much the same way I develop a timeline for all my no-body homicide cases. As the evidence and revelations found their place on one side of the Jesus explosion or the other, my presuppositions and doubts about Jesus were challenged and eventually vanquished.

Now that you understand the investigative template I typically use, let's examine the evidence together as I share my startling findings. As the fuse and the fallout take shape, I'll show you why Jesus still matters—even if you reject the Bible. I predict you'll begin to see Jesus as more than merely a person of interest.

Chapter 2

JESUS, THE AVERAGE ANCIENT?

The Cultural Fuse

Time brings all things to pass.
—AESCHYLUS

Nothing great is produced suddenly.
—EPICTETUS

"I saw this coming even *before* Tammy disappeared . . ." Michelle's voice seemed fragile and emotional over the speakerphone. In our conference room, Kyle was taking notes as I tried to adjust the volume of the call.

"How?" I asked. We had identified Michelle as Steve's half sister, and we located her in Michigan, where she had been living for many years. We called her to ask a few questions about Steve's relationship with Tammy, and we were surprised at Michelle's candor.

"Back in those days Steve was hanging around the wrong crowd. He'd already been married once before, and most of his friends while he was married to Tammy were players, even the ones who were married themselves."

"You mean they were sexually promiscuous?" Kyle tried to clarify.

"Yes, and they were always introducing Steve to girls."

"Do you think he was unfaithful to Tammy?" I asked.

"I *know* he was unfaithful, especially around the time Tammy disappeared," she replied without hesitation.

"How can you be so sure?"

"I accidentally discovered his text messages to some girl named Charley," she replied. "I didn't have a phone that could text in those days, and Steve had just gotten a new phone. He was outside talking to a friend while I was visiting, and he got a text. I was curious about what the text would look like on the new phone. I shouldn't have read it."

She paused.

"But it was obvious Steve was having an affair," she said solemnly. "The messages were quite vulgar."

"About how long was this before Tammy disappeared?" asked Kyle.

"Maybe a month or so? And that's the thing: I distinctly remember him texting Charley that they would be together *soon*. But he was married to Tammy, and they were always together. I couldn't even understand how Steve would have had the time or opportunity to start a relationship behind Tammy's back. But here's the weird thing: after Tammy disappeared, Steve moved this Charley girl into their house within about two weeks!"

"Did you ever contact the police about this?" I asked, even though I knew there was no record of an interview in the original casebook.

"No . . ." she paused again.

I waited for her to offer a reason, but none came. "Why didn't you report any of this?"

"Look," Michelle said, carefully searching for the right words. "I didn't want to believe Tammy was dead, and Steve was family. At the time, I wasn't sure *what* happened. I just knew that *something* happened. I didn't want to believe he would hurt her."

"Then why tell us now?" asked Kyle.

"*You* called *me*. And it's *obvious* at this point. Something bad happened to Tammy, and I'm not covering for Steve anymore. He burned a bridge with me recently, and I don't ever want to see him again."

DOES CHARACTER COUNT AS EVIDENCE?

Jurors are allowed to consider the character and trustworthiness of witnesses and defendants when evaluating their statements.[1] Michelle's testimony reveals something about Steve's character. In a similar way, the character of Jesus can be evaluated by the statements of those who recorded the accounts of his teaching and ministry.

THE CULTURAL FUSE

Over the next few days, Kyle and I wondered if Michelle was telling us the truth about Steve, especially since Michelle was angry with him and wouldn't tell us how he had "burned a bridge" with her. But as we spoke to others, Michelle's version of events was confirmed.

Two strands of the fuse were coming into focus, and both were related to the culture in which Steve was living.

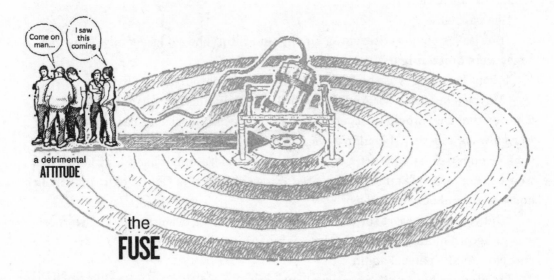

First, Steve's friends created an environment that encouraged the formation of an extramarital relationship. If this aspect of Steve's world hadn't been in place, he may never have initiated the affair.

Additionally, the texting technology played a role in Steve's developing relationship with Charley. Had it been 1990, *prior* to the invention of cellular texting technology and the culture of texting, it would have been much harder for Steve to cultivate an extramarital relationship without detection. The world around Steve—his social group and the timing of the available technology—contributed to the fuse that burned toward Tammy's disappearance.

 ## A COMMUNICATION STRAND

"So why all the interest in ancient *non*-Christian history?" asked Susie as I finished dressing for work.

"I'm trying to figure out why Jesus appeared *when* he did," I responded.

"I've always wondered about that too," added Susie. "If Jesus is God, he could've come whenever he wanted, right? Why not come in the time of Moses? Or much later in history, maybe when we had the ability to tell the world about him on the internet?"

"Well, if he's not God, it wouldn't really matter when he arrived." I was a long way from believing in God or considering Christianity as something that mattered. I still saw Jesus as either a work of fiction or a typical ancient sage.

But Susie's questions rang in my ears for several weeks after our conversation, despite my initial response. Was there an aspect of ancient history—a strand of the "Jesus fuse"—that would identify Jesus as more than an average ancient and explain *why* he came when he did?

I eventually discovered the answer to that question, and part of it was hiding in the history of communication.

While it's true that the internet provides an excellent means by which to communicate claims about Jesus, there's a much older approach that can be just as effective, and you're using it right now. Books and manuscripts are excellent messaging tools. They're inexpensive, portable, easy to produce, and require little in terms of technology. But like much of the information we find on the internet, even the oldest books and documents are dependent on a prior historic invention: writing.

The first and most ancient forms of writing (dating back to around 3500 BCE) are now called *pictographs* (or *proto-cuneiform*). Symbols representing objects were pressed into wet clay with primitive writing tools. When dried, these clay tablets were used to retell events and to serve as trading documents between merchants.[2] But pictographs were limited. They could describe only simple topics that could be easily communicated with visual symbols.

Had Jesus arrived at this point in history (prior to 3500 BCE), complex concepts involving his nature and teaching would have been impossible to communicate in writing. Worse yet, the tablets would have been incredibly fragile, given the nature of clay.

But another advance in writing technology would solve at least one of these problems.

By 3000 BCE, the development of simplified *cuneiforms* allowed writers to communicate concepts by adding *phonograms* (symbols for vowels and syllables) to the communication palette.[3] This allowed writers to better express themselves, but their surfaces (clay tablets) were still fragile and temporary.

That all changed when the ancients began using papyrus.

OBJECTION: WHY DIDN'T JESUS COME LATER IN HISTORY?

If you're active on social media, you probably recognize the crowded, noisy nature of the information age. In addition, technology has advanced to the point that "miraculous" events are easily fabricated in movies and videos. Surveys often find that young people are skeptical and distrusting about many claims made in this environment. Would the message of Jesus be more (or less) likely to resonate in this environment than in the past, when these distractions and innovations were still in the distant future?

The Egyptians can be credited with this communication advance, as they were the first to use papyrus (a writing material made from a reed that grows around the Nile River). Around the same time that cuneiform writing emerged, Egyptians began pressing strips of papyrus at right angles, and this naturally bonding material, once it was exported, became the most popular writing material of the ancient Greek and Roman world. Papyrus, unlike clay tablets, could travel safely.

While these developments were helpful, another advancement would be necessary to further the cause of communication as we know it today. The world was still waiting for a true alphabet.

The Phoenician alphabet is an excellent example of early efforts in this regard. Their alphabet is seen consistently in writings dated to approximately 1050 BCE. It is a relatively simple collection of twenty-two consonants and no vowels. It became the most widely used alphabet in antiquity, modified by several other cultures.[4]

Had Jesus arrived at this point in history (around 1050 BCE), even with these advances in writing technology, it still would have been difficult to communicate the truth about him across the known world. While the Phoenician alphabet was well established, most humans on the planet didn't use it. But other alphabets were on their way.

By 800 BCE, the Greeks, for example, added vowels to make their twenty-seven-letter version of the alphabet, and for the first time, differences between words like *sad*, *said*, and *sod* were clearly understood.

About one hundred years later (700 BCE), the Etruscans, who lived in the region we now call Tuscany, Italy, adopted and modified the Greek alphabet, changing the shape of several letters. When the Romans conquered the Etruscans, they embraced the Etruscan alphabet. By 100 BCE it became the alphabet of the empire, and it followed the Romans to every region they conquered (the Latin alphabet is a direct descendant of the Etruscan). As the Roman Empire conquered the most expansive region of civilization, it also taught the world how to read and write using this alphabet.

The Romans exported another important communication tool in addition to an alphabet: the Greek *language*. Even though the Romans had conquered much of the region, the linguistic legacy of the Greeks still overshadowed the culture.

WORD CHOICES MATTER

As a detective, I commonly use forensic statement analysis to evaluate the word choices of suspects who provide a written statement. But this requires a robust common language and alphabet that allows me to assess potential "deception indicators" in the statement. None of this would have been possible prior to the development of writing and alphabets. Even today we can assess and investigate the claims of the Gospels using forensic statement analysis, thanks to the innovations in writing and language described in this chapter.

A common form of this language, known as Koine Greek,[5] dominated trade and civic interactions throughout the empire.

Even the Jews used it to speak to Gentiles.

Only at this point in history—once the Roman Empire had adopted the Etruscan-modified Greek alphabet, embraced Koine Greek as a common language, and adopted the use of papyrus—could the message of Jesus be effectively communicated with a shared language and letters. Had Jesus arrived prior to 100 BCE, this would *not* have been possible.

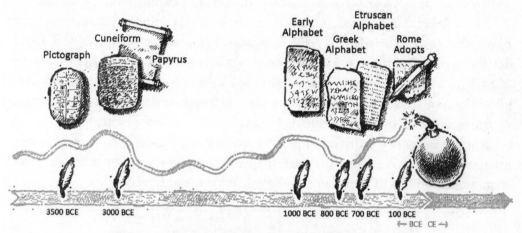

THE COMMUNICATION FUSE

Writing and language alone did not allow the person and message of Jesus to change the world. An even more forceful strand of the fuse was critical. This one required the growth of an empire.

A COLONIZATION STRAND

The Roman Empire began, according to legend, when Romulus and Remus, the twin sons of the war god, Mars, defeated the king of Alba Longa and founded Rome in 753 BCE. Initially a monarchy, Rome became a republic in 509 BCE after its seventh king (an allegedly cruel tyrant named Lucius Tarquinius Superbus) was overthrown in an uprising. Still only a city-state, Rome did not control the entire Italian peninsula until 264 BCE.

Had Jesus appeared at this point in history, his life and message (as he lived and traveled in what is now called Israel) would have been confined to the obscure language and government of the Jewish region. But the growth of the Roman Empire would soon change that.

By 149 BCE (after two wars with the powerful city-state Carthage), Rome also controlled Sicily, the western Mediterranean, and a large portion of Spain. By 146 BCE, Rome conquered Carthage and, as a result, controlled a portion of northern Africa. Rome also defeated King Philip V of Macedonia and possessed what is known today as Greece, North Macedonia, Bulgaria, Albania, Serbia, and Kosovo.[6]

In the years that followed, consuls ruled the empire, setting the stage for several power struggles and murderous, political dramas. Rome was only a "republic" in name during much of this time, and leadership was often divided and contentious. But by 27 BCE, a Roman statesman and military leader named Gaius Octavius defeated all other contending leaders and became the sole leader (and first emperor) of Rome.

He assumed the title of Augustus Caesar.

Augustus dramatically enlarged the empire, capturing Egypt and regions around the Mediterranean. Compare the empire under Augustus with the prior empires of antiquity at their height—Egypt, Persia, and Greece:

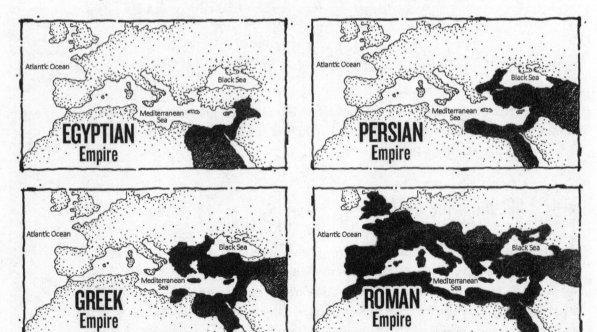

At the pinnacle of Roman rule, most of Europe, Asia Minor, the Balkans, the Middle East, the coast of North Africa, the Mediterranean, and the Black Sea were unified under the same economic, military, and linguistic systems.[7] Had Jesus arrived on the scene prior to 27 BCE, his impact on the "known world" would have been much smaller and more difficult to advance, especially beyond the boundaries of the empires that preceded Rome.

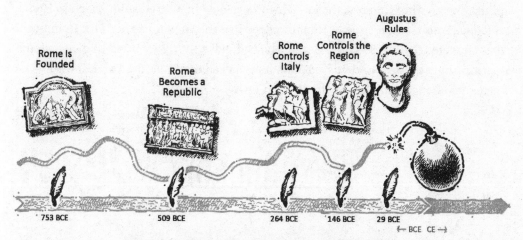

THE COLONIZATION FUSE

The *size* of the Roman Empire allowed Jesus's teaching to spread within its expansive borders, but it was also the *power* of the empire that allowed the message of Jesus to be heard.

 ## A DOMINATION STRAND

Prior to the rule of Augustus, peace was rare among ancient warring nations. In fact, the history of antiquity is cluttered with power struggles and tales of bloodshed.

Starting as early as 3250 BCE, people groups declared and waged war on one another with startling regularity. Few ancient groups were immune from the hostilities. Egyptians, North Africans, Akkadians, Sumerians, Persians, Babylonians, Hittites, Kassites, Assyrians, Jews, Greeks, and Romans repeatedly engaged in brutal warfare. Engaging in more than simple battles, many of these groups waged *generational* wars. Even under the powerful leadership of Alexander the Great (at the height of the Greek Empire), peace—at least on a global level—was elusive.

The wars these nations waged crowded the timeline of history, especially as the appearance of Jesus approached. But that changed under Augustus.

The Roman Empire unified much of the Western world, bringing the entire Mediterranean region under common rule. Many of the same people groups that warred against one another in more ancient times were now in shared submission to Rome.

Under Augustus, a time of Roman peace began, known as the "Pax Romana."[8] It lasted from 27 BCE to 180 CE and allowed Jews living in cities like Jerusalem to retain their culture and customs (so long as residents paid a tax known as the "Fiscus Judaicus" and obeyed the Roman laws).

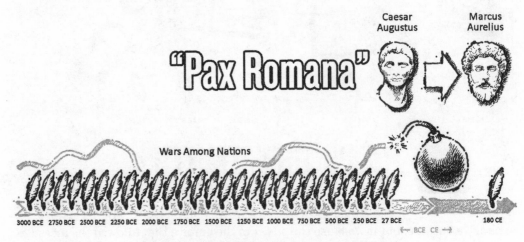

THE DOMINATION FUSE

This small window of Roman peace provided the perfect setting for the teaching and ministry of Jesus of Nazareth. The relative tranquility resulted in a surprising development that would assist those who wanted to spread Jesus's message.

 ## A TRANSPORTATION STRAND

Roman resources previously dispatched to wage war were now reallocated to several domestic improvement projects, including the development of a remarkable system of roads.

The history of transportation set the stage for this technological achievement. Wheels appeared early in history, for example, perhaps as soon as 5000 BCE in ancient Sumer (Mesopotamia). From the same region came the first two-wheeled cart (c. 3000 BCE), usually pulled by donkeys called "onagers."

Four-wheeled carts came later in history (around 2500 BCE) and were used primarily for farming. By 2000 BCE spoke-wheeled chariots emerged in southern Siberia and Central Asia.

These developments certainly aided the ability to move materials and wage war, but their use as "social" transportation devices was limited to the quality of roads in each region. Most roads were little more than cleared pathways, susceptible to weather and war. Had Jesus been born at this time in history, his message would not have traveled far from the region in which he lived.

But as road technology advanced, so did the opportunity to advance the message of Jesus.

Persians were among the first to build significant roads. Darius the Great refurbished an existing roadway and created the "Royal Road" in 500 BCE, connecting regions as far apart as Susa (now the Khuzestan region of Iran) to Sardis (now the Manisa Province in western Turkey). This reduced travel from ninety days on foot to nine days on horseback.

Surprisingly, the powerful Greek Empire contributed little to the advancement of roads, primarily because of Greece's difficult, mountainous, and rocky terrain, their reliance on sea travel for trade, and their inability to protect travelers with official oversight.[9] Until 400 BCE, with some exceptions (like the thoroughfares between major cities and surrounding holy sites), most roads were difficult for wheeled transportation.

Had Jesus arrived at this point in history, his followers would still have faced the limits of transportation within nations in less-than-perfect road conditions. But as before, the Roman Empire provided a solution.

As the Roman Empire grew militarily, so did its need for roads. As a result, Roman roads were widespread and usually well paved. Wherever they conquered, the Romans built long, relatively straight roads to make the movement of military equipment easier. This desire to avoid curves necessitated the advanced

NATURAL AND PROBABLE CONSEQUENCES

According to California Criminal Jury Instructions, a "natural and probable consequence is one that a reasonable person would know is likely to happen if nothing unusual intervenes."[10] In evaluating the cultural fuse leading up to the appearance of Jesus, it is reasonable to ask if Jesus's impact (described in the fallout section) was the inevitable result of the events leading up to his birth or if an unnatural ("unusual") force was involved.

engineering of bridges, tunnels, and viaducts to traverse mountains and valleys. Roman roads were well built and often populated by the military, making them much safer to travel than their Greek counterparts. Spanning nearly 250,000 miles, these roads became a symbol of Rome's power, connecting diverse subcultures within the empire.

Construction of probably the most famous of Roman roads, the Appian Way, was started in 312 BCE. Called by Romans the "Queen of Roads," it set the standard for the many famous roads Romans would build leading up to the lifetime of Jesus.

The Romans weren't the only ones contributing to the advance of transportation. By 130 BCE, the Silk Road (also called the Silk Routes) was formally opened for travel by the Han dynasty of China. This ancient network of connected trade routes would be used to facilitate trade between the East and the West for many centuries.

As the Romans built the infrastructure of secondary roads and perfected the engineering of bridges and tunnels by 100 BCE, the stage was set for the peacetime expansion of the Roman highway system that occurred as Jesus's followers began to share his message and ministry.

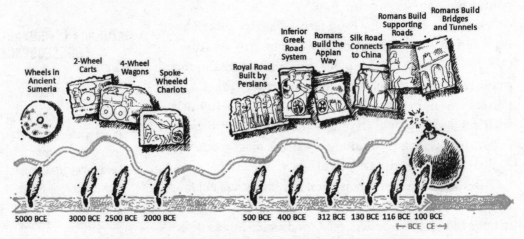

THE TRANSPORTATION FUSE

At this point in history, early in the first century, the Roman Empire had unified and refurbished the road systems of conquered nations, connecting the various systems into a network of roads that spanned the empire from Britain to

Syria. This network provided a new opportunity to trade and share ideas, *even ideas about Jesus*, and it did so largely by laying the groundwork for *another* important development.

A CIRCULATION STRAND

For much of ancient history, the only way to communicate a message was face-to-face (for spoken words) or hand-to-hand (for written documents). Until, of course, the invention of postal services.

According to historical references, the ancient Egyptians may have had a postal service (of sorts) as early as 2000 BCE, but the Persians are typically credited with the first true mail carriers. From around 1700 BCE, the ancient Persian kings needed a way to communicate their decisions, and their relatively primitive courier systems later (under the leadership of King Cyrus the Great in 550 BCE and King Darius I in 521 BCE) became a network of roads and couriers connecting what is now Western Iran to Western Burma.[11]

In China a system for delivering mail emerged early during the Zhou dynasty (c. 1122–c. 221 BCE), but this system was limited regionally and was used primarily by the government to deliver official mail. In a similar way, India, during the Mauryan Empire (322–185 BCE), developed a mail system to transmit political and military intelligence. Greece, during the Hellenistic period (323–30 BCE), developed a system like other ancient empires, but relied heavily on private couriers.

If Jesus had appeared during the period of history in which these empires reigned (from 2000 BCE to 30 BCE), none of these systems would have benefitted him (or his followers) beyond the limited regions each nation occupied.

Once again, Rome would provide a more sophisticated solution.

Augustus created a service called *cursus publicus* from 30 to 25 BCE. At the time of its creation, it was the most advanced system on the planet. It did more than deliver messages; it also transported officials and tax revenues from distant provinces to Rome. The network relied heavily on Rome's superior transportation system (nearly 47,000 miles of new roads were built by Augustus and his successors) and the security and strength the Roman Empire offered. Using the Persian system of "relays," the Romans built forts and stations on their exceptional roads, each positioned about one day's ride apart. The cursus publicus was fast and reliable, especially compared with its predecessors.[12] More importantly, the system was built to circulate information across the geographically expansive Roman Empire, with the ability to reach beyond its borders.

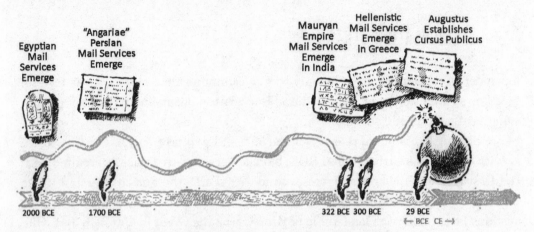

THE CIRCULATION FUSE

By the time Jesus appeared on the scene, the Roman Empire was ready to transmit his message. But more importantly, their attitude toward religion would allow the teaching of Jesus to take root.

 ## A TOLERATION STRAND

Most ancient civilizations were anything but tolerant of the gods of competing groups. Conquered nations were usually forced to adopt the gods of the victors and reject those they had previously worshiped. Had Jesus been born in any of these ancient societies, his emergence as a global religious leader would have been far more difficult.

The Roman Empire, however, was another story.

At its peak, Rome controlled a portion of three continents *and* the Mediterranean Sea. With each conquest, the Romans annexed another culture, along with its languages, traditions, and gods. Rome's early strategy was simple: allow each people group to retain its gods and traditions and embrace these deities as part of the larger Roman pantheon. Rome had done this earlier with the gods of Greece and had, in fact, adopted the Greek gods as their own, "Romanizing" the Greek pantheon.

This effort to tolerate the gods of conquered nations served the Roman Empire well in most cases. Annexed regions were encouraged to worship their own gods, and Rome even built temples and facilitated animal sacrifices to the gods of captured groups. All they expected in return was for the annexed groups to submit to Roman authority and to make offerings (however nominal) to the Roman gods.

But this requirement was not acceptable to Jewish believers within the empire. The Jews were monotheistic and refused to make offerings or take part in Roman religious festivals. Their refusal to present even cursory worship to the gods of Rome tested the tolerance of Roman authorities who saw this worship as a sign of loyalty to the empire.

They made an exception for the Jewish community, however. The Romans conquered Judea in 63 BCE but later allowed the Jews to retain their monotheism, recognizing Judaism as a legal religion. The Romans allowed the Jews to coexist among the conquered people groups, even though they would not worship the Roman gods. Rome *tolerated* Judaism, even if it didn't *trust* it.

In the earliest days of Christianity, Rome did little or nothing to stop its growth, in part because Roman authorities initially saw Christianity as simply a branch of Judaism, partly because of Roman tolerance for local gods in general, and partly because the Christian community was still relatively small. As Christianity grew in the first two decades, Rome may also have tolerated the sect because they hoped it would weaken Judaism.[13]

In any case, a thirty-year window of opportunity opened to spread the message of Jesus (prior to Emperor Nero's maltreatment of Christians in 64 CE).[14] And even though some Roman emperors in the years ahead would persecute Christians, others returned to a version of Roman tolerance, allowing Christianity to flourish in every region under Rome's control.

OBJECTION: CHRISTIANS WERE NEVER REALLY PERSECUTED

The Roman historian Tacitus described the persecution of Christians in Rome (c. 64–68 CE) in Book 15, Section 44 of *Annals* (written c. 116 CE). Modern scholars (even skeptics of Christianity) still regard Tacitus as one of the greatest Roman historians, although in very recent years, some have tried to deny his claims about Christian persecution. But other early manuscripts, including Pliny the Younger's letter to Emperor Trajan, written c. 112 CE, support Tacitus's early report of Christian persecution.

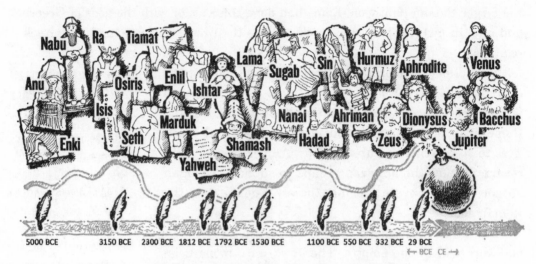

THE TOLERATION FUSE

Jesus arrived at *this* point in human history, when the Roman Empire embraced a version of religious tolerance unique to the history of the ancient world, providing a small window of opportunity. This window allowed Jesus to preach a message his followers could communicate to the world.

SOMETHING WOULD HAPPEN

"I saw this coming even before Tammy disappeared . . ."

Michelle could "read the tea leaves." Even though she wasn't sure *what* would happen, she knew *something* would happen.

As Kyle and I assembled the fuse leading up to Tammy's disappearance, it became all too obvious that Steve's culture and friends were pointing him in the wrong direction. Even Michelle could see it coming.

Any careful investigator of ancient history could also see something was about to happen in what we now call the first century.

A cultural fuse was burning, preparing antiquity for whatever would eventually initiate the Common Era. The Roman Empire had unified much of the known world, adopted a popular language, provided a shared alphabet, established peace, constructed roads, developed the world's best postal service, and embraced just enough religious tolerance to detonate an explosion. Even *before* the arrival of Jesus of Nazareth, it ought to have been apparent to any careful student of history that events within the Roman Empire were aligning for *someone* special to arrive and for *something* special to happen.

Cultural

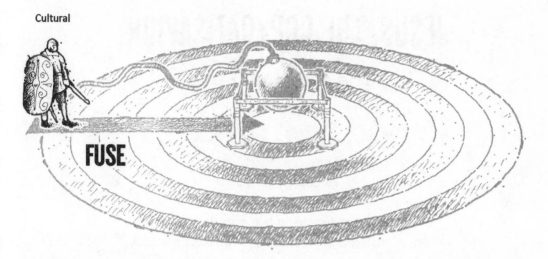

FUSE

But what kind of someone? What kind of something? The more I examined the fuse, the clearer the answers became.

Chapter 3

JESUS, THE COPYCAT SAVIOR?

The Spiritual Fuse

Is man merely a mistake of God's?
Or God merely a mistake of man?
—FRIEDRICH NIETZSCHE

I've come to the conclusion that mythology is really a
form of archaeological psychology. Mythology gives you
a sense of what a people believes, what they fear.
—WIDELY ATTRIBUTED TO GEORGE LUCAS

"That was interesting." Kyle closed the church door behind us as we stepped out into the sunshine. "I'm kinda surprised he was that honest—"

"He's a *pastor,*" I interjected. Kyle had a sarcastic look on his face. He'd known me for years, and during most of that time, we shared the same view of Christians. I wondered if he could recognize a subtle change on my part.

Our continuing investigation of the fuse helped us to understand how and why Tammy disappeared. One of Steve's old friends, Ted, told us that Steve borrowed a large, empty, plastic barrel from his garage. The barrel had a sealable lid; Ted's previous employer used it to store cleaning solution and gave it to Ted when he closed his business in June 1999. According to Ted, Steve borrowed the barrel about a week prior to Tammy's disappearance and never returned it, even after Ted repeatedly asked for it.

This prompted us to look for local businesses that sold acids Steve might have used in Ted's barrel. We knew that murderers had used sulfuric, hydrofluoric, hydrochloric, and nitric acids to partially or completely dissolve their victims, and

Ted's barrel would have resisted most of these acids. Only one chemical store of this nature existed in our part of the county in 2000, and it had been in business only for about six months. The owner was cooperative and agreed to search his records. He called days later to report that there was a single sales receipt, handwritten to Steve, but the employee of the business had failed to write the name of the product Steve purchased. It was written just days before Tammy's disappearance.

While we were waiting for the store owner to call us, we discovered Steve had an older brother, Dennis. That's what had brought us to this church.

"I wonder if Steve was getting cold feet," said Kyle as we entered our unmarked police car and drove away from the church parking lot. "Sounds like it, doesn't it?"

When we learned about Dennis and decided to interview him, he asked us to meet him at the church where he was volunteering. Dennis was unlike Steve in nearly every way. He became a Christian in high school, donated his time to the youth ministry, and eventually became a deacon at the church. Steve, on the other hand, never attended church and showed no interest in God, except, according to Dennis, on *one* occasion.

A few weeks before Tammy vanished, Steve showed up unannounced at Dennis's home. Dennis hadn't seen or spoken to Steve in years, but now Steve wanted to talk. After a few pleasantries, he asked Dennis an unusual question about God.

"Do you think it's possible for a murderer to go to heaven someday?"

Dennis was shocked. "Why do you ask?"

Steve paused, stammered a bit, and then told Dennis he was watching a news story about a convicted killer.

"STATE OF MIND"

What we believe—our motives and desires—is important in determining truth and our level of culpability in criminal matters. For example, a perpetrator's "state of mind" determines the difference between first degree murder, second degree murder, and manslaughter.[1] Do many of us believe in God simply because we desire him to exist? Is this belief simply an errant "state of mind," or is there good evidence to infer his existence?

Dennis offered a response: "That would depend on whether the killer was repentant—in other words, if the murderer confessed, asked God to forgive him, and accepted Jesus as his Savior."

"What if the murderer killed a *baby*?" added Steve.

Dennis remembered feeling uncomfortable when Steve asked this second question, and he began to wonder if Steve or one of his friends had done something terrible. Dennis repeated his response, but Steve still seemed unsatisfied with his answer.

Given the distant nature of their relationship, Dennis didn't learn about

Tammy's disappearance until nearly two years after the fact. For many years he suppressed his concern that Steve might have harmed Tammy. But on the day of our visit, he seemed relieved to tell us his story. The fuse leading up to Tammy's disappearance was clearer with every interview and investigative discovery.

"So Steve was a *Christian*? How many of these 'believers' have we put in jail for murder now?" asked Kyle as he parked the car in the police compound.

"Too many," I replied. "But I'm not sure Steve was a Christian. If so, he definitely wasn't a Christian like his brother."

"It doesn't matter," snarled Kyle. "Seems like almost *everyone* we've taken to jail believes in *some* kind of 'higher power.' They're a bunch of hypocrites. That's why I refuse to believe that garbage."

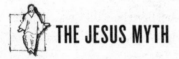 THE JESUS MYTH

"I wish I would have kept my mythology books," I said as I rummaged through the crawl space above the garage, looking through my old college textbooks.

"They're not up there," Susie replied with a librarian-like knowledge of our book collection.

When I bought and read that first Bible, I considered it more akin to mythology than history. As I read the Gospel accounts of Jesus, I rejected the supernatural events they alleged as pure fiction. The Gospels appeared to be an ancient work of mythology, and not even *original* mythology at that. The miracle Jesus performed in Cana, for example, was similar to something I read in college—another miracle in which water was turned into wine. That story seemed vaguely familiar to me, but I remembered a different God performing the miracle: a Greek god known as Dionysus.[2]

According to several ancient myths and sources, Dionysus could create wine from nothing, and water occasionally turned into wine in his presence. The more I thought about it, the more I suspected Jesus's miracle at Cana had been borrowed from Greek mythology. It wouldn't have been the first time a group had borrowed it; the Romans also adopted Dionysus's miracles when they renamed him Bacchus and included him in their pantheon of gods.

"I thought you were studying *Jesus*," Susie said, holding the ladder as I stepped down into the garage.

"I am, but I just want to compare Jesus to some of the myths I read about in college. Why go any further with all this if he's just another myth in a long line of fictions?"

I originally noticed the nearly universal human inclination to believe in "God," a "higher power," or a "Supreme Being" as I began conducting criminal interviews and interrogations. Kyle was right; over the history of my career, most suspects—surprisingly—shared a belief in the Divine, even if they didn't belong to an organized religion.

OBJECTION: JESUS IS A COPYCAT SAVIOR

Scrutiny of pre-Christian mythologies reveals they are less similar to the story of Jesus Christ than skeptics claim. Cynics typically cherry-pick from the attributes of these myths and exaggerate the alleged similarities to construct a profile vaguely similar to Jesus. It is unreasonable to believe that Christian authors would create a story for Jewish readers by inserting pagan mythological elements into the narrative. More importantly, most alleged similarities are extremely general in nature and would be expected from any group of humans considering the existence of God.

Ancient history also reveals this human interest in deities, and many of these gods seem similar to Jesus. In fact, there's an army of "Jesus mythers" (authors, speakers, and videographers) who share my initial suspicions. They're eager to disprove the existence of Jesus by claiming that his story was simply borrowed from prior "dying and rising" savior myths.[3] Most of these borrowed attributes are, however, overstated.[4]

But as I investigated the Jesus "fuse," it was clear that the civilizations that preceded Jesus worshiped gods—*many* gods. Why? Was it the result of their primitive understanding of the world, or something else?

Current research on the issue provides an answer.

A SPIRITUAL FUSE WAS BURNING

 ## THE GOD INSTINCT

The innate human belief in God, a higher power, or a Supreme Being is still evident in the world today, even in places where you might not expect it. A *New York Times* article written by Dr. Preston Greene described the work of philosopher Nick Bostrom, who "made an ingenious argument that we might be living in a computer simulation created by a more advanced civilization."[5]

Bostrom believes our existence is an illusion, that the universe as we know it may be nothing more than a computer simulation.

Does that sound crazy to you? Think again.

Imagine, if you will, a group of today's best computer programmers designing a computer simulation of a historical event, like the signing of the Declaration of Independence. How accurate would their simulation be?

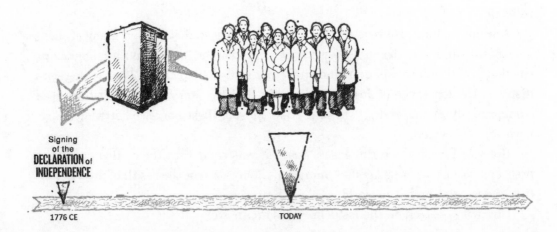

Given our limited computational ability to replicate the past, this simulation may not accurately re-create the setting and characters involved in the signing.

But Bostrom believes a *future* civilization will eventually have the computer technology necessary to create "sophisticated simulations concerning its ancestors," reconstructing the details of history with incredible accuracy and precision.[6]

If this is the case, why *shouldn't* we believe we are one of those ancestry simulations *right now*? Why isn't it reasonable that a future civilization has re-created their *past* (our experience of the *present*) with such accuracy that the re-creation thinks it's real? Bostrom believes that our world—the life we experience today—is just one simulation of many being done in the distant future by a group of scientists studying the past.

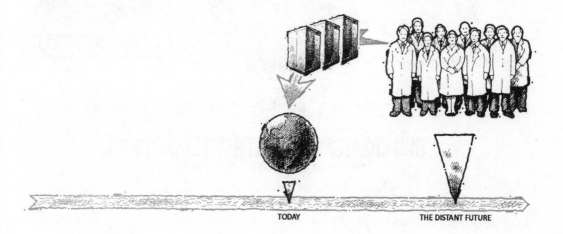

TODAY   THE DISTANT FUTURE

And *that's* not even the interesting part.

According to Dr. Preston Greene, one way to test the theory is to look for anomalies in the computer simulation. For example, a future scientist might make a mistake in the program that would result in a flaw we might experience today. If this theory is true, a single scientist's error in programing might result in a devastating tornado or in some human misbehavior. Greene warns, however, that we *shouldn't* test the simulation. In fact, he says testing the simulation might anger the future programmers who are watching us: "If our universe has been created by an advanced civilization for research purposes, then it is reasonable to assume that it is crucial to the researchers that we don't find out that we're in a simulation. If we were to prove that we live inside a simulation, this could cause our creators to terminate the simulation—to destroy our world."[7]

Greene has inadvertently revealed yet another—albeit more interesting—example of our innate, human belief in a higher power.

Greene imagines a world in which an advanced, creative power (in this case the simulation research team) has the ability to create our world from nothing. He also imagines that human fallenness (in the form of the errant programmer) resulted in the imperfection (the anomalies) we experience in our world. Finally, Greene believes that our creator(s) will ultimately judge us and that we should respect and "fear" them.

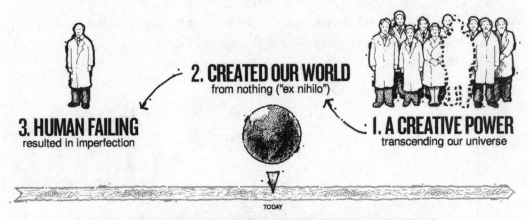

2. CREATED OUR WORLD
from nothing ("ex nihilo")

3. HUMAN FAILING
resulted in imperfection

I. A CREATIVE POWER
transcending our universe

TODAY

4. OUR CREATORS WILL ULTIMATELY JUDGE US
we should respect and "fear" them

Sound familiar? Greene has imagined a new mythology that is obviously similar to many ancient forms of theism.

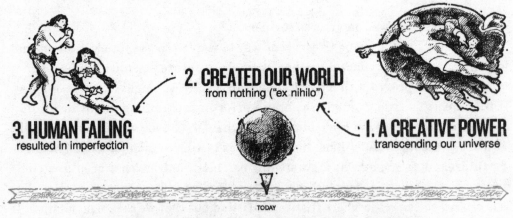

2. CREATED OUR WORLD
from nothing ("ex nihilo")

3. HUMAN FAILING
resulted in imperfection

I. A CREATIVE POWER
transcending our universe

TODAY

4. OUR CREATOR WILL ULTIMATELY JUDGE US
we should respect and "fear" Him

Green's simply replaced classic notions of God with updated placeholders. Greene seeks what most humans pursue: an understanding of the Divine.

A 2012 Pew Research Center Study found that 84 percent of the global population claimed a religious affiliation.[8] And there is good reason to believe that many of the other 16 percent also believe in *some* sort of higher power: "Many of the unaffiliated hold some religious or spiritual beliefs (such as belief in God or a universal spirit) even though they do not identify with a particular faith."[9] A 2017 study confirmed that only 7 percent of the world's population openly claims a strong atheistic or agnostic identity.[10]

Why do so many of us believe in god(s) or higher power(s)? It may be in our genes. University studies in the fields of developmental psychology and the cognitive science of religion now propose that our foundational belief in theism is ingrained in our DNA. Bruce Hood, a professor of developmental psychology at Bristol University, studied the beliefs of children in the United Kingdom and concluded that "children have a natural, intuitive way of reasoning that leads them to all kinds of supernatural beliefs about how the world works."[11] In fact, Hood believes it is futile to encourage people to abandon their beliefs because these come from such a "fundamental level."[12]

Olivera Petrovich, an Oxford University psychologist, surveyed several international studies of children aged four to seven and found that the belief in God as a "creator" is "hardwired" in children and that "atheism is definitely an acquired position."[13]

In an attempt to explain this early belief in God, Deborah Kelemen, a professor of psychology at Boston University (along with PhD student Josh Rottman), surveyed more than a dozen studies and concluded that "evolved components of the human mind tend to lead people towards religiosity early in life."[14]

Paul Bloom, a professor of psychology and director of the Mind and Development Lab at Yale University, writes, "The universal themes of religion are not learned. They emerge as accidental by-products of our mental systems. They are part of human nature. . . . Creationism—and belief in God—is bred in the bone."[15]

OBJECTION: YOU'RE A CHRISTIAN ONLY BECAUSE YOU WERE RAISED THAT WAY

Ancient people groups often adopted the god(s) of their parents and the cultures where they were raised, but this was not true for the young Christian movement. Instead, Christianity emerged in a largely Jewish and pagan culture that was hostile to the claims of Christianity. New believers did not become Christians because Christianity was the default religion of the time. The same can be said for many new believers today. Some of us may have adopted the religion of our parents, but this does not explain the explosive, historic growth of Christianity.

Justin Barrett, from the Centre for Anthropology and Mind at Oxford University, after studying the research of fifty-seven scientists in more than forty studies spanning twenty countries, concluded that "our basic cognitive equipment biases us toward certain kinds of thinking and leads to thinking about a pre-life, an afterlife, gods, invisible beings that are doing things—themes common to most of the world's religions."[16]

God matters to billions of humans across the globe. Humans have a history of thinking about the Divine. As a result, the fuse leading up to Jesus also had a *spiritual* strand. The ancients worshiped a variety of deities, and many of them shared some of the attributes of Jesus. As I examined these ancient deities, I wondered why this would be the case. Was Jesus just another fictional deity in a long line of "copycat" saviors? That's why I was looking for those old mythology textbooks.

✖ COMMON CHARACTERISTICS

I reassembled a library of sorts and began to investigate. I wasn't sure what I would find as I reread each mythology, but along the way I recognized similarities in the narratives. I eventually identified fifteen characteristics commonly shared by ancient deities. These similarities seemed reasonable (and even predictable) given the expectations of people who were "thinking about a pre-life, an afterlife, gods" and "invisible beings that are doing things."

➤ **Inevitable**

In some ancient mythologies, the deity under consideration was *predicted* in some way. His coming was "foretold" by a prophet, another god, or a human author. For example, the birth of Zoroaster, the god worshiped in Persia from 650 BCE to modern times, was allegedly foretold from the beginning of time.[17] This similarity didn't strike me as unexpected, given our modern and ancient interest in divine beings. If humans are predisposed to think about such deities, why would we be surprised that some of us would *expect* their existence and verbalize these expectations?

➤ **Imperial**

In some mythologies, the deity *comes from a royal heritage* in which one or both parents were kings, queens, princes, or princesses. For example, the Greek god Adonis, worshiped from 700 BCE to 450 BCE, was the son of King Theias and his daughter, Myrrha.[18] Upon considering the superior nature of god(s), it seems reasonable that the ancients would see the power and stature of their god(s) as an extension of royal authority.

➤ Inexplicable

Some ancient deities are *born of unnatural means*. Indra, the Tibetan Hindu deity worshiped from 1400 BCE to the present, is said to have been born in a number of unnatural ways (depending on which version of the myth you read), including one account in which he was born from the mouth of the god Purusha.[19] An unnatural birth seems to be another reasonable expectation of humans who think of their deities as exceptional and supernatural in every way, including the ways they emerged into the world.

➤ Insulated

In a few ancient mythologies, the god under consideration is *protected as a child*. The Buddha's parents, for example, prevented him from seeing the ugliness of the world when he was young.[20] It seems reasonable, however, that humans might expect supernatural beings to have *some* experiences that are similar to ours, including the need for protection as an infant.

OBJECTION: IF GOD IS ALL-POWERFUL, WHY DOESN'T HE STOP EVIL?

The ancients believed in god(s) but also experienced suffering, sickness, and violence. If God exists and is all-powerful, why would he allow this? Two common beliefs provide an answer: (1) the reasonable expectation that God and those he saves will live beyond the grave and (2) the expectation that God will ultimately judge the living and the dead. If this is true, justice *will* eventually be served, and peace *will* eventually reign.

➤ Inveigled

Some mythological deities *faced temptation*. For example, demons were said to have tempted and threatened Krishna, the Hindu deity worshiped from 500 BCE to the present, as a child.[21] This common feature of some ancient deities most reasonably reflects a human expectation that our creator(s) would understand and empathize with the experiences of mortals, including our temptations.

➤ Identified

Some ancient deities are *associated with—or identified as—shepherds*. Osiris, the Egyptian god worshiped from 3300 BCE to 30 BCE, was linked to shepherds and illustrated with a shepherd's staff (a "crook").[22] This depiction also seems reasonable given the role of shepherds in ancient culture. If divine beings protect and guide humans, we might expect the ancients to associate them with shepherds.

➤ Incredible

Unsurprisingly, all mythological deities *possess supernatural power*. This power is expressed in different ways. Some, like Quetzalcóatl, the Mesoamerican deity worshiped in the region of

Mexico from 100 BCE to 1550 CE, were believed to have created the world and the first humans.[23] Ancient and modern humans who think about the existence of divine beings are likely to expect them to possess divine powers. Your god's not much of a god if he doesn't have supernatural power. This expectation is the most common characteristic of those who think about the existence of a god.

➤ Interactor

In some mythologies, the deities *engage humans directly*. Tammuz, the Mesopotamian god worshiped from 3000 BCE to 1200 CE, for example, interacts with humans, including, most prominently, a woman named Inanna, her brother Utu, and a local farmer.[24] This kind of interaction also seems like a reasonable inference of humans who expect their divine beings to guide and care for them.

➤ Instructive

Some mythological deities *teach their human followers*. Serapis, the Graeco-Egyptian deity worshiped from 350 BCE to 385 CE, taught his people about agriculture, music, arts, and religion.[25] If divinely powerful beings exist, it seems reasonable that they would have supernatural wisdom and knowledge. We would, therefore, expect to find this attribute in ancient descriptions of gods.

➤ Indemnifier

Many ancient deities *recognize the need for (or require) a sacrifice of some sort*. One example from antiquity, Shangdi, the Chinese deity worshiped from 2230 BCE to 1911 CE, desired animal sacrifices, especially bulls and lambs.[26] This common characteristic of ancient deities reflects a shared (and equally ancient) understanding of human nature. Thoughtful humans understood their propensity to do wrong, and they also understood that this misbehavior deserved punishment. For this reason, they reasonably expected righteous, divine beings to require penance.

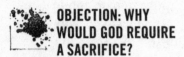

OBJECTION: WHY WOULD GOD REQUIRE A SACRIFICE?

Most ancient religions recognized the imperfect moral nature of humans by requiring a penalty to be paid before believers could appease (or be united with in some way) their god(s). Many of these religions required animal sacrifices to atone for human sin. Christianity did not. Jesus, as God incarnate, paid the price for sin in a way that was different from prior religious systems. Rather than requiring one created being (an animal or human) to die for another, God stepped into history as a human being and paid the price for human sin *on his own*. He replaced the need for repeated sacrifices with a single eternal sacrifice.

➤ Indicted

A few ancient deities *faced a judicial trial of sorts*. In one example, Dionysus, a Greek and Roman god worshiped from 650 BCE to 186 BCE, appeared before King Pentheus on charges of claiming to be God.[27] As before, it seems reasonable for humans to expect god(s) to execute justice, even when judging their own actions. For this reason, it makes sense that judicial settings would appear in some ancient mythologies.

> ## Inviter

A few mythologies also describe a deity who *shares or establishes a divine meal*. According to Mithraic artwork, Mithras, a god worshiped in Persia and Rome from 400 BCE to 380 CE, shared a meal with the Roman sun god, Sol Invictus, and Mithras worshipers also engaged in ritual meals.[28] This expectation among ancient humans also seems reasonable given that a meal provides an opportunity for intimate, interpersonal interaction. If humans desire this kind of relationship with the Divine (and with one another), meal rituals would be a logical choice.

> ## Immortal

Many ancient deities had *the power to defeat death*. Heracles, the Greek god worshiped from 600 BCE to 250 CE, was allegedly killed by his wife Deianira. As the poison she gave him started to eat his flesh, he burned himself to death on a funeral pyre. When his body burned, he ascended to Olympus, where he became an immortal god.[29] Humans who think about the supernatural power of deities would reasonably expect these deities to transcend the limitations of mortality.

> ## Intercessor

Some ancient mythological deities *offered eternal life* to their followers. Zalmoxis, the deity of the Getae and Dacians (present day Romania) worshiped between 500 BCE and 5 BCE, promised immortality to the souls of brave warriors.[30] If immortal deities love the humans they protect (and in many cases created), it seems reasonable to expect these divine beings to provide eternal life for their followers.

> ## Indicter

Finally, some ancient mythologies describe gods who will *judge the living and the dead*. For example, Thakur Jiu, the Santal (northern Bangladesh) deity worshiped from 1000 BCE to the present, is the judge of humans both before and after their death.[31] This expectation also seems reasonable given the common human belief that justice will eventually be served, if not in this life, then in the next.

OBJECTION: WASN'T THE VIRGIN CONCEPTION OF JESUS COPIED FROM PAGAN MYTHS?

The gospel authors are unlikely to have borrowed from the birth narratives of ancient foreign deities. Jewish readers would be unwilling to embrace a god who shared pagan attributes. Early Christian converts, called to live a new life in Christ and to be free of the foolish philosophies and religions of men, would also be unlikely to embrace a god who was explicitly worldly and pagan. A better explanation is that humans expect a supernatural god to enter the world in a supernatural manner, and this expectation was fulfilled in the conception of Jesus.

As I finished my investigation of the mythologies, I recognized that there *were* similarities between Jesus and the mythological deities. The list of the most common attributes of these ancient deities sounded a lot like the Christian description of Jesus:

Predicted by prophecy	Recognized the need for a sacrifice
Born by unnatural means	Established a divine meal
Protected as an infant	Faced a trial
Faced temptation	Had the power to defeat death
Was associated with shepherds	Offered eternal life
Possessed supernatural power	Judge the living and the dead
Engaged and taught humans directly	

At first glance, these common descriptions seemed surprisingly similar to characteristics of Jesus. But a closer examination revealed something entirely different. None of the ancient mythologies possessed *all* the attributes described on this list. At best, a handful of deities displayed ten of the shared characteristics. Most had far fewer (from five to nine). And while these similarities existed *broadly*, the details among the ancient narratives differed *dramatically*. For example, although many ancient deities were said to enter the world unnaturally, the *way* they entered couldn't have been more different. Attis, for example, was conceived when the god Agdistis was castrated and bled into the ground. From this blood, a tree grew, producing almonds that a goddess later collected and held to her bosom, causing her to conceive Attis. Dionysus's father, Zeus, destroyed Dionysus's mother but saved Dionysus by sewing him up in his thigh and keeping him there until Dionysus reached maturity. Krishna was conceived when the Hindu god Vishnu planted two hairs from his head in Krishna's mother's womb. Mithras was born out of solid rock. Quetzalcóatl was conceived when his mother swallowed an emerald.

When you examine the details related to each similarity between Jesus and ancient mythologies, the resemblances begin to vanish. Jesus isn't much like the other gods after all.

The few broad similarities that do exist are reasonable expectations on the part of humans who are thinking diligently about their experience of the world and the existence and nature of supernatural beings. In the same way that Dr. Greene imagines a set of *otherworldly* minds to explain the nature of the universe and creates a set of attributes mirroring classic descriptions of deities, ancient humans arrived at a set of reasonable attributes given their common human expectations. The most common of these attributes—unsurprisingly—was simply the ability of each god to do what we expect of gods: they were able to *perform supernatural acts.* For larger, readable images, refer to case note.[32]

	Osiris	Tammuz	Shangdi	Marduk	Indra	Attis	Thakur Jiu	Adonis	Dionysus	Zoroaster	Heracles	Krishna	Zalmoxis	Mithras	Buddha	Serapis
Inevitable	X									X		X		X	X	
Imperial		X	X	X		X			X	X		X			X	
Inexplicable	X	X		X	X	X			X	X	X	X	X		X	X
Insulated									X	X	X	X	X		X	
Inveigled										X	X	X	X		X	
Identified	X	X				X							X			
Incredible	X	X	X	X	X	X	X	X	X	X	X	X	X	X	X	X
Interactor		X						X		X	X	X			X	X
Instructive	X		X	X					X	X		X	X	X		X
Indemnifier	X	X	X	X	X	X	X			X	X	X		X		X
Indicted								X	X			X				
Inviter	X								X				X			
Immortal	X	X			X	X			X	X		X	X	X	X	X
Intercessor	X	X							X	X		X	X	X		
Indicter	X	X	X	X			X	X								

3300 BCE	3000 BCE	2230 BCE	1800 BCE	1400 BCE	1250 BCE	1000 BCE	700 BCE	650 BCE	650 BCE	600 BCE	500 BCE	500 BCE	400 BCE	400 BCE	350 BCE

← BCE CE →

OSIRIS	TAMMUZ	SHANGDI	MARDUK	INDRA	ATTIS	THAKUR JIU	ADONIS	DIONYSUS	ZOROASTER	HERACLES	KRISHNA	ZALMOXIS	MITHRAS	BUDDHA	SERAPIS

Of these figures, Osiris, Dionysus, Zoroaster, and the Buddha have more in common with one another—and with Jesus—than any of the other ancient mythologies (even though these four deities don't share the *same* ten attributes). Although you may not be familiar enough with Osiris, Dionysus, and Zoroaster to evaluate their true similarity to Jesus, you probably know enough about the Buddha to recognize that any parallels to Jesus are broad and superficial. Few people, for example, would argue that Jesus is simply a re-creation of the Buddha "myth." In the same way, any statement about Jesus's resemblance to other ancient deities is equally unreasonable, especially considering these lesser-known mythological characters possess far fewer shared characteristics.[33]

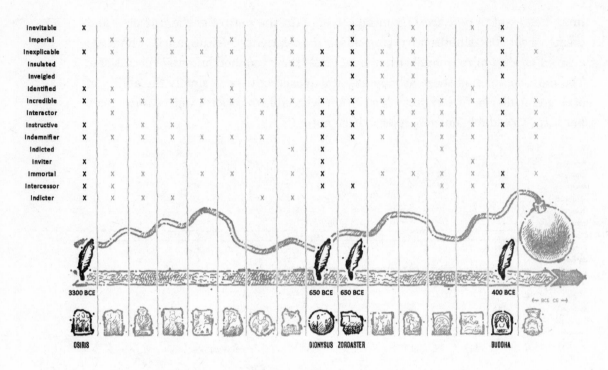

Finally, I found it interesting that Jesus was the one deity who possessed all the attributes found commonly in so many prior ancient mythologies. While the gods of antiquity shared *some* of humankind's expectations of God, Jesus alone personified *all* their expectations.

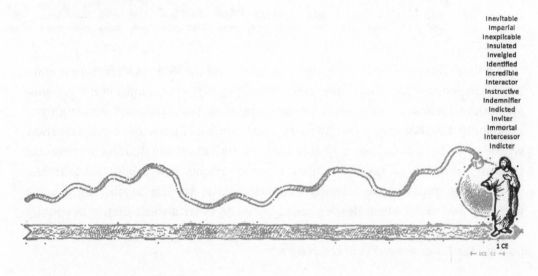

GOD'S MYTH

Why would Jesus be the only deity to possess all the common attributes? Early in my investigation, because of my distrust of the New Testament accounts, I was inclined to believe that the gospel authors simply cobbled the story of Jesus from prior mythologies. But did these authors really know enough about the pantheon of gods (across all history *and* every region) to shape such a tale? Would they really expect Jewish readers to accept a patchwork, pagan "copycat" as their Messiah?

C. S. Lewis, in his own investigation of Christianity, seemed to have considered the same questions. His conclusion was penned in a letter to Arthur Greeves:

> Now the story of Christ is simply a *true* myth: a myth working on us in the same way as the others, but with this tremendous difference that it *really happened*: and one must be content to accept it in the same way, remembering that it is *God's* myth where the others are *men's* myths: i.e. the Pagan stories are God expressing Himself through the minds of poets, using such images as He found there, while Christianity is God expressing Himself through what we call "real things."[35] (emphasis mine)

MYTHS, LIES, AND DETERMINING THE TRUTH

C. S. Lewis was correct when he noted that not all "myths" are untrue. But can a claim about the past contain an untruth yet still tell us something true about the world? Yes, and this is even true in criminal trials. Judges tell jurors, "If you think the witness lied about some things but told the truth about others, you may simply accept the part that you think is true and ignore the rest."[34] Ancient mythological claims about deities contain many untruths, but they also contain the true, reasonable expectations all of us have about God.

Lewis clearly distinguished between two common dictionary definitions of the word *myth*: (1) "a widely held but false belief(s) or idea(s)" and (2) "a traditional story, especially one concerning the early history of a people or explaining some natural or social phenomenon, and typically involving supernatural beings or events."[36] Lewis used the word according to the second dictionary definition, one that doesn't equate *myth* with *false*.

Was Jesus the true myth who embodied the common expectations of all prior mythologies? Was Jesus *God's* myth? If Lewis, as a Christian, recognized the difference between the myths of humanity and the myths of God, to which God was he referring when he wrote that Jesus was "God's myth"? Lewis was referring to the God of *Israel*.

 IT'S NOT JESUS

I was hesitant to read about the God of Israel. The Old Testament seemed volumi-
nous and somewhat obscure. But as I focused on the prophets and leaders chronicled
on the pages of Jewish scripture, I was surprised to discover descriptions of *Jesus*.[37]
Consider, for example, the following list of attributes:

As a baby, he escaped the decree of a king and avoided certain death
He lived in Egypt as a child but later returned to his homeland
He was known by his followers to be both humble and strong
He was tempted while in the wilderness
He was attested by God through signs and wonders
He worked a miracle at the sea
He miraculously fed thousands of people with bread
He spoke God's word and taught God's law from a mountain
He was the mediator between God and his people

This clear, concise description of Jesus preceded him by thousands of years. How
could the ancient author have described Jesus so accurately? The answer? This isn't
a description of Jesus at all. This list describes *Moses*.[38] Strikingly similar to Jesus,
wouldn't you say? There's more. Read the next descriptions:

His name, when translated from Hebrew, means "God saves"
He descended from a man named Joseph
He had a humble, obscure beginning but rose to a place of honor
He was anointed by God
He was filled with God's Spirit
He led and shepherded his people
He did for God's people what Moses could not do
He delivered God's people from the enemies of God
He promised rest and provided it

This appears to be another succinct, ancient description of Jesus, but like the
first, it isn't describing Jesus. This is the Old Testament description of *Joshua*.[39]
Let's investigate another set of attributes:

He was the special object of his father's love

He was underestimated and discounted by his own family

He had the ability to resist a temptation

He fed bread to people to relieve their hunger

He accurately foretold the future

He was sold by someone he trusted for pieces of silver

He was stripped of his robe and delivered to gentiles

He stood before rulers in the assembly

He was falsely accused

His own people did not recognize him

Once again, this ancient list of attributes *sounds* like Jesus, even though it describes *Joseph* from the Old Testament.[40] Let's examine another descriptive list:

He was a descendant of Abraham and of the tribe of Judah

He was born in the town of Bethlehem

He burst onto the scene from an unlikely social position

He was anointed by God to lead his people

He was both shepherd and king

He amazed the elders as a young man

He spent time in the wilderness

He had no place to lay his head

His popularity angered the leaders of the time

He was betrayed by those he served

He trusted God in the face of adversity

This is also an ancient record describing someone other than Jesus (even though it sounds a lot like him). This time, it's an Old Testament description of *King David*.[41] How about these descriptions:

His name, when translated from Hebrew, means "God is salvation"

His ministry started at the Jordan River

He received the Spirit of his Father

He was surrounded by more disciples than his predecessors

He was attested by God with miracles, signs, and wonders

He raised a woman's adult son from the grave

He fed many people with just a few loaves and had more to spare

He healed a leper

He gave sight to the blind

He fed the hungry

He was betrayed for money

Although it sounds like Jesus, this time we're describing the Old Testament prophet *Elisha*.[42] Let's end with this ancient description:

He preached repentance to gentiles

He knew that salvation belongs to the Lord

He slept on a boat during a storm

He acted and the power of God calmed the storm

He chose to sacrifice himself for others

He spent three days in darkness, given up for dead

After three days, he escaped death and taught for forty days

This final description also sounds like Jesus of Nazareth, but it's actually the Old Testament prophet *Jonah*. For larger, readable images, refer to case note.[43]

MOSES	JOSHUA	JOSEPH	DAVID	JONAH
Escaped death and a king's decree as a baby	His name means: "God Saves"	Was the object of his Father's love	Born in the town of Bethlehem	Preached repentance to gentiles
Lived in Egypt as a child but returned	He descended from a man named Joseph	Was underestimated and dismissed by his family	Identified as a shepherd king	Knew that salvation belongs to the Lord
Known by his followers to be humble and strong	Began in obscurity but rose to a position of honor	Was able to resist a temptation	Amazed elders when he was young	Slept on a boat during a storm
Was tempted while in the wilderness	Anointed to lead and shepherd his followers	Fed bread to people when they were hungry	Came on to the scene from an unexpected pedigree	The storm was calmed to the amazement of others
Attested through signs and miracles	He was filled with God's Spirit	Was stripped of his robe and delivered to gentiles	His popularity with the masses angered leaders	He chose to sacrifice himself for others
Worked a miracle with the sea	Did for God's children what Moses could not do	Was sold by someone he trusted for pieces of silver	Anointed by God to lead and shepherd his people	Spent three days given up for dead
Fed thousands miraculously with bread	Brought deliverance from the enemies of God	Stood before rulers in the assembly	Spent time in the wilderness	After the three days, he spent forty days teaching
Spoke the word of God to his followers	Promised and gave rest to his people	Was falsely accused	Had no place to lay his head	
He was the mediator between God and his people			Betrayed by those he served, but trusted God	

Unlike the pagan mythologies that share common, broad characteristics with Jesus, the ancient Jewish religious figures share attributes that are much more distinct and specific. Scholars describe these ancient Jewish figures as "types" of Jesus, foreshadowing the attributes that would later be found in the Messiah.[44] The Israelites knew and admired these leaders and prophets who presented them with characteristics they should eventually recognize in their promised Savior and deliverer. The ancient descriptions of key Jewish leaders presage an important person of interest.

These key figures from history possessed attributes that would become part of the collective consciousness of the Jewish nation. If Jesus were to appear to Israel possessing these characteristics, they would certainly recognize the similarities between Jesus and the most important figures from Jewish history.

But here's where it gets even more interesting.

If we were to combine the broad expectations of non-Jewish mythologies with the foreshadowed attributes of these important Jewish figures, we could create a profile of sorts. This summary, built from collective expectations and common explanations, describes a person of interest:

He was predicted by prophecy

He was a descendant of Abraham and of the tribe of Judah

He descended from a man named Joseph

He was born by unnatural means

He was born in the town of Bethlehem

He burst onto the scene from an unlikely social position

He was the special object of his father's love

His name, when translated from Hebrew, means "God saves"

As a baby, he escaped the decree of a king and avoided certain death

He was protected as an infant

He lived in Egypt as a child but later returned to his homeland

He had a humble, obscure beginning but rose to a place of honor

He amazed the elders as a young man

He spent time in the wilderness

He was tempted while in the wilderness

He faced temptation

He had the ability to resist temptation

His ministry started at the Jordan River

He received the Spirit of his Father

He was underestimated and discounted by his own family

His own people did not recognize him

He was associated with shepherds

He led and shepherded his people

He was both shepherd and king

He was known by his followers to be both humble and strong

He was surrounded by more disciples than his predecessor

He was anointed by God

He was filled with God's Spirit

He was anointed by God to lead his people

He was attested by God with miracles, signs, and wonders

He possessed supernatural power

He miraculously fed thousands of people with just a few loaves of bread and had more to spare

He healed a leper

He gave sight to the blind

He raised a woman's adult son from the grave

He slept on a boat during a storm

He calmed the storm with the power of God

He worked a miracle at the sea

He accurately foretold the future

He engaged and taught humans directly

He spoke God's word and taught God's law from a mountain

He preached repentance to gentiles

He knew that salvation belongs to the Lord

He had no place to lay his head

He recognized the need for a sacrifice

He established a divine meal

His popularity angered the leaders of the time

He was sold by someone he trusted for pieces of silver

He was betrayed by those he served

He faced a trial

He stood before rulers in the assembly

He was falsely accused

He was stripped of his robe and delivered to gentiles

He trusted God in the face of adversity

He chose to sacrifice himself for others

He spent three days in darkness, given up for dead

He had the power to defeat death

After three days, he escaped death and taught for forty days

He offered eternal life

He promised rest and provided it

He was the mediator between God and his people

He did for God's people what Moses could not do

He delivered God's people from the enemies of God

He will judge the living and the dead

This description is eerily similar to the person we know today as Jesus of Nazareth, and this level of detail can be gleaned *not from the New Testament record* but from non-Christian sources that *preceded* the New Testament. If nothing else, the ancients clearly shared common expectations related to divine beings and were intimately familiar with the attributes that those who wrote about Jesus would later document.

 EXPECTING THE UNEXPECTED

As I pondered these ancient descriptions from Jewish and non-Jewish sources, I wrestled with an idea: If God existed, he would certainly know the hopes and history of humans. Would he enter the world in a manner *intentionally* similar to the expectations of the Jews and those of non-Jewish cultures?

WHY?

My own limited, human experience inclined me to believe this might be the case.

As an undercover investigator, I learned to appreciate the relationship between the expected and the expecter. For nearly four years I was part of a surveillance team that allowed me to work in street clothes without any of the restrictions of life in a uniform. As a result, I didn't cut my hair for several years. Toward the end of that assignment, I didn't look much like a detective or police officer.

Around this time, our unit began to investigate a series of residential burglaries. Without a specific suspect in mind, we did the only thing we could do: we surveilled the neighborhoods most recently targeted by the burglars, positioned strategically in unmarked police vehicles. Given the size of the neighborhoods, this approach was far less than ideal. We couldn't watch every street.

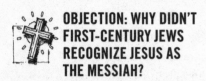

OBJECTION: WHY DIDN'T FIRST-CENTURY JEWS RECOGNIZE JESUS AS THE MESSIAH?

While Jesus met ancient overarching human expectations related to deity, many Jews of the time held a different, inconsistent expectation related to the Messiah. Many Jews who expected a *spiritual savior* and redeemer became Christ followers, but Jews who expected a *temporal king* and conqueror (who would save the nation of Israel and restore the Jewish kingdom) did not. Jesus met the expectations of those who sought eternal, spiritual truth.

Several hours into the second day of surveillance, while watching my assigned thoroughfare and monitoring the regular police traffic on the scanner, I heard our dispatcher detail a police unit to a crime that occurred three blocks from where I was sitting. A victim had just arrived home from work to discover his house had been burglarized. I couldn't believe it happened so close to our fixed surveillance. In frustration I decided to "hop the call" and drive to the victim's location to ask a few questions. I was hoping the caller might have seen a suspect vehicle or could give me some other valuable information I could then relay to the rest of our team. Maybe it wasn't too late to catch the burglars if they were still in the area.

When I arrived at the victim's house, he was standing at the curb, waiting for the marked police unit to arrive. I jumped out of my car, ran up to him, and identified myself as a police officer. He didn't seem to believe me. To be fair, I had shoulder-length hair, hadn't shaved in several days, and was wearing a pair of cargo shorts. I probably wouldn't have cooperated either, had I been in a similar situation.

Minutes later, the police unit arrived, and a uniformed officer approached both of us. Suddenly the victim was eager to provide the information he withheld from me. In that moment I learned a simple rule about expectations: the more the "expected" meets the expectations of the "expecter," the better the response.

Our victim was expecting a uniformed police officer to arrive at his location to take a crime report. Instead, he got a disheveled, unshaven guy in shorts. No wonder he was so uncooperative.

If there *is* a God and he wanted to evoke the best possible response, wouldn't he meet the expectations of the expecters? Jesus possessed all fifteen divine expectations of non-Jewish cultures while robustly personifying attributes of ancient Jewish leaders. Jesus met the expectations of those who were familiar with the Old Testament and those who were not.

THE FUSE SO FAR

As the fuse of history burned toward what we now call the first century, civilizations rose and fell until the Roman Empire set the stage for the inauguration of the Common Era. At the same time, the spiritual expectations of humans began to sketch a thumbnail image of divinity.

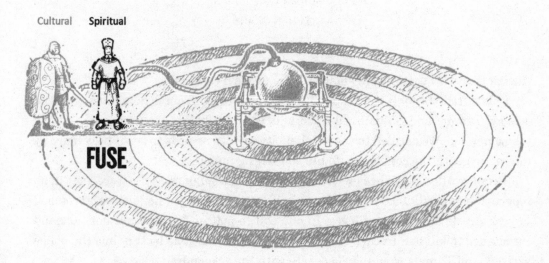

Cultural   Spiritual

FUSE

You can recognize his attributes in the manuscripts of ancient mythologies and the pages of Jewish scriptures. Was this the divine person of interest who divided history and defined our common calendar? Were the years before the Common Era simply the long runway of human expectation? Perhaps antiquity turned a corner when the "expecters" finally met the "expected." If so, the fallout of history would confirm his identity.

It would also confirm the claims of people who *predicted it for centuries.*

Chapter 4

JESUS, THE MISTAKEN MESSIAH?

The Prophetic Fuse

Coming events cast their shadows before.
—DORIS LESSING

A serious prophet upon predicting a flood should
be the first man to climb a tree.
—STEPHEN CRANE

"I wish this stuff would have shown up in our local records."

Kyle sifted through the dispatch logs we received from a neighboring police agency. Tammy and Steve lived in this jurisdiction before moving to our city to take a new job. We decided to search that city's police records to see if they had any interaction with the couple. We found something important.

Tammy called the police on three occasions. Although the calls were logged, no reports were taken. Once the police arrived, Tammy changed her story and refused to give any details to the officers. In one call to police, Tammy said her husband threatened to kill her. In each case, however, Steve was gone by the time the police arrived, and Tammy wouldn't cooperate with the responding officers.

But not all the calls for help came from Tammy.

In one incident, the caller identified herself as Tammy's friend, Brianna Higerstrom. We searched our local files to try to identify Brianna, and given her unusual last name, we found her. We decided to pay her a visit.

She answered the door, and after we identified ourselves, she nearly closed the door in our faces. It took another forty-five minutes, standing on Brianna's porch, to gain her trust and calm her fears. She told us that Steve had always intimidated her and that she never intended to tell anyone about her suspicions.

Kyle and I were eventually able to convince her our investigation would solve the case and protect her in the future.

Brianna was aware of the increasing violence in Tammy's relationship with Steve, although she was never present when it occurred. Tammy shared details of her roller-coaster marriage with Brianna daily, telling her about the intense highs and dark lows. For whatever reason, Tammy remained loyal to Steve, even after being mistreated. She even wanted to have kids with him.

Tammy had confided in Brianna that she was pregnant. Although she wasn't showing yet, Tammy was four months pregnant at the time of her disappearance. No one knew yet, except for Brianna, but Tammy wanted to announce the pregnancy to Steve's family the week she vanished. She asked Brianna to go with her to purchase maternity clothes, but before they could take the shopping spree, Tammy stopped answering her phone. When Brianna drove to Tammy's house, Steve seemed angry that Brianna was asking questions. She kept her suspicions to herself from that moment on.

"Seems like *everyone* was afraid of Steve, doesn't it?" Kyle asked on the way back to the station.

"I wish *Tammy* had been more afraid . . ." I replied. "But this information about the pregnancy makes sense of Steve's conversation with Dennis, and it may begin to explain *why* Tammy vanished when she did."

1   CLEAR AND CLOAKED EVIDENCE

"I'm not impressed."

We had been attending church for several weeks, off and on, studying the evidence from history between the weekly sermons. This week there was a guest speaker. He spent nearly an hour preaching about the Old Testament prophecies related to the Messiah. He claimed these ancient predictions clearly described Jesus of Nazareth, but as I read along with each prophecy, I was . . . *underwhelmed.*

"Just *listen* before you question every little detail," whispered Susie.

According to the speaker, the role of prophecy was important to the first Christians. The Old Testament laid the foundation, as the prophet Isaiah described:

> Remember the former things long past,
> For I am God, and there is no other;
> I am God, and there is no one like Me,
> *Declaring the end from the beginning,*
> *And from ancient times things which have not been done,*
> Saying, "My plan will be established,
> And I will accomplish all My good pleasure."
>   (Isaiah 46:9–10 NASB, emphasis mine)

The New Testament authors understood the role prophecy would play in identifying Jesus as the Jewish Messiah: "As to this salvation, *the prophets who prophesied of the grace that would come* to you made careful searches and inquiries, seeking to know what person or time the Spirit of Christ within them was indicating as He predicted the sufferings of Christ and the glories to follow" (1 Peter 1:10–11 NASB, emphasis mine).

According to the speaker at church that morning, the gospel authors cited Old Testament prophecy fifty-six times to demonstrate that Jesus was the Messiah. He also said there were many more Jewish prophecies (over three hundred[1]) that identified Jesus as the Jewish Savior. But as I tracked along, many of these prophecies seemed to be less powerful than the speaker claimed. He seemed to be confusing important forms of evidence.

Every crime scene provides two types of evidence. Sometimes a piece of evidence points specifically to a suspect with great clarity—fingerprints or DNA evidence, for example. If the suspect's fingerprints or DNA is already in our databases, we can identify him (or her) *before* we make an arrest. "Clear" evidence points unambiguously to the person of interest from the onset.

CLEAR EVIDENCE

Points to the
Person of Interest
from the onset

Time of the crime   Time of the arrest

Some evidence, however, is *less* clear. "Cloaked" evidence is often confusing—it may not point to the suspect at all. Imagine finding a button at the same crime scene, lying on the floor a few feet from the victim's body. Does this belong to the suspect or to the victim? Did it arrive here as a result of the crime, or was it lying in the room before the crime occurred? The button may be useful evidence, or it may be a useless artifact. We won't know for sure until we meet the suspect.

If one of the suspect's shirts is missing a button that matches the one at the crime scene, this piece of evidence will become an important part of our case. While "clear" evidence points to the suspect from the onset (before he is contacted), "cloaked" evidence points to the suspect only in hindsight (after he is identified).

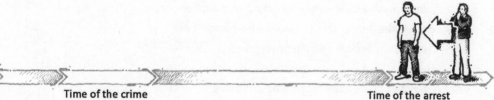

Time of the crime   Time of the arrest

CLOAKED EVIDENCE

Points to the
Person of Interest
in hindsight

This "clear" and "cloaked" distinction is important, and the guest speaker didn't seem to distinguish between the two. At times he cited a biblical passage as if it were a "clear" prophecy, plainly and unambiguously describing and predicting the coming Messiah from the *onset*,[2] when, in fact, it really appeared to be a cloaked description that happened to match Jesus of Nazareth in *hindsight*.

CLEAR PROPHECIES

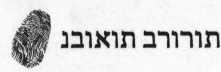

Point to the
Person of Interest
from the onset

Time of
appearance

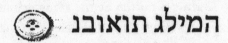

CLOAKED PROPHECIES

Point to the
Person of Interest
in hindsight

Let me give you two examples the speaker provided from the prophet Isaiah. "Isaiah predicted the Savior would lead every nation and usher in eternal peace." He cited Isaiah 2:4 (ESV):

> He shall judge between the nations,
>   and shall decide disputes for many peoples;
> and they shall beat their swords into plowshares,
>   and their spears into pruning hooks;
> nation shall not lift up sword against nation,
>   neither shall they learn war anymore.

This passage seems to be a relatively unambiguous and straightforward description of what God will do in the future. Perhaps that's why it is considered a messianic prophecy even by Jewish believers today.[3] It is a "clear" piece of evidence in our biblical "crime scene."

"Isaiah also said that the Savior would be beaten on his back, have his beard pulled, and would be spat upon." For this prophecy, the speaker cited Isaiah 50:6–7 (ESV):

> I gave my back to those who strike,
>   and my cheeks to those who pull
>   out the beard;
> I hid not my face
>   from disgrace and spitting.
>
> But the Lord GOD helps me;
>   therefore I have not been disgraced;
> therefore I have set my face like a flint,
>   and I know that I shall not be put
>   to shame.

Jewish believers do not accept this passage as a messianic prophecy,[4] and as I read along with the speaker, I could understand why Jews hesitate to include it. The passage, in a straightforward reading, appears to be a description Isaiah is offering about *himself*, not the future Messiah. Would someone reading this passage *prior* to the arrival of Jesus think Isaiah was referring to the coming Savior? This seems unlikely.

"Your detective skepticism is starting to show," Susie said on the way home.

"I'm not saying it isn't good evidence," I replied. "I'm just saying that it's a different *kind* of evidence." The button at the crime scene I described earlier still has incredible value, but unlike a fingerprint, it begins to help us only once we have a suspect in view. In a similar way, the cloaked prophecies are

 OBJECTION: IF THE PROPHECIES ARE SO GOOD, WHY DON'T MORE JEWS ACCEPT THEM?

Jewish believers typically take the following approach when evaluating messianic prophecies:

1. They limit the verses and prophecies they are willing to include in the investigation.
2. They exclude any verse that describes the Messiah —as a person—in any detail.
3. When interpreting the remaining verses, they reject any interpretation that points to a *person* rather than the *nation of Israel* or a *group of people* within the nation.
4. They ignore the "cloaked" verses (which point to a person of interest in hindsight).

But is this approach to the biblical evidence reasonable? Can you imagine doing something similar in a criminal case? Imagine, for example:

1. *Limiting* the evidence you're willing to include in the investigation. What good investigator doesn't want to expand the yellow tape as far as possible to make sure he or she gathers everything?
2. *Disregarding* any evidence that describes the suspect in any detail. What kind of detective would purposely reject the evidence that most clearly and specifically points to a suspect?
3. *Rejecting* any interpretation of the evidence that points to a suspect in favor of an interpretation that points to something *other* than a suspect. Why would a detective try to reinterpret evidence to avoid any inference to a suspect?
4. *Ignoring* all the "cloaked" evidence (which points to a suspect in hindsight). Why wouldn't a good detective want to confirm his or her conclusions with the previously cloaked evidence at the scene?

If Jewish believers approached the evidence for Jesus as they might approach the evidence in a crime scene, they would be far more likely to accept him as the prophesied Messiah.

limited in their ability to *point us* to the Messiah. They may, however, help us *confirm* his identity once we have him in view.

While I am always interested in cloaked evidence, clear evidence leads us more precisely, and more quickly, to a person of interest.

 ## RELIABLE INFORMANTS

This confusion between clear and cloaked evidence wasn't the only distinction the speaker failed to make. He also made no effort to distinguish between two kinds of informants.

All the prophets he mentioned were "informants" of a sort, and as a detective, I understood the value of a good informant. In my years working undercover, I developed several confidential informants who helped me identify robbery and burglary suspects. Many of them were even able to tell me about crimes that hadn't yet occurred.

The best informants are *reliable* informants. This isn't simply a personal distinction; it's a legal definition. A reliable informant is "a person who has a history or 'track record' of providing accurate information to officers. If qualified as 'tested,' he or she will be presumed reliable unless there is reason to believe otherwise."[7] If an informant has given information in the past and this information proved to be true, he or she is now considered reliable. Informants of this nature can be used to authenticate and establish search warrants and are generally more likely to be trusted in a court of law.

The Old Testament also had a criterion for a reliable "informant." Moses defined a reliable prophet in the following manner: "When the prophet speaks in the name of the LORD, and the thing does not happen or come true, that is the thing which the LORD has not spoken. The prophet has spoken it presumptuously; you are not to be afraid of him" (Deuteronomy 18:22 NASB).

If a prophet makes predictions that can be tested (they eventually come to pass), he is considered a true, reliable prophet of God. If he makes a mistake—even *one* mistake—he is not to be trusted. There are several examples of these kinds of

 CAN YOU TRUST INFORMANTS?

Investigators must be careful to test their informants. One way to do this is to examine their motives. Jurors are instructed to examine an informant "with caution and close scrutiny."[5] They are told to "consider the extent to which (an informant's statement) may have been influenced by the receipt of, or expectation of, any benefits."[6] What possible motives would ancient Jewish prophets have to lie about the coming Messiah?

tested, reliable informants in the Old Testament. Many Jewish prophets predicted more than simply the nature of the Messiah; many accurately predicted the events of history.[8]

Title: Reliable Informant (RI or CRI)

Definition: A person who has a history or track record of providing accurate information to officers. If qualified as TESTED, he or she will be presumed reliable unless there is reason to believe otherwise.

U.S. v. Jones (1st Cir 2012)

title: prophet of god
נביא
(han·na·vi)

definition: a person who "speaks in the name of the LORD," if the thing does not come about or come true, that is the thing which the LORD has not spoken. the prophet has spoken it presumptuously; you shall not be afraid of him.

deuteronomy 18:22

The prophet Nahum, for example, predicted the destruction of Nineveh and even predicted the way it would be destroyed. In approximately 614 BCE, Nahum predicted the condition of the Ninevites at the time of their demise:

> They will be entangled among thorns
> > and drunk from their wine;
> > they will be consumed like dry stubble. (Nahum 1:10)

Nahum said the Ninevites would be drunk during their final hours, and the ancient Greek historian Diodorus Siculus later confirmed this.[9]

2 years prior to its destruction

Destruction of Nineveh prophesied

614 BCE   612 BCE

Nahum 3:1-9

The prophet Isaiah was also accurate when he predicted the destruction of Babylon. Between 701 and 681 BCE, Isaiah made a prediction that was not fulfilled until 539 BCE:

> This is what the Lord says to his anointed,
>> to Cyrus, whose right hand I take hold of
> to subdue nations before him
>> and to strip kings of their armor,
> to open doors before him
>> so that gates will not be shut. (Isaiah 45:1)

Isaiah said God would open the gates of Babylon for Cyrus and his attacking army. Despite Babylon's remarkable defenses, which included moats, walls, and watchtowers, Cyrus was able to enter the city and conquer it. He did so by diverting the flow of the Euphrates River into a large lake basin before marching his army across the riverbed and into the city.[10]

Isaiah also predicted Babylon would be turned into a swamp:

> "I will turn her into a place for owls
>> and into swampland;
> I will sweep her with the broom of destruction,"
>> declares the Lord Almighty. (Isaiah 14:23)

When archaeologists excavated Babylon during the 1800s, they discovered that some parts of the city could not be uncovered because they were under a water table, just as Isaiah predicted, confirming his status as a reliable informant.[11]

Nearly 150 years prior to its destruction

Destruction of **Babylon** prophesied

681 BCE   614 BCE 612 BCE   539 BCE
Isaiah 13:1-19

The prophet Ezekiel established his reliability by correctly predicting that Tyre would be attacked by many nations and that the stone, timber, and soil of Tyre would be thrown into the sea: "They will plunder your wealth and loot your merchandise; they will break down your walls and demolish your fine houses and throw your stones, timber and rubble into the sea" (Ezekiel 26:12).

Alexander the Great built a land bridge from the mainland to the island of Tyre when he attacked the city in 332 BCE. It is believed he took the rubble from Tyre's ruins and threw it (stones, timber, and soil) into the sea to build the land bridge.[12]

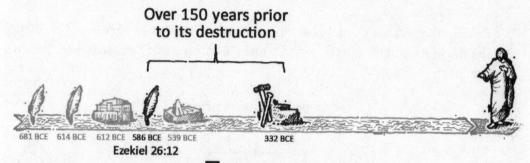

Over 150 years prior to its destruction

681 BCE   614 BCE   612 BCE   **586 BCE**   539 BCE   332 BCE

Ezekiel 26:12

Destruction of Tyre prophesied

Another reliable informant, Jeremiah, predicted the destruction of Edom sometime between 626 and 586 BCE:

> "The terror you inspire
>   and the pride of your heart have deceived you,
> you who live in the clefts of the rocks,
>   who occupy the heights of the hill.
> Though you build your nest as high as the eagle's,
>   from there I will bring you down,"
>   declares the Lord. (Jeremiah 49:16)

Edom's capital city, Petra, was carved in the side of a mountain. Despite this, it was sacked, and the Nabataean Empire no longer exists. It suffered occupation from several ruling powers (including Romans, Muslims, and Christians), but it eventually fell into ruin.[13]

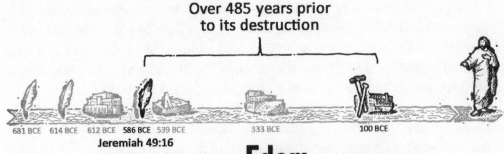

Over 485 years prior
to its destruction

681 BCE   614 BCE   612 BCE   **586 BCE**   539 BCE   333 BCE   **100 BCE**

Jeremiah 49:16

Destruction of **Edom** prophesied

Finally, the prophet Daniel also confirmed his reliability by accurately predicting the fall of Alexander the Great in Daniel 8:5–8, over two hundred years before his demise.[14]

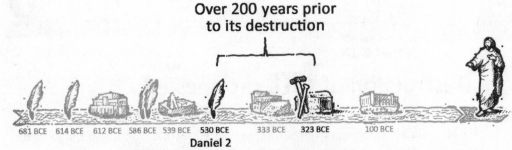

Over 200 years prior
to its destruction

681 BCE   614 BCE   612 BCE   586 BCE   539 BCE   **530 BCE**   333 BCE   **323 BCE**   100 BCE

Daniel 2

End of **Alexander the Great** prophesied

Daniel also predicted the rise of several kingdoms in Daniel chapters 2, 7, 8, 9, 11, and 12.[15]

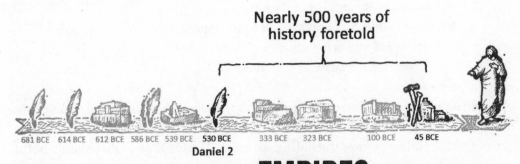

Nearly 500 years of
history foretold

681 BCE   614 BCE   612 BCE   586 BCE   539 BCE   **530 BCE**   333 BCE   323 BCE   100 BCE   **45 BCE**

Daniel 2

Many **EMPIRES** prophesied

CLEAR, RELIABLE, AND EXHAUSTIVE

These five prophets demonstrated themselves to be trustworthy and reliable. They made predictions, and history proved these predictions correct. This doesn't mean the other Old Testament prophets shouldn't be trusted. It just means that without predictions related to history, many of these prophets cannot be tested. I've used many untested informants with great success, but as you might expect, reliable informants are in a category of their own.

As I examined the claims of the speaker, I organized my investigation using several detective principles.

First, I gave clear evidence (prophecies) priority over cloaked. As I read the passages scholars have identified as messianic, I asked myself the question, "If I were reading this prior to the arrival of Jesus, would I clearly understand this as a description of the coming Messiah?" If I could answer yes, I placed it in the "clear" collection.

Second, I gave reliable informants (prophets) priority over the others, even though I collected *every* messianic prediction, placing them in a timeline along the "prophetic fuse."

Third, I examined the prophetic information asking the six investigative questions I ask in every inquiry: what, where, why, how, when, and who? Once the first five questions had been resolved, as in all my investigations, I sought to accurately answer the most important question: Who is the person of interest? My hope in all this was to discover *who* fit the description of the Jewish Messiah and *why* this person of interest arrived *when* he did.

THE MOST ANCIENT PREDICTIONS

Old Testament messianic prophecy is anything but chronologically consistent. Not every generation possessed a prophet who spoke about the coming Messiah. Instead, prophecies of this nature are clustered and unevenly spaced along the fuse leading up to the first century.

The first descriptions of a Jewish person of interest occur, however, prior to any of this historical turmoil. In the years before 1400 BCE, Moses and Job described a coming Savior with the following characteristics (the clear prophecies are printed in bold):[16]

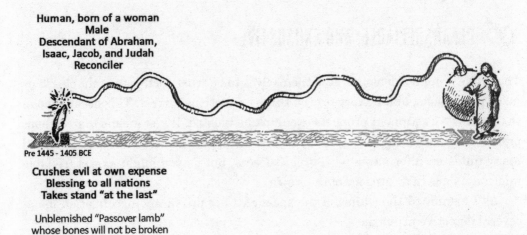

Human, born of a woman
Male
Descendant of Abraham,
Isaac, Jacob, and Judah
Reconciler

Pre 1445 - 1405 BCE

Crushes evil at own expense
Blessing to all nations
Takes stand "at the last"

Unblemished "Passover lamb"
whose bones will not be broken

Even conservatively limiting our list to the clear prophecies, some of our six investigative questions are starting to be answered. But these descriptions aren't yet specific enough to identify the coming Messiah. If our person of interest had come at this point in history, even the Jewish people would not have recognized him, given the scant information Moses and Job provided.[17]

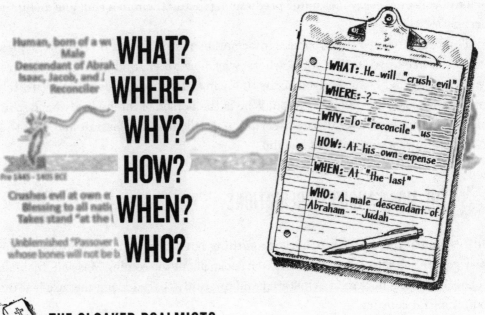

WHAT?
WHERE?
WHY?
HOW?
WHEN?
WHO?

WHAT: He will "crush evil"

WHERE: -?

WHY: To "reconcile" us

HOW: At his own expense

WHEN: At "the last"

WHO: A male descendant of Abraham - Judah

THE CLOAKED PSALMISTS

The next set of prophecies doesn't occur for nearly four hundred years, and they arrive through the quills of the psalmists David, Solomon, and Asaph (written between 1060 and 1015 BCE):[18]

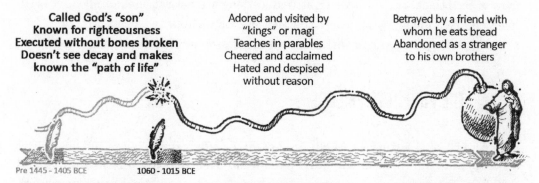

Called God's "son"
Known for righteousness
Executed without bones broken
Doesn't see decay and makes
known the "path of life"

Adored and visited by
"kings" or magi
Teaches in parables
Cheered and acclaimed
Hated and despised
without reason

Betrayed by a friend with
whom he eats bread
Abandoned as a stranger
to his own brothers

Pre 1445 – 1405 BCE   1060 – 1015 BCE

Killed as part of murderous plot
Comes to do the will of the
Father, voluntarily
Accused by false witnesses while
his friends stand far off
Mocked and criticized by people
shaking their heads

Quiet before his accusers
Stripped of his clothing, and
his executors will cast lots
Hands and feet are pierced
Thirsty when he dies, given
vinegar to drink

Prays for his enemies
Forsaken, he cries, "Into your
hands I commit my Spirit"
Dies but defeats death,
rising from the grave
Greater than David, he ascends to
God's right hand and reigns forever

The poetic prose of the psalmists provided more cloaked than clear information, but a few new details (written in bold) can now be added to the growing messianic summary:[19]

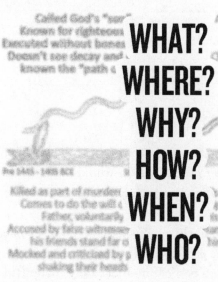

WHAT?
WHERE?
WHY?
HOW?
WHEN?
WHO?

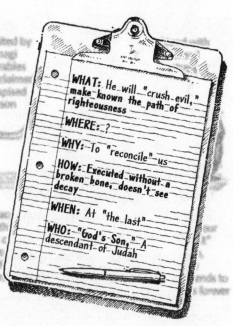

WHAT: He will "crush evil,"
make known the path of
righteousness

WHERE: ?

WHY: To "reconcile" us

HOW: Executed without a
broken bone, doesn't see
decay

WHEN: At "the last"

WHO: "God's Son," A
descendant of Judah

If the Messiah had arrived at this point in history, the description offered so far still would not have made his identity clear. Although the psalmists added a few new descriptions, our six investigative questions are not yet adequately answered, particularly in identifying *where* the Messiah would appear.

But that would change with the next set of prophetic declarations.

THE PROPHETS EMERGE

After a period of silence in which the nation of Israel was divided, the next burst of messianic information came in the two-hundred-year span between 931 and 700 BCE. Several prophets (Samuel, Joel, Hosea, Amos, and Micah) and one proverb writer (Agur son of Jakeh) made proclamations about the coming person of interest:[20]

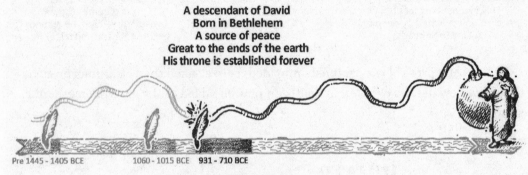

A descendant of David
Born in Bethlehem
A source of peace
Great to the ends of the earth
His throne is established forever

Pre 1445 - 1405 BCE   1060 - 1015 BCE   931 - 710 BCE

Restores the barren land and
makes it abundant and fruitful

Called out of Egypt
Promises the Spirit
Identified as the "Son of God"
who ascends and descends from heaven

Once again, few new pieces of clear information are offered in this period of Jewish history. Aside from the question of where the Messiah would appear, not many other questions are answered with enough detail to accurately identify our person of interest.[21]

As before, if the Jewish Messiah had arrived at this point in history, few people would have recognized him from *clear* messianic prophecy. Much more information was needed, and it was about to arrive from the pen of one incredibly insightful prophet.

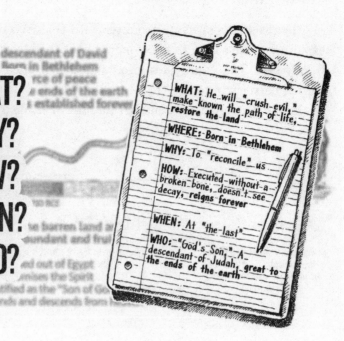

WHAT?
WHY?
HOW?
WHEN?
WHO?

WHAT: He will "crush evil,"
make known the path of life,
restore the land

WHERE: Born in Bethlehem

WHY: To "reconcile" us

HOW: Executed without a
broken bone, doesn't see
decay, reigns forever

WHEN: At "the last"

WHO: "God's Son," A
descendant of Judah, great to
the ends of the earth

ISAIAH ARRIVES

Isaiah prophesied under the reign of four kings of Judah (over the course of about sixty-four years). Maybe that's why he is responsible for more messianic prophecy than any other Jewish prophet.

A descendant of Jesse
Preceded by a forerunner
Called a Nazarene
Comes to Jerusalem to redeem
those who turned from their sins
Brings good news of salvation
Performs miracles

Heals the blind, deaf, mute, and lame
Sets the captives free and comforts
those who are mourning
A shepherd who cares for his sheep
Has the "Spirit of the Lord" and
"Fear of God"
"Numbered with the transgressors"

Despised and forsaken,
and man of sorrows
Oppressed and silent before accusers
Stricken, smitten, a "bruised reed"
His scourging will heal us

Pre 1445 - 1405 BCE   1060 - 1015 BCE   931 - 710 BCE   700 - 681BCE

Bears our griefs and sorrows,
suffers for the sins of others
Is afflicted along with the afflicted,
but redeems and saves them
Pierced through for our sins and
crushed for our iniquities
Dies due to the sins of God's people
Buried in a wealthy man's tomb

Does not remain dead, sees
future generations
Conquers death, hunger, and illness
Defeats evil and tyranny
Causes all the dead to rise again
Reigns forever in mercy
Causes all nations to recognize the
wrongs they did to Israel
Intercedes for sinners and justifies many

Brings justice and peace
Includes and attracts people
from all cultures and nations
Worshiped by all nations
A light to people
"Wonderful Counselor," "Mighty
God," "Everlasting Father," "Prince
of Peace," "King of Kings," and
"Lord of Lords"

He also has a special encounter with God (recorded in Isaiah 6), which may explain why he seems to know more about the Messiah than almost anyone else. In any case, Isaiah provides an abundant list of clear predictions related to the Jewish person of interest.[22]

Isaiah also provided a smaller number of cloaked descriptions:[23]

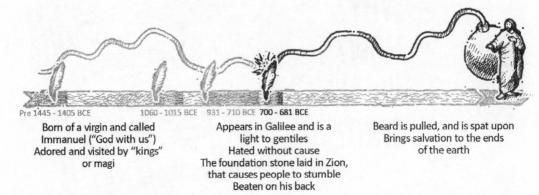

Pre 1445 - 1405 BCE   1060 - 1015 BCE   931 - 710 BCE   **700 - 681 BCE**

Born of a virgin and called
Immanuel ("God with us")
Adored and visited by "kings"
or magi

Appears in Galilee and is a
light to gentiles
Hated without cause
The foundation stone laid in Zion,
that causes people to stumble
Beaten on his back

Beard is pulled, and is spat upon
Brings salvation to the ends
of the earth

Isaiah's robust collection of clear predictions helps us to answer two more investigative questions. Prior to Isaiah, the ancients knew where the Messiah would arrive, but little else by which to identify the coming person of interest.[24]

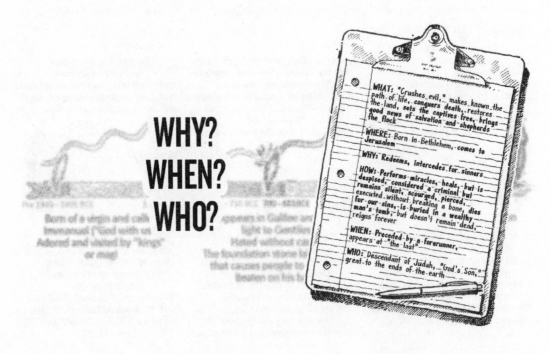

After Isaiah, the ancient Jews knew much more about *what* the Messiah would do and *how* he would do it. While their "clipboard" now contained answers to every question, the prophetic information was still vague and unspecific, especially when attempting to explain *why* the Messiah was coming and, more importantly, *when* he would arrive—two critical questions that wouldn't be answered robustly for centuries to come.

TWO MORE RELIABLE "INFORMANTS"

Another group of prophets and Jewish writers appeared approximately six hundred years before the Common Era. Ezekiel and Jeremiah (who proved to be reliable based on their accurate predictions of history), along with the sons of Kora, Ethan the Ezrahite, and other unnamed psalmists, described the coming person of interest with clear and cloaked predictions:[25]

A descendent of David through Judah
The Good Shepherd
Reigns as king and "does justice
and righteousness"
Ushers in a new era in which God will
forgive their sin

Pre 1445 - 1405 BCE   1060 - 1015 BCE   931 - 710 BCE   700 - 681 BCE   **590 - 539 BCE**

Brings in a new covenant
Restores Israel's cities
Makes the barren land
abundant and fruitful
Destroys the weapons of war
Called "The Lord our righteousness"
Exalted from humility

Conceived by the Holy Spirit
Object of a murderous plot,
but hope lies ahead
Accused by false witnesses
Cut off in his prime while
he is still young
Is resurrected from the grave

While these writers provided several clear prophecies during this time, they offered little *new* information.[26]

Even with these additional prophecies, ancient Jewish readers *still* would have been unable to answer the final three investigative questions related to the Messiah. Most importantly, at this point in history, they would have known extraordinarily little about *when* the Messiah would appear.

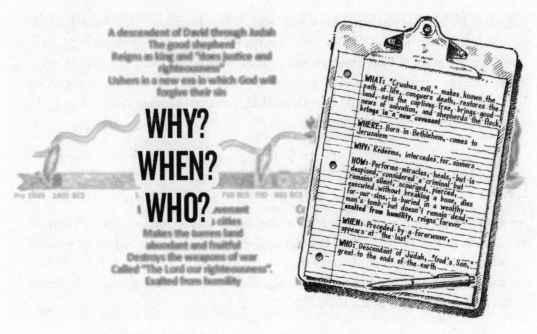

A descendent of David through Judah
The good shepherd
Reigns as king and "does justice and righteousness"
Ushers in a new era in which God will forgive their sin

WHY?
WHEN?
WHO?

...venant
...cities
...
Makes the barren land abundant and fruitful
Destroys the weapons of war
Called "The Lord our righteousness"
Exalted from humility

WHAT: "Crushes evil," makes known the path of life, conquers death, restores the land, sets the captives free, brings good news of salvation, and shepherds the flock, brings in a new covenant

WHERE: Born in Bethlehem, comes to Jerusalem

WHY: Redeems, intercedes for sinners

HOW: Performs miracles, heals, but is despised, considered a criminal but remains silent, scourged, pierced, executed without breaking a bone, dies for our sins, is buried in a wealthy man's tomb, but doesn't remain dead, exalted from humility, reigns forever

WHEN: Preceded by a forerunner, appears at "the last"

WHO: Descendant of Judah, "God's Son," great to the ends of the earth

That would all change when another reliable prophet arrived on the scene.

THE VISIONS OF DANIEL

As a young man, the prophet Daniel was carried off to Babylon when King Nebuchad-nezzar captured Jerusalem. While there, Daniel interpreted the dreams of the king, predicting the history of nations we described earlier. Years later, in the first year of Belshazzar's reign, Daniel had visions of the coming "son of man" (Daniel 7:13).

Brings an end and makes atonement for sin
Brings everlasting righteousness
Fulfills prophecy and anoints a most holy place

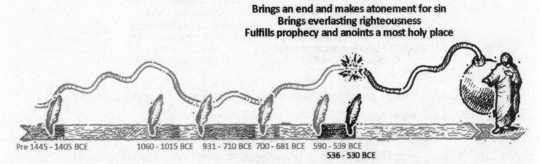

Pre 1445 - 1405 BCE   1060 - 1015 BCE   931 - 710 BCE   700 - 681 BCE   590 - 539 BCE
                                                                    536 - 530 BCE

Appears after a decree to rebuild Jerusalem
Appears before Jerusalem and the temple are destroyed
Will be the "Son of Man," and have an everlasting throne

These visions provided clear data related to the Messiah, including a remarkable prediction about the *timing* of the Messiah's arrival.[27]

Daniel's prediction (recorded in Daniel 9:25–26) provides us with a timeframe in which the Jewish person of interest would appear in history. This timeframe has clear beginning and ending points: "So you are to know and understand that **from the issuing of a decree to restore and rebuild Jerusalem, until Messiah the Prince,** there will be *seven weeks and sixty-two weeks*; it will be built again, with streets and moat, even in times of distress. Then after the *sixty-two weeks,* **the Messiah will be cut off and have nothing**, and the people of the prince who is to come will **destroy the city and the sanctuary**" (NASB, emphasis mine).

Three things are clear from this prediction: First, the Messiah will come sometime *after* a decree is issued to rebuild Jerusalem. Second, the Messiah will then be "cut off" and "have nothing." Finally, all this will happen sometime *before* Jerusalem and the temple are destroyed.

Daniel also narrowed the timeframe by providing two references to "seven weeks and sixty-two weeks," and "sixty-two weeks." But what did Daniel mean by this refence to "weeks"? For the answer to that question and its impact on predicting the Messiah, I will defer to my investigative predecessor, Sir Robert Anderson.

Anderson was the assistant commissioner of the London Metropolitan Police (Scotland Yard) from 1888 to 1901; he was also a theologian and author. He wrote many books related to Christianity, science, and prophecy, including *The Coming Prince*.[28] His observations and calculations related to Daniel's prophecies are enlightening, even if somewhat controversial.[29]

First, to better understand the way Daniel uses the word *weeks*, he cites two Old Testament verses:

In accordance with the number of days that you spied out the land, forty days, *for every day you shall suffer the punishment for your guilt a year*, that is, forty years, and you will know My opposition. (Numbers 14:34 NASB, emphasis mine)

When you have completed these days, you shall lie down a second time, but on your right side, and bear the wrongdoing of the house of Judah; I have assigned it to you for forty days, *a day for each year*. (Ezekiel 4:6 NASB, emphasis mine)

Old Testament prophets commonly counted *years* by a number of *days*. Forty days indicated forty years for Moses and Ezekiel. In a similar way, Daniel described sixty-nine *weeks* when he really meant sixty-nine "weeks' worth" of *days*, and these days are actually *years*.[30]

Using the passages written by Moses and Ezekiel as a guide, Anderson reconstructs Daniel's prophecy:

WHO IS SIR ROBERT ANDERSON?

Sir Robert Anderson was born in Dublin, Ireland, on May 29, 1841. His father was a distinguished elder in the Presbyterian Church of Ireland. He was raised in a devout Christian home but had a crisis of doubt as a teenager. Once he decided Christianity was true, he became friends with some of the greatest Bible teachers of his day, including James Martin Gray, C. I. Scofield, A. C. Dixon, Horatius Bonar, and E. W. Bullinger. He was educated as a lawyer but eventually became a police detective. After a long, celebrated career, he died from the Spanish flu in 1918 at the age of seventy-seven.

> From the issuing of a decree to restore and rebuild Jerusalem, until Messiah the Prince, there will be seven weeks [of years] and sixty-two weeks [of years].
> (Daniel 9:25 NASB)

Daniel claimed there would be sixty-nine "weeks of years" between the issuing of a decree to rebuild Jerusalem and the appearance of the Messiah:

$$7 \text{ weeks} + 62 \text{ weeks} = 69 \text{ weeks}$$
$$69 \text{ weeks} \times 7 \text{ days/years} = 483 \text{ years}$$

According to Anderson's calculations, the Messiah would appear 483 years after the issuing of the decree. But during this time in antiquity, Jewish years were comprised of twelve thirty-day months (Jewish years had 360—not 365—days):

$$483 \text{ years} \times 360 \text{ days} = 173,880 \text{ days}$$

Anderson, therefore, argued that when Daniel wrote, "From the issuing of a decree to restore and rebuild Jerusalem until Messiah the Prince there will be seven weeks and sixty-two weeks," he actually meant, "From the issuing of a decree to restore and rebuild Jerusalem until Messiah the Prince there will be 173,880 days."

According to Anderson, we can now be more specific when trying to determine when the Messiah will appear: Daniel predicts the Messiah will emerge 173,880 days *after* the decree to rebuild Jerusalem and the temple, and sometime *prior* to the next destruction of Jerusalem and the temple.

Let's return now to our prophetic fuse timeline. In 586 BCE Daniel predicted a future decree to rebuild Jerusalem. But when did that decree take place? Anderson points to the Old Testament prophet Nehemiah, who described the decree to restore and rebuild Jerusalem issued "in the month of Nisan in the twentieth year of King Artaxerxes" (Nehemiah 2:1),[31] which is March 5, 444 BCE,[32] according to our Julian calendar.[33] Daniel predicted this decree 142 years prior to its fulfillment.

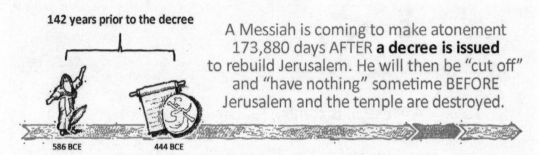

142 years prior to the decree

586 BCE   444 BCE

A Messiah is coming to make atonement 173,880 days AFTER **a decree is issued** to rebuild Jerusalem. He will then be "cut off" and "have nothing" sometime BEFORE Jerusalem and the temple are destroyed.

Daniel made another important prediction. He prophesied that "the people of the ruler who will come will destroy the city and the sanctuary" (Daniel 9:26). This did ultimately occur in 70 CE. Daniel correctly predicted the event 655 years *before* it occurred. This shouldn't surprise us since his predictions related to the sequence of nations have already confirmed his reliability.

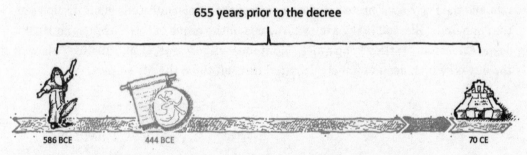

655 years prior to the decree

586 BCE   444 BCE   70 CE

A Messiah is coming to make atonement 173,880 days AFTER a decree is issued to rebuild Jerusalem. He will then be "cut off" and "have nothing" sometime BEFORE **Jerusalem and the temple are destroyed**.

Even if we disagreed about the interpretation of "seven weeks and sixty-two weeks" as 173,880 days, we still have a clear prediction regarding the appearance of the Messiah: According to Anderson, Daniel predicted that the Messiah would appear sometime between 444 BCE and 70 CE.[34]

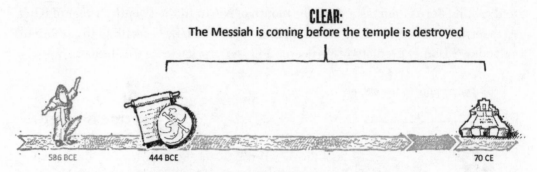

CLEAR:
The Messiah is coming before the temple is destroyed

586 BCE   444 BCE   70 CE

A Messiah is coming to make atonement
173,880 days AFTER a decree is issued to rebuild Jerusalem.
He will then be "cut off" and "have nothing"
sometime BEFORE Jerusalem and the temple are destroyed.

But Sir Robert didn't stop there. Instead, he argued for a much narrower window related to the appearance of the Messiah. He noted that Jesus, on numerous occasions, forbade and prevented his followers from revealing his identity as the Messiah.[35] But on March 30, 33 CE, when he entered Jerusalem on a donkey, he rebuked the Pharisees' protest and encouraged the whole multitude of his disciples as they shouted, "Blessed is the king who comes in the name of the Lord" (Luke 19:38). Jesus even said, "If they keep quiet, the stones will cry out" (Luke 19:40). This was the day on which Jesus publicly declared himself to be the Messiah.

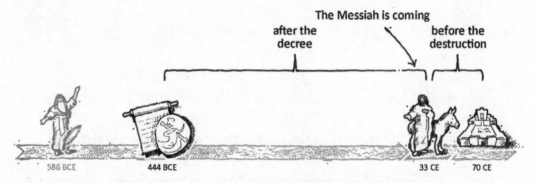

The Messiah is coming
after the
decree
before the
destruction

586 BCE   444 BCE   33 CE   70 CE

A Messiah is coming to make atonement
173,880 days AFTER a decree is issued to rebuild Jerusalem.
He will then be "cut off" and "have nothing"
sometime BEFORE Jerusalem and the temple are destroyed.

Anderson compared the date of the decree (March 5, 444 BCE) with the date of Jesus's declaration (March 30, 33 CE) and observed that the time span from 444 BCE to 33 CE is 476 years (remember 1 BCE to 1 CE is only one year). And if we multiply 476 years × 365.2421879 days per year (corrected for leap years), we get the result of 173,855 days. Close, but not precisely what Daniel predicted (although still remarkable). Now let's add back the difference between March 5 and March 30 (twenty-five days). What is our total? You guessed it: 173,880 days, exactly as Daniel predicted.

Even *without* Anderson's calculations, Daniel's prophecy still helped answer the "when" question by providing a timeframe (after the decree and before the destruction) in which the Messiah would appear.[36]

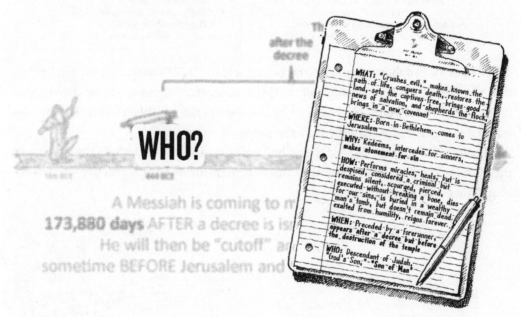

Daniel provided a range of dates (at the very least), and the last Jewish prophets provided a profile that would identify the Jewish person of interest, within Daniel's timeframe.[37]

 THE FINAL DESCRIPTION

The prophets Zechariah, Ezra, and Malachi gave us the final bits of messianic data as the fuse continued to burn toward the Common Era. These last prophecies confirmed the timetable Daniel described:[38]

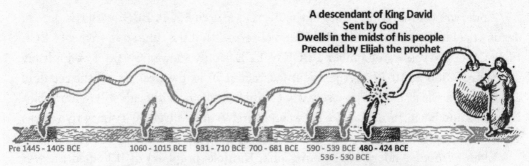

A descendant of King David
Sent by God
Dwells in the midst of his people
Preceded by Elijah the prophet

Pre 1445 - 1405 BCE   1060 - 1015 BCE   931 - 710 BCE   700 - 681 BCE   590 - 539 BCE   **480 - 424 BCE**
                                                                            536 - 530 BCE

Is the cornerstone
Betrayed for thirty pieces of silver,
later thrown to the potter
Mourned for and cried over like
a "firstborn" son
A shepherd who is pierced with a sword
and whose sheep are scattered

Enters Jerusalem while
riding on a donkey
Preceded by a messenger who
will prepare the way
Suddenly enters his temple
Is the light of the world
Sits on the throne forever

Malachi's prophecy is particularly important. In Malachi 3:1, he confirmed that the Messiah would appear before the temple was destroyed (so he could enter it "suddenly") and would be preceded by a messenger, a prophet akin to Elijah, who would act as the marker to identify the person of interest.

Those expecting the Messiah now had specific information to help them identify the messianic person of interest in Daniel's timeframe (even if Anderson was wrong about his precise calculation):[39]

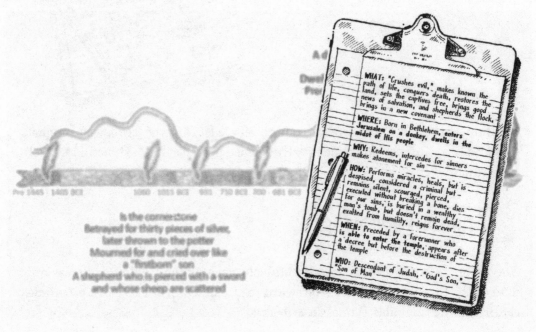

WHAT: "Crushes evil," makes known the path of life, conquers death, restores the land, sets the captives free, brings good news of salvation, and shepherds the flock, brings in a new covenant

WHERE: Born in Bethlehem, enters Jerusalem on a donkey, dwells in the midst of his people

WHY: Redeems, intercedes for sinners, makes atonement for sin

HOW: Performs miracles, heals, but is despised, considered a criminal but remains silent, scourged, pierced, executed without breaking a bone, dies for our sins, is buried in a wealthy man's tomb, but doesn't remain dead, exalted from humility, reigns forever

WHEN: Preceded by a forerunner who is able to enter the temple, appears after a decree but before the destruction of the temple

WHO: Descendant of Judah, "God's Son," "Son of Man"

The information was now complete; they had an adequate description of the Messiah. They knew *what* he would do, *where* he would do it, *why* he was coming, *how* he would accomplish his task, and *when* it would occur. With Malachi's final prophecies, the prophetic fuse burned to a close. Nothing more needed to be said; no additional description was necessary. There was enough information to answer the final and most important question: *Who* is the person of interest?

Jesus of Nazareth arrived in precisely the timeframe Daniel described. Was he the person of interest the prophets predicted? If so, the clear prophecies should have described him from the onset (before his arrival), and the cloaked prophecies should match Jesus in hindsight (after his arrival). The descriptions offered by the clear messianic prophecies answered the first five investigation questions and pointed to a unique who: a person of interest who sounded a lot like Jesus of Nazareth.

But we ought not ignore the cloaked prophecies. To do so would be the equivalent of ignoring the button at our crime scene. Even though these evidences may not have pointed to our person of interest from the onset, they corroborated this person of interest in hindsight. (To be conservative, I've listed Sir Robert Anderson's specific calculation on the cloaked side, even though I could easily have placed it with the clear prophecies):[40]

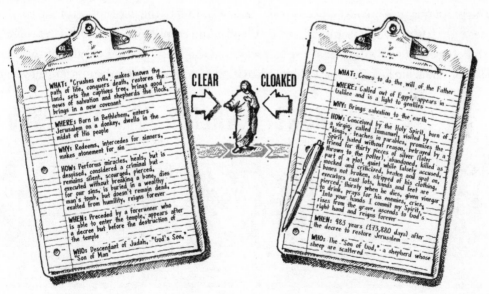

If, just for the sake of argument, we limited ourselves to only the *clear* prophecies from the *reliable* prophets (as we defined them earlier), we would still have a striking picture of a person of interest who resembles Jesus of Nazareth:[41]

ISAIAH
EZEKIEL

A descendant of David through Judah who arrives 483 years after the decree to restore Jerusalem. He will be preceded by a forerunner, conceived by the Holy Spirit, and born of a virgin. He will be visited by "kings" (magi) and called a Nazarene.

He will appear in Galilee, come to Jerusalem, performs miracles, heal the blind, deaf, mute and lame. He will shepherd His sheep and bring a message of peace and salvation.

He will be the "Son of Man," "Wonderful Counselor," "Mighty God," and "Prince of Peace."

He will be hated without a cause, beaten, and abused, and the object of a murderous plot. Despised and forsaken, he will be silent before His accusers, suffer for our iniquities, and pierced through. He will die due to the sins of God's people and will be buried in a wealthy man's tomb.

He will conquer death and come back to life, bringing a new covenant, and making atonement for sin.

JEREMIAH
DANIEL

WHY DID HE APPEAR WHEN HE APPEARED?

The prophetic fuse burned for centuries, slowly adding to the description of the coming Messiah. His arrival was anticipated by the gradual revelations of the Jewish prophets who offered the details necessary to recognize the long-awaited person of interest. Had he come earlier, few would have identified him, given the information they had.

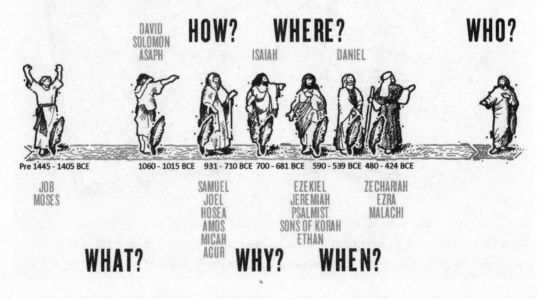

DAVID SOLOMON ASAPH   **HOW?**   **WHERE?**   **WHO?**

ISAIAH   DANIEL

Pre 1445 - 1405 BCE   1060 - 1015 BCE   931 - 710 BCE   700 - 681 BCE   590 - 539 BCE   480 - 424 BCE

JOB   SAMUEL   EZEKIEL   ZECHARIAH
MOSES   JOEL   JEREMIAH   EZRA
                   HOSEA   PSALMIST   MALACHI
                   AMOS   SONS OF KORAH
                   MICAH   ETHAN
WHAT?   AGUR   **WHY?**   **WHEN?**

But by the time the Jewish prophets had completed their description, the first five investigative questions had been answered sufficiently, leaving only the sixth.

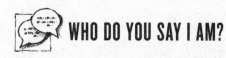

WHO DO YOU SAY I AM?

Susie had been reading through the gospel of Matthew. One evening after the children were asleep, she asked me, "Who do you say Jesus is?"

She read Matthew 16: "When Jesus came into the district of Caesarea Philippi, he asked his disciples, 'Who do people say that the Son of Man is?' And they said, 'Some say John the Baptist, others say Elijah, and others Jeremiah or one of the prophets.' He said to them, 'But who do you say that I am?' Simon Peter replied, 'You are the Christ, the Son of the living God'" (Matthew 16:13–16 ESV).

Peter may have been sure, but I wasn't ready to answer Susie yet.

That pesky "who" question lingered in my mind given the prophecies I had been investigating. I was also thinking about what this case might sound like in a courtroom:

Ladies and gentlemen of the jury, imagine assembling everyone who has ever lived on planet earth. Using the broadest, *clear* list of descriptions from only the *reliable* "informants" we've called as witnesses, let's begin to eliminate the people who don't fit the informants' descriptions.

The prophetic informants said the coming person of interest would be born of a woman. That wouldn't eliminate *anyone*:

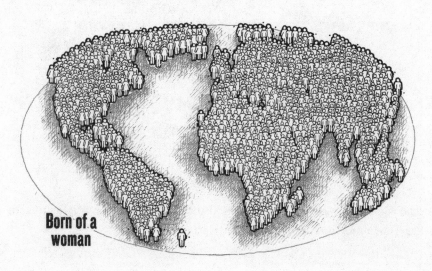

Born of a woman

But the prophets also said the person of interest would be a male. That would cut our candidate group in half (more or less):

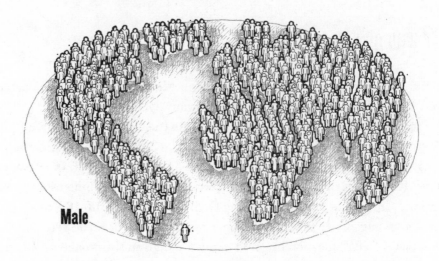

Male

The prophets said he would be a descendant of King David. Without our knowing precisely how many people that would eliminate, it's probably safe to say that millions more would be removed from our list of viable "suspects":

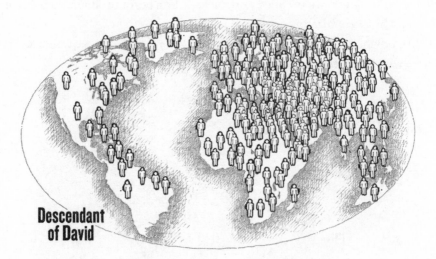

Descendant of David

The coming person of interest was also described consistently as a miracle worker. How many humans fit *that* description?

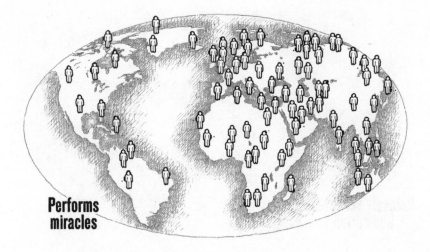

Performs miracles

According to the reliable "informants," our person of interest also appears in a relatively tight timeframe, sometime between the decree to restore the Jewish temple and the next time it's destroyed. Surely a huge group of people would be cut from candidacy by this limitation:

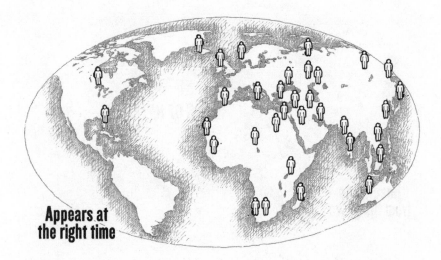

Appears at the right time

According to the reliable prophets, he was also scourged, pierced, executed without broken bones, and buried in a wealthy man's tomb. While there may have been others who fit this description, there could not have been many:

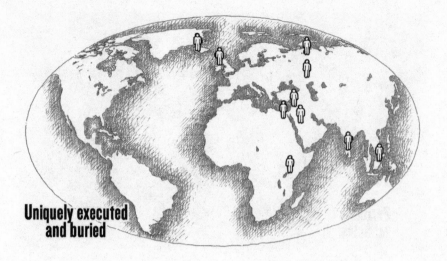

**Uniquely executed
and buried**

And then, according to these same reliable "informants," the Jewish person of interest would also conquer death by rising from the grave. Only one man fits this collective description and meets this final requirement:

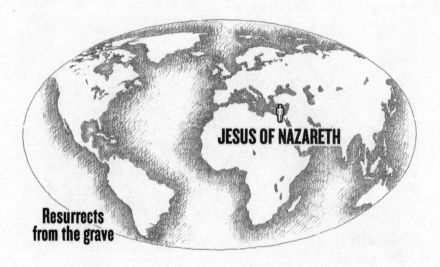

JESUS OF NAZARETH

**Resurrects
from the grave**

Ladies and gentlemen of the jury, I submit that only Jesus of Nazareth fits the description given by the reliable "informants" who have testified in this case . . .

I was wrestling with the obvious: the cultural, spiritual, and prophetic fuses of history burned toward the explosive arrival of the Common Era. Everything in history was about to change.

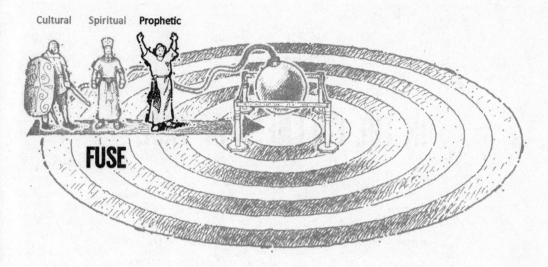

Cultural   Spiritual   **Prophetic**

FUSE

"I'm waiting . . ." said Susie, interrupting my thoughts and breaking the long silence. She was clearly eager to learn more, but I knew there was still a lot to discover.

"It definitely seems compelling so far . . ." I said, searching for words.

I could tell she hoped for more. Like me, she wasn't quite sure Jesus *mattered*, but with every step in my investigation, we inched closer to a decision.

"I'm still working on it," I assured her. "I've almost finished assembling the fuse . . ." That was a true statement, and what I was about to discover would surprise both of us.

Chapter 5

IN THE FULLNESS OF TIME

Jesus Arrives

Some things arrive on their own mysterious hour, on their own
terms and not yours, to be seized or relinquished forever.
—GAIL GODWIN

It is the mark of a good action that it appears inevitable in retrospect.
—ROBERT LOUIS STEVENSON

Weeks into our investigation, we located Steve's first wife, Gabrielle. It was more difficult than we expected. She was living in a small rural suburb of St. Louis.

"So far everyone we've met who had a relationship with Steve had a bad experience with him," said Kyle as he devoured his fourth White Castle slider. This was our first time at this restaurant chain, given that none exist in Southern California. We interviewed Gabrielle for nearly two hours and were now debriefing our conversation over our second order of sliders and fries.

"I'm starting to understand why Steve might have felt a sense of urgency to do something to Tammy," I replied, trying not to get cheese on my notepad.

Gabrielle and Steve met in high school, and she became pregnant with their daughter, Jillian, shortly after they began dating. They married after graduation, but their relationship was violent for the four years they were together.

Toward the end, Steve repeatedly abused Gabrielle until she fled the state with Jillian.

Gabrielle hired an attorney to help her collect child support from Steve, but Steve traveled to Missouri and showed up on her front porch, unannounced. He looked like he had been drinking and told her she would be wise to stop asking for money. He threatened to kill Gabrielle and Jillian if they ever contacted him again. She never did.

"Do you think he would actually have killed his own child?" I asked Gabrielle.

"I'm not sure exactly *what* to think, but I didn't want to test him. I can tell you this: Steve absolutely did not want any more children. He's never visited Jillian in all the years we've been here." Gabrielle fidgeted nervously as she answered our questions. "He told me he wished Jillian had never been born," she whispered.

Twelve-year-old Jillian was watching a video in the next room.

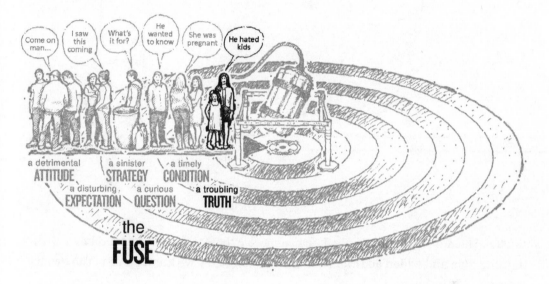

"Yeah, his dislike of kids explains a lot," said Kyle as he finished the last fry and began to clear the table. "Including the *timing* of all this."

Gabrielle's statement added to our understanding of the fuse that burned toward Tammy's disappearance. I began sketching a new timeline on my notepad. This additional chronology would help explain why Tammy disappeared when she did and why Steve may have been involved. I drew a few question marks on either side of a crime scene:

"Okay, we know Tammy disappeared at a particular point in time," I said. "We also know she vanished when she was living in our city with Steve . . ."

"You're not telling me anything I don't already know," interrupted Kyle.

"Yes, but there's a *reason* why it happened in our city when it did—why it didn't happen earlier or later—and the fuse leading up to her disappearance will show us why this was the case." I then drew another timeline with a bomb and a fuse. For larger, more readable sizes for this entire series of images, refer to case note.[1]

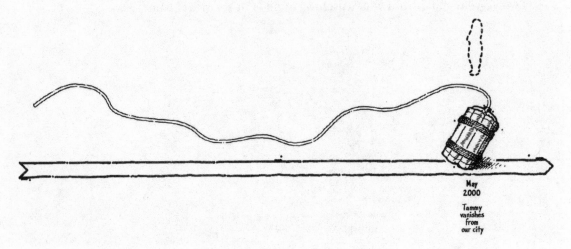

"On the day Tammy vanished, we suspect a 'bomb' exploded," I said as I drew the long fuse and added additional elements. "And now we know some of the events that ignited that fuse . . ."

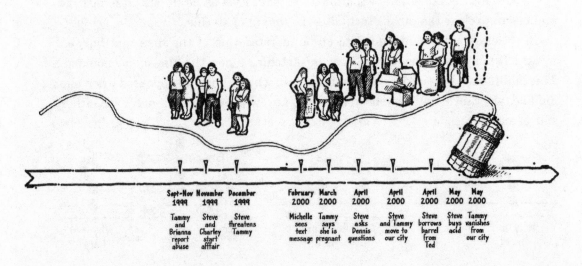

Kyle waited for me to finish the sketch, reminding me along the way of everything we had learned so far. "It's not hard to understand what happened here . . ." he said once we were finished.

"Given the allegations of abuse leading up to May 2000, combined with everything else we've learned, it's reasonable to conclude Steve is responsible for Tammy's disappearance." Finished with this portion of the drawing, I put down my pen, cleared the empty bags and wrappers from our table, and reviewed my notes. We were alone in this part of the restaurant, so I continued to sketch the fuse.

Kyle pointed to the drawing of the barrel and the chemicals. "Now we also know why we never found her body."

"True." I sifted through my notes. "So far all the evidence points to Steve and explains what motivated him, but this fuse can also explain the *timing* of the 'explosion.'"

I resketched another timeline as Kyle tapped his fingers on the table. "Can't you just *tell* me what you're after here?"

"Do I really need to answer that?" My new drawing featured Steve and Tammy with their moving boxes.

"We wouldn't be investigating this case if it had occurred outside our jurisdiction. But have you ever stopped to think about *why* it happened in our town? It happened here because Steve moved closer to a new job at an auto shop that had just opened. That shop didn't even exist in our city until January 2000 . . ." I quickly sketched the auto shop and highlighted the timeline following its opening:

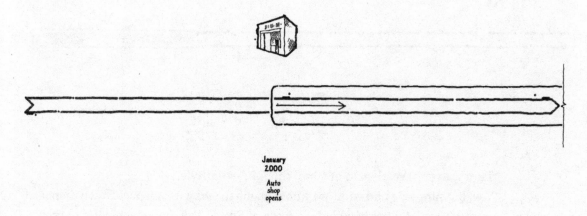

January
2000

Auto
shop
opens

". . . that's the whole reason he and Tammy moved here to begin with." I now highlighted the timeline from Tammy and Steve's arrival in our town:

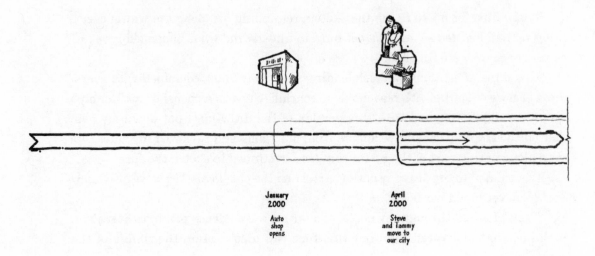

January
2000

Auto
shop
opens

April
2000

Steve
and Tammy
move to
our city

"This is our 'red zone.'" I drew a rectangle on the timeline where the two high-lighted areas overlapped. "If this crime was going to happen in our city, it would have to happen after Steve and Tammy moved here":

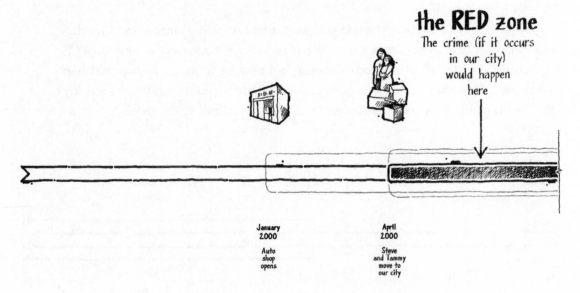

the RED zone
The crime (if it occurs
in our city)
would happen
here

January
2000

Auto
shop
opens

April
2000

Steve
and Tammy
move to
our city

"That's a very broad span of time, though," said Kyle.

"Yes, but now let's add what we know about the way we suspect Steve disposed of Tammy's body." I quickly added a sketch of Steve, Ted, and the plastic barrel.

Kyle could already see where I was headed. "Steve needed a barrel that would hold corrosive chemicals . . ."

"That's right," I replied, drawing the additional facts. "Ted would not have been able to give the barrel to Steve if Ted's boss hadn't first given it to Ted . . ." I highlighted the timeline around the date Ted first got the barrel and the date he gave it to Steve:

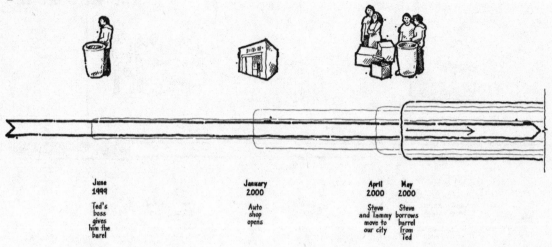

Next, I added a new "red zone":

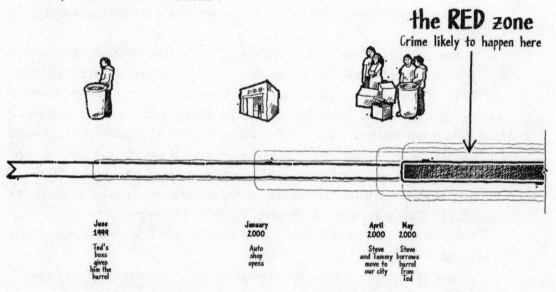

"This *smaller* red zone represents the time in which this crime was most likely to happen," I said. "*After* Steve had access to the barrel."

"*And* the chemicals," added Kyle.

I updated the drawing to include the opening of the chemical store in our town, along with the date Steve bought the chemicals and the new "red zone":

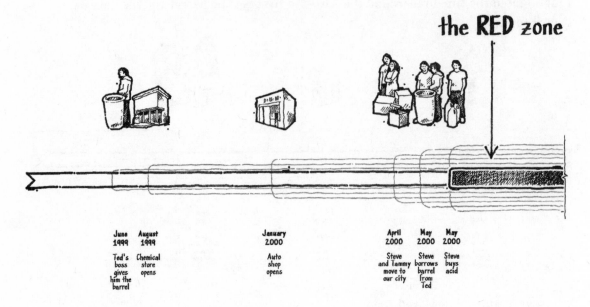

"The zone is shrinking." Kyle sifted his weight in his chair. "But where is all this going?"

"Almost done," I replied. "So far we've described only the events and factors that set the *beginning* of the red zone, but another event determined the *end limit* of this zone." I drew three sketches of Tammy, one with a baby crib and one in which she was obviously pregnant. I then highlighted the timeline as I did before, drawing from right to left, rather than from left to right. "Tammy's pregnancy set a *timer* on the fuse. It's the reason why the crime occurred when it did. If Steve wanted to get rid of her before she gave birth, he would have to do it before November of 2000 . . ."

"And if he wanted to do it before she started to show, he'd have to kill her before June, right?" Kyle pointed to my sketch of Tammy as a pregnant woman.

"Yes, and if he wanted to do it before she could even tell anyone, he would have to act even earlier."

"So you think Steve didn't want anyone to even *know* about the pregnancy?" asked Kyle.

"I don't think Steve knew that Tammy told Brianna, and if he killed her after it was public knowledge, people who knew how he felt about kids might suspect him for her disappearance—even more than they already did."

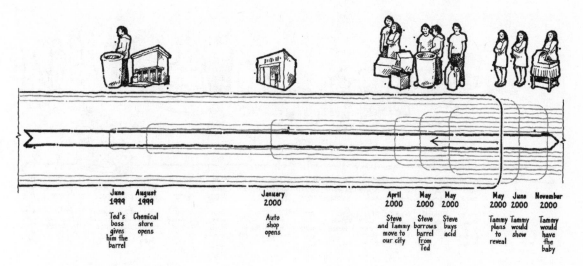

| June 1999 | August 1999 | | January 2000 | | April 2000 | May 2000 | May 2000 | | May 2000 | June 2000 | November 2000 |

Ted's boss gives him the barrel • Chemical store opens • Auto shop opens • Steve and Tammy move to our city • Steve borrows barrel from Ted • Steve buys acid • Tammy plans to reveal • Tammy would show • Tammy would have the baby

I highlighted the updated "red zone":

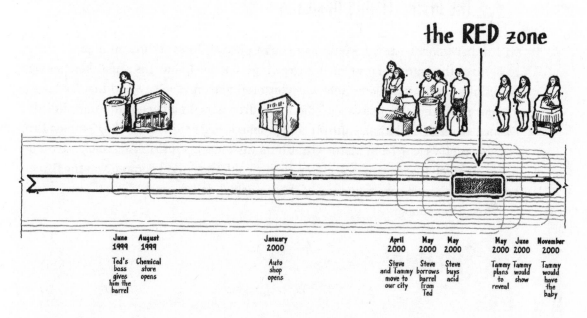

the RED zone

| June 1999 | August 1999 | | January 2000 | | April 2000 | May 2000 | May 2000 | | May 2000 | June 2000 | November 2000 |

Ted's boss gives him the barrel • Chemical store opens • Auto shop opens • Steve and Tammy move to our city • Steve borrows barrel from Ted • Steve buys acid • Tammy plans to reveal • Tammy would show • Tammy would have the baby

"Steve's set of circumstances created a unique red zone. It's much smaller and more specific, and it just happens to be the time in which Tammy disappeared."

"That this crime occurred *in our city—when* it did—makes sense given Steve's unique fuse." I referred back to the original timeline and added a few details. "So far everything—including the timing of this crime—points to Steve as our person of interest."

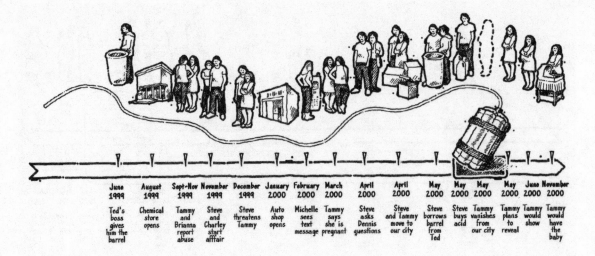

June 1999	August 1999	Sept–Nov 1999	November 1999	December 1999	January 2000	February 2000	March 2000	April 2000	April 2000	May 2000	May 2000	May 2000	May 2000	June 2000	November 2000
Ted's boss gives him the barrel	Chemical store opens	Tammy and Brianna report abuse	Steve and Charley start afffair	Steve threatens Tammy	Auto shop opens	Michelle sees text message	Tammy says she is pregnant	Steve asks Dennis questions	Steve and Tammy move to our city	Steve borrows barrel from Ted	Steve buys acid	Tammy vanishes from our city	Tammy plans to reveal	Tammy would show	Tammy would have the baby

 ## THE DIVINE TIMING OF JESUS

"If I didn't know better, I would say you're putting in overtime on a case." Susie recognized the nature of my timeline drawings, but she knew this set of sketches was different. Our dining room table was cluttered with mythology and history books, and our new Bible sat open at the edge of my drawings. I had been summarizing all I learned about the spiritual, cultural, and prophetic fuses that led up the Common Era.

"It's pretty clear from history that humans have been thinking about God and have imagined him in a number of mythological forms, and I showed you the fifteen general similarities among many of these ancient deities, right?"

"Yes, I remember."

Spiritual

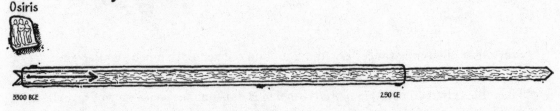

Osiris

3300 BCE

250 CE

I showed her the first sketch. "Let's place the major mythologies on a timeline, including the dates people started—and *stopped*—worshiping them. Let's start with Osiris."

"Osiris worship begins about 3300 BCE and ends around 250 CE," I said as I high-lighted this period of time on the timeline. I used tracing paper overlays to build a series of sketches that highlighted the time span in which each ancient deity was worshiped.

"Look at this collection of deities." My drawing was now half filled with icons of each mythology and long rectangles to highlight their history.[2] "Serapis is the last one I've illustrated."

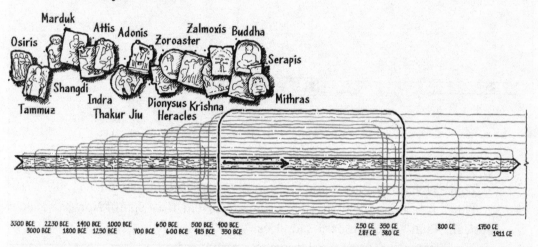

"Each of these mythologies shares a number of similarities with Jesus . . ."

"Does that make you skeptical?" asked Susie. "Do you think Jesus was just copied from these ancient stories?"

"No, the similarities are too broad, and they're the kind of thing you would expect people to include if they were thinking about the nature of God." I pointed to the drawing. "In fact, I'm starting to be the opposite of skeptical. Doesn't it make sense that humans would recognize some true things about God over time and that God would eventually *meet* those expectations?"

"I never thought of it like that." Susie pointed to my stack of sketches and resource materials. "So what's the drawing for?" she asked.

"Well, look at these overlapping time spans for each mythology. If the *true* God wanted to interact with humans by meeting the divine expectations of the greatest number of people possible, he would arrive at a time in which all these expectations and mythological deities overlap. It's a lot like the fuse timelines in my cases. This overlap is what I call the red zone."

Susie picked up the illustration and examined the dates. "So you're saying that if God appeared between 350 BCE and 250 CE, all these groups of religious believers would still have been active?"

Spiritual

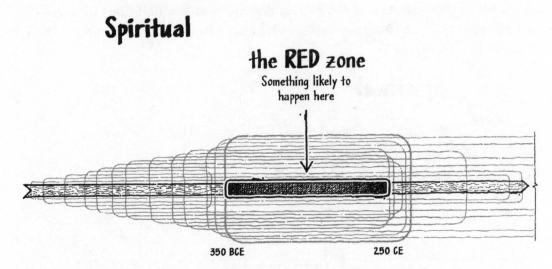

the RED zone

Something likely to happen here

350 BCE   250 CE

"That's right, and they would have similar expectations of God, as well."[3]

"That's interesting, but that's a six-hundred-year time span." Now *she* looked skeptical. "That seems kinda broad, doesn't it?"

"Yes, but I'm not done." I retrieved the drawing, laid a piece of tracing paper on it, and started sketching a second timeline. "Let's now add what I call the cultural fuse. One empire eventually conquered the entire region and set the table for something interesting."

Spiritual + Cultural

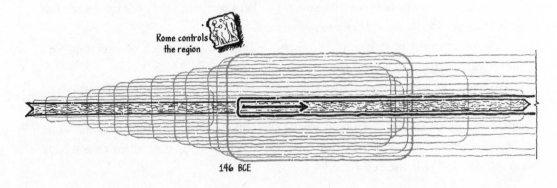

Rome controls the region

146 BCE

"By about 146 BCE, Rome had conquered most of the known world—certainly the entire region around the Mediterranean. They adopted the Etruscan alphabet and the Greek language, providing a common way to communicate throughout the empire. They also built an amazing system of roads that would allow people to travel throughout the region."

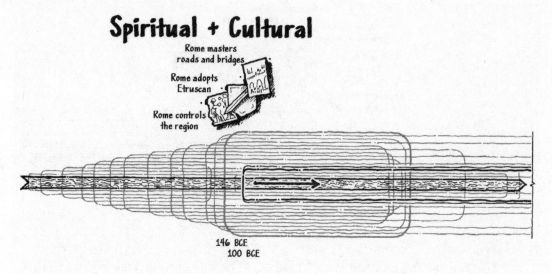

"When Augustus came into power, the Romans created a postal service system called *cursus publicus* and provided a continuous common government until the fall of the empire centuries later."

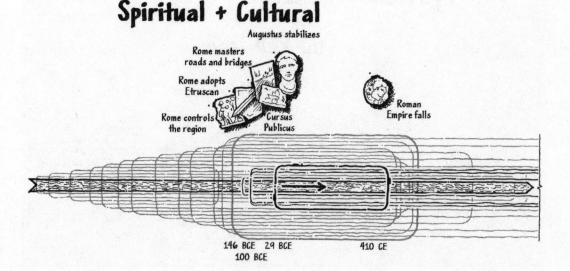

"One more thing," I said as I drew the last aspect of the cultural fuse. "Augustus also initiated *peace* in the region, called the Pax Romana, and it lasted for over two hundred years."

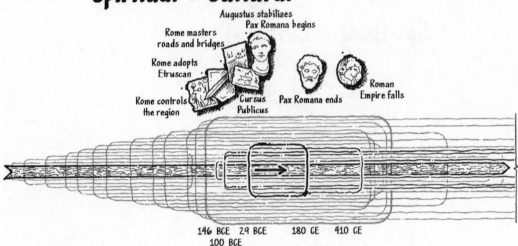

"Do you see the new red zone?" I asked. "There is now an area of overlap that takes advantage of humanity's common expectations of God and *also* leverages the opportunity the Roman Empire provided to spread the news of God's arrival."

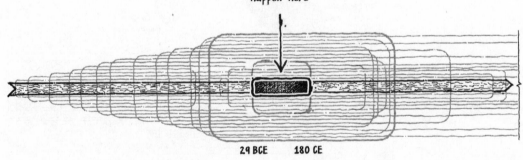

"The red zone is still over two hundred years long . . ."

"Yes, but there's one more fuse," I added as I quickly threw another layer of tracing paper over the drawings. "The Jewish prophets predicted the coming of a person of interest—the Messiah—and one of them provided a range of dates."

I drew an image of Daniel on the tracing paper. "Daniel said the Messiah would come *after* an edict to rebuild Jerusalem and *before* the destruction of the temple":

Spiritual + Cultural + Prophetic

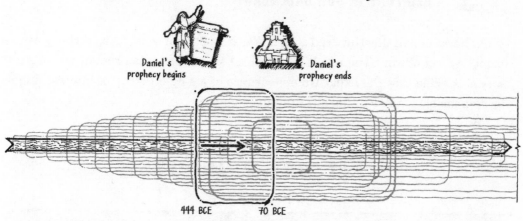

Daniel's prophecy begins

Daniel's prophecy ends

444 BCE   70 BCE

"Now let's look at where all the time spans from the spiritual, cultural, and prophetic fuses overlap."

Spiritual + Cultural + Prophetic

the RED zone

Something likely to happen here

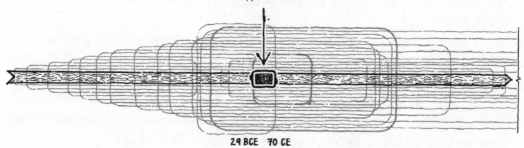

29 BCE   70 CE

"Wow . . ." Susie seemed to be as impressed as I was when I first discovered this tiny window of opportunity.

"Exactly," I responded. "There's a small window that just happens to mark the same place where our calendar changed forever. That explosive moment when BCE turned into CE—it happened right here, in this red zone, and now I think we know why."

A RED ZONE IN OUR CALENDAR

What happened in this tiny "red zone"? Was it a political event? An edict of government? An act of war? The result of a natural tragedy or catastrophe? Or instead, was it possible that the explosive appearance of a single person of interest might be responsible for disrupting our human calendar?

The three-stranded fuse that burned toward the Common Era seemed to make Jesus's arrival inevitable. He met our human expectations, matched the Jewish predictions, and arrived at precisely the right time in the history of the Roman Empire to be shared with the entire known world.

A New Testament writer, the apostle Paul, wrote, "When the fullness of time had come, God sent forth his Son, born of woman, born under the law, to redeem those who were under the law, so that we might receive adoption as sons" (Galatians 4:4–5 ESV).

What did Paul mean when he described Jesus's arrival as coming in the "fullness of time"? Did God send Jesus at just the right moment in history? The fuse certainly seemed to agree.

But every explosion, whether a criminal act or an important historical event, has both a fuse and some fallout, and I still had more to investigate. If Jesus truly mattered, the fallout of history would be cluttered with evidence.

Chapter 6

JESUS, THE UNFOUNDED FICTION?

The Dissemination Fallout

Books are the carriers of civilization. Without books,
history is silent, literature dumb, science crippled,
thought and speculation at a standstill. Without books,
the development of civilization would have been impossible.
—BARBARA TUCHMAN

Christ and the life of Christ is at this moment inspiring the literature
of the world as never before, and raising it up a witness against
waste and want and war. It may confess Him, as in Tolstoi's
work it does, or it may deny Him, but it cannot exclude Him.
—WILLIAM DEAN HOWELLS

Every case has an unexpected twist. Some are more detrimental than others. This one was about to sidetrack our investigation for a month.

"Wow," said Kyle, reading the letter for at least the twentieth time. "This guy was living *right across the street*. He sounds more like the killer than Steve!"

Kyle was right, although I hated to admit it.

Everything in the fuse pointed to Steve as a person of interest, until now. The activities, statements, and facts we uncovered in the weeks and months prior to Tammy's disappearance predicted something bad was about to happen, and Steve was the most reasonable explanation for her disappearance.

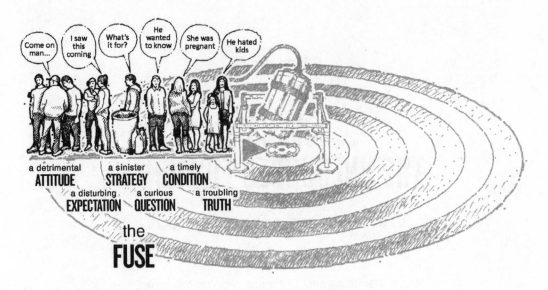

Until Frank Webb complicated matters.

It all started when we returned to Steve and Tammy's old neighborhood and interviewed as many neighbors as we could find. Some remained in the area, others had moved, and one stood out in a disturbing way.

Frank lived directly across the street from Tammy and Steve. He died about a month before we reopened the case, but his daughter, Samantha, still lived there. When we knocked on her door, she told us that her father often talked about Tammy, and after Tammy disappeared, he wrote a letter to Steve. Frank even made a copy of the letter before placing the original in Steve's mailbox. Samantha was cooperative, and after digging through a box in Frank's bedroom, she allowed us to read and photograph it.

Steve,

I am writing to you because I don't want a confrontation. Don't bother coming over here, I won't answer the door. I see that you've packed up all of Tammy's things and put some of them in the trash. She's only been gone a week! Why would you do that? Why not wait to see if she comes back?

I had a very close relationship with Tammy. We talked a lot. She shared her innermost feelings with me. I bet she never told you that. She told me that she was getting ready to leave you. But she said she was afraid of you.

Every day when you were gone at work, she would spend time over here.

She told me about your job at the garage and that she wanted more from life than you could give her.

I know she would have contacted me if she left you on her own. She's never reached out to me. Honestly, I haven't talked to her since she disappeared. Honest. But now I wonder how much you know about her disappearance.

I am praying for you Steve and for Tammy as well. I hope that you do the right thing.

Frank

Frank's letter was cryptic and confusing. The Tammy he described was different from the woman we learned about previously. He also seemed to have an awkwardly close relationship with her, and *that's* what led us to investigate Frank more fully. What we found was troubling.

Frank had been a security guard at a local storage company. One night, on the way home from work, he decided to kidnap a girl. He saw her walking and offered to give her a ride home. Once she got in the car, he pulled out a gun, assaulted her, and then attempted to kill her. Thinking she was dead, he dumped her body on a long embankment overlooking the beach.

His victim survived the attack and later identified him in a jury trial. He served fifteen years for that assault and attempted murder. After his release from prison, he moved in with his grown daughter. That house happened to be across the street from Tammy.

"If he was willing to kill one victim and dump her body, maybe he did the same thing to Tammy." Kyle continued to examine the words Frank used in his letter. "Maybe he was determined to do a better job this time and that's why we never recovered Tammy's body."

Frank's letter was the first piece of data in the fallout portion of our investigation (given that Frank wrote the letter *after* Tammy's disappearance). It provided several new pieces of information. First, Frank was now someone we had to consider as a suspect. We also had to reconsider what we thought we knew about Tammy and her attitude toward Steve. Finally, almost lost in the drama related to Frank was his

EXCULPATORY EVIDENCE

Exculpatory evidence is evidence that tends to excuse, justify, or absolve the defendant in any given case. While Frank's letter certainly complicated our investigation, it did not yet prove that Frank was the real killer. If the evidence pointing to Steve remained strong, he would still be the most likely candidate. In a similar way, if the evidence for the existence and nature of Jesus remains strong, alternative descriptions (like the noncanonical accounts described in this chapter) don't eliminate Jesus as a person of interest.

observation that Steve trashed Tammy's belongings as early as a week after she disappeared. Samantha confirmed that she also saw Steve place boxes containing Tammy's belongings in the trash.

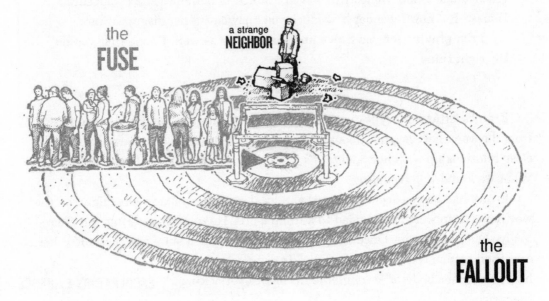

Over the next several days and weeks, Kyle and I continued to investigate Frank and the full nature of the fallout that resulted from Tammy's disappearance. Was Frank's description of Tammy accurate? Was Frank involved in Tammy's disappearance? Would the evidence in the fallout continue to point to Steve as our person of interest?

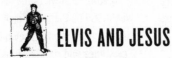 ## ELVIS AND JESUS

"Wow, I never knew Elvis was such a big deal."

Susie and I were watching a documentary on the history of rock and roll. I was embarrassed to admit I didn't really know much about Elvis Presley, aside from my teenage memory of his death in 1977.

"My mom was a fan," replied Susie. "But I didn't know he set all those records."

At the time of his death, Elvis had more number-one albums than any other male recording artist in history.[1] Even today Elvis remains the second "richest dead celebrity" (with over one billion albums sold, earning $39 million in 2019 alone).[2] In the four decades after his passing, hundreds of books were written about Elvis's extravagant career and tragic death.

Authors seeking to retell the story of Elvis typically fall into one of three groups:

1. Presleys (family members and close friends) who liked Elvis
2. Non-Presleys (strangers) who liked Elvis
3. Non-Presleys (strangers) who disliked Elvis

The truthfulness of these Elvis books is closely tied to which of the three groups the author belongs. Some authors favored Elvis; some did not. Some were close to Elvis; some were not. Some were accurate; some were not. You might wonder how someone could write something *untrue* about Elvis and get away with it, but remember, Elvis died in 1977, long before the internet turned the world into an accessible, global community. Unless you happened to live in Elvis's hometown (Memphis, Tennessee), you were probably unlikely to bump into true eyewitnesses who could verify the claims of an author. In addition, some of these Elvis books were written long after living witnesses could fact-check them. As a result, truth and legend emerged, the latter more likely from the pen of someone with a bias as distance and time increased.

Even though a wild variety of fables and tales were written about Elvis, they were crafted upon common features of the *true* Elvis story. A careful reading of every book will reveal core truths related to Elvis's life, accomplishments, and death:

Elvis was born into a poor family in Tupelo, Mississippi

His parents bought him a guitar for his eleventh birthday

His family moved to Memphis when he was thirteen years old

Elvis did a series of recordings with the Memphis Recording Service
   (Sun Studio)

One of his recordings became very popular

He formed a group, performed a live show, and was loved by the crowd

He signed a recording contract with RCA Records

He recorded his first album and the single "Heartbreak Hotel"
   in Nashville

Elvis made his TV debut on *Stage Show*

He starred in a film called *Love Me Tender*

He named his home "Graceland"

He was drafted into the Army and served with pride

He returned home and made a record-breaking album called *G.I. Blues*

He married a woman named Priscilla

He met President Nixon at the White House

He received the Grammy Lifetime Achievement Award

Elvis died at his home, Graceland

Every "tall-tale" *distortion* of Elvis borrows from the truth of the *real* Elvis, an Elvis who really existed, even though late, embellished accounts may exaggerate or misstate the truth. When someone has the kind of cultural impact Elvis had, we should expect there to be significant fallout, including literature written by people who would distort the truth and even co-opt his story for their own advantage.

Something similar happened to Jesus, thousands of years before Elvis ever recorded "Heartbreak Hotel."

My investigation of the fuse leading up to the arrival of Jesus revealed three lines of evidence and expectation.

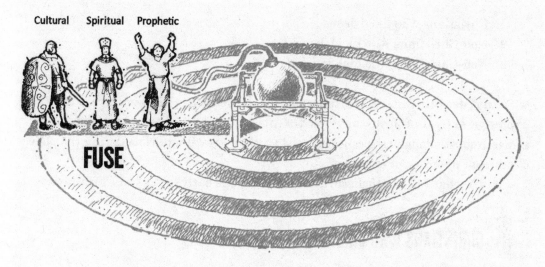

As I investigated the fallout caused by Jesus's life and ministry, I immediately recognized several areas of oversized historical impact, the first of which involved the incredible influence Jesus had on literature:

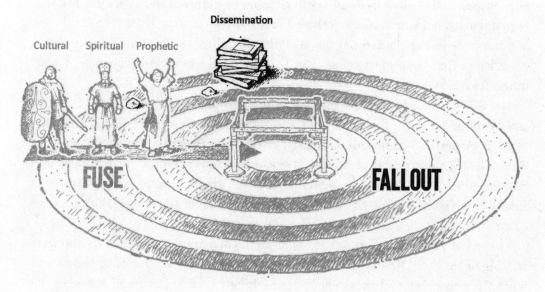

Jesus had a *much* greater literary impact on human history than Elvis. So much so that manuscripts describing Jesus clutter the fallout of the Common Era, and I'm *not* referring to the New Testament documents. Instead, I'm describing literary evidence from three early groups:

1. Christians who liked Jesus
2. Non-Christians who liked Jesus
3. Non-Christians who disliked Jesus

What does this literature tell us about Jesus? What kind of impact did the explosive arrival of Jesus have on the history of world literature, and is this impact robust enough to reconstruct the truth, even without considering the New Testament manuscript evidence?

That's what I hoped to discover as I studied the early history of Christianity.

 ## CHRISTIANS WHO LIKED JESUS

In the first three centuries of the Common Era, early believers lived cautiously within the Roman Empire and—depending on the emperor at the time—experienced some form of hesitant tolerance, general disdain, or intense persecution. Roman authorities would have allowed their citizens to embrace Jesus as yet another regional deity, but Christians worshiped Jesus as the one true God, to the *exclusion* of other gods in the Roman pantheon. This refusal to worship the Roman deities often led to Christian martyrdom. But that changed when two edicts were issued in the fourth century.

In 313 CE emperors Constantine and Licinius issued the Edict of Milan, proclaiming religious tolerance and ending the persecution of Christians.[3] By 380 CE emperors Theodosius I, Gratian, and Valentinian II issued the Edict of Thessalonica, declaring that citizens of the empire "should continue to profess that religion which was delivered to the Romans by the divine Apostle Peter."[4] This edict firmly established Nicene Christianity as *the* religion of the empire, culminating in an amazing transformation of national worship.

Even before Rome embraced Jesus as God, Christians (who liked Jesus) were writing about their Master. The students of the apostles were the first to describe what their teachers told them about Jesus. Ignatius of Antioch and Polycarp, for example, described the Jesus they learned about at the feet of the apostle John, and Clement of Rome described the Jesus he learned about from the apostle Paul.[5] For the next two hundred years, even before Christianity was accepted as the state religion, Christian leaders reiterated the claims of Christianity in letters and manuscripts written to local congregations and to each other. From Barnabas in the late-first century to Arnobius of Sicca in the late third century, the ante-Nicene church fathers wrote about Jesus, repeatedly citing the earliest descriptions offered by the gospel authors.[6]

Unsurprisingly, the story of Jesus had a tremendous impact on early believers, resulting in a significant collection of early literature. While admonishing local congregations, encouraging one another, and writing about the impact Jesus had on their lives, these leaders often quoted from the New Testament. In fact, much of the data the gospel authors offered can be found in the early church literary fallout.

Letters from Christian leaders in the first three hundred years of the Common Era reveal 935 verse quotations from the gospel of Matthew (87.3 percent of the text), 453 verses from the gospel of Mark (66.9 percent of the text), 990 verses from the gospel of Luke (86.0 percent of the text), and 859 verses from the gospel of John (97.8 percent of the text).[7] In addition, church leaders also quoted from many other New Testament documents. This diagram depicts the number of gospels (upper number) and New Testament letters (lower number) quoted by each leader:[8]

Even without any details from the New Testament manuscripts from antiquity, we could reconstruct the gospel authors' claims from the citations, quotes, and descriptions found in this ancient, explosive body of literature. In fact, if we limited our investigation to the earliest leaders who are believed to have had personal contact with the gospel eyewitnesses and authors (Barnabas, Ignatius, Clement of Rome, the Didache authors, Papias, and Polycarp), we could retrieve the important details related to the life, ministry, death, and resurrection of Jesus.[9]

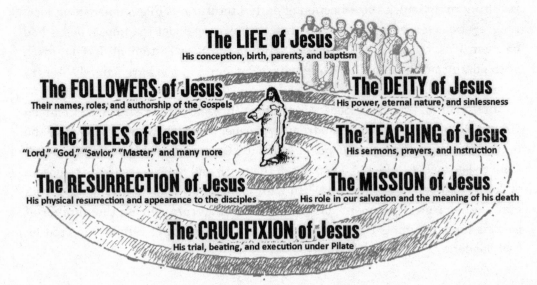

The LIFE of Jesus
His conception, birth, parents, and baptism

The FOLLOWERS of Jesus
Their names, roles, and authorship of the Gospels

The DEITY of Jesus
His power, eternal nature, and sinlessness

The TITLES of Jesus
"Lord," "God," "Savior," "Master," and many more

The TEACHING of Jesus
His sermons, prayers, and instruction

The RESURRECTION of Jesus
His physical resurrection and appearance to the disciples

The MISSION of Jesus
His role in our salvation and the meaning of his death

The CRUCIFIXION of Jesus
His trial, beating, and execution under Pilate

A robust description of Jesus, his teaching, mission, and followers is available *before the early second century*, and by the end of the third century, Jesus followers would quote or reference 3,237 verses from the New Testament gospels.[10] *That's* the kind of early impact Jesus had, and this was *before* Christianity became the religion of the Roman Empire.

If someone truly wanted to erase Jesus from history, they would have to do far more than destroy the New Testament; they would also have to destroy every copy of the many letters and books written in the early centuries of the Common Era by Christians who liked Jesus.

OBJECTION: THE STORY ABOUT JESUS WAS CHANGED OVER TIME

If we trace the story of Jesus through the earliest centuries, comparing the writings of Christians who liked Jesus to one another, one thing is certain: the account of Jesus's life—his miracles and teaching, his nature and his claims—has not changed. The gospel accounts are consistently reiterated, regardless of century or region.

NON-CHRISTIANS WHO LIKED JESUS

While assembling my library of historical Christian documents, I stumbled upon a book in a small used bookstore. It was entitled *The Lost Books of the Bible: Being All the Gospels, Epistles, and Other Pieces Now Extant Attributed in the First Four Centuries to Jesus Christ, His Apostles, and Their Companions, Not Included, by its Compilers, in the Authorized New Testament.*[11] The book cover claimed it contained the work of "several accepted Christian apostles" whose works "were omitted from" the canon of Christian Scripture. I purchased it immediately, suspicious that those who assembled the New Testament might have altered or eradicated the truth about Jesus.

I discovered instead that the book was mistitled. It should have been called *The Lost Untruths about Jesus: Being All the Late Gospels, Epistles, and Other Pieces Written By Non-Christians Who Liked Jesus and Hoped to Alter and Co-Opt His Story for Their Own Religious Purposes, Only to Have True Christians Recognize Them as Forgeries.* I realize this title isn't nearly as provocative, but it is at least more accurate.

Years after the completion of the four canonical gospels (Mark, Matthew, Luke, and John), dozens of noncanonical gospels and writings emerged across the empire. The authors of these texts hoped they would be taken seriously. In fact, religious groups of one kind or another used most of these noncanonical writings *alongside* the gospels of Mark, Matthew, Luke, and John.[12] The authors liked Jesus and recognized his influence and power. But their desire to co-opt the power and authority of Jesus led them to contradict, falsely supplement, or alter the canonical narrative. Groups that embraced the teachings of these texts (many of whom were Gnostic[13]) strayed so far from orthodoxy that they were not recognized or identified as Christians by the earliest church leaders.[14] While the noncanonical authors certainly liked Jesus, these non-Christians sought to co-opt his story for their own purposes.[15]

You might be wondering how someone could write something untrue about Jesus and get away with it. Just like those who lied about Elvis Presley, noncanonical authors waited until people who knew the truth about Jesus were dead, or they wrote their stories far from the region where eyewitnesses could fact-check the narratives. Once again, legend emerged as distance and time increased.[16]

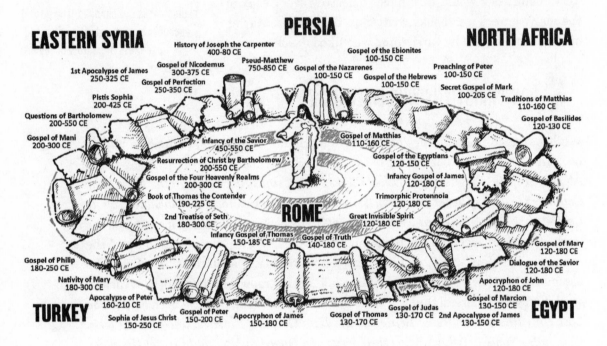

Despite the legendary distortions, these noncanonical documents presupposed and acknowledged the claims of the canonical gospels, just as the legendary distortions of Elvis assumed and affirmed the core truths related to Elvis's life, accomplishments, and death.

 ## CO-OPTING THE TRUTH FOR A LIE

Elvis's life created a tidal wave of fiction, but Jesus's life created much more. Just as the underlying truths related to Elvis can be reconstructed from later, legendary accounts, so too can the foundational truths related to Jesus be reconstructed from late noncanonical fictions.[17] I discovered this as I read *The Lost Books of the Bible*.

The Gospel of Peter, for example, (often described as a Gnostic or "Docetic" narrative) was written after the eyewitnesses of Jesus were dead (likely between 150 and 200 CE). Gnostics generally held a low view of the material universe and the human body, and this late gospel was written to reflect that view. Jesus is therefore described as a spirit whose body was only an illusion. But despite many distortions, the Gospel of Peter affirms many details of the Passion Week as described in Mark, Matthew, Luke, and John. It also lists the names of the disciples and affirms critical features of the canonical gospels, such as the resurrection of Jesus.

Another late narrative, the Gospel of Philip (written between 180 and 250 CE), is similarly Gnostic in its representation of Jesus. The author of this text describes Jesus as the source of secret wisdom (a common feature of salvation in Gnostic groups). Despite this variation from the canonical gospels, the Gospel of Philip acknowledges Jesus as the Savior, Messiah, and "Son of Man" and repeats many verses from the New Testament and the gospels of Matthew and John.

The distorted narratives written by these non-Christians who liked Jesus repeat many common truths from the Gospels, even as they insert unique falsehoods. There are many other late, noncanonical narratives and legendary accounts, and from the common assumptions described in these accounts (the areas where the authors agree on the foundational claims of the canonical gospels), we can retrieve a detailed description of Jesus and his followers. For a more robust description of these texts, consult the Case Notes file for this book, available on the Cold-Case Christianity website (see endnote #18).[18]

These details about Jesus and his followers come *not* from the church fathers but from the authors of *heretical* texts. Even if you destroyed every page of Christian Scripture *and* the writings of *Christians* who liked Jesus, you would still know a lot about him from these *non-Christians* who liked him. But the noncanonical authors weren't the only non-Christians to talk about Jesus. There were others who interacted with Christians in antiquity, and unlike the noncanonical writers, they didn't like Jesus at all.[19]

OBJECTION: EARLY CHRISTIANS ELIMINATED COMPETING ACCOUNTS OF JESUS

Why aren't the noncanonical accounts (the writings from non-Christians who liked Jesus) considered equally authoritative? Were they eliminated solely because they disagreed theologically with Mark, Matthew, Luke, and John? No. More than any other reason, they are disqualified as eyewitness accounts because of their *late* arrival *outside of* the region of Jesus's life and ministry. True eyewitness accounts are written *early* and *within* the region, as were the four gospel accounts we have in the New Testament. For more information about the early dating of the Gospels, read *Cold-Case Christianity*.

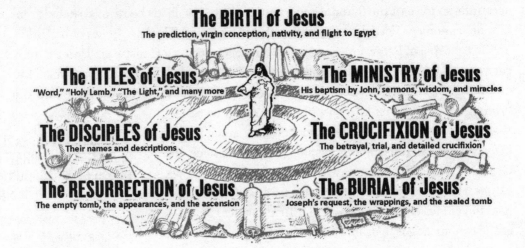

The BIRTH of Jesus
The prediction, virgin conception, nativity, and flight to Egypt

The TITLES of Jesus
"Word," "Holy Lamb," "The Light," and many more

The MINISTRY of Jesus
His baptism by John, sermons, wisdom, and miracles

The DISCIPLES of Jesus
Their names and descriptions

The CRUCIFIXION of Jesus
The betrayal, trial, and detailed crucifixion

The RESURRECTION of Jesus
The empty tomb, the appearances, and the ascension

The BURIAL of Jesus
Joseph's request, the wrappings, and the sealed tomb

THE TRUTH IN A SLANDER

The voices of non-Christians who *disliked* Jesus can be heard on the pages of historical manuscripts. These ancient Roman and Jewish voices were clearly hostile to Christianity, but they inadvertently provided us with additional information about the man they sought to obliterate from history.[20]

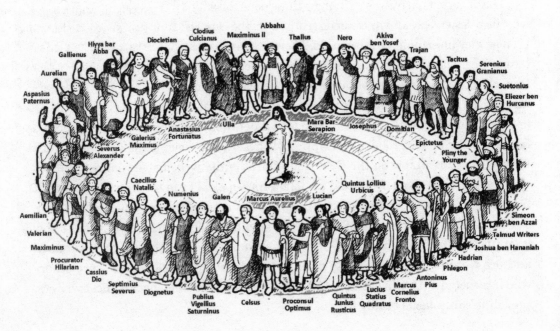

It's impossible to estimate how many hostile nonbelievers came into contact with Christians prior to the edicts of Milan and Thessalonica, but the words of more than fifty of them were documented in ancient manuscripts.[21]

These manuscripts represent authors from many regions within the Roman Empire and beyond. Some were religious; some were not. Thallus, for example, was a Greek-speaking historian. Mara bar Serapion was a Syrian philosopher. Akiva ben Yosef was a Jewish rabbi. Epictetus was a stoic philosopher in what is now known as Turkey. Pliny the Younger was a lawyer and magistrate in a region along the Black Sea. Granianus was an Asian proconsul under Emperor Hadrian. Eliezer ben Hurcanus was an ancient Jewish sage.

It's remarkable to encounter this level of regional, ethnic, and professional diversity among Jesus's most ancient critics, but that's the kind of response he evoked. He was loved deeply by his followers but dismissed or despised by his critics.

From just this group of hostile non-Christians who disliked Jesus, a robust profile of Jesus can be reconstructed. Even though these historical figures typically slandered him, they based their attacks on a set of common claims. These foundational details related to Jesus (and his followers) can be heard from the voices of those who opposed him.[22]

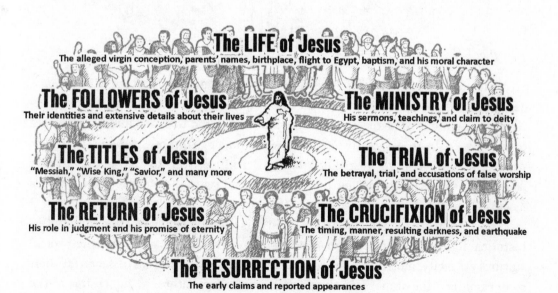

The LIFE of Jesus
The alleged virgin conception, parents' names, birthplace, flight to Egypt, baptism, and his moral character

The FOLLOWERS of Jesus
Their identities and extensive details about their lives

The MINISTRY of Jesus
His sermons, teachings, and claim to deity

The TITLES of Jesus
"Messiah," "Wise King," "Savior," and many more

The TRIAL of Jesus
The betrayal, trial, and accusations of false worship

The RETURN of Jesus
His role in judgment and his promise of eternity

The CRUCIFIXION of Jesus
The timing, manner, resulting darkness, and earthquake

The RESURRECTION of Jesus
The early claims and reported appearances

An incredibly detailed summary of Jesus's life, ministry, death, and resurrection (along with details related to his followers) came from people who *denied* his power and *opposed* the men and women who followed him (visit the Case Notes for the specifics).[23] Even if you silenced the voices of the New Testament authors, you would still have a robust description of Jesus and his followers from ancient, hostile, *non-Christian* voices in the fallout.

The statements of those who followed Jesus, those who later co-opted his name for their own purpose, and those who rejected him provide a tidal wave of information:

This impressive group of historical voices was immediately aware of the impact Jesus had on history. At a time when Christians were pursued, pillaged, and persecuted, we might not expect much information related to Jesus and his followers to survive. Instead, we can reconstruct every major claim of the New Testament without reading a single gospel or letter of Scripture, even though many of these non-Christian authors did their best to co-opt and twist the story of Jesus or were mockingly hostile toward the claims of Christianity.

There are more non-Christian voices in this extrabiblical collection (ninety-two historical figures) than Christian ones (just fifty-one), and regardless of their social stature, ethnicity, motivation, or region, the common description of Jesus (at their core) remained the same.[24] At their foundation, they reiterated the claims of the New Testament authors long before these claims became popular or Christianity became the religion of the empire.

And this explosion of literary activity was only the beginning.

JESUS DOMINATES THE BOOKSHELVES

With every passing century in the Common Era, the number of authors who wrote about Jesus grew exponentially. The dissemination fallout is cluttered with classic literature written by authors who were forever changed by the person and teaching of Jesus.

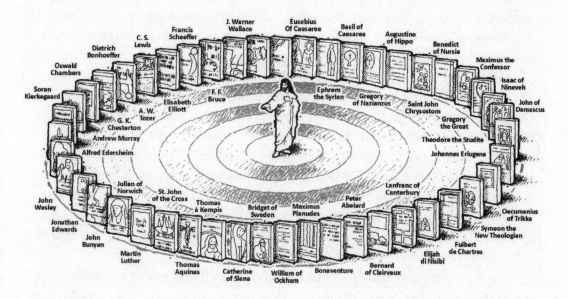

You may not be familiar with the more ancient volumes in this diagram.[25] But if you're a Christian (or even if you aren't), you probably recognize the more recent titles. Human history, and the lives of millions of readers, has been shaped by many of these classic volumes:

History of the Church by Eusebius (c. 330 CE)

The City of God by Augustine of Hippo (405 CE)

The Rule of St. Benedict by Benedict of Nursia (516 CE)

The Imitation of Christ by Thomas à Kempis (c. 1418 CE)

On the Freedom of a Christian by Martin Luther (1520 CE)

The Dark Night of the Soul by St. John of the Cross (c. 1578 CE)

The Pilgrim's Progress by John Bunyan (1678 CE)

Sinners in the Hands of an Angry God by Jonathan Edwards (1741 CE)

Humility by Andrew Murray (1895 CE)

Orthodoxy by G. K. Chesterton (1908 CE)

The Cost of Discipleship by Dietrich Bonhoeffer (1937 CE)

Mere Christianity by C. S. Lewis (1952 CE)

Through the Gates of Splendor by Elisabeth Elliot (1963 CE)

The God Who Is There by Francis Schaeffer (1968 CE)

Some of these books are old, many are ancient, yet all of them are still being published and continue to inspire, correct, and instruct. In *every* century since the appearance of Jesus, iconic books have been written about his life, teaching, death, and resurrection.

The literary fallout Jesus created resulted in the formation of an entire industry. The Bible was the first book ever printed on a printing press, establishing Johannes Gutenberg (the inventor of the movable-type press) as the world's first printed book publisher. Today, books about Jesus are published by nearly *two hundred* publishing houses, a large industry designed to meet the intense interest in Jesus.[26] Compare the number of Christian publishers, for example, with publishing houses representing two religious systems that preceded Christianity by centuries: Hinduism and Buddhism. To these, let's add major religions that followed Christianity: Islam and Bahá'í. These four religious worldviews *combined* cannot boast the number of publishers that have emerged under the Christian banner.[27]

Jesus matters to authors and publishers. He still dominates the publishing industry like no other person of interest. He's inspired more writers—and been the topic of more literature—than any other person in history.

If you don't believe me, ask CIA analyst Peter Dickson.[28] In 1999 Dickson used his considerable investigative skills to identify the historical figure who has been the subject of more books than anyone else. He decided to conduct his search at the Library of Congress in Washington, DC. This is the world's largest library, containing nearly 110 million volumes in every language and format. It houses 532 miles of bookshelves. You read that correctly—532 *miles*. It is the "world's most comprehensive record of human creativity and knowledge."[29] A computerized analysis of eighteen million volumes revealed that there were nearly *twice* as many books about Jesus as his nearest challenger:[30]

1. Jesus (17,239 books)
2. William Shakespeare (9,801)
3. Vladimir Lenin (4,492)
4. Abraham Lincoln (4,378)

5. Napoleon Bonaparte (4,007)
6. Karl Marx (3,817)
7. The Virgin Mary (3,595)
8. Johann Wolfgang von Goethe (3,431)
9. Plato (2,894)
10. Dante Alighieri (2,878)
11. George Washington (2,742)
12. Buddha (2,446)
13. Immanuel Kant (2,410)
14. Martin Luther (2,291)
15. Adolf Hitler (1,989)
16. Georg Wilhelm Friedrich Hegel (1,976)
17. Aristotle (1,696)
18. Richard Wagner (1,680)
19. Alexander Pushkin (1,614)
20. Friedrich Nietzsche (1,613)
21. Sigmund Freud (1,601)
22. Wolfgang Amadeus Mozart (1,592)
23. Gandhi (1,583)
24. John Milton (1,533)
25. Ludwig van Beethoven (1,476)
26. Simón Bolívar (1,467)
27. Thomas Aquinas (1,424)
28. Charles Dickens (1,397)
29. Johann Sebastian Bach (1,361)
30. Miguel de Cervantes (1,348)

When Dickson limited his search to only females, he found that Jesus *continued* to influence the field:[31]

1. The Virgin Mary (3,595)
2. Joan of Arc (545)
3. Jane Austen (544)
4. Queen Victoria (492)
5. Mary, Queen of Scots (477)
6. Elizabeth II (442)
7. George Eliot (434)
8. Elizabeth I (407)
9. Cleopatra (329)
10. Emily Dickinson (310)

As you read this list, you might be wondering if the Library of Congress unfairly favors Jesus because of his influence on Western civilization rather than his warranted impact globally. I wondered the same thing as I investigated the fallout Jesus created in the Common Era. When I first started to research Jesus, the internet was still in its infancy, but today we have the benefit of search engines, including Google Books, "the world's most comprehensive index of full-text books."[32]

This search engine allows us to update Dickson's list in a much more comprehensive, global manner that includes every country, every publisher, and every kind of author (including self-published authors). This global database reveals that Jesus is *still* the subject of more books than anyone else:[33]

1. Jesus (109,000,000 books)
2. George Washington (58,400,000)
3. Plato (27,800,000)
4. Aristotle (21,000,000)
5. John Milton (20,800,000)
6. William Shakespeare (18,700,000)
7. Charles Dickens (16,200,000)
8. Buddha (13,300,000)
9. Martin Luther (13,300,000)
10. Gandhi (12,600,000)
11. Abraham Lincoln (9,340,000)
12. The Virgin Mary (7,400,000)
13. Karl Marx (5,780,000)
14. Richard Wagner (5,400,000)
15. Thomas Aquinas (4,720,000)
16. Napoleon Bonaparte (3,320,000)
17. Adolf Hitler (2,650,000)
18. Immanuel Kant (2,400,000)
19. Johann Wolfgang von Goethe (2,230,000)
20. Friedrich Nietzsche (1,960,000)
21. Dante Alighieri (1,910,000)
22. Miguel de Cervantes (1,600,000)
23. Vladimir Lenin (1,500,000)
24. Johann Sebastian Bach (858,000)
25. Ludwig van Beethoven (797,000)
26. Georg Wilhelm Friedrich Hegel (665,000)
27. Wolfgang Amadeus Mozart (640,000)
28. Simón Bolívar (511,000)
29. Alexander Pushkin (236,000)
30. Sigmund Freud (25,300)

While some of these historical figures have swapped positions from Dickson's original list, Jesus remains at the top. The earliest centuries in the Common Era were cluttered with documents describing Jesus, and he has been the consistent topic of literature ever since. Even today, the dissemination fallout of Jesus is filled with millions of books published about Jesus.

But that's only *part* of the literary fallout.

 ## MOVIE STAR JESUS

Jesus dramatically affected another literary genre in the Common Era fallout. As visual technology progressed, a new category of literature emerged: the screenplay. From the very invention of the "moving picture," Jesus became the focus of writers who were inspired by his impact on culture.

Some of the earliest attempts to create motion pictures featured the life and activity of Jesus. In 1897 Albert Kirchner filmed *La Passion du Christ*, while Mark Klaw and Abraham Erlanger created *The Horitz Passion Play*. These primitive films started an explosion of cinematic activity depicting the life of Jesus.[34]

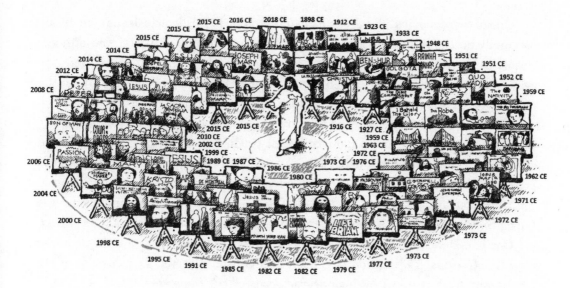

No other religious figure has inspired as many screenplays as Jesus of Nazareth, and this diagram doesn't even include the movies that reflect a Christian worldview but don't specifically reenact his life, ministry, death, and resurrection. Hundreds more have been written describing the lives and experiences of his followers.[35]

Movies tracing only the life of Jesus have been produced in a variety of countries, including Bulgaria, Canada, England, France, Germany, India, Iran, Italy, Jordan, Lebanon, Mexico, Israel, the Philippines, Portugal, South Africa, Spain, and the United States.

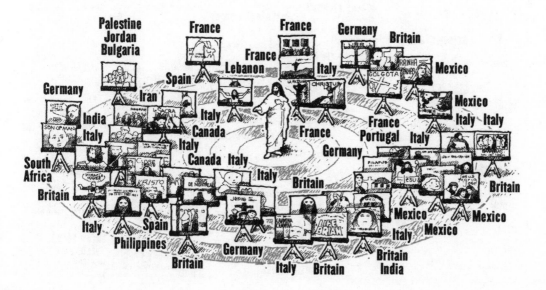

One of these movies, *The Jesus Film* (created in 1979), depicts Jesus's life based primarily on the gospel of Luke. It was filmed on location in Israel and adheres closely to the biblical text. Since its creation, this film has been translated into over 1,800 languages and has been viewed by over 8.1 billion people, making it the most-watched and most-translated motion picture of all time.[36]

Christian movie companies and performers aren't alone in their desire to re-create the story of Jesus. The movie industry's best production companies, directors, and actors have created cinematic depictions of Jesus. Metro-Goldwyn-Mayer, for example, produced *King of Kings* and *Ben-Hur*, Columbia Pictures produced *Godspell*, *Risen*, and *The Star*, Warner Brothers produced *Life of Brian*, Universal Studios produced *Jesus Christ Superstar*, and 20th Century Fox produced *Color of the Cross* and *Son of God*.

Cecil B. DeMille directed *The King of Kings* (1927 version), Martin Scorsese directed *The Last Temptation of Christ*, Mel Gibson directed *The Passion of the Christ*, and Andrew Lloyd Webber scored *Jesus Christ Superstar*.

Richard Burton and Jean Simmons starred in *The Robe*, Charlton Heston appeared in *Ben-Hur*, Orson Welles narrated *King of Kings*, Johnny Cash starred in *Gospel Road: A Story of Jesus*, the Monty Python cast starred in *Life of Brian*, Martin Sheen and Alan Arkin appeared in *The Fourth Wise Man*, Christian Bale starred in *Mary, Mother of Jesus*, Kelsey Grammer appeared in *Killing Jesus*, Ewan McGregor appeared in *Last Days in the Desert*, Joseph Fiennes starred in *Risen*, and Joaquin Phoenix starred in *Mary Magdalene*.[37]

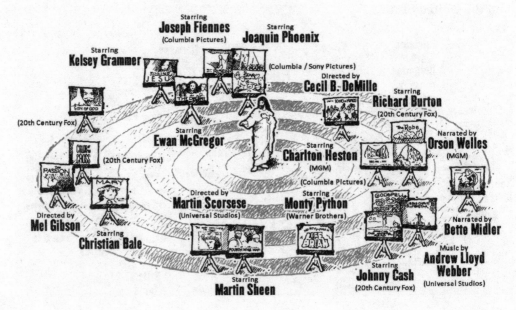

Some of these actors and directors were inspired by Jesus, others were intrigued, and some were infuriated. But whether their movies were complimentary or blasphemous, the core truths of Jesus's life (as described in the Gospels) served as a launching point. In fact, if you compare the common foundational claims of these movies (along with the others we've described) with the claims of the church fathers, you'll find them in agreement. Some of the movies about Jesus are word-for-word reenactments of the gospel accounts.[38]

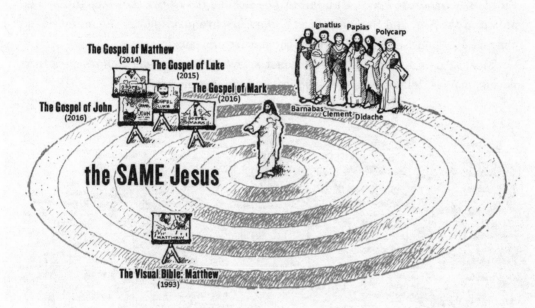

So without a single New Testament document *or* ancient text describing Jesus, you could still reconstruct every detail of Jesus's life, ministry, death, resurrection—*and* his impact on the lives of believers—from the hundreds of screenplays that have been written and movies that have been made in just the past one hundred years. *That's* the kind of impact Jesus had on our collective literary imagination.

But this person of interest didn't only influence books and screenplays that describe the life and ministry of Jesus.

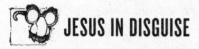 ## JESUS IN DISGUISE

If you're a fan of fictional literature (almost *any* genre of fictional literature, including novels, screenplays, comics, and even video game scripts), you've probably read about Jesus, *even if you didn't know it.* No other person in history has influenced the way authors have crafted their heroes and protagonists. If you look closely at many of history's best-known fictional characters, you'll find attributes of Jesus, even from the pens of authors who didn't know much about the Christian Savior. Either knowingly or unknowingly, writers have borrowed the attributes of Jesus and created what scholars now call "Christ figures." There are *hundreds* of examples throughout the history of literature in *every* genre. Harry in the Harry Potter series, Finny in *A Separate Peace*, Gandalf in *The Lord of the Rings*, Santiago in *The Old Man and the Sea*, and Simon in *Lord of the Flies* are just a few of the many classic characters who resemble and reflect the nature of Jesus.[39]

Most of us are familiar with at least a few of these modern characters from novels, movies, television series, comics, and video games:[40]

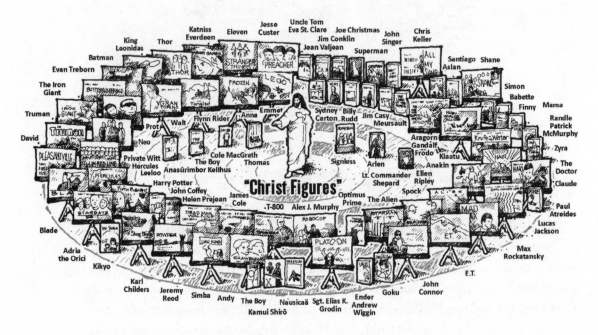

If you were inclined to list the attributes of these fictional characters, you would discover that they share common characteristics. In fact, you would find that the authors, screenwriters, and creators seem to borrow from a singular, common prototype, a person of interest who:

Has a virtuous mother and a divine or royal father
Is born mysteriously and appears to be poor

Possesses some form of dual identity (both "common" and "special")

Has an oddly unknown childhood and is later misunderstood or
    considered crazy

Provides hope to others and has miraculous, supernatural powers

Behaves in an extremely moral manner and/or is celibate

Cares for people who are poor, distressed, or hungry

Sees truth that is hidden to others and is associated with light

Interacts with and is tempted by the devil or an evil force

Is punished and/or dies unjustly for his claims (usually connected to love
    or truth)

Is betrayed by a close friend and is denied by those who knew him

Is depicted at some point with his arms spread (like a cross)

Is reborn in some way physically or emotionally[41]

Jesus *matters* to authors, writers, creators, and screenwriters in the modern era. Either consciously or unconsciously, they've crafted characters that resemble Jesus of Nazareth. Even without Christian Scripture and without the writings of the church fathers or the ancients who liked or disliked Jesus, we'd still be left with this nagging profile and would still have good reason to believe there was an ancient person of interest who dominated creative thought and provided the archetype that would permeate the imagination of humanity for centuries to come.

Once again, that's the kind of influence Jesus had on literature. Even when people didn't write about him *specifically*, they still wrote about him *metaphorically*.

OBJECTION: THERE ISN'T ENOUGH ANCIENT, NON-CHRISTIAN INFORMATION ABOUT JESUS

If you include the noncanonical texts, there are nearly twice as many non-Christian voices as Christian voices in the period preceding the Edict of Milan. In addition, the ancient sources we have for the life and ministry of Jesus are more reliable (and were written much earlier) than the sources we have for the life of Tiberius Caesar, the emperor of Rome who ruled during the latter part of Jesus's lifetime. Some of these sources (like Tacitus), report on both men. If we have enough information to have knowledge about Tiberius Caesar, then we have enough information to have knowledge about Jesus.[42]

DIFFICULT TO ERASE

"You'll figure it out." Susie wasn't just talking about the fallout related to my criminal case. She was also talking about the Jesus fallout. I'd been getting up at four o'clock every morning to investigate the case for Jesus prior to heading off to work.

"Maybe you should sleep in tomorrow," she said. "It's Saturday, you know."

As much as my professional investigations dominated my thoughts, Jesus had become an even larger obsession. He permeated my thinking in much the same way he'd dominated the thoughts of writers and investigators for thousands of years before me.

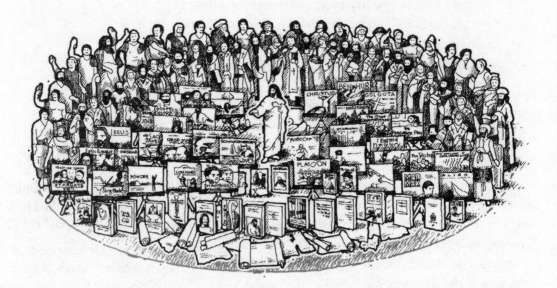

As I investigated the literary fallout caused by the explosive appearance of Jesus, I realized it was nearly impossible to erase him from history. His impact on literature was simply too vast and robust. The facts related to Jesus had been preserved and disseminated throughout the Common Era, in every language, in every culture, and in every genre of literature. No one else in the first century had this kind of impact.

In fact, Jesus had more literary impact than any other person in *all* of history.

But literature isn't the only way Jesus affected humanity, and it isn't the only set of evidences in the fallout. Another creative form of fallout points uniquely to Jesus as the most important person of interest in human history.

Chapter 7

JESUS, THE DREARY DEITY?

The Imagination Fallout

A Christian should use these arts to the glory of God,
not just as tracts, mind you, but as things of beauty to the
praise of God. An art work can be a doxology in itself.
—FRANCIS SCHAEFFER

Today, from countless paintings, statues, and buildings,
from literature and history, from personality and institution, from
profanity, popular song, and entertainment media, from confession
and controversy, from legend and ritual—Jesus stands quietly at
the center of the contemporary world, as he himself predicted.
—DALLAS WILLARD

"Samantha, please forgive us." I handed Frank Webb's daughter the search warrant. After our first interview with Samantha, we knew we'd have to investigate Frank further.

We conducted follow-up investigations all week, and Frank's letter wasn't the only interesting piece of potential evidence we uncovered during our interviews. Another one of Steve and Tammy's neighbors, Sally Broadman, told us she talked to Tammy the day before she disappeared. Tammy said she was excited about a job interview later in the month. The job with BizFax would allow her to work from home and earn significant income.

We telephoned the business and spoke with Spencer Kidman, the man who wanted to interview Tammy. He recalled her and had anticipated hiring Tammy for an important sales job. He talked with her twice on the phone and was expecting her to come in to complete the hiring process. Tammy told him she was extremely interested in the job because it would allow her to work from home, so he was surprised that she never showed up for the meeting or called afterward. Spencer also remembered dialing her home phone number. A man, presumably Tammy's husband, answered and was incredibly angry that Spencer bothered him with a phone call. Spencer never forgot how Tammy's husband treated him.

The missed meeting was yet another factor in the fallout that seemed to indicate that something nefarious had happened to Tammy. Why, if she was so excited about the job, would she *voluntarily* skip the final interview? In addition, Steve's response to Spencer appeared consistent with his involvement in Tammy's disappearance. But while the growing body of evidence in the fallout continued to point to Steve as our person of interest, Frank Webb cast a shadow of doubt on the case.

OBJECTION: YOU CAN'T TRUST OLD MEMORIES

Jurors can evaluate witnesses to determine how well they "remember and describe what happened."[1] But how can a witness be trusted when their testimony occurs *many years* after an event took place? Remember that not all events leave the same impression on witnesses. Some events (such as Spencer's phone call to Tammy's husband) are more memorable than others. Jurors are told to consider the importance of a memory when evaluating the witness. In a similar way, the gospel accounts, even though they were written about Jesus many years after the fact, recall events that were highly unusual and memorable.

That's why we decided to write a search warrant for Samantha Webb's house.

Kyle and I remembered the box in Frank's old bedroom. Samantha sifted through several letters and drawings before retrieving Frank's letter to Steve, and we suspected those materials might be useful.

"Samantha, we're not here to make a mess," said Kyle as he pulled a notepad from his folder. "We just wonder if there might be something in Frank's box that will help us better understand his relationship with Tammy . . . and her disappearance."

"Do you suspect my dad because of his past?" Samantha asked. "He was unstable toward the end of his life, I'll admit that. But I know he didn't have anything to do with Tammy. He was really never out of my sight in those days, and to be honest, he didn't even know Tammy at all."

Frank's box contained many letters. Some were nonsensical and irrational. Frank wrote as though he knew dozens of people intimately, although Samantha said most of the letter recipients were complete strangers. He wrote letters to virtually everyone he met, and most of these notes were pure fiction.

The box also contained drawings.

"Dad was an artist," Samantha said as she watched us sort through the illustrations. "His drawings used to worry me, though."

We could see why.

Frank's sketches were self-portraits, and they were increasingly abstract and distressed. Frank's pastel drawings reminded me of the self-portraits of Vincent van Gogh, who also struggled with mental illness.

"I hardly ever look at dad's old drawings," continued Samantha. "They're too personal for me. Too sad, really."

I added the additional data about Spencer Kidman and Frank's drawings to the fallout section of our diagram.

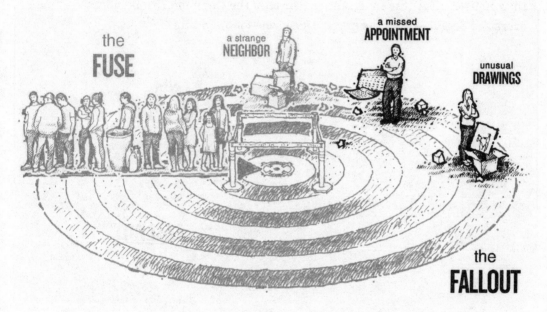

Frank Webb struggled to distinguish truth from his own personal fictions. But was he mentally disturbed enough to harm Tammy?

ART, MUSIC, AND A PLACE TO MEET

"Doesn't it seem strange that so much has been written about Jesus?" Susie had been reading through the New Testament, and after finishing a chapter, she closed her Bible and placed it on her nightstand.

"Not really. A lot's been written about a lot of people," I replied, trying not to admit what seemed increasingly obvious to her.

"Do you remember our trip to Germany before grad school?" she asked. "How many churches did we visit prior to your first year in architecture school?"

"Too many to count," I admitted.

Susie agreed. "Don't you think it's amazing that so much art and architecture was *also* inspired by Jesus?"

Susie had unknowingly initiated yet another one of my investigations into the Common Era fallout. As an unbelieving architecture student, I never stopped to think about the amount of art that Jesus followers generated, even as I admired their artistry. But this imaginative aspect of the Common Era is indebted—to an oversized degree—to Jesus and to those who followed him.

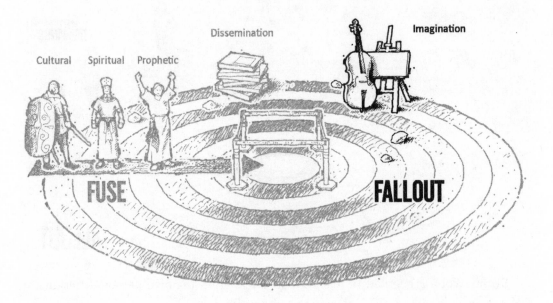

The German vacation Susie described included a visit to Ottobeuren Abbey, a Benedictine monastery in Southern Germany, near the town where Susie was born. It was founded in 764 CE and includes a magnificent basilica that has been described as the "pinnacle of Bavarian Baroque architecture."[2] The interior is nothing short of breathtaking, covered in paintings and housing a magnificent pipe organ above the narthex. Jesus followers have been meeting in this space for centuries, admiring the art and singing to the accompaniment of organ music.

Their experience hasn't been unusual. Christians have been meeting in this way for two thousand years, although they haven't always enjoyed this kind of artistic grandeur. Instead, the early Christians met in simple homes.

Most first-century houses in Israel were single-room residences. They were constructed with thick mudbrick walls built on stone foundations. These walls supported a roof structure built with wood and thatch. Because the building materials were primitive and the climate was warm, most interior spaces were dark with few windows. Thick walls supported the roof. As a result, the inside of the home was significantly cooler and more comfortable than the outdoors.[3]

Adequate for Christian meetings, but hardly inspiring.

These early gathering spaces were nothing like the basilica at Ottobeuren Abbey. They were shadowy, heavy environments that seemed inconsistent with the nature of Jesus, who said, "I am the light of the world. Whoever follows me will never walk in darkness, but will have the light of life" (John 8:12). They were also mired in earthly mudbrick and thatch, even though the apostle Paul wrote, "Our citizenship is in heaven. And we eagerly await a Savior from there, the Lord Jesus Christ" (Philippians 3:20).

How could gathering believers "set [their] hearts on things above, where Christ is, seated at the right hand of God" (Colossians 3:1) in spaces that neither reflected the *light* of Christ nor the *nature* of "things above"? A desire to better reveal the identity of Jesus and the reality of heaven initiated a movement unique in the history of architecture, art, and music.

As Christian groups grew, their creativity and engineering skills were put to the test. How could they build roofs to span greater distances? How could they increase the lighting within these larger spaces? What could they do to create a *heavenly* environment? Early Christian church architects solved the first problem, even if they did little—at first—to solve the second two.

Churches in the first centuries of the Common Era were still relatively dark, uninspiring spaces, although they were much larger than their house church counterparts.[4] But even in these heavy spaces, a simple architectural development would eventually point believers heavenward.

Domes were not unknown to the Greek and Roman world, of course, but they were *mastered* by Christian church builders who stretched the limit of the archetype.[5]

These arched ceiling surfaces provided opportunities to paint images of the angelic realm, and architects designed them to be illuminated in heavenly ways with hidden light wells and strategically placed window openings. Many domes also allowed for the placement of statues, providing yet another artistic avenue for expression. The technology involved in perfecting dome architecture stretched the imagination and engineering skills of designers and builders. The dome at St. Peter's Basilica in Rome is an excellent example.[6]

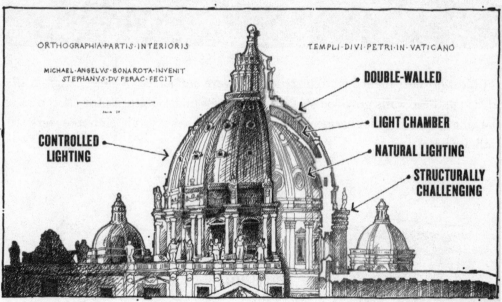

Designed by Michelangelo, the structure of the dome is an artistic and engineering tour de force. He carefully controlled the way in which he allowed light to enter the space by building a double-walled dome with a light chamber. Windows along the base provided another source of controlled light. The result is nothing less than stunning.

So central was the dome to Christian architecture of this period that Rome became known as the "city of domes."[7]

Most of these domed church structures were supported by heavy stone walls. Although these walls provided surfaces for murals and sculptures, they still limited the amount of light that permeated each sanctuary. As a result, churches were still rather dark.

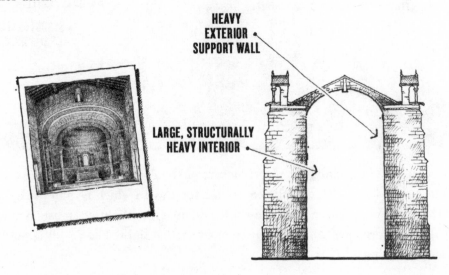

HEAVY EXTERIOR SUPPORT WALL

LARGE, STRUCTURALLY HEAVY INTERIOR

Christian architects and artists thought deeply about how they could allow light to penetrate the heavy walls.

What if the supporting walls (or at least their structural equivalent) could be pushed *outside* the church to allow for the construction of a lighter, *non-weight-bearing* peripheral wall? The "flying buttress" provided church architects with a way to support the roof from stone structures well outside the perimeter of the church. This allowed them to build a secondary, peripheral wall that was windowed.

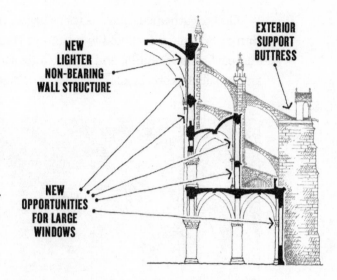

Architects began to reimagine the walls of their churches, creating glass surfaces on secondary walls that were placed alongside (or within the boundaries of) the buttresses.

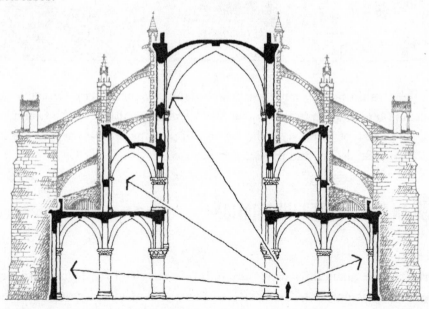

In spaces like these, worshipers had a virtually unobstructed view of window panels, and these new, lighter walls allowed artists to master yet another form of expression: the stained glass window.

Gothic cathedrals such as these began to populate the European landscape. The church became a formidable patron of the arts, churches became display centers and performance halls, and Christian gatherings became the epicenter for artistic and musical expression.

While worship centers such as these became conservatories for the arts, they also became monuments to the impact Jesus had on culture in the Common Era. In fact, no person of interest in the history of persons of interest had the kind of impact Jesus had on art and music.

AN UNEXPECTED INSPIRATION

It started early.

Artists and musicians were immediately inspired by Jesus, and artwork appeared surprisingly soon in Christian history. Consider, for example, the first three hundred years of Christianity, *prior* to the edicts of Milan and Thessalonica. Why would we expect *any* Christian art to emerge and survive in this period? The Christian movement, after all, lacked people, position, property, patronage, permission, and protection.

In the earliest years, Christ followers comprised one of the smallest *people* groups in the empire. How many from this limited group would be artists? Jesus followers also lacked *prestige* and *position* within the culture, which are typically the seedbed of artistic activity. Early Christians didn't even own the *property* on which to create art. Large churches and significant Christian structures like the ones I've described didn't emerge until later in history. These followers also lacked financial *patronage*. Significant, lasting art is usually created at the behest of wealthy patrons. In addition, the earliest believers lacked the *permission* of the government to exercise their beliefs without some form of compromise. To be a Christian in this period of history often meant risking everything without the *protection* of authorities, and active artistry would only serve to identify believers and place them in harm's way.

Given this environment, I wouldn't expect much art to be created (or to have survived) in the first centuries of Christianity, yet significant art *did* emerge and endure.

The early Christians were immediately inspired by Jesus and eventually employed every art media at their disposal to draw, paint, sculpt, and craft images of their Savior. Even those who *opposed* Jesus and his followers were inspired to depict Jesus, if only mockingly. Perhaps the earliest image of Jesus was drawn in this way, illustrating him as a donkey. But shortly thereafter, emerging images of Jesus revealed the adoration of his followers as they illustrated episodes of his life and ministry.[8]

Why did art emerge in this early period when there were relatively few Christians and the environment was less than encouraging? It may simply be that Jesus followers were emboldened by Jesus's message and the promise of eternal life. As Justin Martyr wrote in the second century, "You can kill us, but cannot do us any real harm."[9]

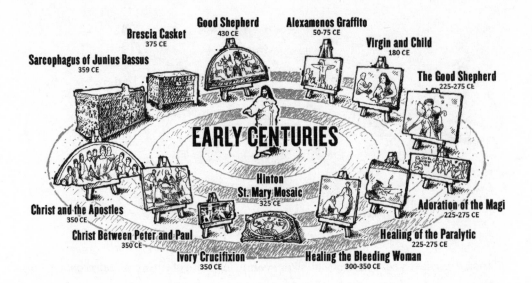

Sarcophagus of Junius Bassus
359 CE

Brescia Casket
375 CE

Good Shepherd
430 CE

Alexamenos Graffito
50-75 CE

Virgin and Child
180 CE

The Good Shepherd
225-275 CE

EARLY CENTURIES

Christ and the Apostles
350 CE

Christ Between Peter and Paul
350 CE

Ivory Crucifixion
350 CE

Hinton
St. Mary Mosaic
325 CE

Healing the Bleeding Woman
300-350 CE

Healing of the Paralytic
225-275 CE

Adoration of the Magi
225-275 CE

Once hostilities toward Christians diminished within the empire, Christian art flourished. Churches were constructed, wealthy patrons emerged, and the Christian population exploded. The setting was perfect for the proliferation of art in every form. This next period of history (typically described as the Early Middle and Middle Ages, from the fifth to fifteenth century CE) saw an increase in artistic expression.

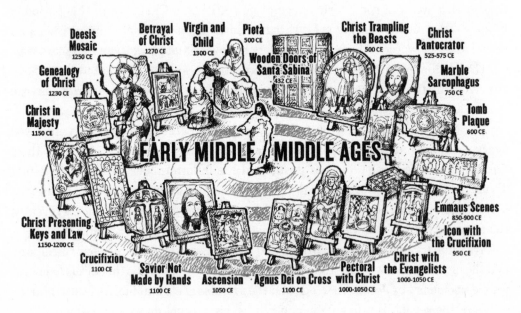

Deesis
Mosaic
1250 CE

Betrayal
of Christ
1270 CE

Virgin and
Child
1300 CE

Pietà
500 CE

Christ Trampling
the Beasts
500 CE

Christ
Pantocrator
525-575 CE

Genealogy
of Christ
1230 CE

Wooden Doors of
Santa Sabina
432 CE

Marble
Sarcophagus
750 CE

Christ in
Majesty
1150 CE

Tomb
Plaque
600 CE

EARLY MIDDLE / MIDDLE AGES

Christ Presenting
Keys and Law
1150-1200 CE

Crucifixion
1100 CE

Savior Not
Made by Hands
1100 CE

Ascension
1050 CE

Agnus Dei on Cross
1100 CE

Pectoral
with Christ
1000-1050 CE

Christ with
the Evangelists
1000-1050 CE

Icon with
the Crucifixion
950 CE

Emmaus Scenes
850-900 CE

Images of Jesus appeared on church doors, in murals, in sanctuaries, on tombs, and in manuscripts.[10] Painters, etchers, sculptors, and architects applied their talents to the story of Jesus. Virtually every aspect of his life, ministry, death, and resurrection inspired these artists to master their craft.

An even more expansive explosion of artistic expression was inevitable, and it occurred in the Renaissance. While the Renaissance (a period in European history that marks the transition between the Middle Ages and modernity—the fifteenth and sixteenth centuries) was inspired in large part by the rediscovery of classical Greek philosophy, Jesus remained the chief inspiration in the arts.

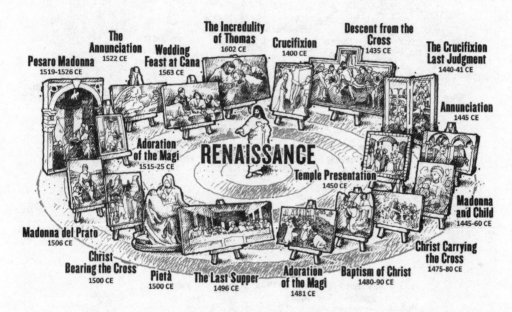

Artists in this period perfected their craft, with Jesus as their subject matter. Many painters, for example, developed and mastered the use of linear perspective by painting New Testament scenes (such as Leonardo da Vinci in his *Last Supper*). Painters also focused on the use of light and shadow and studied anatomy to better perfect the realism of their paintings.[11]

Much of this occurred at the beginning of the modern period, before or alongside the early years of the "scientific revolution." As an atheist investigating Jesus and reviewing my art history books, I wasn't surprised that a religious figure like Jesus would have a creative impact on a largely *religious* world, but as successive generations embraced a more *scientific, secular* mindset, I expected Jesus's inspiration to wane.

It didn't.

Jesus also dominated the modern era of art history, serving as subject matter for believers and unbelievers alike.[12]

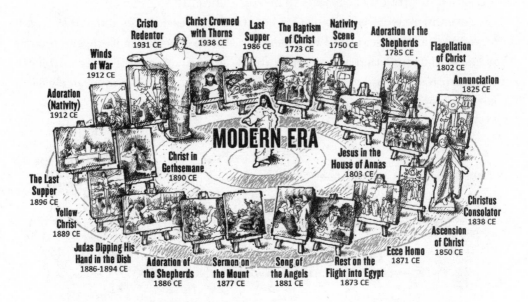

While most expect Jesus to dominate the artistic thought life of Westerners (Europe did, after all, emerge from the vestiges of the Roman Empire), I was surprised to find that Jesus was a global inspiration.[13]

An "A to Z" survey of nations reveals Jesus-inspired artists in every region of the world. No other sacred figure has stirred the imagination in this transcendent manner. Consider, for example, the religious systems that preceded Christianity and are still active today. Indra, Thakur Jiu, Zoroaster, Krishna, and the Buddha had a dramatic head start on Jesus, yet *combined* they haven't had the global impact on art that Jesus has had. Jesus is not just the most inspirational historical figure in the *West*—he's the most inspirational figure in the history of the *world*.

THE EVIDENCE IN THE ARTWORK

Buried within this historic collection of inspired art is an *evidence trail*. The fingerprints of Jesus dominate the art of the earliest centuries of the Common Era. So much so that the truth about Jesus can be completely reconstructed simply from the oldest known Christian paintings and sculptures.

Let's return to our initial thought experiment and imagine that every New Testament document has been destroyed, including the gospel of Mark. This early, brief gospel contains everything you need to know about Jesus, organized into a series of narrative episodes:[14]

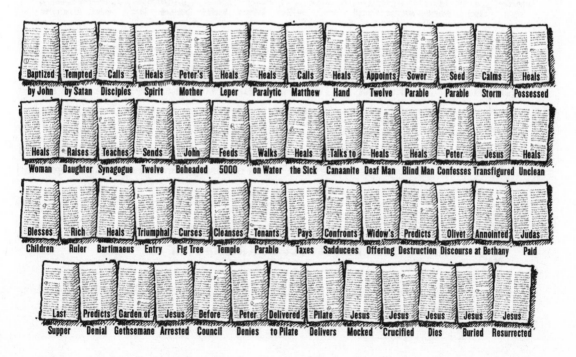

If Mark's gospel, along with every episode it described, was destroyed, it could be reconstructed from the earliest Christian art I've described (most originating from late antiquity to the Middle Ages, and all well before the Renaissance period):[15]

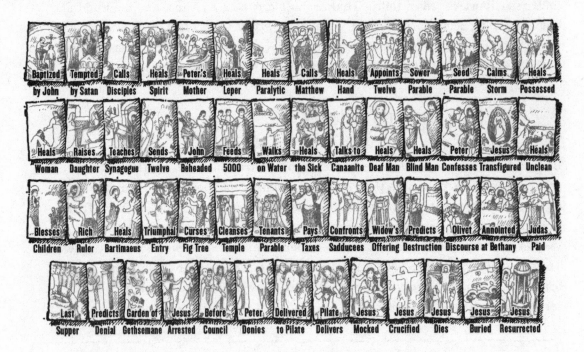

Every important detail about the life and ministry of Jesus—as described in the gospel of Mark—has also been painted or sculpted by inspired artists in the earliest centuries of the Common Era. This is also true of the other gospels. Artists looked to every chapter of every gospel for inspiration. Even if all the New Testament manuscripts were gone, the story of Jesus would remain unless, of course, you were willing and able to destroy two thousand years of art. *That's* what it would take to erase the evidence of Jesus's life and ministry. *That's* how much Jesus has mattered to artists.

EVERY MASTER INFLUENCED BY THE MASTER

Jesus's influence wasn't limited to obscure religious artisans. The greatest painters and artists of history have been inspired by Jesus, from antiquity to modernity.

Art history is typically divided into stylistic periods as artists reimagined their craft in each new generation. Genres of art have emerged over time, each led by its own set of top masters.

Jesus inspired all of them.

Investigate for yourself: perform an internet search of the top three masters in each historic artistic genre. Once you've compiled that list, search to see if they've painted or sculpted Jesus. You'll find that the top masters in every genre were inspired by *the* Master.[16]

The list you assemble from your internet search will be a "who's who" of Common Era artists, but if art hasn't been your interest in the past, you may not be familiar with these creative artisans. As an art student, I admired the work of historic artists in every genre, including these renowned masters:

Duccio (c. 1255–c. 1319 CE)

Giotto (c. 1266–1337 CE)

Donatello (1386–1466 CE)

Jan van Eyck (c. 1390–1441 CE)

Cosimo Rosselli (1439–1507 CE)

Sandro Botticelli (c. 1445–c. 1510 CE)

Leonardo da Vinci (1452–1519 CE)

Albrecht Durer (1471–1528 CE)

Michelangelo (1475–1564 CE)

Giorgione (c. 1478–1510 CE)

Raphael (1483–1520 CE)

Titian (c.1488–1576 CE)

El Greco (1541–1614 CE)
Caravaggio (1571–1610 CE)
Peter Paul Rubens (1577–1640 CE)
Gian Lorenzo Bernini (1598–1680 CE)
Diego Rodríguez Velázquez
(1599–1660 CE)
Philippe de Champaigne
(1602–1674 CE)
Rembrandt (1606–1669 CE)
Anton Raphael Mengs
(1728–1779 CE)
Jean-Honoré Fragonard
(1732–1806 CE)
Benjamin West (1738–1820 CE)
Francisco de Goya (1746–1828 CE)
Alexander Ivanov (1806–1858 CE)
Jean-François Millet (1814–1875 CE)
William Bouguereau (1825–1905 CE)
Domenico Morelli (1826–1901 CE)
John Everett Millais (1829–1896 CE)
Édouard Manet (1832–1883 CE)
Carl Heinrich Bloch (1834–1890 CE)
Edgar Degas (1834–1917 CE)

Paul Cézanne (1839–1906 CE)
Odilon Redon (1840–1916 CE)
Pierre-Auguste Renoir
(1841–1919 CE)
Mary Cassatt (1844–1926 CE)
Paul Gauguin (1848–1903 CE)
Vincent van Gogh (1853–1890 CE)
Alphonse Mucha (1860–1939 CE)
Edvard Munch (1863–1944 CE)
Gustav Klimt (1862–1918 CE)
Wassily Kandinsky (1866–1944 CE)
Emil Nolde (1867–1956 CE)
Henri Matisse (1869–1954 CE)
Paul Klee (1879–1940 CE)
Pablo Picasso (1881–1973 CE)
Marc Chagall (1887–1985 CE)
Georgia O'Keeffe (1887–1986 CE)
Max Ernst (1891–1976 CE)
Marcel Janco (1895–1984 CE)
René Magritte (1898–1967 CE)
Ansel Adams (1902–1984 CE)
Salvador Dalí (1904–1989 CE)
Andy Warhol (1928–1987 CE)

You may not recognize everyone on this list (although, if you're a fan of the Teenage Mutant Ninja Turtles, the names Donatello, Leonardo, Michelangelo, and Raphael will ring a bell), but all of them—that's right, *all* of them—were inspired at some point by Jesus. The renowned masters of every historic period, every artistic genre, and every region of the world painted, sculpted, sketched, or etched Jesus of Nazareth.

This did not have to be the case, and it cannot be said of the leader of any other religious movement. Art as we know it today was forever shaped by the inspiration of Jesus, even when those who were inspired *didn't* claim a Christian identity. No other person in history has been such a person of interest to artists. No other historical figure has received this much artistic attention. No one has *mattered* like Jesus.

AN ADAPTABLE INSPIRATION

Why has Jesus been so broadly inspiring to artists? Perhaps it's because he transcends culture. Artists in every nation have freely reimagined Jesus from their own cultural perspective. He transcends racial, ethnic, and cultural boundaries. Artists have depicted Jesus in every possible cultural, artistic style.

By comparison, search for global images of the Buddha and closely examine what you find. Artists around the globe sculpt statues and paint images of the Buddha in nearly the same artistic language, regardless of their regional or cultural differences.[17] If you didn't know where this art was created, you might assume these images of the Buddha were sculpted or painted in the same region of the world at the same point in history. They were not, even though they conform to the same visual language.

Artists depicting Jesus, on the other hand, have shown him in strikingly different ways, imagining him in a manner specific to their own culture. The *image* of Jesus is adaptable. The imagery of Jesus looks vastly different depending on where and when he is depicted.[18] He became one of us, so we portray him as one of us, regardless of our time, culture, or location.

The truth about Jesus cannot be erased simply by destroying manuscripts and Bibles. It resides in art that spans the globe and transcends history. But even if you were somehow able to burn every painting and smash every statue, Jesus would still emerge as a person of interest in yet another form of artistic expression.

JESUS IN THE HYMNS

Like many American teenagers, I honestly believed I would someday become a rock star. I spent hundreds of hours perfecting the guitar licks I heard on the radio, purchased far more than my fair share of record albums, and eventually owned the best musical equipment I could afford. I formed several bands and learned how to play hundreds of popular songs.

None of them were about Jesus.

All of them, however, were written and originally performed by people who were *inspired* by Jesus, even though I didn't know it at the time.

Music has always been incredibly important to Jesus followers. The earliest believers regularly sang songs, continuing a long Jewish tradition that began in antiquity. Consider, for example, the words of this worship song:

> Oh give thanks to the LORD, for he is good;
>> for his steadfast love endures forever!
>
> Let Israel say,
>> "His steadfast love endures forever."
> Let the house of Aaron say,
>> "His steadfast love endures forever."
> Let those who fear the LORD say,
>> "His steadfast love endures forever." (Psalm 118:1–4 ESV)

If you're a Christian, you might recognize some of these words from a popular Chris Tomlin worship song titled "Forever."[19] Tomlin borrowed many of these lyrics from an ancient source. These words are from Psalm 118. Christians still sing these lyrics, and they have been for thousands of years. Scholars believe that Psalm 118 may have been the hymn Jesus sang with his disciples at the end of the Lord's Supper (Matthew 26:30). Songs have always been an important form of Christian expression.

The earliest Christians continued the tradition of their ancestors and Master. Paul and Silas prayed and sang hymns, for example, even as prisoners (Acts 16:25). Later, Paul and James wrote to early congregations and instructed them to sing.[20]

Aside from the Psalms, other early Christian hymns may also be included in the New Testament letters. When biblical scholars examine these letters in their native languages, they find several passages that seem to be "imported" into the text, as if they represent a series of words, even *lyrics*, that were recited or sung by the earliest believers.[21] This passage, for example, is a beautiful summary of the "mystery of godliness":

> He was manifested in the flesh,
> vindicated by the Spirit,
> seen by angels,
> proclaimed among the nations,
> believed on in the world,
> taken up in glory. (1 Timothy 3:16 ESV)

This passage is a wonderful expression of Jesus's sinless nature: "He committed no sin, neither was deceit found in his mouth. When he was reviled, he did not revile in return; when he suffered, he did not threaten" (1 Peter 2:22–23 ESV).

Are the scholars correct that these passages were songs sung by the earliest believers? Perhaps. One thing is sure: Jesus followers were inspired *by* Jesus to sing songs *about* Jesus *to* Jesus. They borrowed these songs from Old and New Testament Scriptures and quickly began to write their own.

OBJECTION: CHRISTIAN ART IS INFERIOR TO SECULAR ART BECAUSE CHRISTIANITY IS INFERIOR TO SECULARISM

Perhaps you've heard people complain that Christian art, music, or movies are somehow inferior when compared with contemporary secular movies and artists. Without examining specific examples, one thing is certain: some of the greatest art and music in history has been inspired by Jesus and created by Jesus followers. From an artistic standpoint, Jesus is not an irrelevant historical figure who established an uninspiring, inferior worldview, and his followers are not second-tier artists and musicians. The Christian worldview has given birth to some of the greatest writers, artists, and musicians history has ever known.

THE EVIDENCE IN THE HYMNALS

Just as the fingerprints of Jesus can be found in the art of the earliest centuries of the Common Era, so too can they be seen in music. Hundreds of historic hymns were written in the first four centuries of the church, most well before Christianity was safe to sing about.[22]

Embedded in these sacred songs were the simple truths about Jesus. The early church hymns are a rich evidential source of information about Jesus. The broad narrative of Jesus's life, ministry, death, and resurrection can be heard in these songs, along with many rich theological truths that early believers affirmed. In fact, if all the New Testament manuscripts were destroyed, we would still know the following truths about Jesus from Christian hymns sung in the first four centuries.[23]

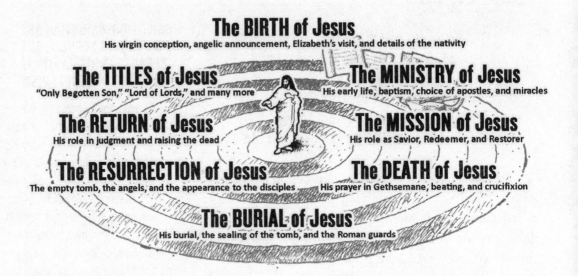

The BIRTH of Jesus
His virgin conception, angelic announcement, Elizabeth's visit, and details of the nativity

The TITLES of Jesus
"Only Begotten Son," "Lord of Lords," and many more

The MINISTRY of Jesus
His early life, baptism, choice of apostles, and miracles

The RETURN of Jesus
His role in judgment and raising the dead

The MISSION of Jesus
His role as Savior, Redeemer, and Restorer

The RESURRECTION of Jesus
The empty tomb, the angels, and the appearance to the disciples

The DEATH of Jesus
His prayer in Gethsemane, beating, and crucifixion

The BURIAL of Jesus
His burial, the sealing of the tomb, and the Roman guards

The Jesus described in ancient hymns matches the Jesus depicted by ancient artists and the Jesus described by the earliest authors of literature. The fallout in the earliest centuries of the Common Era pointed to the same Jesus described on the pages of the New Testament.

 ## MORE THAN JUST CHRISTIAN MUSIC

Jesus inspired more than hymnal music, however. His influence has been felt in every generation of musicians in the Common Era. Much like the history of art, the history of music can also be divided into historic periods representing successive genres of musical expression. And as with the history of art, Christian composers, musicians, and performers dominate the history of music. Even a cursory search of the leading talent in each historic period reveals Jesus followers at the forefront.[24]

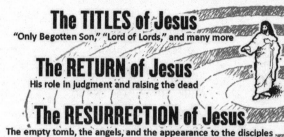

The BIRTH of Jesus
His virgin conception, angelic announcement, Elizabeth's visit, and details of the nativity

The TITLES of Jesus
"Only Begotten Son," "Lord of Lords," and many more

The MINISTRY of Jesus
His early life, baptism, choice of apostles, and miracles

The RETURN of Jesus
His role in judgment and raising the dead

The MISSION of Jesus
His role as Savior, Redeemer, and Restorer

The RESURRECTION of Jesus
The empty tomb, the angels, and the appearance to the disciples

The DEATH of Jesus
His prayer in Gethsemane, beating, and crucifixion

The BURIAL of Jesus
His burial, the sealing of the tomb, and the Roman guards

These contributors were more than musicians and composers. They were *innovators*. They pushed the envelope of their own contemporary forms of musical expression, making structural and compositional changes even as they invented (or added) new musical instruments.[25]

Creatively uninhibited
Updated instruments
Popularly accessible

Voices only
No harmonies
Church-based

Simpler structure
Modern instruments
More creativity
Church, religious
groups, and common
citizens

Simple harmonies
Limited instruments
Music notation
Church, religious
groups, and royalty

Ancient Era

Modern Era

Medieval Era

Romantic Era

Baroque Era

Classical Era
Complex harmonies
Better instruments
Structurally clear

Renaissance Era
Increased harmonies
More instruments
Music in major and minor scales

Complex harmonies, Instrumental music
Church, religious groups, royalty, and the wealthy

Jesus followers creatively changed the course of musical history, systematically advancing forms of expression toward the music we know today. Christ followers led the way, advancing music from:

Pure memorization		Musical notation
Monophony		Harmonization
A cappella	**TO**	Instrumentation
Modal systems		Major and minor scales
Sacred and royal exclusivity		Popular accessibility
Rigid structure		Boundless creativity

You may have noticed, however, that I've truncated this description of music history just short of the generation in which *we* live. Jesus may have affected the musicians and composers of the past, but does he have any impact on musicians today?

 ## JESUS AND THE CONTEMPORARIES

Regardless of your favorite style of popular music (be it jazz, rock, adult contemporary, hip hop, country, rap, punk, synth, or anything in between), Jesus followers dramatically influenced it. All these forms of popular music share key characteristics: musicians singing simple, creative compositions (often emotional and intense) in vocal harmony, accompanied by a wide variety of musical and percussion instruments, performing melodies that are documented in musical notation in major and minor keys.

These common characteristics of contemporary music are the result of generations of adaptations, and Jesus followers led this progress. Wherever you are on the globe today, if you listen to the most popular forms of music, you owe a debt of gratitude to a Jesus follower who, in one small way or another, changed the course of musical history.

Historic Christian musicians, singers, and performers laid the foundation on which modern music stands.

Thousands of years later, Jesus followers are still inspired to sing about Jesus of Nazareth. A brief internet search reveals the depth of the contemporary *Christian* music industry. In the past fifty years, over five hundred artists have contributed to this industry, recording songs numbering into the hundreds of thousands.[26]

People singing	People singing in harmony	People singing in harmony	People singing in harmony	People singing in harmony	People singing in harmony	People singing in harmony	People singing in harmony
	accompanied by instruments	accompanied by a variety of instruments	accompanied by a variety of instruments and percussion	accompanied by a wide variety of instruments and percussion	accompanied by a wide variety of instruments and percussion	accompanied by a wide variety of instruments and percussion	accompanied by a wide variety of instruments and percussion
	documented in musical notation	documented in musical notation	documented in musical notation	documented in musical notation	documented in musical notation	documented in musical notation	documented in musical notation
		major/minor keys	major/minor keys	major/minor keys	major/minor keys	major/minor keys	major/minor keys
					singing simple compositions that are emotional and intense	singing simple, creative compositions that are emotional and intense and accessible to everyone	singing simple, creative compositions that are emotional and intense and accessible to everyone

Ancient   Medieval   Renaissance   Baroque   Classical   Romantic   Modern   YOU

Jesus followers aren't the only artists who have composed or sung music about Jesus, however. Think for a moment about your favorite musical artist over the past fifty to one hundred years. If the artist you have in mind was popular on a national or global level, he or she (or *they* if you're thinking of a band) is probably on this list formed from the *Billboard*, *Rolling Stone*, and IMDb charts of the greatest popular musical artists of all time:[27]

Muddy Waters	Johnny Cash	Simon and Garfunkel
Hank Williams	Carl Perkins	The Everly Brothers
Frank Sinatra	Eric Clapton	Otis Redding
Ray Charles	James Brown	John Lennon
The Drifters	Jerry Lee Lewis	The Stooges
Jackie Wilson	The Four Tops	Booker T. and the MGS
Fats Domino	Patti Smith	Marvin Gay
Al Green	Smokey Robinson	Sly and the Family Stone
Little Richard	Aretha Franklin	Van Morrison
B.B. King	Willie Nelson	Diana Ross and the
Sam Cooke	The Ramones	Supremes
Elvis Presley	Roy Orbison	Bob Dylan

Neil Young	Led Zeppelin	Nirvana
The Temptations	Black Sabbath	Kanye West
Tina Turner	Michael Jackson	Beyoncé Knowles
Rod Stewart	Parliament and Funkadelic	Tupac Shakur
The Supremes	Judas Priest	Jay-Z
Stevie Wonder	Aerosmith	Eminem
Curtis Mayfield	Elvis Costello	Pearl Jam
The Beach Boys	Hall & Oates	Mariah Carey
Janis Joplin	Queen	Mary J. Blige
Righteous Brothers	Earth, Wind & Fire	Tim McGraw
Bob Marley	Eagles	Usher
David Bowie	Van Halen	The Notorious B.I.G.
The Rolling Stones	AC/DC	Outkast
The Kinks	Blondie	Snoop Dogg
Grateful Dead	Talking Heads	Justin Timberlake
Joni Mitchell	The Clash	Wu-Tang Clan
Frank Zappa	Prince	Linkin Park
The Byrds	Dr. Dre	P!nk
Gram Parsons	Whitney Houston	Nickelback
Jimi Hendrix	Def Leppard	Christina Aguilera
Alice Cooper	Madonna	Toby Keith
Lynyrd Skynyrd	Eurythmics	Sean Paul
Velvet Underground	R.E.M.	Lil Wayne
The Who	Jennifer Lopez	50 Cent
Billy Joel	Nine Inch Nails	Alicia Keys
Elton John	Depeche Mode	Lady Gaga
James Taylor	Run-DMC	Fall Out Boy
The Doors	Fergie	The Killers
Pink Floyd	Anthrax	Kelly Clarkson
Bruce Springsteen	Beastie Boys	Ludacris
Tom Petty	Metallica	Avril Lavigne
Creedence Clearwater Revival	Slayer	Katy Perry
	Public Enemy	Rihanna
The Band	Megadeth	Bruno Mars
Carlos Santana	Guns N' Roses	T-Pain
Genesis	Radiohead	Ed Sheeran

Taylor Swift   Kesha   Twenty One Pilots
Carrie Underwood   Justin Bieber

There's a good chance that at least one of your favorite artists is represented here. If you examine the catalog for each of these artists, investigating the titles and lyrics for every song, you might be surprised to find that every one of these artists has recorded a song about Jesus. Every single one.

"Deep Down In My Heart" by Muddy Waters
"Jesus Is Calling" by Hank Williams
"Jesus Is a Rock in the Weary Land" by Frank Sinatra
"Come On Back Jesus" by Willie Nelson
"I'm Not Jesus" by The Ramones
"What Am I Worth" by Roy Orbison
"Why Me Lord?" by Ray Charles
"My Only Desire" by The Drifters
"The First Noel" by Jackie Wilson
"Christmas Is a Special Day" by Fats Domino
"Jesus Is Waiting" by Al Green
"Ride On, King Jesus" by Little Richard
"Jesus Gave Me Water" by B. B. King
"Be with Me Jesus" by Sam Cooke
"Reach Out to Jesus" by Elvis Presley
"Jesus" by Johnny Cash
"Just a Little Talk with Jesus" by Carl Perkins
"We've Been Told" by Eric Clapton
"The Old Landmark" by James Brown
"Jesus Is on the Main Line" by Jerry Lee Lewis
"Away In a Manger" by The Four Tops
"Gloria" by Patti Smith
"Jesus Told Me to Love You" by Smokey Robinson
"What a Friend We Have in Jesus" by Aretha Franklin
"Mrs. Robinson" by Simon and Garfunkel
"Bring a Torch, Jeannette, Isabella" by The Everly Brothers
"Little Ol' Me" by Otis Redding
"God" by John Lennon

"Jesus Loves the Stooges" by The Stooges

"Sweet Little Jesus Boy" by Booker T. and the MGS

"Jesus Is Our Love Song" by Marvin Gaye

"Walking in Jesus Name" by Sly and the Family Stone

"Whenever God Shines His Light" by Van Morrison

"What a Friend We Have in Jesus" by Diana Ross and the Supremes

"Property of Jesus" by Bob Dylan

"Jesus' Chariot" by Neil Young

"Jesus Is Love" by The Temptations

"What a Friend We Have in Jesus" by Tina Turner

"He Come Down" by The Beach Boys

"River Jordan" by Janis Joplin

"He" by The Righteous Brothers

"So Much Things To Say" by Bob Marley

"Bus Stop" by David Bowie

"Just Wanna See His Face" by The Rolling Stones

"Have a Cuppa Tea" by The Kinks

"We Bid You Goodnight" by Grateful Dead

"Passion Play" by Joni Mitchell

"Jesus Thinks You're a Jerk" by Frank Zappa

"Jesus Is Just Alright" by The Byrds

"A Song for You" by Gram Parsons

"The Story of Life" by Jimi Hendrix

"King Herod's Song" by Alice Cooper

"Four Walls of Raiford" by Lynyrd Skynyrd

"Jesus" by Velvet Underground

"Christmas" by The Who

"Goodnight Saigon" by Billy Joel

"Levon" by Elton John

"Fire and Rain" by James Taylor

"When the Music's Over" by The Doors

"The Hero's Return" by Pink Floyd

"Jesus Was an Only Son" by Bruce Springsteen

"Free Fallin'" by Tom Petty

"Walk on the Water" by Creedence Clearwater Revival

"Christmas Must Be Tonight" by The Band

"Black Jesus" by Carlos Santana

"Jesus He Knows Me" by Genesis

"In My Time of Dying" by Led Zeppelin

"After Forever" by Black Sabbath

"Earth Song" by Michael Jackson

"Livin' the Life / Talk about Jesus" by Parliament and Funkadelic

"MC Lars" by Judas Priest

"Street Jesus" by Aerosmith

"Deep Dark Truthful Mirror" by Elvis Costello

"A Lot of Changes Coming" by Hall & Oates

"A Man Called Jesus" by Prince

"Jesus Christ" by U2

"Blood of Christ" by Dr. Dre

"Jesus Loves Me" by Whitney Houston

"Personal Jesus" by Def Leppard

"X-Static Process" by Madonna

"Jack Talking" by Eurythmics

"New Test Leper" by R.E.M.

"It's Hard to Be a Girl" by Jennifer Lopez

"Ringfinger" by Nine Inch Nails

"Personal Jesus" by Depeche Mode

"Christmas Is" by Run-DMC

"What a Time to Be Alive" by Fergie

"Make Me Laugh" by Anthrax

"Dr. Lee, PhD" by Beastie Boys

"Leper Messiah" by Metallica

"Jesus Saves" by Slayer

"What You Need Is Jesus" by Public Enemy

"Captive Honour" by Megadeth

"Sympathy for the Devil" by Guns n' Roses

"I Am a Wicked Child" by Radiohead

"Jesus Doesn't Want Me for a Sunbeam" by Nirvana

"Jesus Walks" by Kanye West

"Say Yes" by Beyoncé Knowles

"Blasphemy" by Tupac Shakur

"Empire State of Mind" by Jay-Z

"Walk on Water" by Eminem

"W.M.A." by Pearl Jam

"Jesus Oh What a Wonderful Child" by Mariah Carey

"Thank You Lord (Interlude)" by Mary J. Blige

"Problems" by Lil Wayne

"Be a Gentleman" by 50 cent

"Fight" by Alicia Keys

"You and I" by Lady Gaga

"Dear Future Self (Hands Up)" by Fall Out Boy

"When You Were Young" by The Killers

"Jesus" by Kelly Clarkson

"Blow It Out" by Ludacris

"Head above Water" by Avril Lavigne

"Take da Wheel" by T.l.

"When There's Nothing Left" by Katy Perry

"Love without Tragedy / Mother Mary" by Rihanna

"Silent Night" by Rod Stewart

"Time and Love "by The Supremes

"Jesus Children of America" by Stevie Wonder

"Jesus" by Curtis Mayfield

"Jesus" by Queen

"Away in a Manger" by Earth, Wind & Fire

"The Last Resort" by The Eagles

"Up for Breakfast" by Van Halen

"Kooler Than Jesus" by AC/DC

"Bermuda Triangle Blues" by Blondie

"Bill" by Talking Heads

"The Sound of Sinners" by The Clash

"I'm Only Jesus" by Tim McGraw

"Oh My God" by Usher

"Get Money" by The Notorious B.I.G.

"13th Floor / Growing Old" by Outkast

"Going Home" by Snoop Dogg

"Cabaret" by Justin Timberlake

"A Better Tomorrow" by Wu-Tang Clan

"Skin to Bone" by Linkin Park

"Here Comes the Weekend" by P!nk
"Not Leavin' Yet" by Nickelback
"Mercy on Me" by Christina Aguilera
"If I Was Jesus" by Toby Keith
"Crick Neck" by Sean Paul
"24K Magic" by Bruno Mars
"Roll in Peace" by T-Pain
"Lately" by Ed Sheeran
"Soon You'll Get Better" by Taylor Swift
"Jesus, Take the Wheel" by Carrie Underwood
"Frenzy" by Kesha
"Otis Freestyle" by Justin Bieber
"Save" by Twenty One Pilots

Some of these songs are flattering to Jesus; some are not. Some are respectful; some are not. Some are historically accurate; some are not. But even recording artists such as The Kinks, Pink Floyd, AC/DC, Megadeth, Public Enemy, The Notorious B.I.G., Outkast, T-Pain, and Black Sabbath have recorded songs that call on the name of Jesus in one way or another (perhaps the funniest song title on this list is Frank Zappa's "Jesus Thinks You're a Jerk"). Some of these artists were inspired by Jesus, some were informed by him, and some were infuriated by him. But Jesus mattered to all of them. They saw Jesus as a person of interest, worthy of their attention.

 ## SINGULARLY INSPIRING

"I'm not sure how I was this involved in the arts and did not see it," I said to Susie one night after dinner. "I studied their work in art school, visited their art overseas, and even played their music in garage bands, yet I never noticed that Jesus had been there all along. These artists and musicians either came out of a Christian tradition or found something inspiring about Jesus."

"Don't feel bad. I missed it too."

Susie and I probably aren't alone. But make no mistake, no other historical person so universally appears in the lyrics of popular music as does Jesus, and no other person in history has inspired the visual arts as has Jesus.

Art and music are interesting and inspiring in large part because of a person of interest who inspired artists and musicians through the ages.

This person of interest cannot be erased from history without also erasing the arts that have consoled us, encouraged us, described us, and inspired us. One is irreversibly connected to—and dependent on—the other. One gives meaning to our *temporal* life; the other offers *eternal* life.

But art and music aren't the only disciplines that shout the name of Jesus. Another entirely unexpected aspect of the Common Era fallout is even more indebted to Jesus, despite what is commonly believed in our culture today.

Chapter 8

JESUS, THE ILLITERATE?

The Education Fallout

It was not by accident that the greatest thinkers
of all ages were deeply religious souls.
—MAX PLANCK

If there be a Creator, and if truth be one of his attributes,
then everything that is true can claim his authorship,
and every search for truth can claim his authority.
—MICHAEL RAMSEY

"So what do you think?" asked Kyle as he finished his turkey sandwich.

"I think we need to get back to our interviews. *That's* what I think," I replied. The timing for this one-week forensic seminar couldn't have been worse. We were almost done interviewing everyone who received a letter or drawing from Frank Webb, and we needed to determine if Frank's mental condition led him to imagine a relationship with Tammy or if Frank was somehow involved in her disappearance.

Instead, we were stuck on a lunch break at a restaurant near the Los Angeles County Crime Lab.

"Well," said Kyle, "*I've* learned a lot." Kyle was right, although I was too impatient to admit it. We were attending a seminar taught by a criminalist in the serology lab, and so far she'd described several new forensic processes that could be used to isolate and test DNA in a variety of mediums and settings. Good stuff, but I couldn't help thinking about Frank and the few loose ends we needed to tie up to move on.

The evidence in the fallout, apart from whatever we might learn about Frank

Webb, continued to point to Steve as the cause for Tammy's disappearance. A week prior to our prescheduled seminar, we interviewed Charley, the woman Michelle said Steve was seeing while married to Tammy. We spent nearly a month investigating Charley to make sure she was no longer in contact with Steve. They hadn't been living together for some time, so we decided it was safe to conduct an interview. We were glad we did.

Charley's description of Steve was like that of Steve's first wife, Gabrielle. Charley often feared for her safety, and after Tammy's disappearance, she quickly regretted her involvement with Steve. He punched her on two occasions and repeatedly threatened her. She was clearly uncomfortable talking about Tammy, but I pressed on.

"Charley, I don't suspect that you were involved in Tammy's disappearance, but I think you know more than you're telling us."

STATEMENTS MADE UNDER "DURESS"

From a legal perspective, "duress" occurs when unlawful pressure is exerted upon a person to coerce them to say or do something they wouldn't otherwise say or do. I was careful to *encourage* Charley to tell the truth, rather than *coerce* her with a threat. The earliest Christians were treated very differently, however. Many were forced—under threat of violence—to recant their faith in Jesus and worship the Roman gods. In criminal trials, statements given under duress are inadmissible.

She remained silent.

"You were lucky, Charley," I continued. "You're still alive. Tammy may not have been as fortunate. If you think of something important or change your mind about helping us, please call me. We're just trying to get to the truth."

I handed her my business card and turned to leave.

"What if he comes after *me*?" she asked.

"If he's in jail for murder, he can't come after you," Kyle replied.

More silence.

"I don't know how, um, if he killed her," Charley finally offered. "But, yes, I think he did something to her. When Tammy disappeared, Steve invited me to move in with him. I asked, 'What about Tammy? She could return any day.' He said, 'Don't worry about her. I took care of it.'

After that I never discussed it with him. I didn't want to believe anything bad about him, but after I moved in and he started to abuse me, I began to look for ways to end the relationship. It was so terrible. I haven't dated anyone since then. I don't think I ever will."

Kyle and I knew we had turned a corner and were close to presenting a case to the district attorney for filing. We added Charley's information to our fallout diagram:

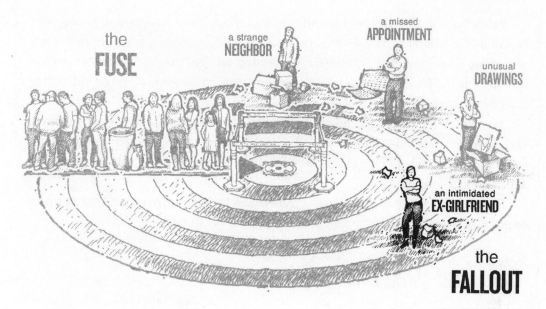

Even though Steve appeared to be our person of interest, we still needed to investigate Frank's role (if he played any), and we couldn't do that until we were done with this one-week seminar.

"Remember," said Kyle as he checked his watch to make sure we weren't late, "you were the one who requested this training over a year ago."

"I'm not opposed to training," I replied. "I'm just opposed to training *right now*."

FOR THE LOVE OF EDUCATION

Each year I was assigned to the detective division, I applied for advanced educational opportunities. My agency sent me to a variety of schools to help me become a better interviewer and investigator. I've always held education in high regard.

But as an atheist I often thought of Christians as people who were *opposed* to modern education.

There weren't many Christians at my police agency, but the most outspoken one, Jason, was a blunt critic of modern education. He and his wife were unhappy with what the public schools were teaching.

DO YOUNG CHRISTIANS LEAVE THE FAITH IN UNIVERSITY?

Studies over the past two decades demonstrate that many Christians (raised in the faith as children) reject their Christian identity by the time they are surveyed in their university years. While it's tempting to infer that universities are responsible for their deconversion, most studies also show that young people start questioning their faith between ten and seventeen years of age. *Parents* have more impact on the beliefs of young Christians than *professors*.[1]

I rode with Jason as a partner on occasion when I was assigned to patrol, and he talked for *hours* about the dangers of public schools and the perils of university education. He complained that public schools and colleges taught principles opposed to Christianity. He also complained that many young Christians left the faith after attending universities.

Jason's conversations left a lasting impression on me as an atheist. In my view back then, Christians—if they were like Jason—were anti-education fanatics who wanted to keep their kids in the dark. Christianity appeared entirely incompatible with a proper education.

But as I continued to study the Common Era fallout, I discovered that nothing could have been further from the truth.

 ## JESUS AS THE CATALYST

Jesus followers *led* the modern education revolution, and they did so because they wished to advance the values of their Master. Education is yet another form of Common Era fallout that points back to Jesus as a person of interest.

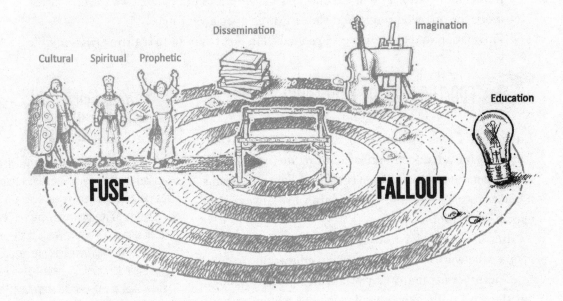

Jesus followers *ignited* education in the Common Era for the following reasons:

Igniter #1: Christ Followers Celebrated the Life of the Mind

Jesus encouraged his followers to worship God with their intellectual and rational abilities. When a skeptical Jewish Pharisee (a sect of Jewish believers that strictly observed the Jewish traditions and law) asked Jesus, "Teacher, which is the greatest commandment in the Law?" Jesus replied, "You shall love the Lord your God with all your heart and with all your soul and with all your *mind*" (Matthew 22:36–37 ESV, emphasis mine).[2]

Jesus was a thinker, and he encouraged his followers to be similarly committed to using their minds, even as an act of worship.

Igniter #2: Christ Followers Collected and Protected Knowledge

The early Christians were also thinkers who studied the Scriptures as the "Word of God" and eventually became known (along with their Jewish predecessors) as "People of the Book." Christians and Jews were students of Scripture. Moses started this educational emphasis many centuries earlier: "These words that I command you today shall be on your heart. You shall *teach them diligently to your children*, and shall talk of them when you sit in your house, and when you walk by the way, and when you lie down, and when you rise" (Deuteronomy 6:6–7 ESV, emphasis mine).

Christians continued this tradition of education. Paul reiterated this emphasis in a letter to his disciple Timothy: "All Scripture is God-breathed and *useful for teaching*, rebuking, correcting and training in righteousness" (2 Timothy 3:16, emphasis mine).

Igniter #3: Christ Followers Were Called to Make Disciples

From start to finish, Jesus and his followers held education in high regard. Jesus's last words to his disciples made this clear: "All authority in heaven and on earth has been given to me. Go therefore and make disciples of all nations, baptizing them in the name of the Father and of the Son and of the Holy Spirit, *teaching them* to observe all that I have commanded you. And behold, I am with you always, to the end of the age" (Matthew 28:18–20 ESV, emphasis mine).

Jesus commanded his followers to *make disciples*, and this required them to become *teachers* of the Word.

OBJECTION: THERE ARE NO OBJECTIVE TRUTHS

Education is predicated on the notion that there are objective truths about mathematics, history, science, and other topics that can be transmitted from one generation to another. Some claim, however, that there are no objective truths. But if this is true, the statement "There are no objective truths" can't be objectively true. Do you see the problem? If there are no objective truths, education becomes nothing more than the transmission of opinions.

Igniter #4: Christ Followers Embraced a "Teaching" Culture

Jesus was both a learner and a teacher. As a child he sat at the feet of instructors in the temple (Luke 2:46), and he later spent his entire ministry teaching his disciples. He prepared his students and sent them to share the truth with others and even used teaching imagery in his illustrations and sermons: "A disciple is not above his teacher, but everyone when he is fully trained will be like his teacher" (Luke 6:40 ESV).

Paul later affirmed the duty to educate the community of saints: "Let the word of Christ dwell in you richly, teaching and admonishing one another in all wisdom" (Colossians 3:16 ESV).

So important was education to the second- and third-century Christians that new believers were "catechized" and educated for lengthy periods of time prior to their baptism. This training period was tailored to each baptismal candidate and could last from weeks to years. Bishops, deacons, elders, and laypeople taught these students from "the Book" on topics related to proper theology and Christian living.[3]

Igniter #5: Christ Followers Embraced Their Responsibility to Learn the Truth

Early Christians understood their personal responsibility as students. They were individually transformed by learning the truth and by using their minds to continually evaluate the will of God as it was described in the Book: "Do not be conformed to this world, but be transformed by the renewal of your mind, that by testing you may discern what is the will of God, what is good and acceptable and perfect" (Romans 12:2 ESV).

Igniter #6: Christ Followers Educated the World to Share the Gospel

Jesus followers took seriously the command to "go therefore and make disciples" (Matthew 28:19 ESV). They branched out into the world and immediately encountered a significant obstacle: discipleship was dependent on the Book, but not every new people group could read. Some groups didn't even possess an alphabet of their own.

This didn't stop Christian missionaries. Ulfilas (c. 311–c. 383 CE), for example, was born into captivity in a region that the Goths controlled (now known as Ukraine, Moldova, and Romania), but he eventually became a Christian bishop and missionary to the region.[4] He evangelized the Goths and invented an alphabet that would allow him to translate the Bible into the Gothic language. This invention made it possible for Goths to read, a foundational skill that laid the groundwork for higher education in the region.

Saint Cyril (826–869 CE) and Saint Methodius (815–885 CE) followed in Ulfilas's footsteps as they made disciples of the Slavic people in Eastern Europe. The Slavs possessed an unwritten language (just like the Goths), so Cyril invented an alphabet to translate the Bible into this language.

More than two hundred million people, representing more than one hundred languages spoken around the world, still use the Cyrillic alphabet.[5] The invention of an alphabet such as this (for the purpose of translating the Bible) opened the doors for education on a global level.

Christians are still translating the Book and creating alphabets, even today. According to the Wycliff Global Alliance, at least part of the Bible has been translated into 3,415 languages (representing 7 billion people), the complete Bible has been translated into 704 languages (representing 5.7 billion people), and the New Testament has been translated into 1,551 languages (representing 815 million people).[6] Jesus followers are largely responsible for advancing literacy across the globe.

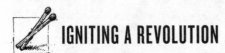 IGNITING A REVOLUTION

These six catalysts ignited an educational revolution in the fallout of the Common Era, a movement driven by "People of the Book" who wanted to share their Book with others. This revolution initiated a series of events that led directly to the creation of humanity's greatest educational institution: the modern university.

If you've attended a college or university, you can thank Jesus (and his followers) for the opportunity. The word *university* is derived from the Latin term *universitas magistrorum et scholarium*. It means, more or less, a community of teachers and scholars. Christians met in communities of teachers and scholars early in history, and these communities grew into universities as we know them today.

While the Greeks and Romans had their own notable instructors and philosophers, they developed no permanent, organized institutions of education like the universities we know today. The creation of formal institutions of learning "represented by faculties and colleges and courses of study, examinations and commencements and academic degrees" sprang out of the Christian community, and it started in antiquity.[7]

The teaching efforts of the disciples and their students, for example, have been captured in an ancient Christian education text known as the Didache ("The Lord's Teaching through the Twelve Apostles to the Nations").

The Didache was used to teach new believers in a "question and answer" approach. Male and female students spent two to three years learning in an instructor's home.[8]

"The Lord's Teaching Through the Twelve Apostles to the Nations"

The Disciples

Didache Author(s)

Men and Women
Two to Three Years
Q & A Methodology
(in the Teacher's Home)

It wasn't long before Christian students were being taught more than theology and godly living. Ignatius of Antioch (the student of the apostle John that I described earlier) encouraged teachers in Christian communities to "'bring up your children in the nurture and admonition of the Lord;' and teach them the holy Scriptures, and also trades, that they may not indulge in idleness."[9]

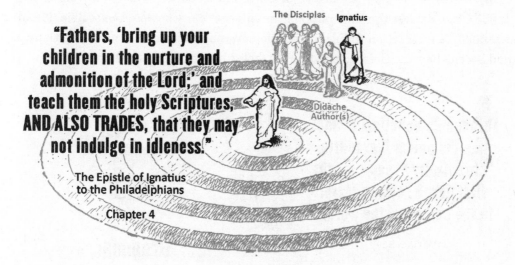

"Fathers, 'bring up your children in the nurture and admonition of the Lord;' and teach them the holy Scriptures, AND ALSO TRADES, that they may not indulge in idleness."

The Disciples   Ignatius

Didache Author(s)

The Epistle of Ignatius to the Philadelphians

Chapter 4

Christian communities, therefore, expanded the scope of their teaching, formalizing the curriculum and placing an emphasis on literary learning.

Justin Martyr (c. 100–c. 165 CE), for example, established formal catechetical schools in Ephesus and Rome and became known as the first great scholar of the

Christian church. Around the same time, Saint Pantaenus the Philosopher (c. 130 –c. 200 CE) established a catechetical school in Alexandria, Egypt. These three schools, strategically placed within the Roman Empire, were influential communities that served as the template for future Christian training centers.

By the time Origen (the "prince of Christian learning" who lived from c. 184 –c. 253 CE) took over the leadership at the catechetical school in Alexandria, it had expanded its instruction to include mathematics and medicine, and "Christianity [had become] for the first time a definite factor in the culture of the world."[10]

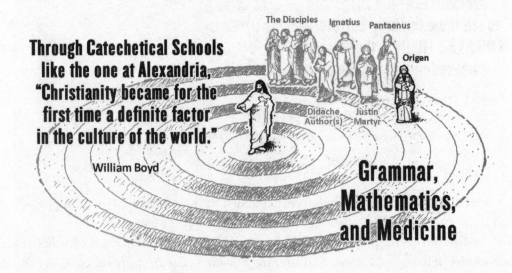

As catechetical schools populated the landscape of the Roman Empire, they grew in stature and scope. The School of Edessa (second century) and School of Nisibis (350 CE), for example, are sometimes referred to as the world's first universities.[11] The School of Nisibis offered instruction in three primary departments: theology, philosophy, and medicine.

Shortly after the formation of these schools, the Pandidakterion (425 CE) was founded, also within the tradition of emerging Christian educational communities. Emperor Theodosius II established the school with thirty-one "chairs" (departments led by notable professors). He included departments for medicine, law, philosophy, arithmetic, geometry, astronomy, music, and rhetoric in both Latin and Greek. The school grew and eventually became the Imperial University of Constantinople, an important Eastern Roman educational institution that survived until the fifteenth century.

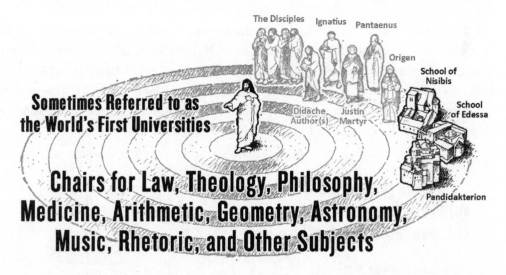

Benedict of Nursia (c. 480–c. 547 CE) significantly raised the educational bar when he established his order's first monastery at Monte Cassino, Italy, in 528 CE (quickly followed by the creation of several additional communities for monks). Benedict encouraged each enclave to collect the literature of antiquity, even texts that were written by non-Christians. As a result, Benedictine monasteries became repositories for Greek and Roman wisdom. Benedict was so committed to this objective that he has become known as "the godfather of libraries," and these literary collections have been described as his monasteries' "armory, similar to the armory of a castle."[12]

"A library was a [Benedictine] monastery's armory, similar to the armory of a castle."

Daniel J. Boorstin

"The Godfather of Libraries"

Cassiodorus (c. 487–c. 585 CE) continued this tradition of libraries when he founded the Vivarium monastery about 554 CE. Like Benedict, he collected manuscripts and directed his monks to copy Christian *and* non-Christian authors. So vast and timely was the collection in his library that without it, much of the wisdom of antiquity would be lost to us today. As the Roman Empire crumbled, Cassiodorus "helped to save the culture of Rome at a time of impending barbarism."[13]

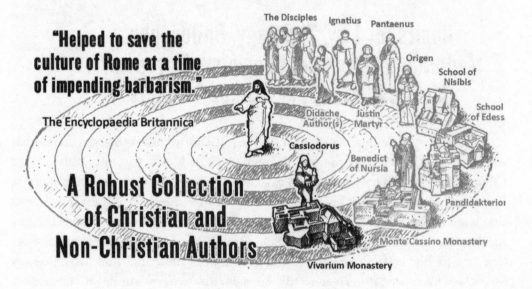

"Helped to save the culture of Rome at a time of impending barbarism."

The Encyclopaedia Britannica

A Robust Collection of Christian and Non-Christian Authors

The crumbling empire led to another important development in education: cathedral schools. Local bishops established these schools as the Roman educational system began to deteriorate. Augustine of Canterbury (c. 520–c. 604 CE), for example, helped establish a cathedral and school in Canterbury (597 CE). Others later emerged in Rochester (604 CE) and York (627 CE). Beverley Grammar School was established shortly thereafter (700 CE) in Beverley, East Riding of Yorkshire, England. These schools are still operating today. In fact, they're the *oldest continuously operating schools in the world*.[14]

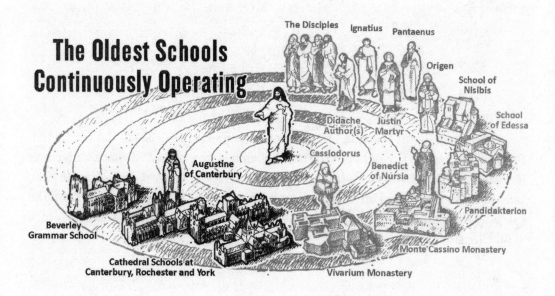

These aren't the only ancient cathedral schools, however. The Gymnasium Paulinum school in Münster, for example, is the oldest school in Germany, and there are many other similar examples. In fact, Charlemagne (the king of the Franks who later became a Roman emperor) issued several decrees *requiring* cathedrals and monasteries to establish schools so that "children [could] learn to read; that psalms, notation, chant, computation, and grammar [could] be taught . . ."[15] using teachers who had "the will and the ability to learn and a desire to instruct others."[16]

Within a few centuries, the first modern universities were established in Bologna, Oxford, and Paris. *All* were founded by Jesus followers.

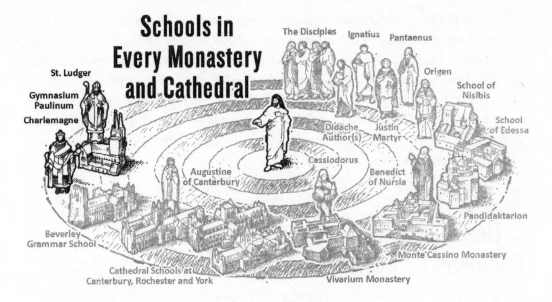

The University of Bologna (established in 1088 CE) still bears the motto, "St. Peter is everywhere the father of the law, Bologna is its mother."[17] Oxford University (founded in 1096 CE) has a motto that includes the opening words to Psalm 27: "The Lord is my light."[18] The University of Paris (founded in 1150 CE) emerged from the cathedral schools of Notre Dame and became "the most celebrated teaching centre of all Christendom."[19]

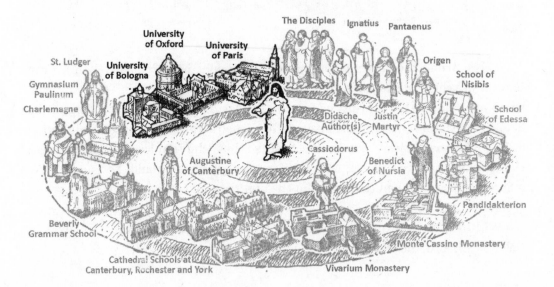

While the University of Bologna is often described as the world's oldest university, Muslims also established two schools in the same period. But nothing approximated the nature of modern universities prior to the universities at Bologna, Oxford, and Paris, and these three *Christian* universities became the model for the universities we know today.[20]

So influential were these three universities that they gave birth to these daughter universities, from which the scientific revolution of the sixteenth and seventeenth century emerged:

University of Cambridge (1209 CE)

University of Palencia (c. 1212 CE)

University of Salamanca (1218 CE)

University of Padua (1222 CE)

University of Toulouse (1229 CE)

University of Orléans (1306 CE)

University of Siena (1240 CE)

University of Northampton (1261 CE)

University of Murcia (1272 CE)

University of Montpellier (1289 CE)

University of Coimbra (1290 CE)

University of Macerata (1290 CE)

University of Alcalá (1293 CE)

University of Lleida (1300 CE)

Sapienza University of Rome (1303 CE)

University of Perugia (1308 CE)

University of Pisa (1343 CE)

Charles University (1348 CE)

Jagiellonian University (1364 CE)

University of Vienna (1365 CE)

Heidelberg University (1386 CE)

University of St Andrews (1413 CE)

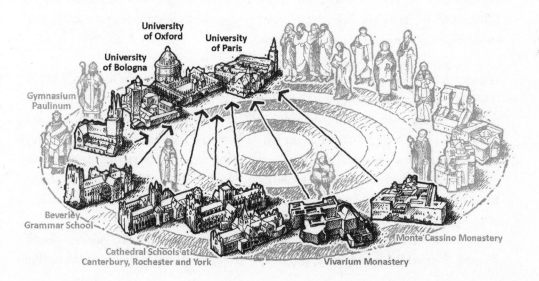

These historic institutions arose from the universities of Bologna, Oxford, and Paris, three educational institutions that descended from monasteries and cathedral schools inspired by Jesus and established by his followers.

Jesus followers had an overwhelming impact on the history of education, and establishing modern universities is only part of the story.

 ## SCHOOL AS YOU KNOW IT

Even if you haven't attended a university, you've experienced the impact of Jesus followers at some point in your education. Christians have been educational innovators:

If you were asked to read books as part of your education (at the primary, secondary, or university level), you can thank Johannes Gutenberg (c. 1400–1468 CE), devoted Jesus follower and the creator of the printing press.[21]

If you benefited from an organized, public educational system in your community, you can thank Johannes Bugenhagen (1485–1558 CE), a Jesus follower who pioneered the organization of schools;[22] Philipp Melanchthon (1497–1560 CE), a theologian who was also a pioneer of public education;[23] John Comenius (1592–1670 CE), a Moravian Brethren bishop (considered the "father of modern education") who advocated for universal education;[24] and Jean-Baptiste de La Salle (1651–1719 CE), a French priest who promoted compulsory education and spent much of his life educating the poor.[25]

If you had access to an education as a child, you can thank Martin Luther (1483–1546 CE), the German theologian and religious reformer who argued for universal education and literacy for children;[26] John Calvin (1509–1564 CE), the French theologian and reformer who advocated for "a system of elementary education in the vernacular for all, including reading, writing, arithmetic, grammar, and religion;"[27] and Friedrich Froebel (1782–1852 CE), the son of a Lutheran pastor who is known as the "father of kindergarten education."[28]

If you found satisfaction in advancing from one grade to the next, you can thank Johann Sturm (1507–1589 CE), the Lutheran layman who introduced the notion of grade levels to motivate students to study so they could earn the reward of advancing to the next level.[29]

If you had access to an education as a person with disabilities, you can thank Charles-Michel de l'Épée (1712–1789 CE), the ordained priest (called the "father of education for the deaf") who developed sign language for use in schools;[30] Laurent Marie Clerc (1785–1869 CE), the committed Christ follower who brought sign language to the United States; Thomas Hopkins Gallaudet (1787–1851 CE), the Congregational clergyman who opened the first school for the deaf in the United States;[31] or Louis Braille (1809–1852 CE), the Catholic priest (known as the "father of education for the blind") who developed a system of reading and writing for the blind and visually impaired.[32]

If you received an education in a foreign land, you can thank the inspiration of Frank Laubach (1884–1970 CE), a Methodist missionary (known as "the apostle to the illiterates") who traveled to more than 100 countries, developed primers in 313 languages, and created a literacy program that has been used to teach nearly 60 million people to read in their own language.[33]

Jesus *matters* to the history of education. Jesus followers laid the foundation for schools as we know them today, from kindergartens to universities.

Christians contributed to the progress of education and founded more universities and colleges than all their religious predecessors. Even though Hindus had a 2,300- to 1,500-year advantage, Jews had a 2,000- to 1,800-year lead, and Buddhists and Zoroastrians had a 600-year head start, Christians established more universities than all the other groups combined, by a magnitude of ten to one.[34]

And universities founded by Christians *still* dominate the educational landscape.

 ## WHERE DO YOU WANT TO GO TO SCHOOL?

Imagine, for example, that your daughter wants to attend one of the best universities in the world. After an internet query of the three leading organizations that rank universities, she collects each organization's top ten candidates and combines the schools into one list (not every organization lists the *same* top ten universities).[35]

Her new combined list includes the top fifteen universities in the world based on the collective rankings of the best university evaluators:

Harvard University   Stanford University
Massachusetts Institute of Technology   University of Cambridge

University of Oxford

Yale University

Columbia University

University of Paris (Sorbonne)

Princeton University

University of Michigan

University of California, Berkeley

California Institute of Technology

University of Pennsylvania

University of Washington

University of Chicago

This is an impressive list of universities, and it represents the finest institutions of learning in the world. Your daughter would be fortunate to attend any of these schools, but would you be surprised to learn that *all of them were founded by Christians, most for the purpose of teaching Christian principles?*[36] It's true.

If your daughter were inclined to personally visit these fifteen campuses and took the time to examine their original buildings and founding charters, she would learn something about the person who inspired their creation. In fact, from just these buildings and charters, your daughter could reconstruct the historical truth about Jesus of Nazareth.

That's right. The original buildings on these campuses typically include chapels and halls that display either images of Jesus or passages from the New Testament. The original charters also reveal truths about Jesus, based on the stated purposes of each university. This is true for more than the top fifteen universities in the world. Christians founded most of the top *fifty* universities. If your daughter were interested, she could examine the buildings and read the charters of the best universities on earth to discover the following truths about Jesus:[37]

The NATURE of Scripture
The authorship of the Gospels, their ability to provide wisdom and "light"

The FOLLOWERS of Jesus
Their names, roles, and activities

The NATURE of Jesus
His deity, role as Redeemer, and title as Son of God

The RESURRECTION of Jesus
The burial, empty tomb, and resurrection appearances

The EARLY LIFE of Jesus
His birth, the flight to Egypt, temple visit, and baptism

The CRUCIFIXION of Jesus
The agony in the garden, the trial, beating, and execution

The TEACHING of Jesus
His sermons and parables, and his preaching at the temple

The MIRACLES of Jesus
Healing the lame, walking on water, raising of Lazarus, the transfiguration, and more

That's an amazing collection of data from an unlikely source, but most of the founders of the world's top fifty universities were devout Christians who regularly preached and wrote about Jesus.[38] Even though many of these schools have abandoned their Christian identity, their buildings and charters tell a different story, unanimously pointing back to the man who inspired their creation.

Any effort to remove Jesus from history would also require the destruction or reconstruction of the world's leading universities. No other historical figure is better represented in university buildings, and bylaws, and founding charters.

AN EDUCATION LIKE OURS

"I can't help but wonder," began Susie one morning over coffee, "what would the educational system in the US look like if Christians hadn't been so interested in creating schools and universities?"

"I'm sure we would have created something, but I'm not sure if it would have been *this* something."

As I shared what I learned with Susie, I could see she was as surprised as I was. Susie and I received a modern education, one that was organized, offered publicly, and began in kindergarten. We learned about reading, writing, arithmetic, and grammar in schools that accommodated students with disabilities and were designed to advance students from one grade to the next. We received university diplomas at institutions where noted scholars were in community with students and ultimately certified our efforts. A Jesus follower at some point in history had shaped every aspect of our education, and neither of us had any idea.

But we were even more surprised by another—closely related—aspect of the Common Era fallout.

OBJECTION: CHRISTIANITY ADVOCATES VIOLENCE TO ADVANCE THE GOSPEL

Skeptics sometimes claim Christians haven't historically advanced the gospel with a well-reasoned, educated approach, but have instead acted violently to force people to convert to Christianity. Have people behaved violently under the Christian banner? Yes. Does the *Christian worldview as taught by Jesus* endorse this approach? No. Christianity grew exponentially in the earliest centuries of the Common Era, when followers of Jesus were powerless, persecuted, and pursued. They simply obeyed the counterintuitive commands of their Master to love their enemies (Matthew 5:44), turn the other cheek (Matthew 5:39), and to pray for those who abused them (Luke 6:28). Christianity grew not as a result of violence, but as Christ followers advanced education across the globe.

Chapter 9

JESUS, THE SCIENCE DENIER?

The Exploration Fallout

If a man is drawn towards honor and courage and endurance,
justice, mercy, and charity, let him follow the way of Christ and find
out for himself. No findings in science hinder him in that way.
—WILLIAM HENRY BRAGG

A scientific discovery is also a religious discovery. There is no
conflict between science and religion. Our knowledge of God is
made larger with every discovery we make about the world.
—JOSEPH H. TAYLOR JR.

"Any idea when the tests will return from the crime lab?" I asked. Another compelling line of evidence from the fallout of Tammy's disappearance came to light as we were finishing our investigation of Frank Webb.

We located the recipients of Frank's letters and drawings. Not a single one had the kind of relationship Frank had imagined, nor had any of them been harmed in any way. We were now convinced that Frank was unconnected to Tammy's case. With that part of our investigation concluded, we were currently focused on a new development.

"Maybe two more weeks," replied Kyle, tapping on his desk calendar.

New evidence surfaced when we interviewed Tyler Boswell, a man who worked with Steve at the auto shop. He told us that Steve hired him for a job about a week after Tammy disappeared. Tyler had a side business as an auto detailer, and Steve asked him to clean his 1996 Chevy Lumina. The request surprised Tyler because he didn't consider the Lumina worthy of an expensive detailing, given its age and the way Steve had treated it. But Steve knew that Tyler had steam-cleaning equipment, and he wanted the car detailed inside and out.

Tyler remembered a notable feature of the Lumina. While vacuuming the trunk, he noticed dark brown stains in the carpeting and what looked like a small acid burn. He steam cleaned the carpet and took extra time to repair the burn. Steve seemed pleased with the results, but he refused to pay Tyler for the additional work. It ruined their friendship.

Using DMV records, we found the Chevy Lumina. We wrote a warrant for the car and brought it to the crime lab. Technicians examined the trunk and found residue from the stains Tyler described. Although he washed the stain from the top of the carpet, Tyler was apparently unable to completely remove the residue from the carpet's backing. Our criminalist collected a sample and determined that the stain was human blood.

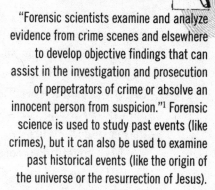

FORENSIC SCIENCE

"Forensic scientists examine and analyze evidence from crime scenes and elsewhere to develop objective findings that can assist in the investigation and prosecution of perpetrators of crime or absolve an innocent person from suspicion."[1] Forensic science is used to study past events (like crimes), but it can also be used to examine past historical events (like the origin of the universe or the resurrection of Jesus).

Now we were waiting for a DNA comparison. By searching the county foster records, we were able to identify and locate Tammy's biological father. We submitted his DNA along with the carpet residue. A familial DNA comparison would tell us—to within a range of certainty—if this was Tammy's blood.

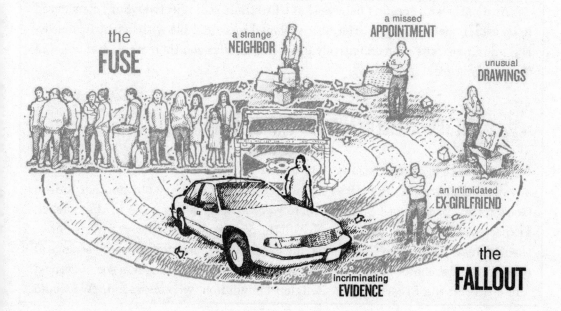

the **FUSE**

a strange **NEIGHBOR**

a missed **APPOINTMENT**

unusual **DRAWINGS**

an intimidated **EX-GIRLFRIEND**

incriminating **EVIDENCE**

the **FALLOUT**

"Sometimes these cases are solved with good old-fashioned detective work, and sometimes they're solved with science," said Kyle.

"Sometimes it's a little of both."

 ## THE INCOMPATIBLE JESUS

Cold cases are cold for a reason. Detectives tried their best to solve the case the first time around, and even though technology has improved over the years, these advances in forensic science haven't typically aided my cases. That's why I was eager to test some of the techniques we learned about in the seminar. If the stains in Steve's trunk were Tammy's blood, this evidence (along with the evidence of the acid burn) would corroborate our suspicions. I'm not opposed to using science to determine the truth.

My Christian coworker Jason seemed to hold a different view.

When he told me about his frustration with his kids' schools, he focused on one aspect of public education that he and his wife found particularly objectionable: the theory of evolution. He rejected the hypothesis and opposed the way it was taught in the public schools in his area.

"They teach it as though it's a fact, when it's just a theory," he said.

"Do you also reject the theory of gravity?" I asked.

As an atheist, I couldn't believe that Christians still rejected what I considered to be established science. Christianity seemed incompatible with scientific discovery, and Christians seemed entirely unwilling to abandon their irrational belief in the supernatural.[2]

 ## SCIENCE, GALILEO, AND THE CHRISTIAN DENIERS

I suspected that *all* Christians held a view like my friend Jason, resisting the advances of science as though every new scientific discovery put another nail in God's coffin. Back then I believed there were already many nails in that casket. I expected science would someday solve all the questions once answered by primitive theologians—*if* stubborn Christians like Jason would just stop opposing science at every turn. I resonated with the statement of Catherine Fahringer, a social activist and officer at the Freedom from Religion Foundation, who once said, "We would be 1,500 years ahead if it hadn't been for the church dragging science back by its coattails and burning our best minds at the stake."[3]

I'll admit that my view about stubborn Christians and primitive theologians was based mostly on what little I knew about the work of Galileo Galilei, his advocacy for heliocentrism (the astronomical model that proposes the earth and planets revolve around the sun), and his treatment at the hands of Catholic leadership.

Galileo (an Italian astronomer who lived in the sixteenth and seventeenth century) was correct in his description of the solar system, but the Catholic Church at the time held to a *geocentric* view of the sun and planets (with the earth at its center). Galileo was investigated as a heretic by the Roman Inquisition in 1615, which rejected heliocentrism as contradictory to the Holy Scripture. Galileo was convicted and spent the rest of his life under house arrest.

This historic episode, along with Jason's statements, seemed to solidify—at least for me—a long-standing Christian tradition of science denial. It seemed to start early, and it appeared to continue today.

But the truth about Galileo and Pope Urban VIII (the man who opposed Galileo's theory) is much more nuanced than I was originally led to believe. The pope was a fan of Galileo many years earlier (when Urban was known as Cardinal Maffeo Barberini) and even defended Galileo on one occasion on an unrelated scientific proposal.[5]

But by the time Galileo published his findings on the heliocentric planetary model, Barberini was Pope Urban VIII. He interviewed Galileo several times after ascending to the position and gave him permission to write about the Copernican heliocentric theory *if* he treated it as a *hypothesis*. But Galileo eventually published his treatise as more than that, and to make matters worse, he included a mocking conversation between characters representing an astronomer and the pope.[6] Galileo's portrayal of the pope's character (named "Simplicio," or "Simpleton" in English) was . . . less than flattering. Urban VIII was not pleased, and Galileo found himself judged as much for his *delivery* as his *content*. By comparison, years earlier, Tycho Brahe and Copernicus also proposed heliocentric systems of their own, but neither suffered the same fate as the obstinate and evocative Galileo.

Any apparent conflict between Roman Catholic leadership and Galileo, therefore,

OBJECTION: CHRISTIANITY IS ANTI-SCIENCE

Christianity isn't anti-science, but it is anti-scientism. Scientism is the belief that science is the only way to know anything. But there are many things we know without the benefit of science at all, like logical and mathematical truths (which precede scientific investigations), metaphysical truths (which determine if the external world is real), moral and ethical truths (which set boundaries for our behavior), aesthetic truths (like determining beauty), and historical truths. Christians believe that science can tell us many important things but not *all* of the important things.[4]

does little to prove that Christianity was (or is) hostile to science. It proves only that these two men had a complex relationship and that the timing of history did not happen to favor Galileo's proposal.[7]

Throughout this conflict with Galileo, Catholic leadership did not see themselves as science deniers. Rather, Pope Urban VIII agreed with the reigning scientific consensus of the time. Urban embraced Ptolemy's view of geocentrism, an understanding of the solar system historically held by natural philosophers as far back as Aristotle. Galileo, Brahe, and Copernicus disagreed with this dominant view of the cosmos and therefore opposed *current scientific thinking* as much as they opposed the *religious leadership* of their day.

The Catholic Church had historically been interested in the latest scientific discoveries and *supported* the natural sciences at the university level. Remember that the first universities were Christian institutions, and "about thirty percent of the medieval university curriculum covered subjects and texts concerned with the natural world."[8] In the centuries leading up to Galileo and Pope Urban VIII, Christian universities, supported financially by the Catholic Church, exposed more people to science than any prior institution or civilization.[9] And the church provided "more financial and social support to the study of astronomy . . . than any other, and probably *all*, other institutions."[10]

Perhaps that's why Galileo, while holding to heliocentrism to the end of his life, never rejected his Catholic identity. He saw no contradiction between his beliefs as a Catholic and his findings as a scientist. Galileo once quoted Cardinal Caesar Baronius, agreeing "that the intention of the Holy Ghost is to teach us how one goes to heaven, not how heaven goes."[11] Galileo believed the Bible had much to say about the nature of the real world, even though it was not intended to provide an exhaustive description of the universe. He was therefore content to live out his life as both a Jesus follower *and* a scientist: "Whatever the course of our lives, we should receive them as the highest gift from the hand of God, in which equally reposed the power to do nothing whatever for us. Indeed, we should accept misfortune not only in thanks, but in infinite gratitude to Providence, which by such means detaches us from an excessive love for Earthly things and elevates our minds to the celestial and divine."[12]

 ## A COINCIDENCE OR A CATALYST

Galileo believed it was possible to pursue science while following Jesus, but after examining the role Jesus followers played in advancing the cause of education, I couldn't help but wonder if Jesus was a coincidence or a catalyst in Galileo's pursuit.

Let me explain. There's a relationship between the progress of science and the appearance of Jesus in history. First, let's chart scientific developments and significant scientists (using their portraits) from 2022 BCE to 2022 CE. Science advanced slowly in the first two thousand years, as the ancients laid the foundation for mathematics and natural philosophy.

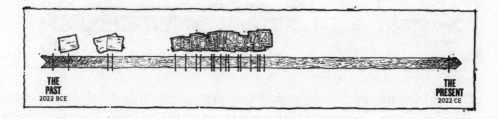

THE
PAST
2022 BCE

THE
PRESENT
2022 CE

But in the next two thousand years, scientific developments progressed at an exponential rate, with several key "bursts" of activity, including the scientific revolution of the sixteenth and seventeenth centuries:[13]

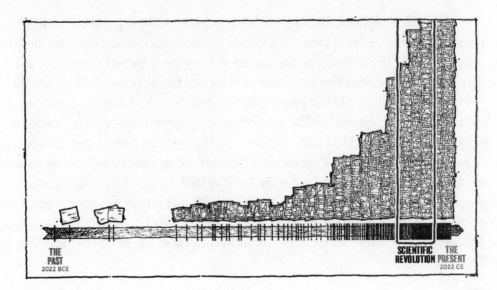

Where does Jesus fall in this timeline? Interestingly, he appears right *before* the growth curve.

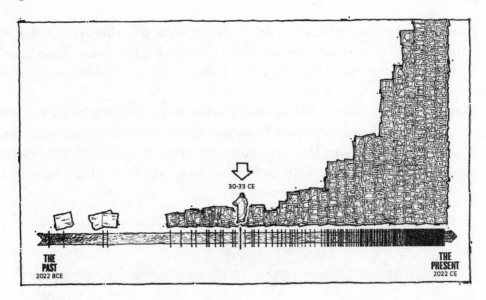

This did not have to be the case. The chart of scientific development could have been different. Jesus could have appeared in the middle of the curve or at the end.

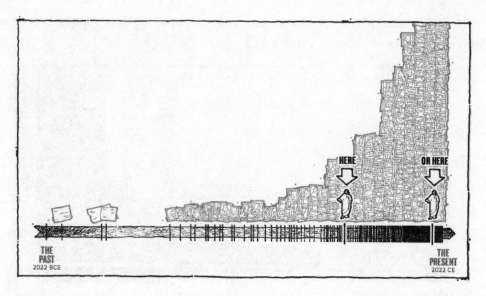

But instead, Jesus appeared just before the growth curve began. Was this a *coincidence* or was Jesus somehow a *catalyst*? The incremental steps in the curve may provide us with a few clues. The first small increase in scientific activity just happens to occur after the Edict of Milan and Edict of Thessalonica. After the Roman Empire ended its persecution of Christians and adopted Christianity as the religion of the empire, science began to advance.

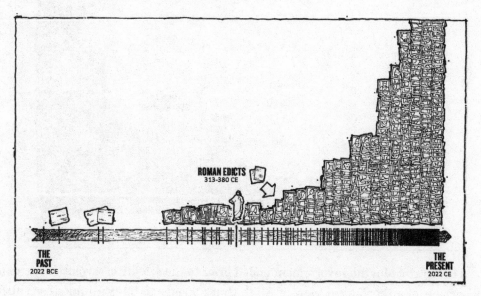

The next "bump" on the chart occurred at the same time monasteries and cathedral schools were being established.

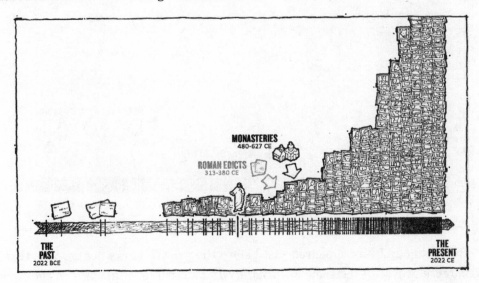

The next increase on the chart appears to have nothing to do with any development within Christianity. Instead, it was caused by Muslim thinkers and scientists who led the sciences in the Middle Ages.

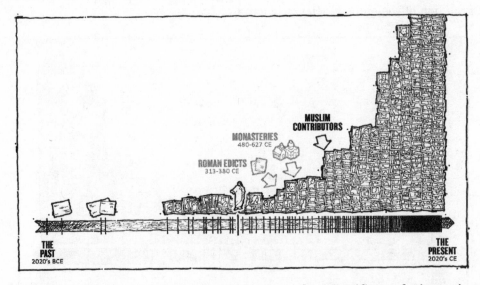

This rate of Muslim involvement ended prior to the scientific revolution, primarily because of a theological view of Allah that appears to have inhibited scientific discovery within the global Islamic community.[14] Christians, however, did not adopt such a view.

The next increase in activity happened to coincide with the Christian founding of the first universities at Bologna, Oxford, and Paris.

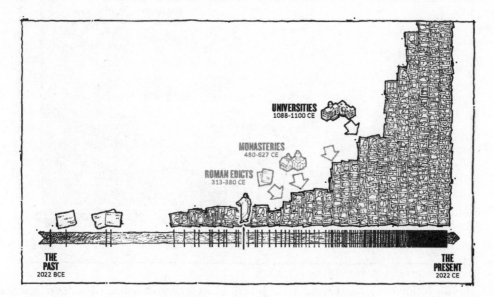

Another increase in scientific activity occurred at about the same time a Jesus follower (Johannes Gutenberg) invented the printing press.

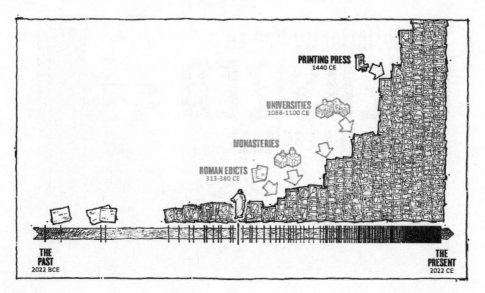

The last impressive explosion of scientific activity occurred at the scientific revolution, and this historic period of discovery happened to coincide with the Protestant Reformation.

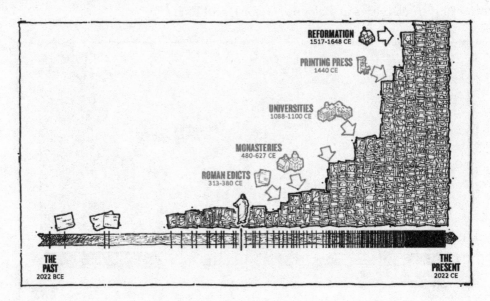

Jesus followers dominated this burst of activity in which modern science emerged and developments in mathematics, physics, astronomy, biology, and chemistry changed the way humans thought about themselves and their world.

Christian scientists dramatically outnumbered all other contributors combined. Why? Was it a coincidence or was there something about the worldview Jesus established that served as a catalyst for this historic Christian contribution? The latter seems to have been the case. Jesus *matters* to the progress of science, and scientific exploration as we know it is yet another piece of Common Era fallout pointing back to Jesus of Nazareth.

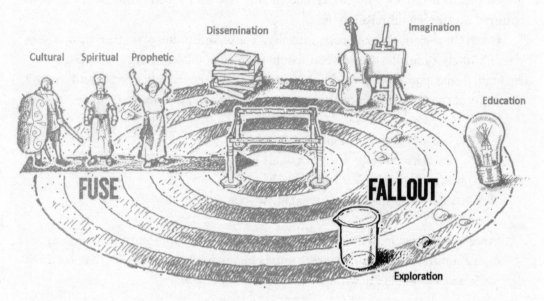

 ## JESUS'S SCIENTIFIC WORLDVIEW

Princeton professor Diogenes Allen once wrote, "We have begun to realize that for its very birth science owed a great deal to Christianity."[15] Why was this the case? What about Jesus's worldview served as the catalyst for science? How did Jesus ignite a scientific uprising?

Igniter #1: Christ Followers Believed Matter Was Good and Worthy of Study

Christ followers believed that matter was worthy of study. As simple as this truth may seem today, ancient thinkers didn't always hold matter (or the material world) in high regard. Pythagoras (a Greek mathematician in the fifth century BCE) believed that numbers, rather than matter, represented the true nature of things. Heraclitus (the fifth century BCE Greek philosopher) believed that everything in the universe was in "flux," making matter impossible. Plato (a Greek philosopher in the fourth century BCE) argued that "forms" (such as beauty) were more real than the material objects that imitated them. Philo (a Jewish philosopher in the first century CE) held that matter was the basis of evil. Gnostics (religious and philosophical believers who flourished in the first and second centuries CE) also believed matter was innately vile.

Given that scientific exploration involves the examination of matter, these views weren't likely to ignite the scientific explosion that followed Jesus's appearance. Instead, Jesus expressed a worldview that held matter in high regard and invited the study of the material world, even as an approach to studying the nature of God:

> The heavens declare the glory of God;
>> the skies proclaim the work of his hands.
> Day after day they pour forth speech;
>> night after night they reveal knowledge. (Psalm 19:1–2)

> Since the creation of the world God's invisible qualities—his eternal power and divine nature—have been clearly seen, being understood from what has been made, so that people are without excuse. (Romans 1:20)

Igniter #2: Christ Followers Believed Their World Was the Product of a Singular, Orderly, Rational God

Ancient polytheistic cultures worshiped a pantheon of erratic, prideful, and chaotic gods. Artistic depictions of these gods typically portray them drinking and carousing in a human, rather than divine, manner.[16]

If our world is ruled by gods such as these, lacking order, discipline, and rationality, why try to explain natural phenomena by way of orderly laws? Worse yet, if *we* are the creation of such gods, how could we ever be certain of our rational capacities to determine the truth about the world around us?

Jesus followers, on the other hand, believed one God ruled the universe in an orderly, rational manner and created us as rational beings in his image.[17] This view led to the birth of science as Christians explored their world, identifying the orderly laws that governed the universe and employing the rationality they received from their Creator.

Igniter #3: Christ Followers Believed God Was Distinct from His Creation

Jesus taught that God *transcended* the material world. Many ancient people groups believed that nature was an extension of the gods, reflecting their moods and proclivities. But if Zeus, for example, was to blame for every incidence of lightning and Poseidon was at fault for the behavior of the ocean, why would we try to explain these phenomena with science? A better explanation would simply be: "Zeus (or Poseidon) did it!"

But Jesus endorsed a worldview that described God as greater than *but distinct from* his creation, working through predictable natural processes in such a way that humans could study these processes. This view of the world allowed Jesus followers to study and investigate their environment without simply attributing every phenomenon to an unpredictable deity.

Igniter #4: Christ Followers Were Motivated by Their Desire to Worship the God of the Universe

Most secular scientists today are driven by their sincere love of science and discovery. While this is a noble motivation, it pales when compared with the inspiration of early Christian scientists who saw their work as an act of divine devotion and holy worship.

Johannes Kepler (the German mathematician, astronomer, and theologian who was a key figure in the scientific revolution) described his work in the following manner: "I was merely thinking God's thoughts after him. Since we astronomers are priests of the highest God in regard to the book of nature, it benefits us to be thoughtful, not of the glory of our minds, but rather, above all else, of the glory of God."[18]

Jesus followers were driven by more than professional desire or personal interest. Their scientific enthusiasm was inspired by a holy devotion.

Igniter #5: Christ Followers Believed They Could Better Understand God by Observing His Activity in the "Book of Nature"

Let's return for a moment to the statement of Galileo: "The intention of the Holy Ghost is to teach us how one goes to heaven, not how heaven goes."[19]

The first part of his statement ("The intention of the Holy Ghost is to teach us how one goes to heaven") describes *special revelation* (that is, the "book of Scripture.") But the second part of Galileo's statement ("how heaven goes") describes the *natural revelation* observed in our world (the "book of nature," so to speak).[20]

Christian scientists held *both* books in high regard. They wanted to read these books correctly, understand them clearly, and share them precisely. They considered their scientific findings to be revelations about the nature and activity of God in the natural world. Wernher von Braun (the "father of space science" and the primary scientist involved in the development of the US space program) described this effort: "Although I know of no reference to Christ ever commenting on scientific work, I do know that He said, 'Ye shall know the truth, and the truth shall make you free.' Thus, I am certain that, were He among us today, Christ would encourage scientific research as modern man's most noble striving to comprehend and admire His Father's handiwork."[21]

Igniter #6: Christ Followers Pursued Physical and Intellectual Investigations of Their Environment

Much of science in antiquity was *intellectual* rather than *physical*.[22] Long before the word *science* was used to describe the endeavor, it was known as "natural philosophy." Most Greeks and Romans, for example, considered manual labor fit only for slaves. If ancient scientific theories were to be tested, empirical research (involving manual activity) would be required.

This kind of empirical research (involving physical experiments) emerged quickly, however, in the earliest Christian educational facilities. The University of Bologna, for example, began dissecting human cadavers regularly in the Middle Ages.

This shift from purely intellectual reasoning toward physical experimentation is unsurprising given that many of the earliest university professors and lecturers were Christian monks who had been steeped in a tradition of physical labor and didn't view matter as inherently evil. These monks weren't afraid to get their hands dirty, and they saw empirical research as an extension of their physical work and divine duty.[24]

OBJECTION: THERE ARE NO GOOD REASONS TO BELIEVE IN MIRACLES

A miracle is commonly described as an event "that is not explicable by natural or scientific laws."[23] Given that definition, most cosmologists (even atheist cosmologists) already believe in at least one miracle. The standard cosmological model for the origin of the universe (the theory most astrophysicists accept) is big bang cosmology. This model describes a universe that came into existence from *nothing*. If all space, time, and matter came into existence from nothing, the cause of the universe must itself be nonspatial, nontemporal, and nonmaterial. That means the cause of the universe *is not explicable by natural or scientific laws*. Since the cause and the origin of the universe already falls into the definition of "miraculous," why would anyone doubt the veracity of other miracles?

Igniter #7: Christ Followers Created a Place to Advance the Sciences

Finally, scientific experimentation and discovery blossomed when like-minded scholars and students gathered in the context of modern universities. These institutions were the invention of Jesus followers (as described in the last chapter). Without this educational advancement, scientific discovery would not have flourished, nor would scientific information have been transmitted effectively from one generation to the next. When Christians established modern universities, they ignited the progress of science.

These seven attributes of the worldview Jesus initiated account for an obvious truth: Jesus followers have had an *oversized* impact on the sciences.

 ## THE RICH HISTORY OF JESUS FOLLOWERS

While the truth that Jesus followers had a huge impact on science is clear to me today, it wasn't when I was an atheist. Growing up, I never associated historic scientists with Christianity, largely because my teachers and professors failed to describe the Christian identity of key scientific figures.

But anyone willing to do a simple online search will discover the shockingly robust contribution of Jesus followers in the sciences. Don't trust me for this claim; do your own investigation. Begin by simply searching for the foremost scientists in every century of the Common Era. Compile your list, then take the time to investigate the religious beliefs of each figure. It won't be easy, as their Christian identity has often been removed from their online profile. But if you're diligent, you'll assemble a *massive* collection of key Jesus-following contributors—a "hall of fame" of Christian scientists.

THE "HALL OF FAME"

THE REST OF THE UNSUNG SCIENTISTS

Your list would just be the tip of the Christian scientist "iceberg." For every well-known Christian scientist you find, *thousands* more worked in relative anonymity.

Make no mistake: what I'm about to describe is only a *fraction* of the oversized impact Christians have had on the sciences.

THE CHRISTIAN "HALL OF FAME"

Even in the earliest, least active centuries of the Common Era, Jesus followers contributed to scientific discovery. If there were a Christian Scientist Hall of Fame (similar, say, to the Pro Football Hall of Fame in Canton, Ohio), filled with sculpted busts for each honoree, the rotunda honoring the most ancient contributors would celebrate several important Jesus followers:

Christians in the earliest period of the Common Era, when science was in its infancy, contributed to the physical sciences, medicine, mathematics, physics, and philosophy.[25] This group of twelve "hall of famers" also includes a standout: John Philoponus, the Byzantine Christian philosopher who theorized about the nature of light and stars and is now known as the "father of the modern kalam cosmological argument."[26]

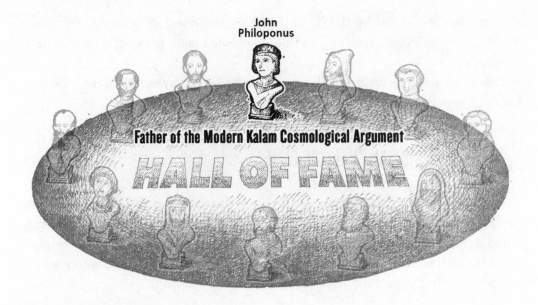

As subsequent scientific thinkers built on the discoveries and advancements of their predecessors, the number of Christian scientists grew. In our imaginary hall of fame, the rotunda dedicated to scientists in the Early Middle Ages would include nearly twenty contributors in the disciplines of medicine, astronomy, physiology, mathematics, toxicology, surgery, horology, geography, and cosmology:[27]

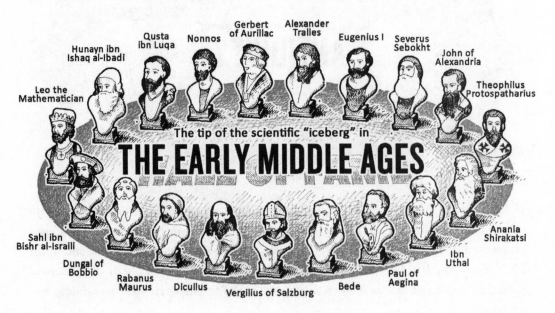

This group has three standouts of its own: Theophilus Protospatharius (the "father of urology"), Anania Shirakatsi (the "father of the natural sciences in Armenia"), and Paul of Aegina (the "father of early medical books").

Many of these early scientists were physicians. The impact of Christ followers on the medical sciences (and the formation of modern hospitals) cannot be overstated.[28] Hospitals, as we know them today, emerged from the efforts of Christ followers.[29] Most of the oldest hospitals operating in the world were formed by Christians, and institutions formed by Jesus followers are still recognized as the "largest non-government provider of health care services in the world."[30]

Scientific activity blossomed in the Middle Ages, and while Muslims were active during this period, they weren't the only group engaged in these disciplines. Christian activity exploded as well. Our hall of fame rotunda dedicated to this period of history celebrates the activity of over fifty Jesus followers.[31]

Christians contributed to every area of scientific exploration, and many of them revolutionized their respective disciplines.

Special honorees in this room include the "fathers" of evidence-based medicine, experimental science, geometry, trigonometry, computation theory, chemistry, anatomy, and many other scientific disciplines.

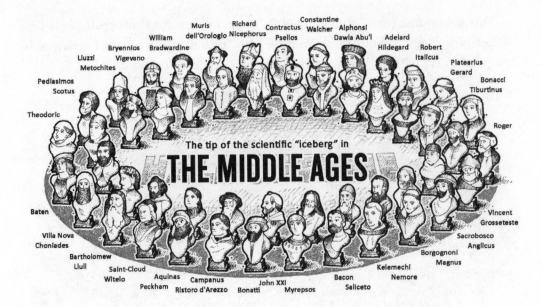

Although Muslim contributions diminished in the next period of history, Jesus followers continued to shape scientific thought at a rapid pace, especially as Christian universities multiplied. Our hall of fame rotunda representing the Early Renaissance is filled with the busts of over sixty key contributors:[32]

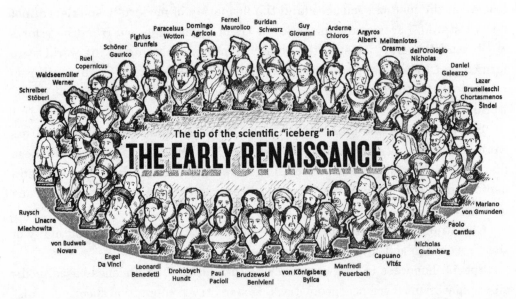

New scientific disciplines emerged, and older disciplines advanced. In addition to the scientific fields already described, Christians contributed to pathologic anatomy, anthropology, geology, botany, ichnology, paleontology, cartography, meteorology, zoology, and mineralogy. Many of these contributors are still considered "fathers" in their fields:

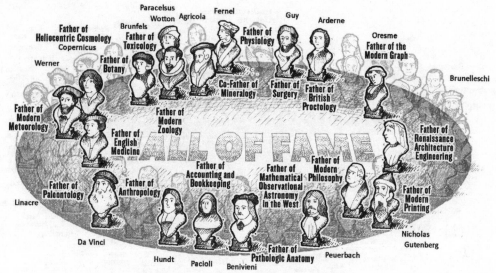

But the collective work of Christian scientists through the Early Middle Ages, Middle Ages, and Early Renaissance was dwarfed by the degree to which Jesus followers contributed to the scientific revolution of the sixteenth and seventeenth centuries. Christians *dominated* this period of scientific advancement in which every modern discipline emerged. With well over two hundred busts honoring the scientists of this period, this rotunda wouldn't even have room for visitors:[33]

This hall of fame rotunda would be *very* crowded. Fathers and co-fathers of *every* major school of science are in this historic group of Jesus followers.[34]

Whatever your fascination with science, your area of interest was probably founded by—or owes a huge debt of gratitude to—a Christian who worked during the scientific revolution. These founders and "fathers" transformed the landscape of scientific discovery, and many of them established the first scientific societies and academies.[35]

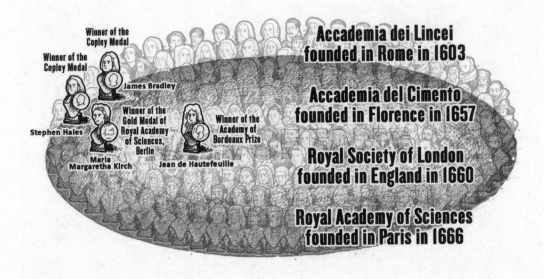

These societies eventually started issuing awards for excellence in science, and this continues, even today. Several of the Christian honorees in the scientific revolution rotunda at our hall of fame were among the first recipients of these awards.[36]

The disproportionate contribution of Jesus followers during the scientific revolution is undeniable. But if you would have described this for me when I was an atheist, I would probably have been unimpressed. I would likely have responded, "Well *of course* Christians were involved in the sciences back then. Almost everyone in Europe was a Christian in those days!" (I hadn't yet seen the evidence that Christianity was the *catalyst* for the explosion of science, rather than a *coincidence*.) "But once humans discovered the power of science to explain the universe, I'll bet Christians didn't influence science anymore."

My suspicion was that Darwin changed the religious landscape of science. His theory of evolution eliminated the need for God, didn't it? As Richard Dawkins wrote, "Darwin made it possible to become an intellectually fulfilled atheist."[37] Given this reality, I was sure the number of Jesus followers involved in the sciences would decrease once naturalistic evolution replaced God as a driving explanation.

I was wrong.

Jesus followers also dominated the late modern (even post-Darwin) era. This rotunda in our hall of fame would have to be the largest yet, holding nearly 450 honorees from the "tip" of the Christian scientist "iceberg".[38]

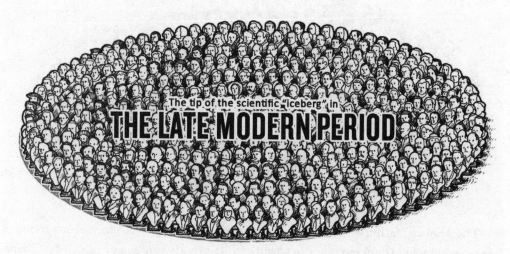

As Darwin's work developed and was eventually published, Jesus followers contributed to the conversation. Some agreed with Darwin's conclusions (to one degree or another), and some did not. Many saw no incompatibility between evolution and the claims of Christianity, and notable Christians engaged or contributed to the proposal. Several even became known as the "fathers" of evolutionary disciplines:[39]

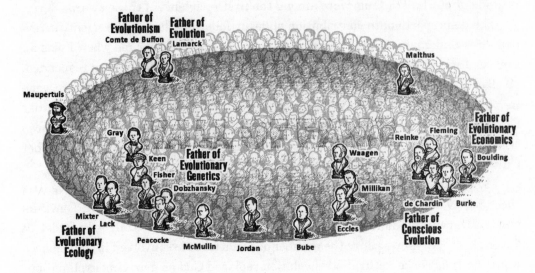

The number of Christ followers who founded or pioneered scientific disciplines in the late modern period (and later became known as "fathers" of their areas of expertise) is staggering.

The science "fathers" in this room of our hall of fame are too numerous to label here, and most of them earned the world's most prestigious science awards. These award-winning "fathers" and "mothers" of science were raised as Christians and saw no contradiction between their Christian identity and their scientific endeavors, even though Darwin's work was familiar to them.

And Christians' enthusiastic involvement in the sciences continues to this day.

While the men and women we've covered so far are no longer alive, there is a *new* group of hall of fame inductees right around the corner. These accomplished Jesus followers (already well over one hundred standouts in the earliest years of this latest era of scientific discovery) are just as celebrated as their predecessors, and all of them are still alive.[40]

This latest group is on pace to be the most awarded group of Christian thinkers (by percentage) in *any* era. They are founders of new disciplines and international award winners.

These new inductees into our hall of fame include the fathers of x-ray astronomy, nuclear reprogramming, the MRI, modern superluminal light theory, the Genome Project, and the Perl computer language, along with eleven living Nobel Prize winners. Christ followers are still initiating, elevating, or perfecting *every major field of scientific study*. Christians excel in scientific disciplines, devoutly studying new chapters in the "book of nature" and, as Kepler said, serving as "priests of the highest God" and "thinking God's thoughts after him."[41]

Consider the following list of disciplines and categories of discovery. While it may be tempting to flip through this list quickly, *resist that temptation*. Take the time to examine the diversity and significance of the disciplines listed here. Jesus *matters* to the sciences. The history of scientific exploration was forever changed as Jesus followers studied the "book of nature." Christians are the "fathers" and founders of these disciplines:[42]

Scientific Disciplines

Co-Father of Modern Science

Father of Experimental Science

Father of Modern Physics

Father of Theoretical Physics

Father of Flavor Physics

Father of Atomic Physics

Father of Atomic Energy and Nuclear Physics

Father of Acoustics (Physics)

Father of Geometrical Acoustics (Physics)

Father of Theoretical Kinematics (Physics)

Father of Hydrodynamics (Physics)

Father of the Atomic-Molecular Theory (Physics)

Co-Fathers of Modern Astronomy

Father of Galactic Astronomy

Father of Southern Astronomy

Father of X-Ray Astronomy

Father of Modern Observational Astronomy

Father of Lunar Topography (Astronomy)

Father of Astrophysics

Father of Modern Theoretical Astrophysics

Father of Heliocentric Cosmology

Father of Big Bang Cosmology
Father of Biology
Father of Modern Biology
Father of Cell Biology
Father of Microbiology
Co-Fathers of Embryology (Biology)
Father of Cytology (Biology)
Father of Bacteriology (Biology)
Father of Nuclear Reprogramming (Biology)
Father of Hemodynamics (Biology)
Father of Modern Neuroscience (Biology)
Father of Centrosome Research (Biology)
Co-Fathers of Modern Genetics (Biology)
Father of the Genome Project (Biology)
Father of Modern Parasitology (Biology)
Father of Toxicology (Biology)
Father of Intelligent Design (Biology)
Father of Modern Chemistry
Father of Modern Coordination Chemistry
Father of Acetylene Chemistry
Father of Pneumatic Chemistry
Father of Lipid Chemistry
Father of Catalysis (Chemistry)
Father of Chemurgy (Chemistry)
Father of Chemical Energetics (Chemistry)
Father of Experimental Electrospray (Chemistry)
Father of Modern Human Anatomy
Father of Pathologic Anatomy
Father of Anatomical Study
Father of Modern Anatomical Pathology (Anatomy)
Co-Fathers of Physiology
Co-Fathers of Modern Physiology
Father of Comparative Physiology
Father of Physiological Optics
Father of Modern Oceanography
Father of Modern Hydrography

Father of Fluid Mechanics

Father of Modern Biomechanics

Father of Hydrostatics (Mechanics)

Co-Fathers of Quantum Mechanics

Co-Fathers of Meteorology

Co-Fathers of Modern Meteorology

Father of Tropical Meteorology

Father of Modern Zoology

Co-Fathers of Ichthyology (Zoology)

Father of Ethology (Zoology)

Co-Fathers of Modern Entomology

Father of Entomology of Living Insects

Father of American Descriptive Entomology and Conchology

Father of Botany

Father of Modern Plant Classification (Botany)

Father of Plant Pathology (Botany)

Co-Fathers of Paleontology

Father of Ichnology (Paleontology)

Father of Micropaleontology

Father of Modern Metallurgy

Father of Modern Experimental Optics and Optical Mineralogy

Father of Modern Crystallography

Co-Fathers of Mineralogy

Father of Geology

Father of Glacial Geology

Father of Scientific Archaeology

Father of Old-World Archaeology

Father of Egyptology

Father of Optometry

Father of Anthropology

Father of Modern Cartography

Mathematics

Father of Modern Number Theory

Father of Modern Mathematics

Father of Modern Algebra
Father of Geometry
Father of Analytic Geometry
Father of Kinematic Geometry
Father of Descriptive Geometry
Father of Non-Euclidean Geometry
Co-Father of Trigonometry
Father of Calculus
Father of Differential Calculus
Father of Infinitesimal Calculus
Co-Father of Tensor Calculus
Father of Logarithms
Father of the Analysis of Algorithms
Father of the First Predictive Algorithm
Father of Modern Mathematical Analysis
Father the Fibonacci Sequence
Father of the Modern Graph
Father of Accounting and Bookkeeping

Scientific Philosophies
Father of Modern Philosophy
Father of Modern Epistemology
Father of Modern Philosophy of Science
Father of the Scientific Inductive Method
Father of Modern Analysis
Father of Dimensional Analysis and Model Analysis
Father of Modern Statistics and Experimental Design
Father of Theory-Ladenness
Father of Modern Demography
Father of the Kalam Cosmological Argument
Father of the Neo-Lamarckism School of Thought
Father of Transcendental Thomism

Regional Sciences
Father of Mathematical and Observational Astronomy in the West

Father of Russian Science
Father of the Exact and Natural Sciences in Armenia
Father of Scientific Thought in Oxford
Father of Modern Science in India
Father of Natural History in Canada
Father of Modern Natural Science in Mexico
Father of Scientific Natural History in Germany
Father of European Medicine
Co-Fathers of American Chemistry
Co-Fathers of American Botany
Fathers of Canadian Botany
Father of South African Botany
Father of East African Botany
Father of German Botany
Father of English Botany
Father of Italian Botany
Father of British Geology
Father of American Gynecology
Father of American Neurology
Father of Jamaican Ornithology
Father of Mining Engineering in Chile
Father of French Archaeology
Father of Scientific Archaeology in Suffolk
Father of Archaeology of Egyptian Antiquities
Father of Italian Rural Meteorology
Father of British Proctology
Father of English Medicine
Father of the French Experimental Method

Evolutionary Theory

Father of Evolutionism
Father of Evolution
Father of Evolutionary Genetics
Father of Conscious Evolution
Father of Evolutionary Ecology
Father of Evolutionary Economics

Medicine

Father of Evidence-Based Medicine
Father of Thoracic Medicine
Father of Preventive Medicine
Father of Physiology and Modern Experimental Medicine
Father of Nuclear Medicine
Father of Electromedicine
Father of Medical Microscopy
Father of Urology
Father of Serology
Father of Gynecology
Father of Neuropathology and Alzheimer's Disease
Father of Surgery
Father of Modern Surgery
Father of Antiseptic and Aseptic Surgery
Father of Modern Pathology
Father of Solid Organ Transplantation
Father of Surgical Transplantation
Father of Modern Pediatrics
Father of Modern Nutrition
Father of the X-Ray
Father of the MRI
Father of the Somatic Mutation Theory of Carcinogenesis
Father of the Voluntary Health Agency Movement

Electricity, Energy, and Electromagnetics

Father of Electronics
Father of Electricity and Magnetism
Father of the Electrical Battery
Father of Battery Technology and Magnetism
Father of Energetics
Co-Fathers of Thermodynamics
Father of Quantum Electrodynamics
Father of Magnetometry and the Black Hole Concept
Co-Fathers of Electromagnetism
Father of Electromagnetics and Field Theory

Father of Statistical Thermodynamics and Electrodynamics

Father of the Dynamo and Electric Motor

Father of Wireless Telegraphy

Co-Fathers of the Radio

Father of Wireless Technology and Radio Transmission

Driving and Flying

Father of Engines

Father of the Automobile

Father of Basic Flying

Father of Aviation and Aeronautics

Father of Modern Space Flight

Computer Sciences

Father of Computation Theory

Father of Computer Science

Father of Theoretical Computer Science

Father of Modern Computers

Father of Perl Computer Language

Father of IBM OS/360

Co-Mother of the BASIC Programming Language

Father of Digital Humanities

Engineering and Technology

Father of Electrical Engineering

Father of Optical Engineering

Father of Renaissance Architecture and Engineering

Father of Hydraulics

Father of Ergonomics

Father of the Metric System

Father of Nanotechnology

Father of the Nuclear Reactor and the Nuclear Age

Other Cool Stuff

Father of Hydrogen Peroxide

Father of Polyvinyl Chloride (PVC)

Father of Sugar Processing

Father of Modern Beekeeping

Father of Modern Cattle Farming

Father of the Barometer

Father of the Spectrometer

Father of the Chronograph (Stopwatch)

Father of the Laser

Father of the Pendulum

Father of the Printing Press

Father of the Modern Parachute

Father of the Gregorian Calendar

Father of the Modern Submarine

Father of Nitric Oxide and Viagra

Father of Modern Fly-Fishing

Jesus followers didn't simply *contribute* to the sciences, they *founded and led* the sciences. That's why so many of them have been award winners. Christians have claimed the world's most prestigious scientific awards, winning medals and prizes from over one hundred scientific institutions, societies, academies, associations, and universities.[43]

The prize of prizes is the Nobel Prize.

While it's difficult to determine the religious affiliation of every Nobel Prize winner, statistics were gathered at the 100th anniversary of the Prize. Given the impressive collection of scientists in our hall of fame, you may not be surprised to find that most Nobel Prize winners have, in fact, been Jesus followers:[44]

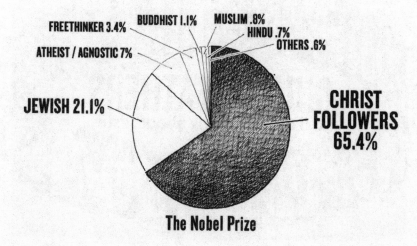

The Nobel Prize

This graph represents *every* category of Nobel Prize winners (including, for example, the Nobel Peace Prize, 78.3 percent of which were awarded to Jesus followers). When the sciences are isolated, Christians have received 72.5 percent of the Nobel Prizes in chemistry, 65.3 percent of those awarded for physics, and 62 percent of those awarded in medicine.[45] The worldview Jesus initiated ignited a *firestorm* of scientific activity, and this activity continues to win the most prestigious awards on the planet.

DO YOU TRUST THESE GUYS?

In my conversations with Jason, he seemed to trust his pastor more than he trusted scientists. I held just the opposite view, and if recent polls are accurate, most people would have agreed with me rather than Jason.

In a 2019 poll (taken *before* the coronavirus pandemic and the social and political unrest of 2020), Americans were asked about their level of trust in a variety of institutions and experts.[46] Scientists topped the list of trusted authorities, ahead of the military, police officers, public school officials, religious leaders, university professors, journalists, business leaders, and politicians (in that order). If a scientist says it, most people are inclined to believe it.

Perhaps that's why I initially rejected the claims of Christianity. I expected the primitive theologians and church fathers to have something to say about Jesus, but I didn't trust their authority. I trusted scientists, whom I assumed had nothing to do with Jesus.

But as I researched and identified the nearly one thousand premier scientists I've described in this chapter, I realized that these Christ followers *also* had something to say about Jesus. Many of them wrote extensively about their faith and the man they believed was the Son of God.

I challenge you to take the time to read what the "science fathers" had to say about Jesus (you'll find the details in the *Case Notes*). You might be surprised to find that the central claims of Christianity related to Jesus can be reconstructed from the writings of these eminent scientists, including the following details:[47]

The EARLY LIFE of Jesus
His virgin conception, the nativity details, historical dating, and baptism

The TITLES of Jesus
"Christ," "Mediator," "High Priest," and many more

The TEACHING of Jesus
His divine wisdom, parables, teachings, and sermons in detail

The NATURE of Jesus
His full deity and fully human nature

The MINISTRY of Jesus
His sinless nature, travels, and gathering of disciples

The MIRACLES of Jesus
Healing the sick, raising the dead, commanding nature

The MISSION of Jesus
His role as Savior, Redeemer, and leader of the church

THE DISCIPLES and Jesus
Their names and extensive descriptions of their interaction

The PREACHING of Jesus
His preaching in Galilee and the Sermon on the Mount

The ASCENSION of Jesus
His ascension and position in heaven with God the Father

The CRUCIFIXION of Jesus
Extensive details about the trial, beating, and execution

The RESURRECTION of Jesus
The empty tomb, his resurrection appearances, and teaching over forty days

That's what you would know about Jesus if every New Testament manuscript were destroyed and all you had were the writings of the most accomplished scientists of history.

Of all the evidential summaries I've offered so far—including the church fathers' writings, the claims of the Gnostics and the ancient non-Christians, the works of artists and hymn writers, and the historical documents of university campuses—this list from scientists is the most robust summary of Jesus. In every significant claim related to Jesus, the science fathers *agree* with the church fathers.

That's right, men and women who founded the disciplines of physics and chemistry, biology and cosmology, evolutionary genetics and quantum mechanics *also* believed that Jesus performed miracles and rose from the grave. They were certain that the supernatural author of the laws they studied had the power to intervene in the natural world and that he had done so in the person of interest known as Jesus of Nazareth. As George Ellis, an astrophysicist who collaborated on the Hawking–Penrose singularity theorems, once wrote, "God's nature is revealed most perfectly in the life and teachings of Jesus of Nazareth, as recorded in the New Testament of the Bible, who was sent by God to reveal the divine nature, summarized in 'God is Love.'"[48]

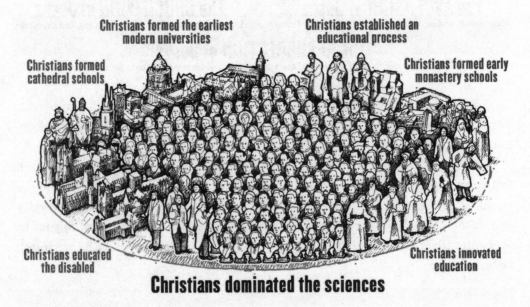

I was shocked to discover Jesus followers' impact on education and the sciences. The Common Era fallout is filled with educational and scientific activity that points back to Jesus as a person of interest.

Jesus matters to the history of science. At some point I found myself asking, "If I trust scientists as much as I claim, why am I unwilling to take seriously what the world's foremost scientists have to say about Jesus?"

But as I pondered this question, others popped into my mind. If Jesus was as "divine" as these scientists claimed, why are there so many diverse world religions and alternative claims about God? If Jesus truly is the person of interest of the Common Era, wouldn't the other world religions also recognize him in this way? What do other religious systems say about Jesus?

This last set of questions led me to a powerful conclusion.

Chapter 10

JESUS, THE ONE AND ONLY?

The Exaltation Fallout

In Jesus Christ, the reality of God entered into the reality
of this world. . . . Henceforth one can speak neither of God nor
of the world without speaking of Jesus Christ. All concepts of
reality which do not take account of Him are abstractions.

—DIETRICH BONHOEFFER

Buddha simply said, "I am a teacher in search of the truth."
Jesus said, "I am the Truth." Confucius said, "I never claimed to
be holy." Jesus said, "Who convicts me of sin?" Mohammed said,
"Unless God throws his cloak of mercy over me, I have no hope."
Jesus said, "Unless you believe in me, you will die in your sins."

—ANONYMOUS

It finally came down to this.

Kyle and I were standing on Steve's front porch, waiting for him to answer the door. We purposely scheduled our prior interviews to minimize the possibility that anyone would tell Steve we had been asking questions. We didn't want him to know we had reopened the case until this moment, and after phone calls to everyone we had interviewed so far, we were certain Steve had no idea we were coming.

Steve had only been questioned in 2000, and we chose to take a unique approach with this second interview. We decided to tell Steve we were simply investigating a missing persons case, without any reference to a possible murder. We thought this strategy might reduce Steve's hesitancy to talk to us and prevent him from seeing himself as a possible suspect. In essence, we were going to "play dumb."

"Do I know you guys?" Steve asked after opening the door.

"Steve Hayes?" I asked. "Sorry to bother you, sir. We're from the police department, and we've been tasked with clearing a bunch of old backlogged cases, and today we're checking off some of the old missing persons reports."

"Is this about Tammy?" he asked.

"Yes," said Kyle. "This won't take long. We just figured she probably returned years ago—sometimes people forget to notify us—and we didn't have a current phone number for you, so we thought we would update the case and get it off our list. You know, so we can move on the next one."

"Well . . ." he started, "She's not here. I haven't thought about her in years."

"Really?" I said, trying to act surprised. "She never called or came back for her things?"

"Tammy was a wandering type. She never liked to stay put for very long. She wanted to travel. I just figured she decided to leave me and see the world." Kyle and I knew Tammy had never been described like this in any of our prior interviews.

"Okay," I replied. "Can you give me a list of friends or relatives we could contact to learn more about her?" I could already tell Steve was getting impatient. But before he could answer my question, his cell phone rang. He reached into his pocket, answered the phone, and briefly turned away from us to exchange a few words with the caller. "Dude, can I call you back in a few minutes? I have two homicide detectives standing on my porch . . ." He hung up and turned back toward us.

"Look, it's been a ton of years since Tammy left. I really don't have any information for you. Sorry." Steve then abruptly closed the door in our faces.

"Wow," said Kyle as we drove back to the station. "That didn't go like I thought it would."

"No, but he gave us some interesting data, if you think about it."

In just a few sentences, Steve had revealed information consistent with his involvement in Tammy's disappearance.

First, when notified that we were investigating the case, he didn't say something like, "That's so great. I would like to know what happened because she never returned," or "Thank God you guys haven't forgotten about her," or even, "I want some closure on this; it's bugged me for years." Instead, he said coldly, "I haven't thought about her in years." That's an unexpected response, unless of course Steve was responsible for Tammy's disappearance.

He also modified Tammy's nature after the fact, describing her now as a wandering soul who wanted to travel the world. This new version of Tammy certainly made her disappearance sound more reasonable, but it didn't match anyone else's description of her nature.

Finally, Steve told the caller he was talking to *homicide detectives*, even though we didn't identify ourselves that way and didn't give him a business card with that title. We intentionally told him we were trying to clear "a bunch of old backlogged cases," including missing persons reports. Why jump to the conclusion that this was a homicide investigation?

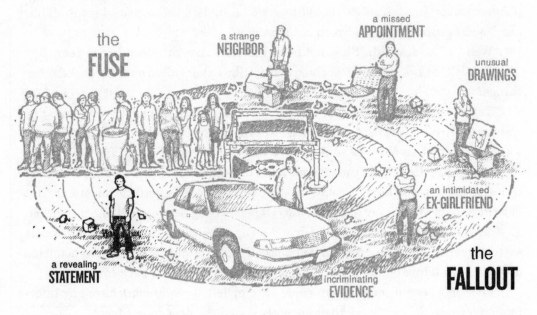

These small details might not have been conclusive, but they certainly added to the evidence and data we were gathering in the fallout. Would our cumulative case from the fuse and the fallout be enough to convince the district attorney to file the case? Would a jury think the evidence from the fuse and the fallout was conclusive? That remained to be seen.

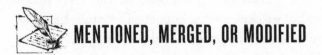 ## MENTIONED, MERGED, OR MODIFIED

"Do you ever wonder if all this would have been different if we were living someplace else?" asked Susie, pointing to the tall stack of research books piled up in the corner of our bedroom.

"What do you mean?"

"Well, if we had been raised in a Muslim country, would you be investigating Islam?"

"Maybe," I replied. "But even if we had been raised in a Muslim country, we still would have learned a lot about Jesus . . ."

I was surprised to discover yet another way Jesus affected the fallout of the Common Era, and this line of evidence involved groups, like Muslims, who don't include the New Testament in their collection of holy writings.

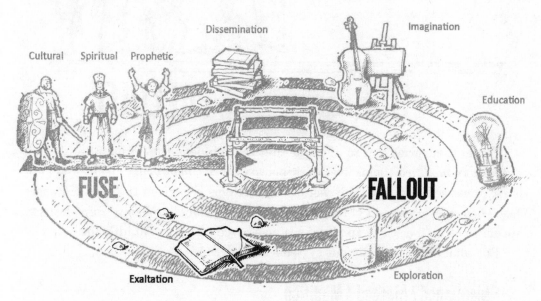

Jesus matters to religious believers around the world, even if they reject the claims of Christianity. Consider for a moment the appearance of Jesus in history:

His explosive entry on our timeline was preceded by the fuse and resulted in the fallout I've described so far. After Jesus inaugurated Christianity, several other world religions and spiritual worldviews also appeared on the timeline, including Islam, Bahá'í, Ahmadiyya, and New Age spirituality.

Would it surprise you to discover that the religions that came after Jesus's appearance *modified* themselves in response to Jesus, *mentioned* his life and ministry, or *merged* him into their worldview? Perhaps not, given the kind of impact Jesus had on every aspect of the Common Era. We should probably *expect* Jesus to appear in other theistic or spiritual systems based on his global influence.

But what about the religious systems that preceded Jesus?

Would you be surprised to discover that these ancient religions also modified, mentioned, or merged Jesus into their worldviews? As it turns out, they did.

You might be asking, "How could the early religions in this illustration acknowledge or include Jesus if he hadn't yet been born?" While it's true the earliest worshipers of Indra, Attis, Heracles, Krishna, Mithras, and the Buddha knew nothing about Jesus, as these faith systems survived into the Common Era, they found themselves accommodating Jesus in one manner or another.

FUSE   FALLOUT

After the inauguration of Christianity, these ancient religions found themselves contending with Jesus's overwhelming impact. Some responded by *modifying* their practices and beliefs to mimic Christianity, some simply *mentioned* Jesus, and others found a way to *merge* him into their worldview. Let's begin by examining the response of religions that preceded Jesus.

 ## JESUS MENTIONED AND MERGED IN HINDUISM

Hinduism traces its roots back to the Iron Age of India (twelfth to sixth centuries BCE).[1] It is a remarkably diverse religious system without a single founder. Given the many varieties of Hinduism (each embracing a complex and divergent set of views), it is difficult to isolate a single, unified set of beliefs, but one thing is certain: modern Hindus acknowledge Jesus and have merged him into their worldview.

> ### Jesus Is Considered a Sadhu

Most Hindus evaluate "spirituality" based on behavior and practice. Virtues such as tolerance, love, nonviolence, self-sacrifice, and humility are held in high esteem and considered to be characteristics of "holy men" known as *sadhus*.[2] Many Hindus, using this broad criteria, see Jesus (called "Ishu") as a "Hindu saint" because of his life and teaching.[3] Some

OBJECTION: ALL GOD EXPECTS OF US IS SINCERITY

Is sincerity more important to God than accuracy? Imagine that you and I are hiking and discover a poisonous hemlock plant. Since it looks like parsley, you decide to eat some of it. You sincerely believe the plant is parsley. Will your sincerity protect you from harm? Most of us understand the value of truth and sincerity. Both are important, but sincerity without truth can lead you to the wrong place and endanger your life.

Hindus also believe that Jesus spent time in India as a young man (during the years missing from the Gospels) learning the basic philosophy of yoga so he could return to Israel as a sadhu.

➤ Jesus Is Considered an Acharya

The Sanskrit word *acharya* means "one who teaches by example."[4] For many Hindus, Jesus provides an example of someone who engaged and practiced a spiritual life (much like the example set by Krishna).[5]

➤ Jesus Is Considered Divine

Some Hindus acknowledge Jesus as divine, even if he is not seen as *uniquely* divine. Hindus often worship many gods and goddesses, and some include Jesus in their list of deities, considering him the perfect example of "self-realization."[6] Many see Jesus as a "God-man" of sorts, even while acknowledging other examples such as Rama, Krishna, and the Buddha.[7]

➤ Jesus Is Considered a Wise Teacher and Model of Morality

Most Hindus respect Jesus's teaching, and some have even committed themselves to his instruction. Mahatma Gandhi, for example, greatly admired the moral philosophy of Jesus (particularly as expressed in the Sermon on the Mount).[8] He considered Jesus a superior source of moral truth and an expression of the "spirit and will of God."[9]

Even though Hinduism began long before Jesus's arrival, Hindus acknowledge Jesus as a divine sadhu and acharya:

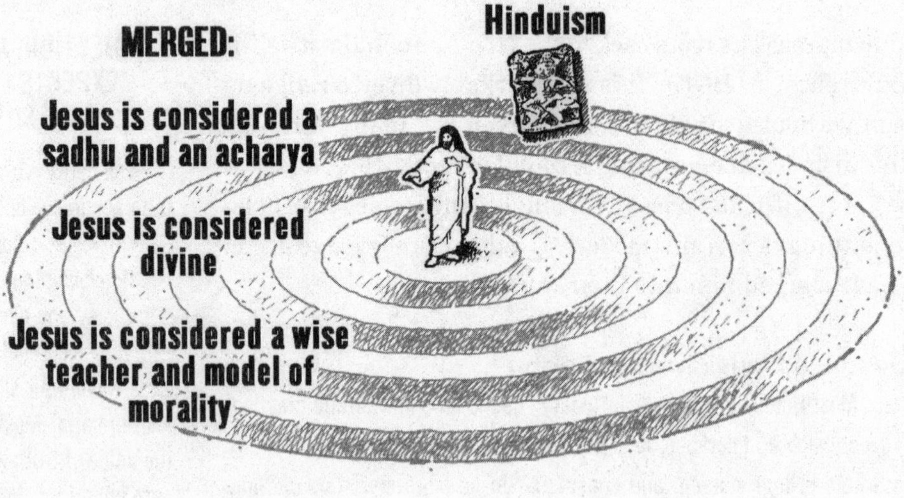

Hinduism also *mentions* and acknowledges many episodes and truths found in the Christian Scriptures:

➢ Many Details of Jesus's Life Are Acknowledged

Hindus acknowledge episodes from the gospel narratives, including Jesus's birth in a stable, the visit of the magi, his ability to perform miracles (such as walking on water and healing the sick), and his public sermons.

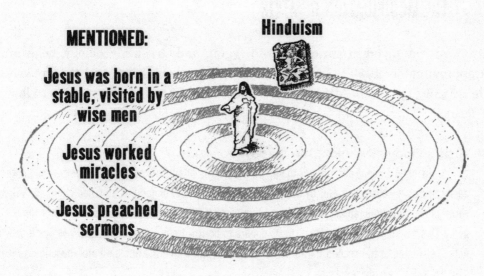

Because of the way Hindu leaders (like Mahatma Gandhi) have mentioned Jesus and merged him into their own religion, *1.16 billion* Hindus in these regions of the world have had the opportunity to hear about Jesus, *even within the context of Hinduism.*[10]

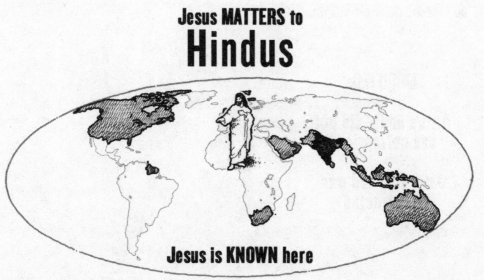

Jesus *matters* to Hindus who have *merged* Jesus into their system, and they continue to *mention* and acknowledge key episodes of the New Testament gospels.

THE MODIFICATION OF ATTIS

Attis was worshiped in antiquity in Phrygian and Greek mythology, beginning in approximately 1250 BCE. After the appearance of Jesus and the growth of Christianity, the cult of Attis *modified* the nature of Attis to incorporate attributes of Jesus.

➤ Attis's Body "Did Not See Decay"

In the most ancient accounts of the myth, no description of Attis says that his body would not rot, decay, or become corrupted. But by the second century of the Common Era, this had changed. A Greek writer of the time, Pausanias, now included this new attribute of Attis in his description of the Greek god.[11] This modification of the Attis story appears to borrow from a passage of the New Testament in Acts 2:31 (dated to the second half of the first century), in which the apostle Peter, describing Jesus, said, "Nor did his body see decay."

➤ Attis Died and Was Resurrected

Related to that modification of the myth, second-century worshipers (as early as 133 CE) developed a purification right for members symbolizing "rebirth." This reflected a new view of Attis as a god who died and was reborn (or resurrected).[12]

The cult of Attis has long been abandoned, but history records how much Jesus mattered to Attis worshipers.

The cult modified its notions of Attis in response to the overwhelming influence of Jesus and his followers.[13]

MODIFYING HERACLES

Heracles was a divine hero in Greek mythology (known more popularly as Hercules in Roman times). The earliest evidence we have for the worship of this Greek god dates to the sixth century BCE. In the most ancient descriptions of Heracles, he behaved in a morally questionable manner, participating in multiple marriages and affairs, committing several questionable killings, and conceiving many children out of wedlock. But by the second century, some aspects of the Heracles mythology had changed.

> ### Heracles Is a Paragon of Virtue
> Philosophers and writers in the late first century, *after* Christianity had already arrived in the Roman Empire, began to imagine Heracles as "a paragon of the wise man and the incarnation of all virtues," much like the sinless description of Jesus.[14]

> ### Heracles Is the "Logos"
> One stoic philosopher in this period of the Common Era also described Hercules for the first time as "the Logos infused in all things, which gives nature both its power and its cohesion,"[15] a clear parallel with the way John described Jesus in his gospel,[16] as well as how Paul described Jesus in his letter to the Colossians.[17]

> ### Heracles "Walked on Water"
> A fourth-century Roman emperor, Flavius Claudius Julianus (commonly known as Julian), rejected Christianity and continued to worship the Roman gods. In recrafting the Hercules myth, he added to Hercules's "mighty deeds" an episode in which Hercules crossed the sea without getting wet, similar to the way Jesus walked on water.[18]

> ### Heracles Is a Member of a "Trinity"
> Julian also described the relationship between Jupiter, Athena Pronaia, and Heracles "so that the divine triad thus sketched out closely resembles a Trinity."[19]

➤ Heracles Ascended into Heaven

Justin Martyr, a second-century Christian apologist, described several episodes of plagiarism in the Greek and Roman myths, including a version of Heracles's death in which he ascends into heaven in a manner similar to Jesus.[20]

MODIFIED:

Heracles is a paragon of virtue

Heracles is the "Logos"

Heracles "walked on water"

Heracles ascended into heaven

Heracles is a member of a "trinity"

Indra (Hinduism)

Attis

Heracles

While the worship of Heracles ended many centuries ago, Jesus mattered enough to this ancient religion that its followers were willing to modify the nature and life of Heracles in response to Jesus's influence.

 ## KRISHNA MODIFIED

Although Krishna is a Hindu deity, a modern form of Krishna worship (the Hare Krishna movement) emerged well after the appearance of Jesus. Even the ancient description of Krishna was modified after Gnostic gospel authors and Christian missionaries exposed Krishna worshipers to the story of Jesus in the Common Era.

➤ Krishna Is the Sole Deity

While Krishna originally appeared within Hinduism as one of many gods, Krishna worshipers later identified him as the *sole* deity. This "post-Christian phase in Hinduism" is "indebted to Christianity."[21]

➤ Krishna Was Born of a Virgin, and a Tyrant Ordered the Killing of Innocent Infants

Modern writers cite similarities in the birth stories of Krishna and Jesus, describing Krishna's mother, Devaki, for example, as a virgin. In another similarity to the Christian birth narrative, Kansa (a tyrant ruler of the Vrishni kingdom) is said to kill innocent infants, recalling the actions of Herod in the New Testament. Scholars believe that any similarity between the Hindu and Christian birth narratives was "borrowed" from Christianity.[22]

➤ Krishna's Birthday Is Celebrated with Christian Imagery

Hindus also celebrate the birth of Krishna with symbolism familiar to Christians. Krishna birth scenes typically include images of Devaki lying in a stable with Krishna surrounded by shepherds and farm animals, while deities and demigods hover in the air (like Christian images of angels). According to scholars, this celebration "is an imitation of the Christian festival."[23]

➤ Krishna Was a Shepherd or "Herdsman"

Krishna's identification as a herdsman is also considered a modification of the Krishna mythology that appears to have been borrowed from Christian sources.[24]

➤ Krishna Defeated a Demon Similar to Satan

Another part of the Krishna narrative describes him defeating a serpent demon named Kaliya. Scholars also believe this story is a corruption of Jesus's victory over Satan.[25]

➤ Krishna Raised a Dead Son to Life

In the *Jaimini Bharata*, a thirteenth-century version of the Hindu epic *Mahâbhârata*, Krishna is described as raising a dead son to life in a manner similar to the way Jesus raised a dead son in the gospel of Luke (7:11–17). This late addition to the Krishna narrative has also been borrowed from Christianity.[26]

Krishna worshipers, like those of Attis and Heracles, modified the nature of Krishna after Christianity began to grow as a global movement.

A modern version of Krishna worship, known as Krishna Consciousness or the Hare Krishna movement, focuses on "an awareness of and affection for the Supreme Person, Krishna," as "the culmination of all forms of yoga, knowledge, meditation, and spirituality."[27] Claiming to be a monotheistic branch of the spiritual tradition that dates back to Krishna himself, this modern version incorporates the teaching of Sri Chaitanya Mahaprabhu (a fifteenth-century

Indian saint) and A. C. Bhaktivedanta Swami Prabhupada (a twentieth-century Indian spiritual teacher).

MODIFIED:
Krishna is the sole deity
Krishna was born of a virgin and a tyrant ordered the killing of innocent infants
Krishna's birthday is celebrated with Christian imagery
Krishna was a shepherd or "herdsman"
Krishna defeated a demon similar to Satan
Krishna raised a dead son to life

Indra (Hinduism)

Attis

Heracles

Krishna

Even though it centers on the person of Krishna, today's Hare Krishna movement merges Jesus into their religious system in several important ways.

➤ Jesus Is the Perfect Guru

Srila Prabhupada and others within the Hare Krishna movement accept Jesus and honor him with the title of "guru." They describe him as the "perfect guru," a trusted representative of God and someone who has shown us how to love and serve him.[28]

➤ Jesus Was Sent by God

Hare Krishna believers also believe God sent Jesus to reveal himself to humanity.[29]

➤ Jesus Is the "Son of God" and "Lord"

Leaders and members of Krishna Consciousness acknowledge Jesus as the "Son of God" and "Lord." Although they don't assign exclusive deity to him, they give him "all honor" as "a pure representative of God" and "our guru, our spiritual master."[30]

The Hare Krishna movement accommodates the existence of Jesus as it merges him into their spiritual worldview:

MERGED:

Jesus is the perfect guru

Jesus was sent by God

Jesus is the "Son of God" and "Lord"

Indra (Hinduism)

Attis

Heracles

Krishna

The Hare Krishna movement also mentions many episodes and claims from Christian Scripture.

➤ The New Testament Records True Events

Hare Krishna leaders and believers accept and recite many of the episodes described in the New Testament, including Jesus's sermons, parables, miracles, interactions, and travels, in addition to the crucifixion narrative. While they often reinterpret Jesus's meanings or actions, many details from the Gospels can be reconstructed from the statements of these leaders and believers.[31]

MENTIONED:

The sermons, parables, miracles, interactions, travels, and crucifixion of Jesus

Indra (Hinduism)

Attis

Heracles

Krishna

Jesus and his followers have widely affected ancient and modern forms of Krishna worship. Today, *one million* Hare Krishna members recognize Jesus as an important guru based on the teaching of Srila Prabhupada and other Hare Krishna leaders.

THE MODIFICATION OF MITHRAS

Mithraism blossomed in Rome from the first to the fourth century, bringing it into contact with the earliest Christians who also lived in the region. The worship of Mithras, the central god of the religion, began centuries earlier in Persia, but little is known about the religious system before it appeared in Rome.[32] When it did arrive in the West, Mithraism changed from its prior, Persian form.[33] What caused the modification? The powerful influence of Jesus and his followers. Roman Mithraic believers modified their practices and beliefs in two ways:

➤ **Believers Achieved Eternal Life through a Blood Sacrifice**

Mithraic believers met in small temples and celebrated a rather gruesome ritual. A bull was slaughtered directly over each new believer. The blood of the sacrificed bull would *cover* the initiate. In one Mithraic temple, the words *in aeternum renatus* ("reborn for eternity") were inscribed near the location of the ritual. This is similar to the Christian belief that eternal life is attained through the "blood of the Lamb." The Mithraic inscription was written in 375 CE, well after Christianity was established in the region. According to scholars, this concept of attaining eternal life through a blood sacrifice was borrowed from Christianity.[34]

➤ **Believers Observed a Communion Ceremony**

Roman Mithraic believers also regularly celebrated a less grisly ritual: a sacred meal with bread and wine. The Mithraic liturgy appears late in history, well after Christians were established in Rome.[35]

The nature of Mithraic rituals changed after Jesus's appearance:

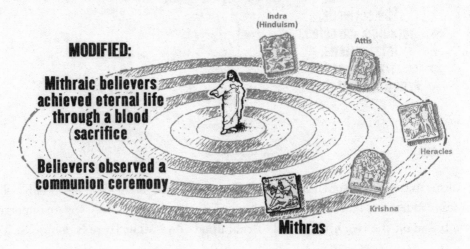

MODIFIED:

Mithraic believers achieved eternal life through a blood sacrifice

Believers observed a communion ceremony

Indra (Hinduism)

Attis

Heracles

Krishna

Mithras

Although Mithraism did not stand the test of time, it did experience a period of modification in Rome under the influence of Jesus and his followers.

BUDDHISM MERGED AND MENTIONED

While Buddhism is based primarily on the teachings of Siddhartha Gautama (known as the Buddha), it incorporates a variety of religious traditions, beliefs, and practices. Like Hinduism, Buddhism provides no singular, unified view of Jesus, although many Buddhists have merged and included him in their worldview.

➤ **Jesus Is an "Enlightened Man"**

Most Buddhists acknowledge and respect Jesus's self-sacrificial life and the compassion he showed toward those who were in spiritual need. Under Buddhism, this kind of compassion is the key to happiness and enlightenment. For this reason, many Buddhists, including fourteenth-century Zen master Gasan Jōseki, refer to Jesus as an "enlightened man" in the Buddhist tradition.[36]

➤ **Jesus Is a _Bodhisattva_**

The current Dalai Lama (Tenzin Gyatso, the foremost spiritual leader of Tibetan Buddhism) has described Jesus as a _bodhisattva_, a term typically used to describe someone on a journey toward Buddhahood, or someone who is able to reach nirvana but delays doing so out of compassion for others who are suffering.[37]

➤ **Jesus Is a Wise Teacher**

Most Buddhists also respect Jesus's teaching to a high degree, especially Jesus's instruction related to loving one's neighbor and his call to demonstrate kindness and forgiveness. The substance of Jesus's teaching was particularly impressive to the Dalai Lama.[38] He considered the instruction of Jesus to be in accord with Buddhist values.

Buddhism provides a "place" for Jesus within its traditions, merging him into the Buddhist worldview. At the very least, Jesus is considered a wise, moral teacher, and to many Buddhist leaders and believers, Jesus is an enlightened man or _bodhisattva_ journeying toward Buddhahood. Buddhists consider Jesus in an extremely favorable light.[39]

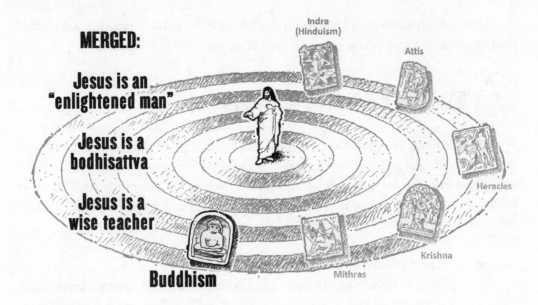

Just as importantly, Buddhist leaders (including the Dalai Lama) have spoken and written publicly about many of the episodes and claims of the New Testament accounts.[40]

➤ Jesus Lived as Described in the New Testament

Buddhist leaders acknowledge Jesus's sermons, parables, interactions, travels, miracles, crucifixion, and even the resurrection. The Dalai Lama has acknowledged the following biblical episodes in his written and public statements:

The Sermon on the Mount

The interaction between Jesus and his mother, brothers, and sisters

The parable of the growing seed

The transfiguration[41]

The sending of the twelve apostles

Jesus's claim that he spoke with God's authority

Mary's observation of the risen Christ in the garden[42]

The value Buddhists place on the person of Jesus is grounded in their acknowledgment of the New Testament. Jesus matters to Buddhist leaders such as the Dalai Lama who mention the gospel accounts, honoring Jesus as a wise teacher, an "enlightened man," and a *bodhisattva*.

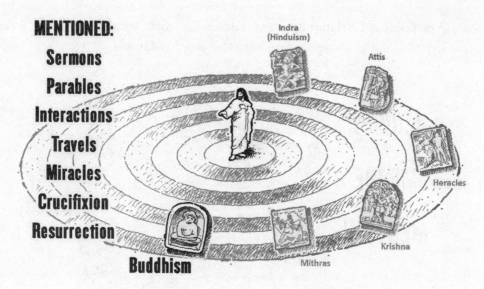

MENTIONED:

Sermons

Parables

Interactions

Travels

Miracles

Crucifixion

Resurrection

Over *506 million* Buddhists know something about Jesus from the teaching of their leaders. Even though Buddhism preexisted Christianity, Buddhists in these regions of the world are familiar with Jesus as a person of interest:[43]

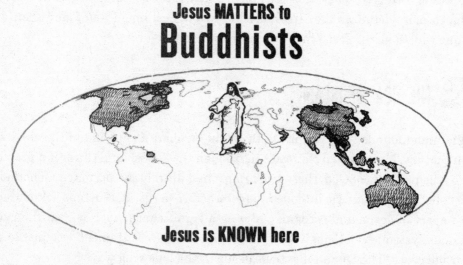

Jesus MATTERS to
Buddhists

Jesus is KNOWN here

THE ONES THAT FOLLOWED

Jesus and his followers affected the religious systems that *preceded* Christianity in three important ways: believers and leaders in these religions either *modified* their beliefs in response to Christianity, *merged* Jesus into their worldviews, or *mentioned* the history of Jesus as it was described in the New Testament.

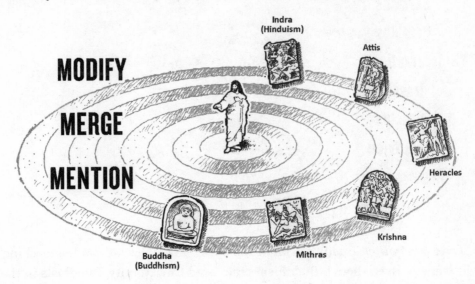

The religions that *followed* Jesus in history were also dramatically influenced by Jesus of Nazareth. They accepted and *mentioned* the foundational truths of Jesus in much more detail as they referenced the New Testament and found their own unique way to *merge* Jesus into their religious worldviews.

 THE "ISA" OF ISLAM

Muhammad founded the Islamic faith on the Arabian Peninsula in the early seventh century. Muhammad claimed that though the Jewish and Christian prophets were true prophets of God, these two groups had ultimately corrupted monotheism (the belief in one God). He intended to restore it. As a result, Muslims acknowledge the impact of Jesus and recognize him as a significant person within their own religious system, even though they reinterpret the New Testament accounts to suit their purposes. The Qur'an mentions Jesus in the following ways:

➤ Jesus Was Born of a Virgin Named Mary
The Qur'an describes Mary as a virgin prior to her miraculous conception. A conversation between Mary and Allah is recorded in the Qur'an, and Mary is told that she will conceive without the benefit of human involvement.[44]

➢ **Jesus Was Sinless**

The Muslim scripture also describes Jesus as a "faultless" or "pure" son who had Allah's unique "protection" from Satan.[45]

➢ **Jesus Was a Wise Teacher**

Muslims acknowledge that Jesus was a divinely wise teacher. So powerful was the teaching of Jesus that his disciples were filled with compassion and mercy and became "helpers" of God.[46]

➢ **Jesus Was a Miracle Worker**

Muslims believe Jesus performed many miracles, including the healing of a blind man and a leper and restoring the dead to life.[47]

➢ **Jesus Ascended to Heaven**

Islam also acknowledges the biblical claim that Jesus ascended into heaven in bodily form.[48]

These details related to the life and ministry of Jesus can be gleaned from a source most people consider hostile to the Christian worldview: the Qur'an.

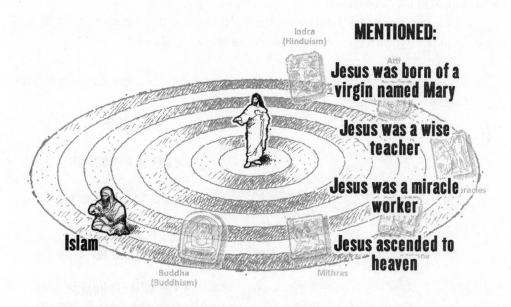

In addition to mentioning Jesus, Islam also incorporates and merges him into its theology. For the following reasons, Jesus is also a person of interest to Muslim believers:

➤ Jesus Is a Prophet

Jesus is held in high regard within the Muslim worldview. Islam affirms Jesus (known as "Isa" or "Eesa") as one of God's most important prophets.[49]

➤ Jesus Is to Be Revered

According to a legend, when Muhammad eliminated all the images of other gods in a shrine he was cleaning, he refused to destroy the statue of Mary and the infant Christ.[50] Jesus remains in a position of respect and reverence within Islam. When Muslims speak the name of Jesus today, they typically say either, "*Hazrat Eesa*" ("revered Jesus") or "*Eesa alai-hiss-salaam*" ("Jesus, peace be upon him").[51]

➤ Jesus Is the Messiah and a Messenger of God

In Islam, Jesus is considered the Messiah (*al-Masih*) and a messenger of God (Allah) who was sent to guide the children of Israel (*Bani Isra'il*) with a new scripture, the gospel.[52]

➤ Jesus Will Sit Beside God During the Final Judgment

Islam recognizes that Jesus will be an important part of the final judgment of humans.[53]

➤ Jesus Will Come Again

Islam acknowledges that Jesus will return in the future (during the latter days). The Hadith (a collection of sayings from Muhammad) describes this second coming of Jesus.[54]

Jesus matters to Muslims who honor and revere him as a prophet and messenger of God:

Islam *mentions* and *merges* Jesus as an important person of interest. As many as *1.9 billion* Muslims in these regions know something about Jesus because of how he is described in the Qur'an:[55]

Jesus MATTERS to
Muslims

Jesus is KNOWN here

 ## JESUS AS A "MANIFESTATION"

Bahá'u'lláh, a nineteenth-century Persian religious leader, claimed to be a messenger and "manifestation" of God as he founded the Bahá'í Faith in 1863. Bahá'u'lláh believed that religious history had been revealed through a series of similar messengers, and he considered himself the last in the series. Bahá'u'lláh recognized the leaders of prior religious movements and believed these men revealed the progressive truth of God to each generation. With this perspective, Bahá'u'lláh accepted many of the claims of Christianity, affirming and mentioning many characteristics of Jesus.

➤ Jesus Was Born of a Virgin

Bahá'u'lláh affirmed that Jesus was born of a virgin through the Holy Spirit, just as the New Testament claims.[56]

 ### OBJECTION: ALL RELIGIONS LEAD TO THE SAME PLACE

There are unreconcilable differences between the historic views of God. Christians believe that Jesus is God; Jews do not. Both groups could be wrong, but they can't both be right, given that their claims are contradictory. Christians believe that Jesus died on the cross and then rose from the grave. Muslims deny this claim. Again, both groups can't be correct. Christians believe in a personal God; Buddhists are pantheistic and deny the existence of a personal God. Yet again, both groups could be wrong, but they can't both be right. Why would anyone believe that all religions lead to God when none of them agree on essential claims?

➢ A Star Announced the Birth of Jesus

Bahá'u'lláh believed that celestial signs and wonders would precede God's important messengers. Bahá'í believers, therefore, accept that a star announced Jesus's birth.[57]

➢ John the Baptist Prepared the Way for Jesus

Bahá'u'lláh also believed that these messengers would be introduced by human precursors. He acknowledged the existence and ministry, for example, of John the Baptist.[58]

➢ John Baptized and Set an Example for Christians

Bahá'u'lláh taught that John initiated the practice of baptism and that Jesus's followers later continued the tradition.[59]

➢ Jesus Rejected Worldly Materialism

Bahá'í believers respect that Jesus shunned earthly belongings and material wealth, citing New Testament passages such as Mark 10:21 and Matthew 10:9–10.[60]

➢ Jesus Is the Divine "Son of God"

The Bahá'í religion recognizes the "divine origin," "Sonship," and "Divinity of Jesus Christ."[61]

➢ Jesus Worked Miracles

The Bahá'í Faith acknowledges Jesus's ability to perform miracles, including his healing of the sick and blind,[62] and his healing of the paralytic[63] and the leper.[64]

➢ Jesus Said, "Render to Caesar the Things That Are Caesar's"

Bahá'u'lláh, in navigating his own relationship to the government of his time, referenced Mark 12:17 as an example of the model Jesus set for addressing the relationship between believers and the government.[65]

➢ Peter Was an Important Apostle

Bahá'u'lláh also accepted and recognized the importance of Peter as an apostle and disciple of Jesus.[66]

➢ Jesus Promised the Counselor (or Comforter) Would Come

Bahá'u'lláh quoted John 16:5–7 in his writings, affirming Jesus's promise of the Holy Spirit to his disciples.[67]

➢ Jesus Prayed in the Garden of Gethsemane

In comparing his struggles to those of Jesus, Bahá'u'lláh described and affirmed the scene of Jesus in the garden of Gethsemane on the night before his arrest.[68]

➤ Jesus Faced a Trial

Bahá'u'lláh wrote about the gospel accounts related to Jesus's trial, impressed by the way Jesus retained his composure as the "Son of Man" even under intense pressure.[69]

➤ Jesus Died on a Cross

Unlike Muslims who lived in the region around him, Bahá'u'lláh affirmed the bodily death of Jesus on the cross.[70]

➤ The Death of Jesus Redeems Believers

Bahá'u'lláh taught that Jesus's death on the cross was redemptive as a "sacrifice" for the "sins and iniquities of all the peoples of the earth."[71]

➤ Jesus Was "Resurrected"

Bahá'u'lláh rejected the idea of a physical, literal resurrection but referenced the claims of the New Testament while interpreting them in a symbolic way. He argued that resurrection day was simply a symbol for spiritual awakening.[72]

➤ Jesus Ascended into Heaven

Bahá'u'lláh affirmed the ascension of Jesus, but in a non-Christian manner, believing that Jesus ascended to heaven as soon as he died on the cross.[73]

MENTIONED:

Jesus was born of a virgin

A star announced the birth of Jesus

John the Baptist prepared the way for Jesus

John baptized and set an example for Christians

Jesus rejected worldly materialism

Jesus is the divine "Son of God"

Jesus worked miracles

Jesus said, "Render to Caesar the things that are Caesar's"

Peter was an important apostle

Jesus promised the Counselor (or Comforter) would come

Jesus prayed in the garden of Gethsemane

Jesus faced a trial

Jesus died on a cross

The death of Jesus redeems believers

Jesus was "resurrected"

Jesus ascended into heaven

Bahá'í

Muhammad (Islam)

Buddha (Buddhism)

Mithras

Krishna

Heracles

Indra (Hinduism)

These teachings of the New Testament accounts are mentioned in the writings of Bahá'u'lláh, even though he reinterprets them in his own way. The claims about Jesus, including the New Testament verses in which they appear, can be reconstructed from the writings of Bahá'u'lláh.

Beyond affirming the New Testament claims, Bahá'u'lláh incorporated or merged Jesus into the Bahá'í religious system in several significant ways:

➢ Jesus Is a "Manifestation" of God

The Bahá'í consider Jesus to be one of several historic "manifestations" of God (messengers who reflect divine attributes into the human world for the benefit of humans).[74]

➢ Jesus Is a Wise Teacher Who Spoke for God

Because Jesus is considered an important "manifestation," his words and teaching matter. Bahá'u'lláh described Jesus's teaching as deep wisdom from God himself.[75]

Jesus mattered to Bahá'u'lláh because he saw Jesus as a messenger of God and a wise teacher of divine truth.

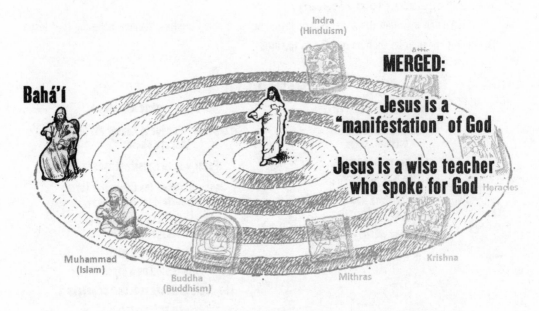

Nearly two thousand years after Jesus taught in a small corner of the Roman Empire, his presence and words still *matter* to *five million* Bahá'ís in these regions across the globe:[76]

Jesus MATTERS to
Bahá'ís

Jesus is KNOWN here

JESUS, THE AHMADI PROPHET

Mirza Ghulam Ahmad founded the Islamic Ahmadiyya movement in the late nineteenth century. His book *Jesus in India*, published shortly after his death in 1908, outlines the core tenets of the Ahmadiyya movement.[77] Ahmad believed Jesus survived the crucifixion and later traveled to India to preach as a prophet. The Ahmadiyya movement mentions and affirms the Christian New Testament and most of its claims, describing Jesus specifically in the following ways:[78]

> ➤ **Jesus Was a Prophet of God**
>
> Like traditional Muslims, the Ahmadiyya movement recognizes Jesus (called *"Yus Asaf"*) as a prophet of God and the Messiah of the Israelites as foretold by Moses.

> ➤ **Jesus Was Born of a Virgin**
>
> Ahmadi Muslims affirm the virgin birth of Jesus, recognizing Mary's statement to the angel: "How can I have a child when no man has touched me and neither have I been unchaste?" (as described in the Qur'an 19:21).

> ➤ **Jesus Was the "Son of God"**
>
> Ahmadi Muslims refer to Jesus as the "Son of God," affirming several passages from the Bible, including Psalm 2:7, Luke 3:38, and Mark 13:32. However, they don't accept this term as an indication of Jesus's divinity. Instead, they see it as an expression that applies to several Jewish and Christian figures in history.[79]

➤ **Jesus Prayed in the Garden**

Ahmadi Muslims acknowledge the gospel accounts of Jesus in the garden on the night before his trial, and Ahmad specifically quoted from Mark 14:36, Matthew 21:22, Matthew 7:7–9, and Luke 22:43.

➤ **Jesus Faced a Trial**

Ahmad affirmed the trial of Jesus, reciting and describing passages from Matthew chapters 26 and 27.

➤ **Jesus Was Crucified**

While acknowledging the gospel passages that describe the crucifixion, burial, and resurrection, Ahmad claimed that Jesus survived the attempted execution and was simply unconscious when he was removed from the cross.[80] All the postcrucifixion appearances, according to Ahmadi Muslims, were encounters with the resuscitated Jesus prior to his teaching in India.

Ahmadi Muslims know something about Jesus from the writings of their master. The broad outline of Jesus's life and ministry as described in the New Testament is mentioned and affirmed in the writings of Mirza Ghulam Ahmad:

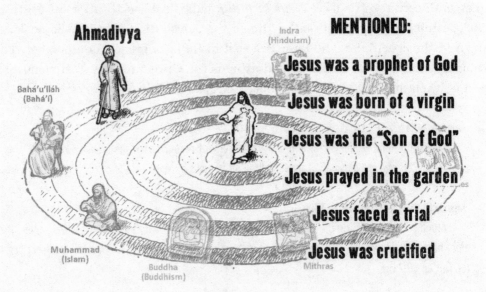

But Ahmad did more than mention Jesus as a person from history. Jesus matters to Ahmadi Muslims because he provides the moral teaching Ahmad believed would ultimately reform Islam. Ahmad merged the teaching of Jesus into an Islamic worldview:

➤ **Jesus Is a Wise Teacher**

Ahmadi Muslims acknowledge Jesus as a divinely wise teacher whose instruction is to be followed. In fact, the person (and teaching) of Jesus was the subject of Ahmad's book and the impetus for blending the instruction of Jesus with traditional Muslim practices. Ahmadi Muslims believe Islam is the final dispensation for humankind but that it needs reform. They also believe Ahmad appeared as a spiritual and temporal leader to restore religion and justice, bearing qualities of Jesus that would revitalize Islam and provide the moral structure for peace.

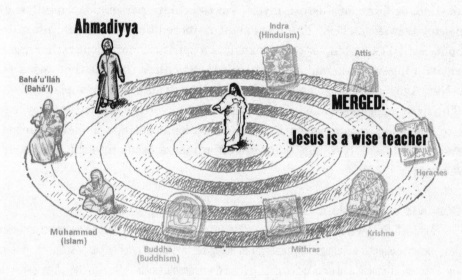

Today *twenty million* Ahmadi Muslims in these regions of the world know something about Jesus:[81] Ahmadis are yet another group to whom Jesus *matters*.

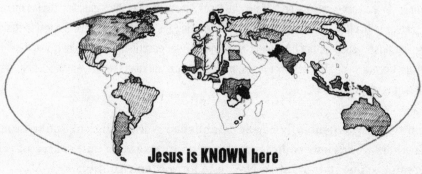

 ## NEW AGE JESUS

The New Age movement became popular in occult and metaphysical religious communities at the end of the twentieth century. Leaders in the movement looked forward to a "new age" of love, enlightenment, personal transformation, and healing. New Age practitioners are typically engaged in tarot reading, astrology, yoga, meditation, or forms of Eastern mysticism to achieve personal, societal, or even planetary transformation. The movement is incredibly diverse and pluralistic, without central leadership or orthodoxy. It is a spiritual movement rather than an organized religion. This makes it difficult to articulate the role that Jesus plays with New Age believers, given that no two believers may agree completely.

The movement has waned in the twenty-first century, but for those who still look to it for inspiration, several recurrent notions continue to elevate Jesus as a person of interest. New Age believers often merge Jesus into the movement in these ways:

➤ Jesus Is an Excellent Spiritual Example

Although New Agers reject the exclusive claims of world religions, they do venerate and elevate Jesus as an exemplar of human spirituality.[82] In doing so, they often refer to the description of Jesus in the Gospels, affirming and mentioning details from these accounts along the way. New Age leader Helen Schucman found Jesus so inspiring that she claimed to have "channeled" him, and Deepak Chopra has described Jesus as embodying "the highest level of enlightenment," or "God-consciousness."[83]

➤ Jesus Is an Excellent Teacher

Many New Age believers admire and embrace Jesus's teaching, especially as it relates to loving one's enemies, the hypocrisy of the rich and religious leaders, the rights of women and children, and the treatment of the poor or oppressed.[84] Many cite Jesus's instruction in the Sermon on the Mount, affirming the content of the New Testament gospels and elevating the teaching of Jesus alongside that of other "cosmic Christs" such as the Buddha or Muhammad.[85] In describing the "divinely inspired" teaching of Jesus, Chopra said, "The words of Jesus, no matter how you read them or which version, ring with a truth that is very profound."[86]

Even those who generally reject established world religions make "room" for Jesus in their worldview, embracing Jesus as an example and source of truth as they attempt to merge him into a New Age form of spirituality:

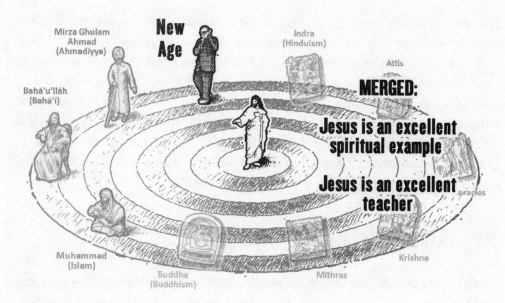

 ## JESUS, ACCORDING TO EVERYONE ELSE

Jesus's impact on global faith systems cannot be overestimated. Modern religions *mention* or *merge* Jesus into their teachings, and ancient religions often *modified* their beliefs to reflect Jesus's influence. Along the way, these religions continue to exalt Jesus and provide us with information to reconstruct his story.

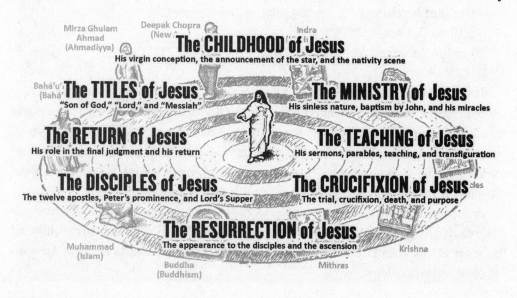

Even if every New Testament were destroyed, we could still reconstruct a lot of information about Jesus from the scripture and statements of *competing* religious systems.[87]

The result would be an impressive and robust description of Jesus, and it comes from *non-Christian* religious leaders and believers.[88] If you wanted to remove any trace of Jesus from human history, you'd also have to scrub the scriptures and statements of religious people all over the world. These non-Christians consider Jesus a divinely wise teacher, a model of morality, a *sadhu, acharya, bodhisattva,* "guru," "manifestation," or prophet of God. Jesus *matters* to *billions* of religious people, even if they don't claim a Christian identity.[89]

 ## JESUS AS A WORLDWIDE PHENOMENON

Consider, for example, the number of people whom Jesus of Nazareth has influenced or affected in some way. The Pew Research Center has been keeping a tally and projection on religious believers from an estimated 7.7 billion people who populate the planet today.[90] How many know something about Jesus from their respective religious worldviews? Let's start with the *non-Christians* we've described so far:

   1.16 billion Hindus
   1 million Hare Krishnas
   506 million Buddhists
   1.9 billion Muslims
   5 million Bahá'ís
   20 million Ahmadi Muslims

If we add the *2.3 billion* global Christians to this group, *5.89 billion* people are affected today—to some extent—by the person and teaching of Jesus. Think about that for a moment. Virtually every corner of the known world has heard about Jesus in one way or another. This collective map combines the prior maps of each religious worldview. The map now represents those areas where Jesus could be known, even if people in these regions had *no* access to a New Testament:

Jesus matters to people all over the globe, even to people who've never read the Gospels. If all the Christian Bibles were destroyed, we'd still be able to reconstruct the story of Jesus from the scriptures, writings, and statements of *non-Christian* religions and their leaders.

Jesus MATTERS to
Religious People Around the World

Jesus is KNOWN here

For people interested in God, spirituality, or religion, Jesus is a great place to start, given that he is the common thread in so many religious systems and spiritual worldviews. Jesus *matters* to people who seek transcendent truths.

 ## THE ONE-DIRECTIONAL INFLUENCER

"I'm hearing this verse in a different way now." Susie had just finished reading the Gospels and recalled an oft-quoted verse from the gospel of John: "Jesus said, 'No one comes to the Father except through me.'"

"How does it seem different?" I asked. Susie knew I had been researching how other religions perceived Jesus, and I had been updating her along the way.

"Jesus doesn't make room for other religions, other gods, or other . . . *paths*. He doesn't accommodate them in any way. He never even *refers* to them."

Susie's observation was strikingly true. While the person of Jesus impressed the leaders of other religious worldviews, the gods, goddesses, prophets, mystics, and religious leaders of these faith systems failed to impress Jesus. Many of these world religions preceded

OBJECTION: THINKING JESUS IS THE ONLY WAY TO GOD IS NARROW-MINDED

Christians don't claim Jesus is the only way to God. *Jesus* claimed he was the only way to God. He said, "I am the way and the truth and the life. No one comes to the Father except through me" (John 14:6). That's an exclusive claim, but what if it's true? Doctors claim isoniazid is the only cure for tuberculosis. That's also an exclusive claim. Are they being narrow-minded? What if their claim is simply true? Isn't it more important to investigate the claim than to dismiss it out of hand because you think it's narrow-minded?

Christianity, yet none of the New Testament writers mentioned their names or merged their claims.

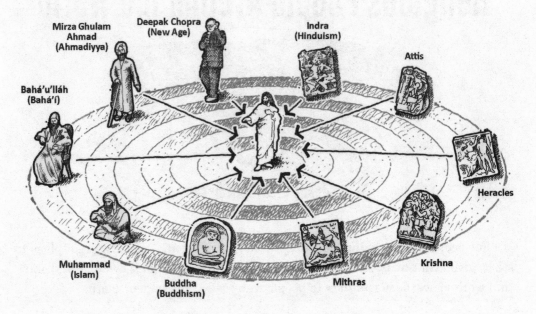

In the years since Christianity was established, many other world religions emerged. While these worldviews all acknowledged Jesus in some way, Christianity didn't modify its claims to embrace their prophets, "manifestations," or deities.

The religions of the world made room for Jesus, but Jesus never budged. His teaching mattered to the other religions, but Krishna, the Buddha, Muhammad, Bahá'u'lláh, and Ahmad *combined* didn't have a similar impact on Christianity. *That*, I thought, was remarkable.

"Maybe it's because the other religions aren't true," said Susie after a long pause.

And there it was: the relationship between what's *true* and what *matters*. I found myself back at the beginning, remembering my first church visit, wondering how a pastor could think Jesus mattered.

Maybe it was because the pastor knew something about the fuse and the fallout of the Common Era. Maybe he knew Christianity was true.

POSTSCRIPT: THE UNLIKELIEST OF SUSPE

Jesus, the Person of Interest

No one else holds or has held the place in the heart of the
world which Jesus holds. Other gods have been as devoutly
worshipped; no other man has been so devoutly loved.
—JOHN KNOX

As the centuries pass, the evidence is accumulating
that, measured by His effect on history, Jesus is the
most influential life ever lived on this planet.
—KENNETH SCOTT LATOURETTE

District Attorney Don Kingsley closed his notebook and faced the jury for the last time. His final argument included a powerful description of the evidence in our case, including the DNA comparison that identified Tammy's blood in the trunk of Steve's old Chevy Lumina. As Don confidently finished his rebuttal of the defense argument, I did my best to assess the attitude of the jury. Were they convinced Tammy was dead? Were they satisfied that Steve was responsible for her death? Was the evidence in the fuse and the fallout sufficient to make the case?

"Before I finish," continued Don as he stepped from the podium and approached the jury, "I want to ask you one final question: If you are convinced that Tammy was murdered, who else could have committed this crime *other* than Steve?"

I was sitting directly behind Don's podium at the prosecution table. Steve sat anxiously at the table to my right, along with his defense attorney.

"Tammy didn't have any enemies. No one had a motive to hurt Tammy *other* than Steve. Nobody else purchased the acid or borrowed the barrel. Only Steve disposed of Tammy's belongings prematurely, he's the only one who tried to have Tammy's blood removed from his car, and only Steve inadvertently acknowledged she was murdered in his interview with detectives."

Steve was clearly uncomfortable at this point in the rebuttal. He fidgeted with his hands and avoided eye contact with the jury. Don pressed on.

"Steve is *unique*, ladies and gentlemen. He alone accounts for all the evidence in the fuse and the fallout. There *is* no other candidate for Tammy's murder. Steve Hayes killed Tammy and disposed of her body. We're asking you to consider *all* the evidence in this case and provide justice for Tammy by finding Steve guilty of her murder."

I was impressed with Don's effort, especially since he was initially reluctant to file the case. Without a body, Don knew he would have to prove *two* claims: first, that Tammy was murdered (rather than just missing), and second, that Steve was the murderer. In my experience, not many prosecutors are willing to take no-body homicide cases to trial, but Don believed there was enough evidence (in the fuse and the fallout) to get a conviction.

The next three days tested Don's certainty.

As the jury deliberated and failed to return a verdict, Don and I wondered if there was a problem. A day passed. Then two. Then three. Still no verdict.

On day four, we sat at a local restaurant and wondered if the jury was hung. We ordered lunch and sat through the afternoon lull, occasionally ordering a soft drink or two to justify our lingering presence. Don seemed to be losing his confidence in the case. From his perspective, the longer the deliberation, the more likely a hung jury or a "not guilty" verdict. I tried to reassure him.

"VERDICT"

Juries consider the evidence presented in a trial, determine the facts of the case, and render a decision. Their ruling is called a "verdict." Juries render verdicts even though they may have unanswered questions. In fact, when jurors are selected, they are instructed that the "standard of proof" is "beyond a *reasonable* doubt" (rather than "beyond a *possible* doubt").[1] *Possible* doubts shouldn't stop jurors from deciding about a suspect's guilt, and they shouldn't stop you from making a decision about Jesus. Ask yourself, "What is the most reasonable inference from the evidence?"

"Don, put yourself in the position of a juror; if Tammy were your wife or your daughter or your sister, would the evidence in the fuse and the fallout be enough to convince you that she was murdered and that Steve was the killer?"

"Of course," he replied without hesitation.

"That's my view as well," I said. "Maybe they're just thoroughly reviewing everything to make sure they do their due diligence. This is a murder case, after all . . ."

"You're right," he replied. "I bet they'll come back tomorrow."

 **WHY JESUS?**

Steve wasn't the only unique subject of an investigation. My examination of the Common Era fuse and fallout revealed something exceptional about Jesus as well. Even though the evidence in the fuse and the fallout pointed strongly to Steve as Tammy's killer, it was nothing compared with the evidence in the Common Era fuse and fallout that pointed to Jesus.

The more I studied this evidence, the more I questioned my presuppositions about Jesus and the New Testament. The explosive impact of Jesus had forever changed the things I valued most as an atheist (and as a "creative")—literature, the arts, music, education, and science. There was simply no denying this truth. Jesus and his followers *transformed* the development of these disciplines. This conclusion was obvious to me, and it changed my skepticism of the Christian Bible.

The *nonbiblical* evidence from history alone gives us a clear picture of the catalyst who inaugurated the Common Era. Which person of interest, in the history of interesting persons, could cause such an explosion? Consider this list of historical figures from the first century:

Antonia Minor	Julia Agrippina	Titus
Augustus Caesar	Kujula Kadphises	Trajan
Boudica	Livia Drusilla	Trung Sisters
Caligula	Ming of Han	Vespasian
Livilla	Nero Claudius	Vitellius
Claudia Octavia	Caesar (Nero)	Valeria Messalina
Claudius	Marcus Cocceius Nerva	Vipsania Agrippina
Decebalus	Marcus Salvius Otho	Major
Domitian	Nedum Cheralathan	Wang Mang
Galba	Pontius Pilate	Yax Ehb Xook
Guangwu of Han	Lucius Aelius Seianus	Yuan An
Heraios	Tiberius	Zhang of Han

While these diverse figures from the past are important, none of them had the impact Jesus did on the Common Era. Now consider this list of significant national leaders from a much broader range in history:

George Washington	Elizabeth I of England	Frederick Barbarossa
Alexander the Great	Leif Ericson	Friedrich Wilhelm von Steuben
Nelson Mandela	William the Conqueror	
Napoleon Bonaparte	Frederick the Great	Cnut the Great
Augustus Caesar	Attila the Hun	Erik the Red
Charlemagne the Great	Sultan Mehmed II	Charles XII of Sweden
Julius Caesar	Theodoric the Great	William of Orange
Catherine the Great	Dmitry Donskoy	Philip II of Macedon
Otto von Bismarck	Suleiman the Magnificent	Gustav I of Sweden
Winston Churchill		Vladimir Lenin
Mustafa Kemal Atatürk	Gustavus Adolphus	Isabella I of Castile
	Hannibal Barca	Frederick I of Prussia
Alfred the Great	Ragnar Lodbrok	Niccolò Machiavelli
Genghis Khan	Joseph Stalin	Mao Zedong
	Queen Victoria	

There are some grand names on this list of world leaders, but none was grand enough to serve as the catalyst for the Common Era, and all of them *combined* didn't have the impact that Jesus had on literature, the arts, music, education, science, and religion. Speaking of religion, consider this list of deities and religious leaders:

Horus	Indra	Thesan
Muhammad	Quetzalcóatl	Bahá'u'lláh
Osiris	Attis	Aita
Tammuz	Hephaestus	Confucius
Joseph Smith	Mithras	The Báb
Shangdi	Krishna	Dalai Lama
Marduk	Cronus	Zhang Guotao
Artemis	Zoroaster	Swedenborg
Adonis	Sabbatai Zevi	The Buddha
Demeter	Zeus	Al-Mahdi
Jupiter	Minerva	Serapis
Gandhi	Dionysus	Heracles
Vulcan	Thakur Jiu	
Zalmoxis	Baldur	

Even the world's most famous gods and spiritual leaders haven't had the *combined* impact on history that Jesus had when he claimed to be the Savior. But Jesus wasn't alone in this claim to messiahship. In the years that followed Jesus, many other people also claimed this identity:

Simon bar Kokhba	Moses al-Dar'i	David Reubeni
Moses of Crete	Eve Frank	Sabbatai Zevi
Abu Isa	Moses Botarel of Cisneros	Asher Lammlein
Yudghan		Shukr Kuhayl I
Abraham ben Samuel Abulafia	Menachem Mendel Schneerson	Judah ben Shalom
Serene	Jacob Joseph Frank	Moses Guibbory

I suspect none of the names in this group of alleged messiahs is familiar to you. That's because they had little or no impact on the Common Era.

Why, then, did *Jesus* have more impact than anyone else?

Jesus was born in a tiny, irrelevant town in the Roman Empire and raised in another small village. He had to walk from one place to the next, and as an adult he never traveled more than two hundred miles from the town where he was born.

He had none of the resources people use today to make an impact: no social media platform, no podcast audience, no clever videos, and no website. He didn't even have the resources people used in the *first century* to make an impact: he never held a political office, never ruled a nation, never led an army, and never authored a book.

His family was insignificant. The locals suspected he was an illegitimate son, his mother was a poor peasant woman, and his father couldn't afford much. Jesus didn't receive an expensive education, never married, never had children, never owned a home of his own, and didn't possess much more than the clothes on his back.

As an adult, his own brother was suspicious of his ministry, a work that ended after just three short years. Public opinion turned against him, most of his followers abandoned him, one disciple betrayed him, and another denied him. He was rejected by the religious, hunted by the powerful, mocked and unjustly persecuted by his enemies. He suffered an unfair trial, was publicly humiliated, brutally beaten, and unduly executed in the most horrific way.

Even then, the few followers who remained had to *borrow a grave* to bury him.[2]

Yet *this* is the man who changed history, inaugurated the Common Era, and forever transformed the most important and revered aspects of human culture. How is it possible that a single man—a man like *Jesus*—could have this impact?

A VERDICT RENDERED

At 4:00 p.m. on the fourth day of deliberation, Don received a text from the court clerk. Our jury was prepared to deliver their verdict. Before I tell you how they decided, ask yourself the question I posed to Don earlier at the restaurant: "If Tammy were your daughter, sister, or friend, would the evidence in the fuse and the fallout have been enough to convince you that she was murdered and that Steve was her killer?"

It should have. It was certainly enough for the jury.

They found Steve guilty even though Tammy's body was missing, there wasn't any evidence from a crime scene, and not a single person witnessed the killing. Despite these evidential deficiencies, the jury convicted Steve of Tammy's murder. The evidence from the fuse and the fallout was sufficient.

Years later, at Steve's first parole hearing, he confessed to the murder and provided the location where he disposed of the barrel that contained Tammy's remains. I was notified of this admission, and we searched for the barrel unsuccessfully.

The dump site where Steve buried it had since been transformed from a landfill to a graded foundation for new homes. As with many of my cold cases, the passing of time thwarted this aspect of the investigation.

But I was satisfied that the evidence from the fuse and the fallout revealed the truth about Tammy's disappearance. Even though this evidence was persuasive, the jurors later told us that they would have been much more confident about their verdict (and their deliberations would have been shorter) if *eyewitnesses* had seen and testified about Tammy's murder.

A DECISION MADE

As I reflected on the fuse and fallout related to Jesus, I was similarly persuaded that Jesus was history's *unique* person of interest. The fuse leading up to the Common Era anticipated and predicted his arrival, and the fallout related to literature, the arts, music, education, science, and world religions demonstrated his unparalleled impact. The appearance of Jesus was the singular event that changed human history.

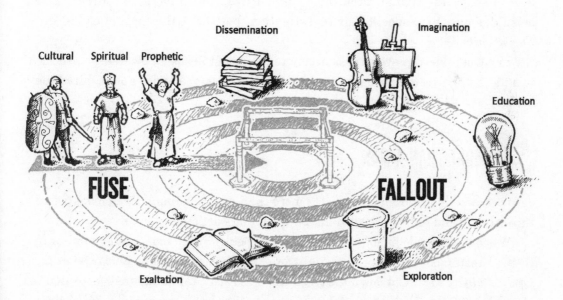

But as with the jury in Steve's criminal trial, I *also* would have preferred testimony from eyewitnesses who saw Jesus's life, death, and resurrection before rendering a verdict. Christians believe the New Testament gospels contain that kind of eyewitness testimony, but when I started investigating Jesus, I didn't trust the Bible and I was unwilling to rely on it for information.

But the evidence from the fuse and the fallout *alone* exposed two important truths: First, *no person* had the kind of impact Jesus had on history. Second, every reconstruction of the Jesus story from the literature, art, music, education, and science fallout describes Jesus as *God incarnate*.

Was that true? Was it possible that Jesus was something *more* than a man? Would the gospel eyewitness accounts provide some context and explain why the explosive appearance of Jesus inaugurated the Common Era? That's the question that caused me to suspend my skepticism of the Bible and investigate the Gospels.

I began by *testing* them.

Were these ancient documents penned early enough to have been written (or sourced) by true eyewitnesses? Could they be corroborated in some way? Were the authors honest and accurate over time? Did the writers possess a bias that would cause them to lie? I evaluated the Gospels using this same four-part template I used to assess eyewitnesses in criminal trials. In the end, the Gospels *passed* this reliability test, adding additional evidence to explain why Jesus—the unlikeliest of suspects—inaugurated the Common Era. (Much more, of course, could be said about this aspect of my investigation, but that's the topic of *Cold-Case Christianity*.)[3]

The Gospels—the eyewitness accounts of ancient Jesus followers—helped me to understand why the appearance of Jesus changed our calendar and inspired the world.

MORE THAN A MAN

Jesus showed his followers he was far more than a mere human. He demonstrated this directly and indirectly, with his words and his actions.

When Jesus made public claims, he didn't speak *for* God in a manner similar to the Old Testament prophets. Jeremiah, for example, proclaimed, "*This is what the* Lord *Almighty says*: 'Cut down the trees and build siege ramps against Jerusalem'" (Jeremiah 6:6, emphasis mine).[4] Jesus, on the other hand, never used expressions such as "This is what the Lord says . . ." Instead, he would say, "*Very truly I tell you,* a time is coming and has now come when the dead will hear the voice of the Son of God and those who hear will live" (John 5:25, emphasis mine).[5] While human prophets spoke *for* God, Jesus spoke *as* God.

Jesus also identified himself as otherworldly. He told his disciples and listeners, "You are from below; I am from above. You are of this world; I am not of this world" (John 8:23).[6] He also claimed a divine domain and authority over angels when he said, "The Son of Man will send out his angels, and they will weed out of his kingdom everything that causes sin and all who do evil" (Matthew 13:41).[7]

Jesus claimed equality with God, saying, "I and the Father are one" (John 10:30).[8] He even identified himself as the great "I am" (the name God used to identify himself to Moses) when he said, "Before Abraham was born, I am!" (John 8:58).[9]

Jesus also *acted* as though he was God. In a Jewish culture that considered it blasphemous to accept the worship of humans, Jesus repeatedly received the worship of others.[10] The wise men worshiped Jesus at his birth, a leper worshiped him after being healed, a synagogue ruler worshiped him after the raising of his daughter, the disciples worshiped him in the boat, the mother of James and John worshiped him when asking a favor, a blind man worshiped him after receiving his vision, and the women worshiped him after leaving the empty tomb.[11] Jesus accepted this worship consistently as though he was God.

OBJECTION: JESUS DIDN'T THINK HE WAS GOD

Jesus *spoke* as though he was God, *equated* himself to God, *accepted the worship* of others as though he was God, *described himself* as God using the Jewish title "I am," and even *claimed to have God's power to forgive sins*. It's one thing to reject Jesus's claims; it's another to deny he made them. Given the nature of Jesus's assertions, only one option remains: each of us must decide if the claims of Jesus are *true*.

The Gospels also include several passages in which Jesus was described as having the *power* of God. According to the gospel authors, Jesus had the power to *create*, the power to *forgive*, the power to *grant eternal life*, and the power to *judge sin*.[12] Only God has that kind of power.

Finally, according to the eyewitnesses, Jesus *rose from the grave*.[13] This alone demonstrated Jesus was—and is—*more than human*.

The jury decided the truth about Steve from the fuse and fallout *without* any testimony from eyewitnesses. How much easier should it have been for me to make a decision about Jesus *with* this information from the gospel eyewitness accounts? The fuse and fallout related to Steve was persuasive, but the fuse and fallout related to Jesus is phenomenal. Add the testimony of the gospel eyewitnesses, and the case is *overwhelming*.

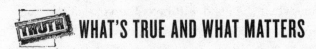

WHAT'S TRUE AND WHAT MATTERS

The early church leaders knew what they were doing when they divided the calendar into BC and AD. Our current terms fail to explain the reason why human history changed so dramatically. The period BCE is better described as BC (the period "before Christ"), and the years we now refer to as part of the Common Era (CE) are better labeled as AD (*Anno Domini*, or the "year[s] of our Lord"). While the designations BC and AD may seem like artifacts from the past, they are a far more accurate description of history's timeline, given that they reference the divine person of interest who divided history.

Our calendars demonstrate that Jesus still matters (and *ought* to matter), even if you're *not* a believer:

He matters because he inspired more literature than any other person in history. More books, scripts, and screenplays have been written about Jesus than anyone else. His story has so captured the human imagination that "Christ figures" have been written into *non-Christian* literature. From the earliest books and writings, the story of Jesus could be reconstructed in nearly its entirety, even if every New Testament manuscript was unavailable to us.

He matters because he was the catalyst for the visual arts, inspiring painters and sculptors in every generation, genre, style, and nation. No one has affected the arts like Jesus, and from these paintings, etchings, and sculptures, the story of Jesus—every episode as described in the Gospels—could be reconstructed, even if every Bible was destroyed.

He matters because he has been the topic of more songs, hymns, and symphonies than any other figure in history. Jesus's followers innovated and changed the nature of music forever, and musicians and singers in every musical style continue to sing about him. From their lyrics, the life of Jesus—along with the rich theology of the Christian worldview—could be reconstructed, even without access to the New Testament.

OBJECTION: IF CHRISTIANITY WERE TRUE, THERE WOULDN'T BE SO MANY DENOMINATIONS

Christianity isn't the only worldview held by people who disagree with each other. Even atheists hold disagreements about secondary issues, although all of them agree God does not exist. Atheists differ in their views, leading to a variety of categorizations and descriptions, including implicit atheists, explicit atheists, iconoclastic atheists, pragmatic atheists, and many more. Like Christians who disagree on secondary issues, people who hold an atheistic worldview (or, for that matter, a Hindu, Buddhist, or Muslim worldview) have similar disagreements. Are we to conclude, then, that *every* worldview is untrue because of these human disagreements?

He matters because his teaching set the standard for moral reform and initiated a worldview that led to the flourishing of education. His followers established monasteries, cathedral schools, and ultimately universities that continue to educate people to this day. From their campus buildings and founding charters, Jesus's life and teaching could be reconstructed, even if no Bibles were available.

He matters because he established a worldview that encouraged exploration and motivated his followers to investigate the natural revelation of God, resulting in an explosion of scientific discovery, the scientific revolution, and an unparalleled history of excellence in the sciences. From the writings of the "science fathers"—the vast majority of whom were Jesus followers—Jesus's life, ministry, and mission could be reconstructed, even if all the Christian Bibles were destroyed.

He matters because his influence on spiritual seekers and religious thinkers is so overwhelming that every major world religion either mentions or merges him into their theological system. From the scriptures of *non-Christian* religions and their leaders' statements, the life of Jesus could be reconstructed, even without access to the New Testament.

Looking at the evidence I had compiled of Jesus's claims and impact, I couldn't help but draw the obvious conclusion: Only if Jesus was truly *more* than a man, if he was *God incarnate* as that first pastor and the gospel authors claimed, would his unparalleled impact on history make sense. Wouldn't we *expect* God to inspire the ancients to think about him and the Jews to prophesy about him? Wouldn't we *expect* history to align to his arrival? Wouldn't we *expect* God to have an explosive impact on the most important aspects of human existence? Wouldn't we *expect* him to reorder our calendar and transform our history?

Jesus had that kind of impact—the impact we would expect from God. The fuse and the fallout of the Common Era simply confirm the existence and deity of Jesus as described in the New Testament.

Christian authors, artists, musicians, educators, and scientists had known for years what I was just discovering: Jesus doesn't matter *because he influenced the world*; Jesus influenced the world *because he matters*. Everything that was important to me as an atheist was ultimately indebted to Jesus, the man who was *with* God and *is* God and *through whom* "all things were made" (John 1:3). Jesus is who he said he was: God incarnate.

That truth turned the world upside down. It turned my world upside down as well.

OUR PERSON OF INTEREST

"Everyone accounted for?" I asked as Susie hopped into the passenger seat of our van.

"Yes," she replied, "All thirty-two of them."

As our caravan of vehicles and students pulled away from the local rescue mission after a day serving at the food bank, everyone was tired but satisfied they had contributed to an important work.

From Susie's perspective, my conversion to Christianity seemed miraculous, especially given my attitude toward God for the first eighteen years of our relationship. But the evidence in the fuse and the fallout, coupled with the writings of the New Testament, convinced me that the gospel claims about Jesus (and his claims about himself) were true, and I understood the relationship between what's *true* and what *matters*. I ultimately attended seminary and became a youth pastor and a lead pastor. Service trips—like the one we were taking to the rescue mission—became a regular feature of our lives.

After investigating history and testing the Gospels, I knew I had a decision to make. Would I continue to ignore the person of interest who was responsible for everything I valued? Or would I acknowledge him as the *source* of nearly everything that matters? I decided to trust what history revealed about Jesus. I came to trust what the Gospels said about Jesus and what Jesus said about himself. Perhaps more importantly, I also decided to trust what the New Testament said about *me*.

OBJECTION: BEING A GOOD PERSON IS ALL THAT REALLY MATTERS TO GOD

Are you a good person? Have you ever lied? Have you ever taken something that wasn't yours? Have you ever even *thought* about such things? I don't know many people who are arrogant enough to say they've never done *anything* wrong. If being a good person is all that matters, then you and I don't matter because we aren't consistently "good." If an all-powerful God exists, it's reasonable to believe he has the power to eliminate moral imperfection. How, then, can morally imperfect humans be united with a morally perfect God? Christianity offers a solution: God came to us in human form. Jesus took the punishment he didn't deserve to provide us with access we can't earn.

I became painfully aware of my own imperfections and the perfect, holy nature of God. At first, the distance between these two realities seemed prohibitively vast.

But the promise of Jesus is much greater than a pledge to transform literature, art, music, education, and science. It's a promise to transform the status and heart of every believer.

Our moral imperfection differentiates and separates us from God, yet he came to us in the person of Jesus to offer a remedy.[14] Those of us who recognize the truth about Jesus can accept his offer to reunite us with God. *On the cross* Jesus paid the price for our moral imperfection. The perfect Being who had the power to create, forgive, grant eternal life, and judge sin took the penalty *we deserve* and exchanged it for the position and status *he deserves*.[15] Those of us who are willing to trust Jesus, accept the offer of forgiveness, and follow him will be forever reconciled to God.[16]

That decision *matters*, and it ultimately leads to *a life that matters*.

I'm a Christian today because Christianity is true. *Demonstrably* true. The evidence of history screams Jesus from every significant human achievement and every meaningful aspect of culture. Even on days when being a Christian is difficult (and those days are sure to increase given our culture's growing rejection of Christianity), my high regard for truth leaves me no alternative but to embrace Jesus as history's person of interest and my personal savior.[17]

Jesus is in the business of changing hearts and minds, creating something from nothing, turning apathy into conviction, and molding hopelessness into meaning. He's done it for thousands of writers, artists, musicians, educators, and scientists. He's done it for millions of believers, just as he did for me.

He can do it for you as well.

CASE NOTES

Preface

1. For an interesting exposition on this issue, please refer to Dallas Willard's talk, "Jesus: The Smartest Man Who Ever Lived?" (La Miranda, CA: Biola University Christian Apologetics Program, 2006), CD.

Chapter 1: The Fuse and the Fallout

1. As an example, judges in jury trials in California instruct jurors to consider the defendant's motive that may be part of the fuse leading up to a crime. "Having a motive may be a factor tending to show (that the defendant is guilty/ [or] that an (allegation/ [or] special circumstance) is true). Not having a motive may be a factor tending to show (the defendant is not guilty/ [or] that an (allegation/ [or] special circumstance) is not true)." Judicial Council of California, *Judicial Council of California Criminal Jury Instructions* (New York: Matthew Bender, 2021), CALCRIM No. 370, https://www.courts.ca.gov/partners/documents/calcrim-2021.pdf.
2. Judges in California jury trials also instruct jurors to consider the evidence they may find *after* the commission of a crime. For example, "If the defendant tried to hide evidence or discourage someone from testifying against (him/her), that conduct may show that (he/she) was aware of (his/her) guilt," "If the defendant tried to create false evidence or obtain false testimony, that conduct may show that (he/she) was aware of (his/her) guilt," "If the defendant fled [or tried to flee] (immediately after the crime was committed/ [or] after (he/she) was accused of committing the crime), that conduct may show that (he/she) was aware of (his/her) guilt." *Judicial Council of California Criminal Jury Instructions*, CALCRIM No. 371 and 372.
3. Prior to the BCE/CE designations, most of the world used BC ("before Christ") and AD (*Anno Domini*, or "In the year of our Lord").

Chapter 2: Jesus, the Average Ancient?

1. Judicial Council of California, *Judicial Council of California Criminal Jury Instructions* (New York: Matthew Bender, 2021), CALCRIM No. 350, https://www.courts.ca.gov/partners/documents/calcrim-2021.pdf.
2. For more information about how the Sumerians used pictographs, refer to Paul Kriwaczek, *Babylon: Mesopotamia and the Birth of Civilization* (New York: St. Martin's, 2012), as cited at World History Encyclopedia, s.v. "Writing," by Joshua J. Mark, April 28, 2011, https://www.ancient.eu/writing/.

3. For more information about the development of cuneiform, refer to Andrew Robinson, *The Story of Writing: Alphabets, Hieroglyphs & Pictograms*, 2nd ed. (London: Thames & Hudson, 2007).

4. Most scholars describe the Phoenician alphabet as the first alphabet and the ancestor of the modern Hebrew, Arabic, Cyrillic, Greek, and Latin alphabets. For the purpose of this study, I am citing the ancient Phoenician alphabet as it became the basis for much richer and robust modern alphabets that allow writers to describe people and events with greater clarity. Another excellent resource for information on the development of writing: Steven Roger Fischer, *A History of Writing* (London: Reaktion, 2004). And visit World History Encyclopedia, s.v. "Writing," by Joshua J. Mark, April 28, 2011, https://www.ancient.eu/writing/.

5. For more information on the history of the Greek language, refer to the work of Brian Joseph at The Ohio State University: Brian D. Joseph, "Greek, Ancient," OSU Department of Linguistics, accessed April 3, 2021, https://www.asc.ohio-state.edu/joseph.1/articles/gancient.htm.

6. Even the ancients were astonished at the speed with which the Roman Empire conquered the world. Polybius, a Greek historian of the Hellenistic period, wrote, "For who is so worthless or indolent as not to wish to know by what means and under what system of polity the Romans in less than fifty-three years have succeeded in subjecting nearly the whole inhabited world to their sole government—a thing unique in history?" Polybius, *Histories* 1.1.5, available here: "Polybius *The Histories*, Book I," Bill Thayer's Web Site, last modified December 10, 2016, http://penelope.uchicago.edu/Thayer/E/Roman/Texts/Polybius/1*.html.

7. For an ancient perspective of Roman history, read Suetonius's *The Twelve Caesars*, trans. J. C. Rolfe (Mineola, NY: Dover, 2018). For a modern perspective, read Mary Beard's *SPQR: A History of Ancient Rome* (New York: Liveright, 2016).

8. "Not only was war banished from the greater part of the world, but internally the provinces were safer and more settled because of the peace brought by Rome and its emperors." Adrian Goldsworthy, *Pax Romana: War, Peace and Conquest in the Roman World* (New Haven, CT: Yale University Press, 2017), 185.

9. For more information about the nature of early Greek roads, refer to Robin Watts and Zishan Parks, *Development of Tourism and Travel Industry* (Essex, UK: Ed-Tech, 2018), 94.

10. *Judicial Council of California Criminal Jury Instructions*, CALCRIM No. 403.

11. Ancient historian Herodotus, when describing the speed with which couriers could use roads like the Royal Road, wrote, "There is nothing in the world which travels faster than the Persian couriers. The whole idea is a Persian invention, and works like this: riders are stationed along the road, equal in number to the number of days the journey takes—a man and a horse for each day. Nothing stops these couriers from covering their allotted stage in the quickest possible time—neither snow, rain, heat, nor darkness. The first, at the end of his stage, passes the dispatch to the second, the second to the third, and so on along the line, as in the Greek torch-race which is held in honour of Hephaestus." Herodotus, *Histories*, trans. Aubrey de Sélincourt (New York: Penguin, 1972), 556.

12. Much has been written about the speed of the Roman postal service and, given their superior roads, their ability to deliver messages even faster than the Persians. From antiquity, Byzantine Greek scholar Procopius wrote, "The couriers appointed for the

work, by making use of relays of excellent horses, when engaged in the duties I have mentioned, often covered in a single day, by this means, as great a distance as they would otherwise have covered in ten." Procopius, *Secret History*, XXX. In modern times, Stanford Mc Krause, assessing the speed of Roman couriers, concluded that a nonurgent messenger could travel thirty-eight to sixty-two miles a day and up to one hundred miles or more each day in urgent situations. Refer to Stanford Mc Krause, *Life in Ancient Rome*, ed. Cambridge Stanford Books (self-pub., Brainy Bookstore Mckrause, n.d.), and A. M. Ramsey, "The Speed of the Roman Imperial Post," *Journal of Roman Studies* 15 (1925): 60–74.

13. Tertullian (writing in the second century) describes Tiberius Caesar's effort to legalize Christianity before the Roman senate. According to this disputed account, Tiberius threatened "wrath against all accusers of the Christians." Tertullian, *Apology*, chap. 5, available here: "Apology," New Advent, accessed April 5, 2021, https://www.newadvent .org/fathers/0301.htm.

14. A great fire burned in Rome in 64 CE, burning down Nero's palace. Rumor quickly spread that Nero started the fire to create the need for a new, grander palace. Nero blamed the Christians for the fire and used them as a scapegoat to distract this blame. As a result, Christians were persecuted in gruel manner for many years. Refer to Tacitus, *Annals* 15.44, available here: "Tacitus *Annals*, Book XV (continued)," Bill Thayer's Web Site, last modified April 2, 2016, https://penelope.uchicago.edu/Thayer/E /Roman/Texts/Tacitus/Annals/15B*.html.

Chapter 3: Jesus, the Copycat Savior?

1. Judicial Council of California, *Judicial Council of California Criminal Jury Instructions* (New York: Matthew Bender, 2021), CALCRIM No. 520, https://www.courts.ca.gov /partners/documents/calcrim-2021.pdf.

2. For more information about Dionysus, read Walter F. Otto's classic, *Dionysus: Myth and Cult* (Bloomington, IN: Indiana University Press, 1995).

3. For a defense of the existence and historicity of Jesus from someone who is skeptical of the *deity* of Jesus (yet still recognizes the strength of the historical evidence), refer to Bart D. Ehrman, *Did Jesus Exist? The Historical Argument for Jesus of Nazareth* (New York: HarperOne, 2012).

4. As an example, Mark Thomas of the Atheists of Silicon Valley once presented my students with the following description of a god:

> Born of a virgin, in a cave, on December 25
> His birth was attended by shepherds
> He was considered a great traveling teacher and master
> He had twelve companions (or disciples) and promised his followers immortality
> He performed miracles and sacrificed himself for world peace
> He was buried in a tomb and after three days rose again
> His followers celebrated this event each year at the time of his resurrection (and this date later became Easter)
> He was called the Good Shepherd and was identified with both the lamb and the lion
> He was considered to be the way, the truth, and the light; the Logos; the Redeemer; the Savior; and the Messiah

His followers celebrated Sunday as his sacred day (also known as the Lord's Day)
His followers celebrated a Eucharist, or Lord's Supper

He then revealed that this was a description of Mithras, not Jesus. Thomas's description was, however, nearly completely untrue of Mithras. For more information, refer to my book *Forensic Faith: A Homicide Detective Makes the Case for a More Reasonable, Evidential Christian Faith* (Colorado Springs: Cook, 2017), 89.

5. Preston Greene, "Are We Living in a Computer Simulation? Let's Not Find Out," *New York Times*, August 10, 2019, https://www.nytimes.com/2019/08/10/opinion/sunday/are -we-living-in-a-computer-simulation-lets-not-find-out.html.

6. Greene, "Are We Living in a Computer Simulation?"

7. Greene, "Are We Living in a Computer Simulation?"

8. Pew Research Center, *The Global Religious Landscape: A Report on the Size and Distribution of the World's Major Religious Groups as of 2010*, December 2012, https:// assets.pewresearch.org/wp-content/uploads/sites/11/2014/01/global-religion-full.pdf.

9. Pew, *The Global Religious Landscape*, 9.

10. Ariela Keysar and Juhem Navarro-Rivera, "A World of Atheism: Global Demographics," in *The Oxford Handbook of Atheism*, eds. Stephen Bullivant and Michael Ruse (Oxford: Oxford University Press, 2017).

11. Arthur Martin, "Why We Are Born to Believe in God: It's Wired into the Brain, Says Psychologist," *Daily Mail*, September 7, 2009, https://www.dailymail.co.uk/news/article -1211511/Why-born-believe-God-Its-wired-brain-says-psychologist.html.

12. Martin, "Why We Are Born to Believe in God."

13. Refer to Barney Zwartz, "Infants 'Have Natural Belief in God,'" *Sydney Morning Herald*, July 26, 2008, https://www.smh.com.au/national/infants-have-natural-belief -in-god-20080725-3l3b.html; More can also be learned from Dr. Olivera Petrovich's book, *Natural-Theological Understanding from Childhood to Adulthood: Essays in Developmental Psychology* (London: Routledge, 2019).

14. Patrick McNamara and Wesley Wildman, eds., *Science and the World's Religions*, vol. 2, *Persons and Groups* (Santa Barbara: Praeger, 2012), 207.

15. Paul Bloom, "Is God an Accident?," *The Atlantic*, December 2005, https://www.the atlantic.com/magazine/archive/2005/12/is-god-an-accident/304425/.

16. Beth Azar, "A Reason to Believe," *American Psychological Association* 41, no. 11 (December 2010): 52, https://www.apa.org/monitor/2010/12/believe.

17. For more information about Zoroaster and his birth, refer to a newer volume: Mary Boyce, *Zoroastrians: Their Religious Beliefs and Practices*, 2nd ed., The Library of Religious Beliefs and Practices (London: Routledge, 2001).

18. Roman poet Ovid wrote about the manner in which Myrrha conceived Adonis in his book *Metamorphoses* (Book X), available online here: "*Metamorphoses* Book X (A.S. Kline's Version)," Electronic Text Center, University of Virginia Library, accessed June 23, 2020, https://ovid.lib.virginia.edu/trans/Metamorph10.htm. For more information on Adonis and other Greek gods, refer to Karl Kerényi, *The Gods of the Greeks* (London: Thames & Hudson, 1980).

19. For an introductory (and entertaining) view of Indra and other Hindu gods, read this newer reference: Swami Achuthananda, *The Reign of the Vedic Gods*, The Galaxy of Hindu Gods 1 (Queensland, Australia: Relianz, 2018). An online summary of the

Indra mythology can be found at the *World History Encyclopedia*, s.v. "Indra," by Mark Cartwright, August 8, 2013, https://www.ancient.eu/Indra/.

20. For more information on the Buddha (the founder of Buddhism), worshiped from 600–400 BCE to the present, refer to this more current volume: Vishvapani Blomfield, *Gautama Buddha: The Life and Teachings of the Awakened One* (London: Quercus, 2011).

21. This newer volume is a good resource for information about Krishna: Vanamali, *The Complete Life of Krishna: Based on the Earliest Oral Traditions and the Sacred Scriptures* (Rochester, VT: Inner Traditions, 2012).

22. An excellent current resource for Osiris: Bojana Mojsov, *Osiris: Death and Afterlife of a God* (Malden, MA: Blackwell, 2005). An online image of the staff (the "crook") can be seen here: *World History Encyclopedia*, accessed June 23, 2020, https://www.world history.org/img/r/p/500x600/775.jpg.

23. For information about Quetzalcóatl, refer to Ignacio Bernal, *Mexico Before Cortez: Art, History, Legend* (New York: Doubleday, 1975). And for a more current resource, see Alfredo López Austin, *The Myth of Quetzalcoatl: Religion, Rulership, and History in the Nahua World,* trans. Russ Davidson and Guilhem Olivier (Boulder: University Press of Colorado, 2015).

24. This interaction is described in a poem entitled "Inanna Prefers the Farmer" and can be accessed at the Electronic Text Corpus of Sumerian Literature: "Dumuzid and Enkimdu: Translation," ETCSL, University of Oxford, accessed June 23, 2020, http://etcsl.orinst.ox.ac.uk/section4/tr40833.htm. For more information about Tammuz (also known as Dumuzi), refer to this newer resource: Stephanie Dalley, *Myths from Mesopotamia: Creation, the Flood, Gilgamesh, and Others*, Oxford World's Classics (Oxford: Oxford University Press, 2009).

25. For more information about Serapis (and other Egyptian deities), refer to Geraldine Pinch, *Egyptian Mythology: A Guide to the Gods, Goddesses, and Traditions of Ancient Egypt* (Oxford: Oxford University Press, 2002).

26. The Chinese emperor continued to sacrifice a bull to Shangdi at the Temple of Heaven in Beijing each year until 1911. For a beginner's guide to Shangdi and other Chinese mythologies, refer to Anne M. Birrell, *Chinese Mythology: An Introduction* (Baltimore: Johns Hopkins University Press, 1999). For a comparison of Shangdi and the God of the Bible, see Chan Kei Thong and Charlene L. Fu, *Finding God in Ancient China: How the Ancient Chinese Worshiped the God of the Bible* (Grand Rapids: Zondervan, 2009).

27. The clash between Dionysus and Pentheus did not end well for Pentheus. He ultimately died and was torn to pieces. For more on Dionysus, refer to Walter F. Otto, *Dionysus: Myth and Cult* (Bloomington: Indiana University Press, 1995).

28. Many experts believe these Mithraic meal rituals may have been borrowed from Christian practices as Mithraism developed in Rome in the first two centuries (refer to chapter 10). For more information on Mithras, read David Ulansey, *The Origins of the Mithraic Mysteries: Cosmology and Salvation in the Ancient World* (New York: Oxford University Press, 1991) and John R. Hinnells, ed., *Mithraic Studies: Proceedings of the First International Congress of Mithraic Studies*, 2 vols. (Lanhan, MD: Rowman & Littlefield, 1975).

29. For an updated version of a classic description of the Heracles myth, read Diodorus Siculus, *Ancient Greek Myths: A Classic Account of the Origin of the Gods, Dionysus, Heracles, Jason and the Argonauts, Theseus and the Minotaur, Oedipus, and More*, trans. Charles Henry Oldfather (n.p.: Omo Press, 2019). This work is also available

online: "Diodorus Siculus: The Library of History," Bill Thayer's Web Site, last modified September 16, 2017, https://penelope.uchicago.edu/Thayer/E/Roman/Texts/Diodorus_Siculus/home.html.

30. Herodotus describes Zalmoxis in his *Histories* 4.93–96. Refer to the 1921 translation of Herodotus from the Loeb Classical Library, available here: "Herodotus Book IV: chapters 83–98," Bill Thayer's Web Site, last modified December 4, 2019, http://penelope.uchicago.edu/Thayer/E/Roman/Texts/Herodotus/4d*.html. (Zalmoxis is described as Salmoxis in this translation.)

31. Finding authoritative information on the Santal deities is difficult, but this resource is helpful to understand their myths, folklore, and culture: Abraham Mathew, *Life of Santal Tribe: With Special References to Their Religious Practices, Teachings, Rites and Rituals* (self-pub., Amazon Asia-Pacific Holdings Private Limited, 2018).

32. For larger, more readable images, please visit https://coldcasechristianity.com/selected-images-from-person-of-interest/.

33. For larger, more readable images, please visit https://coldcasechristianity.com/selected-images-from-person-of-interest/.

34. *Judicial Council of California Criminal Jury Instructions*, CALCRIM No. 105.

35. Lewis to Arthur Graves, October 18, 1931, in *The Collected Letters of C. S. Lewis, ed. Walter Hooper, vol. 1, Family Letters 1905-1931* (San Francisco: Harper, 2004), 977.

36. Lexico, s.v. "myth," accessed June 27, 2020, https://www.lexico.com/en/definition/myth.

37. For another resource describing Jesus as a recurring type and figure in the Old Testament (along with predictions related to the coming Messiah), refer to David Limbaugh, *Finding Jesus in the Old Testament* (Washington, DC: Regnery, 2015).

38. For a discussion of the similarities between Jesus, Moses, and Elisha, refer to Jeremy Tetreau, "Jesus, Elisha, and Moses: A Study in Typology" (master's thesis, Liberty University, 2018), https://digitalcommons.liberty.edu/cgi/viewcontent.cgi?article=1799&context=honors.

39. For another list of similarities, see W. Clarkson, "Joshua and Jesus: Resemblance and Contrast," Pulpit Commentary, Electronic Database, accessed June 25, 2020, https://biblehub.com/sermons/auth/clarkson/joshua_and_jesus_resemblance_and_contrast.htm.

40. A more expansive list of similarities can be found here: From notes by Bill MacDonald, "A Comparison between Joseph and Jesus," Jews for Jesus, July 1, 1985, https://jewsforjesus.org/publications/newsletter/newsletter-sep-1985/a-comparison-between-joseph-and-jesus.

41. For a more detailed look at the similarities between David and Jesus, refer to James M. Hamilton Jr., "The Typology of David's Rise to Power: Messianic Patterns in the Book of Samuel," Julius Brown Gay Lecture, The Southern Baptist Theological Seminary, accessed June 25, 2020, http://d3pi8hptl0qhh4.cloudfront.net/documents/JBGay/the_typology_of_davids_rise_to_power2008-03-101.pdf.

42. For a discussion of the similarities between Jesus, Moses, and Elisha, refer to Tetreau, *"Jesus, Elisha, and Moses."*

43. For larger, more readable images, please visit https://coldcasechristianity.com/selected-images-from-person-of-interest/.

44. Even secular sources recognize the academic tradition of "typology": Wikipedia, s.v. "typology (theology)," last modified January 21, 2021, https://en.wikipedia.org/wiki/Typology_(theology).

Chapter 4: Jesus, the Mistaken Messiah?

1. Many websites list these prophecies. For example: "More than 300 Messianic Prophecies and Scripture References that Match Yeshua!," Refiners Fire, accessed July 1, 2020, https://therefinersfire.org/prophecies.htm; "The First Coming of the Messiah: Messianic Prophecies Summary," Teaching Hearts, accessed July 1, 2020, http://www.teachinghearts.org/dre17hdan09b.html; "351 Old Testament Prophecies Fulfilled in Jesus Christ," New Testament Christians, accessed July 1, 2020, https://www.newtestamentchristians.com/bible-study-resources/351-old-testament-prophecies-fulfilled-in-jesus-christ/.

2. Michael F. Bird describes what I refer to as "clear" prophecy in the following way: "We identify an Old Testament text as 'messianic' when the plain sense of the text (i.e., its semantic and linguistic operation) designates a figure with royal qualities who is sent by God, and also that either the text itself was treated as messianic in postbiblical interpretation, or else the pattern of activity that the figure embodies corresponds to a pattern of activity often expected of messianic figures in antiquity." Michael F. Bird, *Are You the One Who Is to Come? The Historical Jesus and the Messianic Question* (Grand Rapids: Baker Academic, 2009), 46.

3. Why don't more Jews accept the messianic prophecies described in the New Testament? A simple internet search can help us answer this question. Here are the messianic prophecies that modern Jewish believers commonly accept, based on Jewish groups who have established an online presence (i.e., Jews for Jerusalem, https://j4j.me/; Aish HaTorah, https://www.aish.com/; Chabad.org, https://www.chabad.org/; Judaism 101, http://www.jewfaq.org/index.shtml): The Messiah restores the barren land and makes it abundant and fruitful (Amos 9:13–15), leads all nations and ushers in eternal peace (Isaiah 2:4), is worshiped by all nations (Isaiah 2:11–17), is a descendant of King David through Jesse and Judah (Isaiah 11:1), has the "spirit of the Lord" and a "fear of the Lord" (Isaiah 11:2), defeats evil and tyranny (Isaiah 11:4), restores peace on the earth (Isaiah 11:6–9), includes and attracts people from all cultures and nations (Isaiah 11:10), conquers death, hunger, and illness forever (Isaiah 25:7–8), causes the dead to rise again (Isaiah 26:19), is a "bruised reed" who is not "snuff[ed] out" (Isaiah 42:1–4), brings justice to the earth (Isaiah 42:1–4), is a light to people around the world (Isaiah 42:6), takes the barren land and makes it abundant and fruitful (Isaiah 51:3), gives the Jewish people eternal joy and gladness (Isaiah 51:11), is a messenger of peace who announces salvation (Isaiah 52:7), causes all nations to recognize the wrongs they did to Israel (Isaiah 52:13–15), comes to Jerusalem to redeem the descendants of Jacob who have turned from their sins (Isaiah 59:20), ushers in the restoration of Israel's cities (Ezekiel 16:55), takes the barren land and makes it abundant and fruitful (Ezekiel 36:29–30), ushers in an era in which weapons of war will be destroyed (Ezekiel 39:9), is a descendant of David who reigns as king and "do[es] what is just and right" (Jeremiah 23:5), is a descendant of Judah called "The Lord Our Righteous Savior" (Jeremiah 23:6), ushers in a new era in which Israel will have direct access to the law of God through their minds and hearts and God will forgive their sins (Jeremiah 31:33–34), is a descendant of David (Jeremiah 33:15), ushers in an era in which people will turn to the Jews for spiritual guidance (Zechariah 8:23), and is a descendant of King David (1 Chronicles 22:8–10; 2 Chronicles 7:18).

   Interestingly, the messianic prophecies Jews accept account for only 36 percent of the "clear" prophecies I've described so far. In other words, even though the most straightforward reading of the prophecies points to a coming redeemer, restorer, or eternal "king," Jews deny this reading and interpretation. Unsurprisingly, they reject all the "cloaked" prophecies. Of those they accept, many of them refer not to a *person* of interest but to a *nation* of interest: the nation of Israel. Jewish believers are more likely to embrace prophecies that predict the restoration of Israel, in power and status, than other messianic prophecies. The accepted prophecies are very limited in their ability to answer the six investigative questions required to identify a Messiah at all. Jews typically accept only a few prophecies that describe the Messiah in any detail.

And what about our reliable "informants," Isaiah, Ezekiel, Jeremiah, and Daniel? Most of the accepted prophecies come from these reliable sources, but interestingly, Jews reject the prophecies of Daniel. While they acknowledge that Daniel made some accurate predictions, many refuse to acknowledge him as a prophet because his book is not included in the prophets section of the Torah ("What is a Prophet?," Judaism 101, accessed March 9, 2021, http://www.jewfaq.org/prophet.htm). Daniel's prophecies, if you remember, are the most time-specific prophecies related to the Messiah. In any case, Daniel's prophecies are curiously missing given his reliable status. Additionally, modern Jews are even selective about *which* prophecies they will accept from the remaining three reliable prophets. For example, they typically reject prophecies from over half the chapters where Isaiah clearly predicts a coming "person of interest." This is also true for the "clear" prophecies of Ezekiel. Modern Jewish believers accept prophecies from two chapters, while rejecting prophecies from three. In a similar way, they reject one of Jeremiah's chapters in terms of its prophetic claims. Modern Jewish believers reject the more specific prophecies of Isaiah, Ezekiel, and Jeremiah, even though they find them reliable enough to accept the less specific prophecies I've listed here. Why? How are they able to reject some while accepting others? Refer to the sidebar on page 69 to read about the approach Jewish believers use to evaluate messianic prophecies.

4. For an in-depth description of messianic prophecies, the manner in which Jewish believers evaluate and reject these prophecies, and a response to the objections of Jewish believers, refer to Michael L. Brown, *Answering Jewish Objections to Jesus*, 5 vols. (Grand Rapids: Baker, 2000–2015).

5. Judicial Council of California, *Judicial Council of California Criminal Jury Instructions* (New York: Matthew Bender, 2021), CALCRIM No. 336, https://www.courts.ca.gov /partners/documents/calcrim-2021.pdf.

6. *Judicial Council of California Criminal Jury Instructions*, CALCRIM No. 336.

7. Refer to "United States v. Jones," Oyez, accessed March 9, 2021, https://www.oyez.org /cases/2011/10-1259.

8. Skeptics, in response to these predictions of historical events, may simply argue that they were added by editors after the historical events occurred, resulting in an altered text that only *appears* to be an accurate prophesy. But if these predictions were added later, we would expect them to be much clearer and detailed in nature. In addition, we would expect many more "alterations" to exist in an effort to establish *every* prophet as a reliable source. This is simply not the case.

9. Siculus wrote, "It happened at this very time that the king of the Assyrians, who was unaware of the defection of the Bactrians and had become elated over his past successes, turned to indulgence and divided among his soldiers for a feast animals and great quantities of both wine and all other provisions. Consequently, since the

whole army was carousing, Arbaces, learning from some deserters of the relaxation and drunkenness in the camp of the enemy, made his attack upon it unexpectedly in the night." Diodorus Siculus, *Library of History* 2.26.4, updated June 2, 2020, http://penelope.uchicago.edu/Thayer/E/Roman/Texts/Diodorus_Siculus/2A*.html.

10. For more information about how Cyrus accomplished this, refer to Gauthier Tolini, *"Quelques éléments concernant la prise de Babylone par Cyrus le Grand," Achaemenid Research on Texts and Archaeology* (November 2005), https://www.academia.edu/803050/_Quelques_%C3%A9l%C3%A9ments_concernant_la_prise_de_Babylone_par_Cyrus_le_Grand_octobre_539_av._J.-C._ARTA_2005.003.

11. Researcher Harriet Crawford wrote, "The remains of Hammurabi's own city at Babylon are, unfortunately, almost inaccessible as the water table has risen too high to allow them to be explored." Harriet Crawford, "Architecture in the Old Babylonian Period," in *The Babylonian World*, ed. Gwendolyn Leick (New York: Routledge, 2009), 89.

12. This bridge is still in existence today. Refer to Ned Stafford, "How Geology Came to Help Alexander the Great," *Nature*, May 14, 2007, https://www.nature.com/news/2007/070514/full/070514-2.html.

13. Today the ruin of Petra is part of Jordan. Refer to Mati Milstein, "Petra," *National Geographic*, accessed July 4, 2020, https://www.nationalgeographic.com/history/article/lost-city-petra.

14. Refer to Daniel 8:5–8: "As I was thinking about this, suddenly a goat with a prominent horn between its eyes came from the west, crossing the whole earth without touching the ground. It came toward the two-horned ram I had seen standing beside the canal and charged at it in great rage. I saw it attack the ram furiously, striking the ram and shattering its two horns. The ram was powerless to stand against it; the goat knocked it to the ground and trampled on it, and none could rescue the ram from its power. The goat became very great, but at the height of its power the large horn was broken off, and in its place four prominent horns grew up toward the four winds of heaven."

The identity of this king who would defeat Media and Persia was made clear to Daniel later in the revelation: "The two-horned ram that you saw represents the kings of Media and Persia. The shaggy goat is the king of Greece, and the large horn between its eyes is the first king" (Daniel 8:20–21). The "first king" of Greece was none other than Alexander the Great. True to the prediction, Alexander defeated the Persians by 333 BC but died "at the height of [his] power." He was only thirty-two years old. Historians debate the cause of his death (between alcoholic liver disease, fever, strychnine poisoning, or typhoid fever), but one thing is certain: after Alexander's death, his empire was divided (among Cassander in the west, Seleucus in the east, Lysimachus in the north, and Ptolemy in the south), just as Daniel predicted.

15. Daniel provides five main apocalyptic prophecies/visions:

Nebuchadnezzar's prophetic dream (2:31–45)
Vision of four great kingdoms and kingdom of Most High (7)
Vision of Ram and Goat (8)
Seventy weeks (9:24–27)
Broken and divided kingdom and deliverance of saints (11:2–12:4)

Depending on how these prophecies and visions are interpreted, Daniel is describing the rise and fall of the Babylonians, Medes, Persians, and Greeks, or the rise and fall of the Babylonians, Medes, Persians, Greeks, and Romans. In either case, Daniel successfully predicts the governing empires of the region several hundred years before they rose in history.

For more information about this sequence of nations described by Daniel, refer to Hank Hanegraaff, *Has God Spoken? Memorable Proof of the Bible's Divine Inspiration* (Nashville: Thomas Nelson, 2011), chapter 12: "Succession of Nations," 113–27.

16. "Clear" prophecies: The Savior—Redeemer—will take his stand "in the end" (Job 19:25–27), be a human, born of a woman, reconcile people to God, crush evil at his own expense (Genesis 3:15), be the descendant of Abraham and through him all nations will be blessed (Genesis 12:3), be the seed of Isaac (Genesis 17:19), be a blessing to the nations (Genesis 18:18), be a descendant of Abraham (Genesis 22:18), be a descendant of Abraham's son Isaac (Genesis 26:1–5), be a descendant of Isaac's son Jacob (Genesis 28:13–14), be a descendant of Jacob's son Judah (Genesis 49:10), be a star coming out of Jacob (Numbers 24:17). "Cloaked" prophecies: The Savior will be an unblemished "Passover lamb" whose bones will not be broken (Exodus 12:5, 46).

17. For a larger, more readable version of this image, refer to https://coldcasechristianity .com/selected-images-from-person-of-interest/. The summary of clear claims provided at this point in history by Moses and Job:

> WHAT: He will "crush evil"
> WHERE: ?
> WHY: To "reconcile" us
> HOW: At his own expense
> WHEN: At "the last"
> WHO: A male descendant of Abraham–Judah

18. "Clear" prophecies: Psalm 34:19–20 written by David (The Savior will be executed without having a bone broken), Psalm 132:11 written by David (The Savior will be the seed of David), Psalm 2:1–12 written by David (The Savior will be called God's son), Psalm 16:8–11 written by David (The Savior will not see decay, and he will make known the "path of life"), Psalm 45:2, 6–7 written by David (The Savior will be known for his righteousness). "Cloaked" prophecies: Psalm 31:4–5 written by David (The Savior will cry, "Into your hands I commit my Spirit"), Psalm 31:11 written by David (The Savior will be abandoned), Psalm 31:13 written by David (The Savior will be killed as part of a murderous plot), Psalm 35:11 written by David (The Savior will be accused by false witnesses), Psalm 35:19 written by David (The Savior will be hated without reason), Psalm 109:4 written by David (The Savior prays for his enemies), Psalm 68:18 written by David (The Savior will ascend into the heavens to give gifts), Psalm 22:1 written by David (The Savior will be forsaken and cry out to God), Psalm 22:6 written by David (The Savior will be despised), Psalm 22:7–8 written by David (The Savior will be mocked by people shaking their heads), Psalm 22:14 written by David (The Savior will die), Psalm 22:15 written by David (The Savior will be thirsty when he dies), Psalm 22:16 written by David (The Savior's hands and feet will be pierced), Psalm 22:17–18 written by David (The Savior will be stripped of his clothing and his executors will cast lots for his clothing), Psalm 110:1–4 written by David (The Savior will be greater than David; he will ascend to God's right hand and reign forever), Psalm 118:17–18 (The Savior will defeat death), Psalm 118:22–24 written by David (The Savior will become

the cornerstone, even though he was previously rejected), Psalm 118:25–29 written by David (The Savior will be cheered and acclaimed), Psalm 55:12–14 written by David (The Savior will be betrayed by a friend), Psalm 30:3 written by David (The Savior will be brought up from death), Psalm 38:11 written by David (The Savior's friends will stand far off), Psalm 38:12–13 written by David (The Savior will be quiet before his accusers), Psalm 40:6–8 written by David (The Savior will say he came to do the will of the Father. He will submit voluntarily), Psalm 41:9 written by David (The Savior will be betrayed by a friend with whom he eats bread), Psalm 41:10 written by David (The Savior will be raised up), Psalm 69:4 written by David (The Savior will be hated without cause), Psalm 69:8 written by David (The Savior will be a stranger to his own brothers), Psalm 69:9 written by David (The Savior will be stung by criticisms), Psalm 69:21 written by David (The Savior will be given vinegar to quench his thirst), Psalm 72:10, 15 written by Solomon (The Savior will be adored and visited by "kings" or magi), Psalm 78:1–2 written by Asaph (The Savior will teach in parables).

19. The summary of clear claims provided by psalmists at this point in history:

> WHAT: He will "crush evil," **make known the path of righteousness**
> WHERE: ?
> WHY: To "reconcile" us
> HOW: **Executed without a broken bone, doesn't see decay**
> WHEN: At "the last"
> WHO: **"God's Son,"** a descendant of Judah

20. "Clear" prophecies: 2 Samuel 7:12–17 (The Savior will be a descendant of David, and his throne will be established forever), Amos 9:13–15 (The Savior will restore the barren land and make it abundant and fruitful), Micah 5:2–5 (The Savior will be born in Bethlehem, and he will be a source of peace and great to the ends of the earth). "Cloaked" prophecies: Joel 2:28–29 (The Savior will promise the Spirit), Hosea 11:1 (The Savior will be called out of Egypt), Proverbs 30:4 (The Savior will be identified as the "Son of God" who ascends and descends from heaven). For larger, more readable images, please visit https://coldcasechristianity.com/selected-images-from-person-of-interest/.

21. The summary of clear claims provided at this point in history by Samuel, Joel, Hosea, Amos, Micah, and Agur son of Jakeh:

> WHAT: He will "crush evil," make known the path of life, **restore the land**
> WHERE: **Born in Bethlehem**
> WHY: To "reconcile" us
> HOW: Executed without a broken bone, doesn't see decay, **reigns forever**
> WHEN: At "the last"
> WHO: "God's Son," a descendant of Judah, **great to the ends of the earth**

22. "Clear" prophecies: Isaiah 2:4 (The Savior will lead all nations and usher in eternal peace), Isaiah 2:11–17 (The Savior will be worshiped by all nations), Isaiah 9:6–7 (The Savior will be a descendant of David who will be called Wonderful Counselor, Mighty God, Everlasting Father, and Prince of Peace. He will reign forever), Isaiah 11:1 (The Savior will be called a Nazarene, and he will be a descendant of Jesse, a descendant of Judah. He will be descended from King David), Isaiah 11:2 (The Savior will have the "spirit of the Lord," and he will have a "fear of God"), Isaiah 11:4 (The Savior will

be defeat evil and tyranny), Isaiah 11:6–9 (He will restore peace on the earth), Isaiah 11:10 (He will include and attract people from all cultures and nations), Isaiah 16:4–5 (The Savior will reign in mercy), Isaiah 25:7–8 (The Savior will conquer death forever. There will be no more hunger or illness), Isaiah 26:19 (The Savior will cause all the dead to rise again), Isaiah 28:16 (The Savior will be a foundation stone laid in Zion), Isaiah 32:1–4 (The Savior will be the King of Kings and Lord of Lords), Isaiah 35:4–6 (The Savior will perform miracles. He will heal the blind, the deaf, the mute, and the lame), Isaiah 40:10–11 (The Savior is a shepherd who cares for his sheep), Isaiah 42:1–4 (The Savior will be a "bruised reed." He will not "snuff out." He will bring justice to the earth), Isaiah 42:6 (The Savior will be a light to people around the world), Isaiah 51:3 (The Savior will take the barren land and make it abundant and fruitful), Isaiah 51:11 (The Jewish people will experience eternal joy and gladness), Isaiah 52:7 (The Savior will be a messenger of peace who announces salvation), Isaiah 52:13–15 (The Savior will cause all nations to recognize the wrongs they did to Israel), Isaiah 53:1–3 (The Savior will be despised and forsaken and a man of sorrows), Isaiah 53:4 (The Savior will bear our griefs and sorrows. He will be stricken, smitten, and afflicted), Isaiah 53:5 (The Savior will be pierced through for our sins and crushed for our iniquities. The Savior's scourging will heal us), Isaiah 53:4–6 (The Savior will suffer for the sins of others), Isaiah 53:7 (The Savior will be oppressed and silent before his accusers), Isaiah 53:8 (The Savior will die because of the sins of God's people), Isaiah 53:9 (The Savior will be buried in a wealthy man's tomb), Isaiah 53:10–11 (The Savior will see future generations. He will not remain dead but will justify many), Isaiah 53:12 (The Savior will be "numbered with the transgressors" and intercede for sinners), Isaiah 59:20 (The Savior will come to Jerusalem to redeem the descendants of Jacob who have turned from their sins), Isaiah 61:1–2 (The Savior will bring good news. He will set the captives free and comfort those who mourn), Isaiah 63:8–9 (The Savior will be afflicted along with the afflicted, but he will redeem and save them).

23. "Cloaked" prophecies: Isaiah 7:13–14 (The Savior will be born of a virgin and will be called Immanuel, "God with us"), Isaiah 8:14 (The Savior will be a stone that causes people to stumble), Isaiah 9:1–2 (The Savior will appear in Galilee and be a light to Gentiles), Isaiah 40:3–4 (The Savior will be preceded by a forerunner), Isaiah 49:6 (The Savior will bring salvation to the ends of the earth), Isaiah 49:7 (The Savior will be hated without cause), Isaiah 50:6–7 (The Savior will be beaten on his back. His beard will be pulled, and he will be spat upon), Isaiah 60:3, 6 (The Savior will be adored and visited by "kings" or magi).

24. The summary of clear claims provided at this point in history by Isaiah:

> WHAT: "Crushes evil," makes known the path of life, conquers death, restores the land, sets the captives free, brings good news of salvation, and shepherds the flock
>
> WHERE: Born in Bethlehem, comes to Jerusalem
>
> WHY: Redeems, intercedes for sinners
>
> HOW: Performs miracles, heals, considered a criminal but remains silent, is despised, scourged, pierced, executed without breaking a bone, dies for our sins, is buried in a wealthy man's tomb, but doesn't remain dead, reigns forever
>
> WHEN: Preceded by a forerunner, appears at "the last"
>
> WHO: Descendant of Judah, "God's Son," great to the ends of the earth

25. "Clear" prophecies: Ezekiel 16:55 (The Savior will usher in the restoration of Israel's cities), Ezekiel 21:26–27 (The Savior will be exalted from humility), Ezekiel 34:23–24 (The Savior will be a descendant of King David and will be the Good Shepherd), Ezekiel 36:29–30 (The Savior will take the barren land and make it abundant and fruitful), Ezekiel 39:9 (The Savior will usher in an era in which weapons of war will be destroyed), Jeremiah 23:5 (The Savior will be a descendant of David. He will reign as king and "do justice and righteousness"), Jeremiah 23:6 (The Savior will be called "The Lord our righteousness." He will be a descendant of Judah), Jeremiah 31:31–32 (The Savior will bring in a new covenant), Jeremiah 31:33–34 (The Savior will usher in a new era in which the people of Israel will have direct access to the law of God through their minds and hearts and God will forgive their sin), Jeremiah 33:15 (The Savior will be a descendant of David). "Cloaked" prophecies: Jeremiah 31:15 (The Savior will be the object of a murderous plot, but hope lies ahead), Jeremiah 31:22 (The Savior will be conceived by the Holy Spirit), Psalm 27:12 (The Savior will be accused by false witnesses), Psalm 49:15 written by the sons of Korah (The Savior will be resurrected), Psalm 89:3–4, 27–29, 35–37 written by Ethan the Ezrahite (The Savior will be exalted as the seed of David), Psalm 89:45 written by Ethan the Ezrahite (The Savior will be cut off in his prime while he is still young), Psalm 102:24 (The Savior will be cut off in his prime while he is still young).

26. The summary of clear claims provided at this point in history by Ezekiel and Jeremiah, along with psalmists, the sons of Korah, and Ethan the Ezrahite:

> WHAT: "Crushes evil," makes known the path of life, conquers death, restores the land, sets the captives free, brings good news of salvation, and shepherds the flock, **brings in a new covenant**
> WHERE: Born in Bethlehem, comes to Jerusalem
> WHY: Redeems, intercedes for sinners
> HOW: Performs miracles, heals, but is despised, considered a criminal but remains silent, scourged, pierced, executed without breaking a bone, dies for our sins, is buried in a wealthy man's tomb, but doesn't remain dead, **exalted from humility**, reigns forever
> WHEN: Preceded by a forerunner, appears at "the last"
> WHO: Descendant of Judah, "God's Son," great to the ends of the earth

> For larger, more readable images, please visit https://coldcasechristianity.com/selected-images-from-person-of-interest/.

27. "Clear" prophecies: Daniel 7:13–14 (The Savior will be the "Son of Man," and he will have an everlasting throne), Daniel 9:24 (The Savior will come to bring an end to sin, to make atonement for sin, to bring everlasting righteousness, to fulfill prophecy, and to anoint a most holy place), Daniel 9:25 (The Savior will appear after a decree to restore and rebuild Jerusalem. There will be sixty-nine weeks of years (483 years) between the decree and the appearance of the Savior), Daniel 9:26 (The Savior will appear before Jerusalem and the temple is destroyed again).

28. For more information about Anderson's work on the prophecy, refer to Sir Robert Anderson, *The Coming Prince: The Marvelous Prophecy of Daniel's Seventy Weeks Concerning the Antichrist* (n.p.: Trumpet, 2014).

29. Sir Robert Anderson's interpretation of Daniel's seventy sevens prophecy is *not* universally accepted. Kim Riddlebarger (PhD from Fuller Theological Seminary and

visiting professor of systematic theology at Westminster Seminary), for example, believes the scriptural symbolism of "seven," "seventy," and "week" should lead us to interpret the Daniel passage in a different way. Riddlebarger argues that Daniel's seventy sevens prophecy ushers in an ultimate Jubilee and eternal Sabbath. Under this interpretation, the seventy sevens refer to a symbolic period of time, not a woodenly literal period of time as Anderson described. Refer to Kim Riddlebarger, *A Case for Amillennialism: Understanding the End Times* (Grand Rapids: Baker, 2013), ch. 12.

30. The translators of the NIV recognized this truth, translating "weeks" as "sevens."

31. In 464 BC Artaxerxes, a Persian king, ascended to the throne while the Israelites were in captivity. Nehemiah, the Jewish prophet and cupbearer to King Artaxerxes, was deeply concerned about the ruined condition of Jerusalem after the defeat of the Jews (Nehemiah 1:1–4). As a result, he petitioned the king: "Send me to Judah, to the city of my fathers' graves, that I may rebuild it. . . . So it pleased the king to send me" (Nehemiah 2:5–6 ESV).

32. Once again, not everyone agrees that decree of King Artaxerxes (described in Nehemiah 2:1) is the decree Daniel is referencing in his prophecy. Riddlebarger, for example, believes that Daniel, Ezra, Nehemiah, and Isaiah reference the original decree that the Jews to leave Babylon, return to Jerusalem, and rebuild the temple as foretold by Jeremiah (and hinted at in Daniel 1:21; 2 Chronicles 36:21–22; and Isaiah 44:28). Cyrus the Great was responsible for this decree in 538 BCE.

33. The Jewish calendar month was Nisan, and since no day is given, it is reasonable to assume the date would be understood as the first, the Jewish New Year's Day. In the Julian calendar we presently use, the corresponding date would be March 5, 444 BCE.

34. Even if we disagree on Anderson's literal approach to dating the prophecy, his interpretation of "seven," "seventy," and "week," and his use of the decree of King Artaxerxes (rather than that of Cyrus the Great), the range of Daniel's prophecy limits the arrival of the Messiah to a timespan between 538 BCE and 70 CE at most, and between 458–444 BCE and 70 CE at the least.

35. Jesus frequently performed miracles and swore his disciples to silence, saying his "hour has not yet come" (John 2:4; 7:6).

36. The summary of clear claims provided at this point in history by Daniel:

> WHAT: "Crushes evil," makes known the path of life, conquers death, restores the land, sets the captives free, brings good news of salvation and shepherds the flock, brings in a new covenant
>
> WHERE: Born in Bethlehem, comes to Jerusalem
>
> WHY: Redeems, intercedes for sinners, **makes atonement for sin**
>
> HOW: Performs miracles, heals, but is despised, considered a criminal but remains silent, scourged, pierced, executed without breaking a bone, dies for our sins, is buried in a wealthy man's tomb, but doesn't remain dead, exalted from humility, reigns forever
>
> WHEN: Preceded by a forerunner, **appears after a decree but before the destruction of the temple**
>
> WHO: Descendant of Judah, "God's Son," **"Son of Man"**

37. For a larger, more readable version of this image, refer to https://coldcasechristianity.com/selected-images-from-person-of-interest/.

38. "Clear" prophecies: Zechariah 2:10–13 (The Savior is coming and will be sent by God. He will dwell in the midst of his people), Zechariah 8:23 (The Savior will usher in an era in which peoples of the world will turn to the Jews for spiritual guidance), Zechariah 9:9 (The Savior will enter Jerusalem while riding on a donkey), 1 Chronicles 22:8–10 written by Ezra (The Savior will descend from King David), 2 Chronicles 21:7 written by Ezra (The Savior will be a descendant of David who will be on the throne forever), 2 Chronicles 7:18 written by Ezra (The Savior will descend from King David), Malachi 3:1 (The Savior will be preceded by a messenger who will prepare the way for the Lord. The Savior will suddenly enter his temple), Malachi 4:2–3 (The Savior will be the Light of the World), Malachi 4:5–6 (The Messiah would be preceded by Elijah the prophet). "Cloaked" prophecies: Zechariah 10:4 (The Savior will be the cornerstone), Zechariah 11:12–13 (The Savior will be betrayed for thirty pieces of silver. The money was thrown to the potter), Zechariah 12:10 (The Savior will be pierced. People will mourn for him and weep over him like a "firstborn" son), Zechariah 13:6–7 (The Savior will be a shepherd who is pierced with a sword and whose sheep are scattered), 1 Chronicles 17:11–14 written by Ezra (The Savior will be a descendant of David who will be on the throne forever).

39. For a larger, more readable version of this image, refer to https://coldcasechristianity.com/selected-images-from-person-of-interest/. The summary of clear claims provided at this point in history by Malachi:

> WHAT: "Crushes evil," makes known the path of life, conquers death, restores the land, sets the captives free, brings good news of salvation and shepherds the flock, brings in a new covenant
>
> WHERE: Born in Bethlehem, **enters Jerusalem on a donkey, dwells in the midst of his people**
>
> WHY: Redeems, intercedes for sinners, makes atonement for sin
>
> HOW: Performs miracles, heals, but is despised, considered a criminal but remains silent, scourged, pierced, executed without breaking a bone, dies for our sins, is buried in a wealthy man's tomb, but doesn't remain dead, exalted from humility, reigns forever
>
> WHEN: Preceded by a forerunner who **is able to enter the temple,** appears after a decree but before the destruction of the temple
>
> WHO: Descendant of Judah, "God's Son," "Son of Man"

40. For a larger, more readable version of this image, refer to https://coldcasechristianity.com/selected-images-from-person-of-interest/. Clear prophecies cited here:

> WHAT: "Crushes evil," makes known the path of life, conquers death, restores the land, sets the captives free, brings good news of salvation and shepherds the flock, brings in a new covenant
>
> WHERE: Born in Bethlehem, enters Jerusalem on a donkey, dwells in the midst of his people
>
> WHY: Redeems, intercedes for sinners, makes atonement for sin
>
> HOW: Performs miracles, heals, but is despised, considered a criminal but remains silent, scourged, pierced, executed without breaking a bone, dies for our sins, is buried in a wealthy man's tomb, but doesn't remain dead, exalted from humility, reigns forever

WHEN: Preceded by a forerunner, Elijah, is able to enter the temple, appears after a decree but before the destruction of the temple

WHO: Descendant of Judah, "God's Son," "Son of Man"

Cloaked prophecies cited here:

WHAT: Comes to do the will of the Father

WHERE: Called out of Egypt, appears in Galilee and is a light to gentiles

WHY: Brings salvation to the earth

HOW: Conceived by the Holy Spirit, born of a virgin, called Immanuel, visited by "kings," teaches in parables, promises the Spirit, hated without reason, betrayed by a friend for thirty pieces of silver (later thrown to the potter), abandoned, killed as part of a plot, quiet while falsely accused, mocked and criticized, beaten and spat on, bones not broken, stripped of his clothing, executors cast lots, hands and feet are pierced, thirsty when he dies, given vinegar to drink, prays for his enemies, cries, "Into your hands I commit my Spirit," rises from the grave, ascends to God's right hand and reigns forever

WHEN: 483 years (173,880 days) after the decree to restore Jerusalem

WHO: The "Son of God," a shepherd whose sheep are scattered

41. For a larger, more readable version of this image, refer to https://coldcasechristianity
.com/selected-images-from-person-of-interest/. The summary of prophecies from "reliable informants" (Isaiah, Ezekiel, Jeremiah, and Daniel):

A descendant of David through Judah who arrives 483 years after the decree to restore Jerusalem. He will be preceded by a forerunner, conceived by the Holy Spirit, and born of a virgin. He will be visited by "kings" (magi) and called a Nazarene.

He will appear in Galilee; come to Jerusalem; perform miracles; heal the blind, deaf, mute, and lame. He will shepherd his sheep and bring a message of peace and salvation.

He will be the "Son of Man," "Wonderful Counselor," "Mighty God," and "Prince of Peace."

He will be hated without a cause, beaten, and abused, and the object of a murderous plot. Despised and forsaken, he will be silent before his accusers, suffer for our iniquities, and pierced through. He will die due to the sins of God's people and will be buried in a wealthy man's tomb.

He will conquer death and come back to life, bringing a new covenant and making atonement for sin.

Chapter 5: In the Fullness of Time

1. For larger, more readable images, please visit https://coldcasechristianity.com/selected
-images-from-person-of-interest/.

2. The dating for the diagram illustrated here is based on data for each ancient mythology as described in our comprehensive Case Note PDF file, downloadable here: https://cold
casechristianity.com/case-notes-for-person-of-interest/.

3. In this visual summary, the overlap includes every ancient mythology *except* Marduk (worshiped from 1800 BCE to 485 BCE). Marduk was the God of the Babylonians, and

once Babylon was destroyed, Marduk worship ended. Babylonians did, however, become members of other societies and adopted the gods of those cultures (included in the diagram). The "red zone" I've drawn here still accurately includes the greatest number of concurrent worshipers from all groups (including Marduk worshipers).

Chapter 6: Jesus, the Unfounded Fiction?

1. During his lifetime, Elvis set several significant records:

   > Most US hit singles (149)
   > Most US No. 1 albums by a male solo artist (9)
   > Most weeks on UK singles chart (111 hits over 1,149 weeks)
   > Most consecutive weeks on UK singles chart (100)
   > Most "certificates" held by a single artist (132 gold, 70 platinum, and
   >   33 multiplatinum)
   > Most platinum albums (70)
   > Elvis remains the second richest dead celebrity (over 1 billion albums sold,
   > $39 million in 2019 alone). Elvis is second only to Michael Jackson.

   It should be noted that some of these records have now been eclipsed since Elvis's death. For more information about the records Elvis held, refer to "Elvis in the Guinness World Record book," Elvis.net, accessed March 10, 2021, https://www.elvis.net /guinness/guinnessframe.html and Zack O'Malley Greenburg, "The Top-Earning Dead Celebrities of 2019," *Forbes*, October 30, 2019, https://www.forbes.com/sites/zackomalley greenburg/2019/10/30/the-top-earning-dead-celebrities-of--2019/.

2. Greenburg, "The Top-Earning Dead Celebrities of 2019."

3. In 311 CE Emperor Galerius issued an edict of toleration regarding Christians in which they were granted an "indulgence": "Wherefore, for this our indulgence, they ought to pray to their God for our safety, for that of the republic, and for their own, that the commonwealth may continue uninjured on every side, and that they may be able to live securely in their homes." The Edict of Milan, however, sought also to restore meeting places and properties that had been taken from Christians: "The same shall be restored to the Christians without payment or any claim of recompense and without any kind of fraud or deception." Both texts available here: "Galerius and Constantine: Edicts of Toleration 311/313," Internet History Sourcebooks Project, accessed April 6, 2021, https://sourcebooks.fordham.edu/source/edict-milan.asp.

4. The text of the Edict of Thessalonica is available here: "Edict of Thessalonica," *World Heritage Encyclopedia*, Project Gutenberg Self-Publishing Press, accessed August 1, 2020, http://www.gutenberg.cc/articles/Edict_of_Thessalonica.

5. For more evidence related to the relationship between John and his students (Ignatius and Polycarp) and Paul and his student (Clement), refer to my book *Cold-Case Christianity: A Homicide Detective Investigates the Claims of the Gospels* (Colorado Springs: Cook, 2013), 213–38.

6. For larger, more readable images, please visit https://coldcasechristianity.com/selected -images-from-person-of-interest/. Another valuable resource on the ante-Nicene church fathers is Cyril C. Richardson, ed., *Early Christian Fathers* (New York: Touchstone, 1996). Some scholars doubt the early dating and authenticity of the Gospel of Barnabas. But John Dominic Crossan argues for an early date because the New Testament writers

neither explicitly nor tacitly refer to the Epistle of Barnabas. As a result, he argues for a date as early as the late first century CE:

> Richardson and Shukster have also argued for a first-century date. Among several arguments they point to the detail of "a little king, who shall subdue three of the kings under one" and "a little excrescent horn, and that it subdued under one three of the great horns" in Barnabas 4:4–5. They propose a composition "date during or immediately after the reign of Nerva (96–8 C.E.) . . . viewed as bringing to an end the glorious Flavian dynasty of Vespasian, Titus, and Domitian . . . when a powerful, distinguished, and successful dynasty was brought low, humiliated by an assassin's knife" . . . [and that this] "would argue for an early date, perhaps even before the end of I C.E." (John Dominic Crossan, *The Cross That Spoke: The Origins of the Passion Narrative* [New York: HarperCollins, 1992], 121).

In addition, Jay Curry Treat, writing in *The Anchor Bible Dictionary*, cites the following: "Since Barnabas 16:3 refers to the destruction of the temple, Barnabas must be written after 70 C.E. It must be written before its first undisputable use in Clement of Alexandria, ca. 190. Since 16:4 expects the temple to be rebuilt, it was most likely written before Hadrian built a Roman temple on the site ca. 135. Attempts to use 4:4–5 and 16:1–5 to specify the time of origin more exactly have not won wide agreement. It is important to remember that traditions of varying ages have been incorporated into this work." Jay Curry Treat, *The Anchor Bible Dictionary*, ed. David Noel Freedman, vol. 1 (New York: Doubleday, 1992), 613–14.

7. Based on research conducted by Steve Morrison, "Early Christian New Testament Quotes before Nicea I (325 A.D.)," Bible Query, accessed January 4, 2020, https://www.biblequery.org/Bible/BibleCanon/EarlyChristianNTQuotes.xlsx.

8. For larger, more readable images, please visit https://coldcasechristianity.com/selected-images-from-person-of-interest/. For a summary of early church leaders and the New Testament books from which they quoted or referenced, refer to our comprehensive Case Note PDF file, downloadable here: https://coldcasechristianity.com/case-notes-for-person-of-interest/.

9. For larger, more readable images, please visit https://coldcasechristianity.com/selected-images-from-person-of-interest/. For the characteristics of Jesus cited by Ignatius, Polycarp, and Clement of Rome, refer to my book *Cold-Case Christianity*, 217–23. For the others and for the details that can be retrieved from the writings of these early leaders, refer to our comprehensive Case Note PDF file, downloadable here: https://coldcasechristianity.com/case-notes-for-person-of-interest/.

10. Based on Morrison, "Early Christian New Testament Quotes before Nicea I (325 A.D.)."

11. Solomon J. Schepps, *The Lost Books of the Bible: Being all the Gospels, Epistles, and Other Pieces Now Extant Attributed in the First Four Centuries to Jesus Christ, His Apostles, and Their Companions, Not Included, by its Compilers, in the Authorized New Testament* (New York: Testament Books / Random House, 1979).

12. Many early religious groups rewrote, edited, or created their own narrative of Jesus to affirm a theological belief held by the group. If, for example, a sect of believers held to the idea that matter is inherently corrupt or evil, they wrote gospels describing Jesus as an immaterial spiritual being, denying the physicality of Jesus described in the canonical gospels.

13. The word *Gnosticism* is rooted in the Greek word *gnosis*, which means "knowledge" or "to know." But unlike the Christian definition of *intellectual* knowledge, gnostic knowledge is "mythical" and comes through an esoteric, secret knowledge spoken privately by Jesus or one of his followers. This secret knowledge is the basis for salvation. This differed dramatically from the Christian belief in redemption through the death and resurrection of Jesus. Many Gnostic groups also believed in a lesser creator of the material world (a demiurge) in addition to a more transcendent god. They also held a low view of this inferior creator god, the material universe, and the human body. Unsurprisingly, because of these dramatic differences, early church leaders warned their followers to avoid these late texts and deemed them heretical. By the end of the second century, Gnostics either abandoned their Christian identity or were expelled from the church.

14. The earliest disciples of Jesus and leaders of the church knew that these late-appearing gospels were fraudulent. Early leaders such as Polycarp, Irenaeus, Hippolytus, Tertullian, and Epiphanius wrote about most of the noncanonical gospels when they first appeared in history, identifying them as heretical frauds. Irenaeus, writing in 185 CE about the growing number of noncanonical texts, said there were "an unspeakable number of apocryphal and spurious writings, which they themselves have forged, to bewilder the minds of foolish men, and of such as are ignorant of the Scriptures of truth." Irenaeus, *Against Heresies 1.20*, in *The Ante-Nicene Fathers,* eds. Alexander Roberts, James Donaldson, and A. Cleveland Coxe, vol. 1 (Buffalo, NY: Christian Literature, 1885). This work is available online: "Against Heresies (Book I, Chapter 20)," New Advent, accessed March 12, 2021, https://www.newadvent.org/fathers /0103120.htm. Those who were closest to the action knew the late noncanonical texts were not to be trusted.

15. The authors of the noncanonical gospels allowed their theological presuppositions to corrupt their work. Many of the noncanonical texts were written by Gnostic authors utilizing the pseudonym of an apostle to legitimize the text while co-opting the person of Jesus to legitimize their theology. As a result, Jesus was often portrayed as the source of hidden, esoteric wisdom communicated in sayings or dialogues with a selected disciple who was privileged enough to be "enlightened." In addition, Jesus was often described as a "Docetic" immaterial spirit without a body, forcing the author to account for the appearance of a bodily death at the crucifixion or other physical appearances described in the New Testament.

16. For larger, more readable images, please visit https://coldcasechristianity.com/selected -images-from-person-of-interest/. To review the names and dates of the noncanonical gospels, refer to endnote 18 below. The gospels found in the New Testament appeared very early in history. There is good reason to believe that Mark's gospel was written as early as 50 CE and that John's gospel was written no later than 70 CE. These texts appeared early enough to be eyewitness accounts of Jesus's life, just as they claim to be. By comparison, the entire catalog of noncanonical gospels were written much later in history (The Gospel of Thomas, for example, was written from 110–180 CE, the Gospel of Mary from 120–180 CE, and the Gospel of Judas from 130–170 CE). The noncanonical gospels appear far too late to have been written by eyewitnesses to the life of Jesus.

17. Another excellent resource for these texts is Paul Foster, ed., *The Non-Canonical Gospels* (London: T&T Clark, 2008).

18. To review what the noncanonical gospels say about Jesus, despite their unique distortions, and to review the overlapping assumptions of the noncanonical gospels and the facts that can be reconstructed from them, refer to our comprehensive Case Note PDF file, downloadable here: https://coldcasechristianity.com/case-notes-for-person-of-interest/.

19. For larger, more readable images, please visit https://coldcasechristianity.com/selected-images-from-person-of-interest/.

20. For larger, more readable images, please visit https://coldcasechristianity.com/selected-images-from-person-of-interest/.

21. Some of these ancient manuscripts are Roman in origin, others are Jewish, and some are Christian. Before you reject the Christian sources as biased, recognize that many non-Christian, hostile voices have been reliably and accurately recorded by Christian authors. Celsus, for example, was a second-century Greek philosopher who opposed Christianity. He wrote a document entitled *On the True Doctrine*. The only evidence we have for the existence of Celsus (or the existence of this document) comes from a *Christian* source (Origen of Alexandria's ancient response, *Contra Celsum*). No serious scholar doubts the existence of Celsus or the content of his attack on Christianity (see, for example, the manner in which both are assumed as accurate here: Britannica, s.v. "Celsus," accessed March 10, 2021, https://www.britannica.com/biography/Celsus, and here: Encyclopedia.com, s.v. "Celsus," accessed March 10, 2021, https://www.encyclopedia.com/people/philosophy-and-religion/philosophy-biographies/celsus. In a similar way, other ancient, hostile, non-Christians have been recorded by Christian authors. Our list of hostile voices therefore includes those who have been recorded in this way.

22. For larger, more readable images, please visit https://coldcasechristianity.com/selected-images-from-person-of-interest/. To review the statements of the ancient non-Christian voices related to Jesus and his followers and a complete list of these voices, refer to our comprehensive Case Note PDF file, downloadable here: https://coldcasechristianity.com/case-notes-for-person-of-interest/.

23. Our comprehensive Case Note PDF file is available for download here: https://coldcasechristianity.com/case-notes-for-person-of-interest/.

24. For a complete list of the Christian and non-Christian sources cited here, refer to our comprehensive Case Note PDF file, downloadable here: https://coldcasechristianity.com/case-notes-for-person-of-interest/.

25. For an excellent list of early church writings, see Matthew Barrett's article "The Well-Trained Theologian: Essential Texts for Retrieving Classical Christian Theology," *Credo*, April 1, 2020, https://credomag.com/2020/04/the-well-trained-theologian-essential-texts-for-retrieving-classical-christian-theology/, and his PDF document (with an excellent set of hyperlinks to each document), accessed April 5, 2021: https://www.dropbox.com/s/rfcr23ikrhyx4q5/Final-Well%20Trained%20Theologian-Matthew%20Barrett.pdf?dl=0. Here are just a few of the books that have been written about Jesus:

> *The History of the Church* by Eusebius of Caesarea (c. 330 CE)
>
> *Hymns on Paradise* by Ephrem the Syrian (c. 360 CE)
>
> *On the Holy Spirit* by Basil of Caesarea (c. 365 CE)
>
> *On God and Christ: The Five Theological Orations and Two Letters to Cledonius* by Gregory of Nazianzus (c. 365 CE)
>
> *On the Providence of God* by Saint John Chrysostom (c. 410 CE)

The City of God by Augustine of Hippo (c. 426 CE)

The Rule of St. Benedict by Benedict of Nursia (516 CE)

The Book of Pastoral Rule by Gregory the Great (c. 575 CE)

On the Cosmic Mystery of Jesus Christ by Maximus the Confessor (c. 640 CE)

On the Ascetical Life by Isaac of Nineveh (c. 680 CE)

On Holy Images by John of Damascus (c. 730 CE)

On the Holy Icons by Theodore the Studite (c. 815 CE)

The Voice of the Eagle by Johannes Eriugena (c. 860 CE)

Commentary on the Apocalypse by Oecumenius of Trikka (c. 990 CE)

On the Mystical Life: The Ethical Discourses by Symeon the New Theologian (c. 995 CE)

A Prayer of Saint Fulbert of Notre Dame by Fulbert de Chartres (c. 1010 CE)

The Book to Dispel Worry by Elijah di Nisibis (c. 1030 CE)

Mediaeval Continuation by Lanfranc of Canterbury (c. 1070 CE)

On Loving God by Bernard of Clairvaux (c. 1120 CE)

Ethical Writings by Peter Abelard (c. 1130 CE)

The Journey of the Mind to God by Bonaventure (1259 CE)

Cum Graecis Commentariis by Maximus Planudes (c. 1290 CE)

Predestination, God's Foreknowledge, and Future Contingents by William of Ockham (c. 1324 CE)

Revelations of St. Bridget on the Life and Passion of Our Lord and the Life of His Blessed Mother by Bridget of Sweden (c. 1370 CE)

The Dialogue by Catherine of Siena (c. 1378 CE)

The Imitation of Christ by Thomas à Kempis (1418 CE)

Summa Theologica by Thomas Aquinas (1485 CE)

On the Freedom of a Christian by Martin Luther (1520 CE)

The Dark Night of the Soul by St. John of the Cross (1578 CE)

Revelations of Divine Love by Julian of Norwich (1670 CE)

The Pilgrim's Progress by John Bunyan (1678 CE)

Sinners in the Hands of an Angry God by Jonathan Edwards (1741 CE)

A Plain Account of Christian Perfection by John Wesley (1766 CE)

Fear and Trembling by Søren Kierkegaard (1843 CE)

The Life and Times of Jesus the Messiah by Alfred Edersheim (1883 CE)

Humility by Andrew Murray (1884 CE)

Orthodoxy by G. K. Chesterton (1908 CE)

My Utmost for His Highest by Oswald Chambers (1924 CE)

The Cost of Discipleship by Dietrich Bonhoeffer (1937 CE)

The Pursuit of God by A. W. Tozer (1948 CE)

Mere Christianity by C. S. Lewis (1952 CE)

Through Gates of Splendor by Elisabeth Elliot (1957 CE)

The God Who Is There by Francis Schaeffer (1968 CE)

The Canon of Scripture by F. F. Bruce (1988 CE)

And purely tongue in cheek:

Cold-Case Christianity, *God's Crime Scene*, and *Forensic Faith* by J. Warner Wallace (2013–2017 CE)

26. For a partial list of Christian publishing companies that reflect the magnitude of the literary fallout Jesus caused, refer to our comprehensive Case Note PDF file, downloadable here: https://coldcasechristianity.com/case-notes-for-person-of-interest/.

27. To get an idea of the number of publishers that exist in each religious worldview, visit the following sites for Buddhism: "Buddhist Book Publishers," Purify Mind, http://purifymind.com/Publishers.htm; "Buddhist Books Websites," BuddhaNet, http://www.buddhanet.net/l_books.htm; and Wikipedia's entry on Buddhist Publishing Companies, https://en.wikipedia.org/wiki/Category:Buddhist_publishing_companies; for Hinduism: "Religion Publishers' Directory of India," Publishers Global, https://www.publishersglobal.com/directory/india/subject/religion-publishers; and for Islam: "17 Top Islamic Book Publishing Companies," Writing Tips Oasis, https://writingtipsoasis.com/islamic-book-publishing-companies/; and "Islamic Book Publishers," The Halal Life, https://thehalallife.co.uk/islamic-book-publishers/. All sites accessed April 9, 2021.

28. For more information related to Peter Dickson's research, see Martin Kettle, "When Fame Is an Open Book," *Guardian*, September 13, 1999, https://www.theguardian.com/world/1999/sep/14/martinkettle.

29. Encyclopedia.com, s.v. "Library of Congress," accessed August 14, 2020, https://www.encyclopedia.com/literature-and-arts/journalism-and-publishing/libraries-books-and-printing/library-congress.

30. Kettle, "When Fame Is an Open Book."

31. Kettle, "When Fame Is an Open Book."

32. Google Books, https://books.google.com/.

33. I conducted this search using Google Books (https://books.google.com/) on February 4, 2020. Keep in mind, however, that these statistics vary on a daily basis based on the tagging and publisher's listing of books for each historical figure.

34. For larger, more readable images, please visit https://coldcasechristianity.com/selected-images-from-person-of-interest/. For a partial list of Jesus films illustrating the impact Jesus had on screenplays and motion pictures, refer to our comprehensive Case Note PDF file, downloadable here: https://coldcasechristianity.com/case-notes-for-person-of-interest/.

35. Even a cursory search of Christian movie titles on Wikipedia reveals 371 titles. See Wikipedia, s.v. "List of Christian Films," accessed August 15, 2020, https://en.wikipedia.org/wiki/List_of_Christian_films.

36. "Official Jesus Film Project Ministry Statistics," Jesus Film Project, May 27, 2020, https://www.jesusfilm.org/about/learn-more/statistics.html; Franklin Foer, "1979 Bible Film is the Most-Watched Movie of All Time," *New York Times*, July 22, 2003, 1AR; and Giles Wilson, "The Most Watched Film in History," *BBC News*, July 21, 2003, http://news.bbc.co.uk/2/hi/uk_news/magazine/3076809.stm.

37. For larger, more readable images, please visit https://coldcasechristianity.com/selected-images-from-person-of-interest/.

38. The following depictions of Jesus's life contain the gospel accounts as screenplays:

> *The Visual Bible: Matthew* (1993)
> Director: Regardt van den Bergh / Producer: Chuck Bush
>
> *The Visual Bible: The Gospel of John* (2003)
> Director: Philip Saville / Producers: Garth H. Drabinsky, Chris Chrisafis

The Gospel of Matthew (2014)
Director: David Batty / Producers: Brent Ryan Green, Mart Green, Hannah Leader

The Gospel of John (2015)
Director: David Batty / Producer: Hannah Leader

The Gospel of Luke (2015)
Director: David Batty / Producer: Hannah Leader

The Gospel of Mark (2016)
Director: David Batty / Producer: Hannah Leader

39. An excellent resource for information related to the Christ figures in *Star Trek, Star Wars, I, Robot, The Fifth Element, Lost, Tron, Pleasantville, The Matrix, The Terminator, Planet of the Apes, Doctor Who,* and Marvel Comics is James L. Papandrea, *From Star Wars to Superman: Christ Figures in Science Fiction and Superhero Films* (Manchester, NH: Sophia Institute, 2017). Here are several examples of Christ figures in fictional literature:

Uncle Tom and Eva Saint Clare in Harriet Beecher Stowe's novel *Uncle Tom's Cabin* (1852)
Sydney Carton in Charles Dickens's novel *A Tale of Two Cities* (1859)
Jean Valjean in Victor Hugo's novel *Les Misérables* (1862)
Prince Myshkin in Fyodor Dostoevsky's novel *The Idiot* (1869)
Jim Conklin in Stephen Crane's novel *The Red Badge of Courage* (1894)
Billy Budd in Herman Melville's novel *Billy Budd* (1924)
Joe Christmas in William Faulkner's novel *Light in August* (1932)
Superman in Jerry Siegel and Joe Shuster's DC Comic series (1938)
Jim Casy in John Steinbeck's novel *The Grapes of Wrath* (1939)
John Singer in Carson McCullers's novel *The Heart is a Lonely Hunter* (1940)
Meursault in Albert Camus's novel *The Outsider* (1942)
Chris Keller in Arthur Miller's screenplay *All My Sons* (1947)
Aragorn, Gandalf, and Frodo Baggins in J. R. R. Tolkien's novel *The Lord of the Rings* (1949)
Aslan in C. S. Lewis's *The Chronicles of Narnia series* (1950–1956)
Klaatu in Edmund H. North's screenplay *The Day the Earth Stood Still* (1951)
Zyra in Sydney Boehm's screenplay *When Worlds Collide* (1951)
Santiago in Ernest Hemingway's novel *The Old Man and the Sea* (1952)
Shane in A. B. Guthrie Jr.'s screenplay *Shane* (1953)
Simon in William Golding's novel *Lord of the Flies* (1954)
Babette in Karen Blixen's novel *Babette's Feast* (1958)
Finny in John Knowles's novel *A Separate Peace* (1959)
Mama in Lorraine Hansberry's play *A Raisin in the Sun* (1959)
The Boy in Jakub Goldberg, Roman Polanski, and Jerzy Skolimowski's screenplay *Knife in the Water* (1962)
Randle Patrick McMurphy in Ken Kesey's novel *One Flew Over the Cuckoo's Nest* (1962)
The Doctor in Sydney Newman's television series *Doctor Who* (1963)

Paul Atreides in Frank Herbert's novel *Dune* (1965)

Claude in Michael Weller's screenplay *Hair* (1967)

Lucas Jackson in Frank Pierson and Donn Pearce's screenplay *Cool Hand Luke* (1967)

George Taylor in Michael Wilson and Rod Serling's screenplay *Planet of the Apes* (1968)

Anakin Skywalker in George Lucas's screenplays *Star Wars: Episodes I-VI* (1977–2005)

Max Rockatansky in James McCausland and George Miller's screenplay *Mad Max* (1979)

Ellen Ripley in Dan O'Bannon's screenplay *Alien* (1979)

Spock in Jack B. Sowards's screenplay *Star Trek II: The Wrath of Khan* (1982)

E.T. in Melissa Mathison's screenplay *E.T. the Extra-Terrestrial* (1982)

Flynn in Steven Lisberger and Bonnie MacBird's screenplay *Tron* (1982)

The Alien in Bruce A. Evans and Raynold Gideon's screenplay *Starman* (1984)

John Connor in James Cameron and Gale Anne Hurd's screenplay *The Terminator* (1984)

Optimus Prime in Jim Shooter and Dennis O'Neil's backstory for *Transformers* (1984)

Goku in Akira Toriyama's *Dragon Ball* series (1984)

Andrew "Ender" Wiggin in Orson Scott Card's novel *Ender's Game* (1985)

Sergeant Elias K. Grodin in Oliver Stone's screenplay *Platoon* (1986)

Alex J. Murphy in Edward Neumeier and Michael Miner's screenplay *RoboCop* (1987)

Nausicaä in Hayao Miyazaki's manga comic *Nausicaä of the Valley of the Wind* (1987)

The T-800 in James Cameron and William Wisher's screenplay *Terminator 2: Judgment Day* (1991)

Kamui Shirō in Satsuki Igarashi, Nanase Ohkawa, Tsubaki Nekoi, and Mokona's manga comic series *X* (1992)

Kahless in Ronald D. Moore and James E. Brooks's screenplay *Star Trek: The Next Generation,* "Rightful Heir," Season 6, Episode 23 (1992)

The Boy in Lois Lowry's novel *The Giver* (1993)

Andy in Stephen King and Frank Darabont's screenplay *Shawshank Redemption* (1994)

Simba in Irene Mecchi, Jonathan Roberts, and Linda Woolverton's screenplay *The Lion King* (1994)

James Cole in David and Janet Peoples's screenplay *Twelve Monkeys* (1995)

Jeremy Reed in Victor Salva's screenplay *Powder* (1995)

Sister Helen Prejean in Tim Robbins's screenplay *Dead Man Walking* (1995)

Karl Childers in Billy Bob Thornton's screenplay *Sling Blade* (1996)

Kikyo in Rumiko Takahashi's manga comic *Inuyasha* (1996)

John Coffey in Stephen King's short story *The Green Mile* (1996)

Harry Potter in J. K. Rowling's Harry Potter series (1997)

Adria the Orici in Brad Wright and Jonathan Glassner's television series *Stargate SG-1* (1997)

Leeloo in Luc Besson and Robert Mark Kamen's screenplay *The Fifth Element* (1997)

Hercules in Ron Clements and John Musker's screenplay *Hercules* (1997)

Blade in David S. Goyer's screenplay *Blade* (1998)

David in Gary Ross's screenplay *Pleasantville* (1998)

Private Witt in Terrence Malick's screenplay *The Thin Red Line* (1998)

Truman in Andrew Niccol's screenplay *The Truman Show* (1998)

Neo in Lana and Lilly Wachowski's screenplay *The Matrix* (1999)

The Iron Giant in Tim McCanlies and Brad Bird's screenplay *The Iron Giant* (1999)

Prot in Charles Leavitt's screenplay *K-Pax* (2001)

Anasûrimbor Kellhus in R. Scott Bakker's *The Prince of Nothing series (2004–2006) and The Aspect-Emperor* series (2009–2017)

Sonny in Jeff Vintar and Akiva Goldsman's screenplay *I, Robot* (2004)

Jack Shephard in J. J. Abrams, Jeffrey Lieber, and Damon Lindelof's television series *Lost* (2004–2010)

Evan Treborn in J. Mackye Gruber and Eric Bress's screenplay *The Butterfly Effect* (2004)

The Boy in Cormac McCarthy's novel *The Road* (2006)

King Leonidas I in Zack Snyder, Kurt Johnstad, and Michael B. Gordon's screenplay *300* (2007)

Lieutenant Commander Shepard in Drew Karpyshyn, Casey Hudson, and Preston Watamaniuk's *Mass Effect* video game series (2007–2017)

Bruce Wayne/Batman in Jonathan and Christopher Nolan's screenplay *The Dark Knight* (2008)

Walt in Nick Schenk's screenplay *Gran Torino* (2008)

Arlen in Peter V. Brett's novel *The Warded Man* (2008)

Katniss Everdeen in Suzanne Collins's *The Hunger Games* series (2008–2010)

Cole MacGrath in Sucker Punch Productions' *inFAMOUS* video game (2009)

Thomas in James Dashner's novel *The Maze Runner* (2009)

Signless in Andrew Hussie's webcomic *Homestuck* (2009)

Flynn Rider in Dan Fogelman's screenplay *Tangled* (2010)

Thor in Ashley Miller, Zack Stentz, and Don Payne's screenplay *Thor* (2011)

Anna in Chris Buck, Jennifer Lee, and Shane Morris's screenplay *Frozen* (2013)

Emmet in Phil Lord and Christopher Miller's screenplay *The Lego Movie* (2014)

Eleven in Matt and Ross Duffer's television series *Stranger Things* (2016)

Jesse Custer in Sam Catlin, Evan Goldberg, and Seth Rogen's television series *Preacher* (2016)

40. For larger, more readable images, please visit https://coldcasechristianity.com/selected -images-from-person-of-interest/.

41. For more information on identifying Christ figures, refer to this more robust profile and: "How to Identify a Christ Figure," Mill Valley School District, accessed March 12, 2021, https://www.mvschools.org/cms/lib03/CA01001212/Centricity/Domain/132/How %20to%20identify%20a%20Christ%20Figure%20in%20literature.doc.

42. "The story of [Tiberius Caesar's] reign is known from four sources, the *Annals* of Tacitus and the biography of Suetonius, written some eighty or ninety years later, the brief contemporary record of Velleius Paterculus, and the third-century history of Cassius

Dio. These disagree amongst themselves in the wildest possible fashion, both in major matters of political action or motive and in specific details of minor events. . . . But this does not prevent the belief that the material of Tacitus can be used to write a history of Tiberius." A. N. Sherwin White, *Roman Society and Roman Law in the New Testament: The Sarum Lectures 1960–1961* (Eugene, OR: Wipf & Stock, 2004), 187–88. In addition, New Testament scholar Justin Bass describes the evidence in this manner: "Tiberius was the most powerful man in the world of his day. Jesus was one of the poorest, belonging to the peasant class as a Jewish carpenter. He even died the most shameful death, a slave's death, on a cross during Tiberius' reign. Yet we have far more reliable written sources and closer to the time of Jesus' actual life and death than this Caesar of Rome." Justin Bass, *The Bedrock of Christianity: The Unalterable Facts of Jesus' Death and Resurrection* (Bellingham, WA: Lexham, 2020), cited at Sean McDowell, "The Historical Evidence for Jesus vs. Tiberius Caesar," Sean McDowell, May 22, 2020, https://seanmcdowell.org/blog/the-historical-evidence-for-jesus-is-greater-than-for-caesar#_ftn1.

Chapter 7: Jesus, the Dreary Deity?

1. Judicial Council of California, *Judicial Council of California Criminal Jury Instructions* (New York: Matthew Bender, 2021), CALCRIM No. 105, https://www.courts.ca.gov/partners/documents/calcrim-2021.pdf.

2. For more on the basilica at Ottobeuren Abbey, refer to Wikipedia, s.v. "Ottobeuren Abbey," last modified January 23, 2021, https://en.wikipedia.org/wiki/Ottobeuren_Abbey; or "Ottobeuren Abbey," Bavaria, accessed September 7, 2020, https://www.bavaria.by/experiences/city-country-culture/churches-monasteries/ottobeuren-abbey/.

3. For more on the nature of first-century churches in Israel, refer to Clifford Merton Jones, ed., *New Testament Illustrations: Photographs, Maps, and Diagrams* (London: Cambridge University Press, 1966), 61; and "Ancient Houses—What Were They Like?," Jesus's Story, accessed September 7, 2020, https://www.jesus-story.net/nazareth-houses/.

4. Excellent examples are Romanesque churches like the rural church of São Pedro de Lourosa: Paul M.R. Maeyaert, "Central nave of the Church of São Pedro de Lourosa (Coimbra)," July 2009, photograph, Wikipedia, accessed September 7, 2020, https://en.wikipedia.org/wiki/Portuguese_Romanesque_architecture#/media/File:PM_33274_P_Lourosa.jpg; and the Church of Igreja de São Fins de Friestas: José Antonio Gil Martínez, "Interior," November 2011, photograph, Wikipedia, accessed September 7, 2020, https://pt.wikipedia.org/wiki/Igreja_de_S%C3%A3o_Fins_de_Friestas#/media/Ficheiro:Mosteiro_de_Sanfins_de_Friestas.jpg.

5. There are many amazing examples of Christian dome architecture, from early primitive domes like the one at the Arian Baptistry in Ravenna, Italy: Petar Milošević, "Ceiling mosaic of Arian Baptistry," April 2015, photograph, Wikipedia, accessed September 7, 2020, https://en.wikipedia.org/wiki/Arian_Baptistery#/media/File:Arian_Baptistry_ceiling_mosaic_-_Ravenna.jpg; to the Gesu Jesuit Church Golden Dome Cupola in Rome, surrounded by windows and painted with heavenly images: Livio Andronico, "Dome," May 2015, photograph, Wikipedia, accessed September 7, 2020, https://en.wikipedia.org/wiki/Church_of_the_Ges%C3%B9#/media/File:Dome_of_Church_of_the_Ges%C3%B9_(Rome).jpg.

6. The plans for the dome are on display at the Metropolitan Museum in New York: Etienne DuPérac, "Speculum Romanae Magnificentiae: Longitudinal Section Showing

the Interior of Saint Peter's Basilica as Conceived by Michelangelo," 1569, print, The Met, New York, accessed September 7, 2020, https://www.metmuseum.org/art/collection /search/364511.

7. Travel sites for the city of Rome still tout this title: "Rome, the City of Domes," Walks inside Rome, accessed September 7, 2020, https://www.walksinsiderome.com/blog/about -rome/rome-the-city-of-domes/.

8. To review a few artistic highlights from this period of ancient Christian history, refer to our comprehensive Case Note PDF file, downloadable here: https://coldcasechristianity. com/case-notes-for-person-of-interest/.

9. Justin Martyr, *The First Apology of Justin, the Martyr*, Chapter 45, in *Early Christian Fathers*, ed. Cyril C. Richardson (New York: Touchstone, 1996). This work is available online: "*The First Apology of Justin, the Martyr*: The Text," Christian Classics Ethereal Library, accessed August 31, 2020, https://www.ccel.org/ccel/richardson/fathers.x.ii.iii.html.

10. To review a limited survey of Christian art during this period demonstrating the prolific diversity of creativity that dominated the Early Middle Ages, refer to our comprehensive Case Note PDF file, downloadable here: https://coldcasechristianity.com /case-notes-for-person-of-interest/.

11. To review a brief sample of art created in the Renaissance, refer to our comprehensive Case Note PDF file, downloadable here: https://coldcasechristianity.com/case-notes-for -person-of-interest/.

12. To review a sample of Christian art from the post-Renaissance, modern period, demonstrating the diversity of style, culture, and media used during this period, refer to our comprehensive Case Note PDF file, downloadable here: https://coldcase christianity.com/case-notes-for-person-of-interest/.

13. To review examples of how Jesus inspired art across the globe, refer to our comprehensive Case Note PDF file, downloadable here: https://coldcasechristianity.com/case-notes-for -person-of-interest/.

14. In *Cold-Case Christianity*, I make a case for the early dating of Mark, circa 45–50 CE. J. Warner Wallace, *Cold-Case Christianity: A Homicide Detective Investigates the Claims of the Gospels* (Colorado Springs: Cook Publishers, 2013), 160–171.

15. To review the ancient paintings, murals, etchings, and sculptures used to re-create the episodes in the gospel of Mark, refer to our comprehensive Case Note PDF file, downloadable here: https://coldcasechristianity.com/case-notes-for-person-of-interest/.

16. To review examples of how Jesus inspired every genre of art (along with the top masters in every genre), refer to our comprehensive Case Note PDF file, downloadable here: https://coldcasechristianity.com/case-notes-for-person-of-interest/.

17. To review descriptions of the images of the Buddha that demonstrate the homogenous nature of Buddhistic art across cultures, refer to our comprehensive Case Note PDF file, downloadable here: https://coldcasechristianity.com/case-notes-for-person-of-interest/.

18. To review descriptions of the art that demonstrates the diversity of genre and style in Jesus illustrations across nations, refer to our comprehensive Case Note PDF file, downloadable here: https://coldcasechristianity.com/case-notes-for-person-of-interest/.

19. "Forever," MP3 audio, track 2 on Chris Tomlin, *The Noise We Make*, Sparrow/sixstep, 2001.

20. Paul instructed local congregations to sing in a particular way: "What then, brothers? When you come together, each one has a hymn, a lesson, a revelation, a tongue, or an interpretation. Let all things be done for building up" (1 Corinthians 14:26 ESV),

"And do not get drunk with wine, for that is debauchery, but be filled with the Spirit, addressing one another in psalms and hymns and spiritual songs, singing and making melody to the Lord with your heart" (Ephesians 5:18–19 ESV). James also instructed congregations to continue singing: "Is anyone among you suffering? Let him pray. Is anyone cheerful? Let him sing praise" (James 5:13 ESV).

21. For more information on the early New Testament hymns, refer to Matthew E. Gordley, *New Testament Christological Hymns: Exploring Texts, Contexts, and Significance* (Downers Grove, IL: IVP Academic, 2018).

22. To review the Christian hymns used to assemble data about Jesus, refer to our comprehensive Case Note PDF file, downloadable here: https://coldcasechristianity.com /case-notes-for-person-of-interest/.

23. For larger, more readable images, please visit https://coldcasechristianity.com/selected -images-from-person-of-interest/. To review the details about Jesus that can be retrieved from the aforementioned hymns, refer to our comprehensive Case Note PDF file, downloadable here: https://coldcasechristianity.com/case-notes-for-person-of-interest/.

24. For larger, more readable images, please visit https://coldcasechristianity.com/selected -images-from-person-of-interest/. To review the periods of music history characterized by prominent Christians who contributed to the growth and development of musical style, refer to our comprehensive Case Note PDF file, downloadable here: https://cold casechristianity.com/case-notes-for-person-of-interest/.

25. For larger, more readable images, please visit https://coldcasechristianity.com/selected -images-from-person-of-interest/. To review the Christian innovators who helped advance the cause of music by contributing in a number of significant ways, refer to our comprehensive Case Note PDF file, downloadable here: https://coldcasechristianity.com /case-notes-for-person-of-interest/.

26. For larger, more readable images, please visit https://coldcasechristianity.com/selected -images-from-person-of-interest/. To review a partial list of 508 Christian recording artists (from 1950 to the present), refer to our comprehensive Case Note PDF file, downloadable here: https://coldcasechristianity.com/case-notes-for-person-of-interest/.

27. To review the list of the 148 greatest recording artists of all time (along with their songs about Jesus), refer to our comprehensive Case Note PDF file, downloadable here: https://coldcasechristianity.com/case-notes-for-person-of-interest/.

Chapter 8: Jesus, the Illiterate?

1. For more information about the departure of young people from Christianity, read the data posted on our Cold-Case Christianity website: J. Warner Wallace, "UPDATED: Are Young People Really Leaving Christianity," Cold-Case Christianity, January 12, 2019, https://coldcasechristianity.com/writings/are-young-people-really-leaving-christianity/. And for more information about the plight of young Christians and how we can better prepare them for university and beyond, see by Sean McDowell and J. Warner Wallace, *So the Next Generation Will Know: Preparing Young Christians for a Challenging World* (Colorado Springs: Cook, 2019).

2. For more on the manner in which Jesus repeated the words of Moses from Deuteronomy 6:5 but replaced Moses's use of the word *might* with the word *mind*, see my book *Forensic Faith: A Homicide Detective Makes the Case for a More Reasonable, Evidential Christian Faith* (Colorado Springs: Cook, 2017), 33–34.

3. Descriptions of the educational (catechism) process preceding baptism is described in the works of Augustine (*On the Merits and the Forgiveness of Sins*, *On the Catechising of the Uninstructed*, and Sermon 224), Ambrose (*On the Mysteries and The Treatise on the Sacraments*), Tertullian (*On Baptism*), Hippolytus (*A Text for Students*), and the Didache. For more information, refer to L. L. Mitchell, "The Development of Catechesis in the Third and Fourth Century: From Hippolytus to Augustine," in *A Faithful Church: Issues in the History of Catechesis*, eds. John H. Westerhoff and O. C. Edwards Jr. (Harrisburg, PA: Morehouse, 1981), 48–78.

4. Ulfilas's parents were Cappadocian Greeks who were enslaved by the Goths, and Ulfilas was either born into captivity or made captive when very young.

5. For more information, refer to D. James Kennedy and Jerry Newcombe, *What If Jesus Had Never Been Born?*, (Nashville: Thomas Nelson, 1994), 42.

6. For updated statistics, refer to "2020 Scripture Access Statistics," Wycliffe Global Alliance, accessed April 6, 2021, https://www.wycliffe.net/resources/statistics/.

7. For more on the limitations of Greek and Roman institutions of education, refer to Charles H. Haskins, *The Rise of Universities* (New York: Holt, 1923), 3.

8. For more information on the early use of the Didache, see Clayton N. Jefford, ed., *The Didache in Context: Essays on Its Text, History, and Transmission* (Leiden: Brill, 1995).

9. See Ignatius, *The Epistle of Ignatius to the Philadelphians*, in *The Ante-Nicene Fathers*, eds. Alexander Roberts and James Donaldson (Grand Rapids: Eerdmans, 1981), 1:81.

10. W. M. Ramsay, *The Church in the Roman Empire Before A.D. 170* (London: Hodder & Stoughton, 1893), 345.

11. For more, refer to *Wikipedia*, s.v. "School of Nisibis," last modified February 25, 2021, https://en.wikipedia.org/wiki/School_of_Nisibis.

12. Daniel J. Boorstin, *The Discoverers: A History of Man's Search to Know His World and Himself* (New York: Random House, 1983), 492–93.

13. *Britannica*, s.v. "Cassiodorus," accessed September 17, 2020, https://www.britannica.com/biography/Cassiodorus.

14. See a comprehensive list of the oldest schools in the world at Wikipedia, s.v. "List of Oldest Schools," last modified March 24, 2021, https://en.wikipedia.org/wiki/List_of_oldest_schools.

15. Pierre Riché, *Daily Life in the World of Charlemagne* (Philadelphia: University of Pennsylvania Press, 1988), 191.

16. Charlemagne, from his *"De litteris colendis,"* in *Translations and Reprints from the Original Sources of European History*, trans. D. C. Munro, vol. 6, bk. 5 (Philadelphia: University of Pennsylvania Press, 1900), 12–14. Also found here: "Charlemagne: Letter to Baugaulf of Fulda, c. 780–800," Internet History Sourcebooks Project, accessed April 6, 2021, https://sourcebooks.fordham.edu/source/carol-baugulf.asp.

17. This motto is still listed on the University's Wikipedia page: *Wikipedia*, s.v. "University of Bologna," accessed September 20, 2020, https://en.wikipedia.org/wiki/University_of_Bologna.

18. This is described at the university's website: "What Does the University's Motto 'Dominus Illuminatio Mea' Mean?," University of Oxford, last modified June 28, 2017, https://uni-of-oxford.custhelp.com/app/answers/detail/a_id/121/~/what-does-the-universitys-motto-dominus-illuminatio-mea-mean?. As John Dickerson describes, "looking to God as provider and director was the principle on which Oxford was

founded." John Dickerson, *Jesus Skeptic: A Journalist Explores the Credibility and Impact of Christianity* (Grand Rapids: Baker, 2019), 92.

19. For more, refer to *Britannica*, s.v. "Universities of Paris I–XIII," accessed September 20, 2020, https://www.britannica.com/topic/Universities-of-Paris-I-XIII.

20. J. K. Hyde, the professor of medieval history at the University of Manchester until he died in 1986, noted that all universities in the world are based on the three prototypes offered at Oxford, Paris, and Bologna. For more on this, refer to Thomas Bender, ed., *The University and the City: From Medieval Origins to the Present* (New York: Oxford University Press, 1988), 13. Charles Haskins observed that our modern universities are the "lineal descendant of medieval Paris and Bologna." For more on this, refer to Charles Homer Haskins, *The Rise of Universities* (New York: Henry Holt, 1923; London: Routledge, 2017), 5. Citation refers to the Routledge edition.

21. Gutenberg wasn't the first Westerner to develop a printing press, but he was the first to create the kind of press that made the mass production of books possible. He once said, "I know what I want to do: I wish to manifold [print] the Bible." For more on this, see Kennedy and Newcombe, *What If Jesus Had Never Been Born?*, 43.

22. Bugenhagen was also called the "father of the Deutsche volkschule" (the German public school). For more information, refer to Lars P. Qualben, *A History of the Christian Church* (New York: Thomas Nelson, 1958), 241.

23. For more information, refer to Douglas H. Shantz, "Philipp Melanchthon: The Church's Teacher, Luther's Colleague," *Christian Info News* (February 1997).

24. For more information, refer to John Comenius, "A Brief Proposal Regarding the Renewal of Schools in the Kingdom of Bohemia," in *J. A. Comenius: Selections from His Works* (Prague: Statni Pedagogicke Nakladatelstvi, 1964), 28.

25. For more on Jean-Baptiste de La Salle's role in education, refer to Gabriel Compayré, *The History of Pedagogy*, trans. W. H. Payne (Boston: D.C. Heath, 1896), 262.

26. Luther scolded parents who neglected the education of their children, writing, "I shall really go after the shameful, despicable, damnable parents who are not parents at all but despicable hogs and venomous beasts devouring their own young." Martin Luther, "Introduction: A Sermon on Keeping Children in School," in *Luther's Works: The Christian in Society III*, trans. Charles M. Jacobs, ed. Robert Schultz (Philadelphia: Fortress, 1967), 46:211.

27. Qualben, *A History of the Christian Church*, 270.

28. For more information about Friedrich Froebel's contribution to education, refer to Harry Good and James D. Teller, *A History of Western Education* (Boston: Houghton Mifflin, 1948), 281–85.

29. For more information on Johann Sturm, refer to Lewis Spitz and Barbara Sher Tinsley, *Johann Sturm on Education* (St. Louis: Concordia, 1995), 85. Sturm was convinced that students needed to be taught Christian values, and that without them all education was a waste of time. For more on this, refer to refer to Good and Teller, *A History of Western Education*, 153.

30. Michel de l'Épée developed sign language specifically for use in schools. He was motivated by a desire for deaf people to hear the gospel of Jesus Christ. For more information on this, refer to Harlan Lane, *When the Mind Hears: A History of the Deaf* (New York: Random House, 1984), 58.

31. For more information, refer to Richard A. Tennant and Marianne Gluszak Brown,

The American Sign Language Handshape Dictionary (Washington, DC: Clerc Books / Gallaudet University Press, 1998), 10.

32. Braille saw his work with the blind as a holy mission. On his deathbed, he said, "I'm convinced that my mission is finished on earth; I tasted yesterday the supreme delight; God condescended to brighten my eyes with the splendor of eternal hope." Alvin J. Schmidt, *How Christianity Changed the World* (Grand Rapids: Zondervan, 2001), 183.

33. A summary of Frank Charles Laubach's work can he found at *Wikipedia*, s.v. "Frank Laubach," last modified April 2, 2020, https://en.wikipedia.org/wiki/Frank_Laubach.

34. I conducted an internet search of universities in March 2020 and found 76 Buddhist, 52 Hindu, and 143 Jewish institutions. A search for Christian universities revealed 2,868 institutions.

35. "World University Rankings," The Center for World University Rankings, accessed September 22, 2020, https://cwur.org/; "U.S. News Best Colleges," U. S. News and World Report, accessed September 22, 2020, https://www.usnews.com/best-colleges; and "The 100 Best Universities in the World Today," The Best Schools, July 29, 2019, https://the bestschools.org/rankings/best-universities-world-today.

36. To review a summary of the Christian foundations for each university, refer to our comprehensive Case Note PDF file, downloadable here: https://coldcasechristianity.com /case-notes-for-person-of-interest/.

37. For larger, more readable images, please visit https://coldcasechristianity.com/selected -images-from-person-of-interest/. To review details about Jesus and his followers that can be discerned from campus buildings and charters, refer to our comprehensive Case Note PDF file, downloadable here: https://coldcasechristianity.com/case-notes-for-person-of-interest/.

38. To review what some university founders spoke or wrote about Jesus, refer to our comprehensive Case Note PDF file, downloadable here: https://coldcasechristianity.com /case-notes-for-person-of-interest/.

Chapter 9: Jesus, the Science Denier?

1. "Forensic Science," United States Department of Justice, last modified January 15, 2021, https://www.justice.gov/olp/forensic-science.

2. For a robust defense of theism (the existence of God) from science and philosophy, please read my book *God's Crime Scene: A Cold-Case Detective Examines the Evidence for a Divinely Created Universe* (Colorado Springs: Cook, 2015). In it, I present the evidence for intelligent design and demonstrate the insufficiencies of evolutionary processes.

3. Annie Laurie Gaylor, "Catherine Fahringer," Freedom from Religion Foundation, accessed September 28, 2020, https://ffrf.org/news/day/dayitems/item/14551-catherine -fahringer.

4. In addition, scientism is self-refuting. The statement, "Science is the only way to really know the truth," cannot be verified by science. This statement is a philosophical proclamation that defies its own claim: it cannot be verified or confirmed as "true" through any scientific examination or method. For people who make this claim, there is at least one truth they can know without the benefit of science: that science is the only way to really know the truth!

5. Barberini initially admired Galileo's intelligence and sharp, biting sense of humor. In 1611 he even defended Galileo's view on floating bodies, even though another leader, Cardinal Gonzaga, opposed Galileo.

6. When Barberini became pope in 1623, he conducted six interviews with Galileo. In these meetings, Urban gave Galileo permission to write about the Copernican *hypothesis*. But when Galileo published *Dialogue Concerning the Two Chief World Systems* in 1632, it contained the mocking description of a pope (named Simplicio) who held the Aristotelian views Galileo had previously debunked in his treatise. Urban never forgave Galileo for this indiscretion.

7. For a brief summary of Galileo's interaction with the Catholic Church, refer to Dinesh D'Souza, "An Atheist Fable: Reopening the Galileo Case," in *What's So Great about Christianity* (Carol Stream, IL: Tyndale, 2008). Also, Richard J. Blackwell, *Galileo, Bellarmine, and the Bible* (Notre Dame: University of Notre Dame Press, 1991).

8. Edward Grant, "Science and the Medieval University," in *Rebirth, Reform, and Resilience: Universities in Transition, 1300–1700*, eds. James M. Kittelson and Pamela J. Transue (Columbus: Ohio State University Press, 1984), 68–102.

9. "Between 1150 and 1500, more literate Europeans had had access to scientific materials than any of their predecessors in earlier cultures, thanks largely to the emergence, rapid growth, and naturalistic arts curricula of medieval universities." Michael H. Shank, "Myth 2: That the Medieval Christian Church Suppressed the Growth of Science," in *Galileo Goes to Jail and Other Myths about Science and Religion*, ed. Ronald L. Numbers (Cambridge: Harvard University Press, 2009), 26–27.

10. John Heilbron, *The Sun in the Church: Cathedrals as Solar Observatories* (Cambridge: Harvard University Press, 1999), 3. Also refer to David C. Lindberg and Ronald L. Numbers, eds., *When Science and Christianity Meet* (Chicago: University of Chicago Press, 2003).

11. Galileo Galilei to the Grand Duchess Christina of Tuscany, letter, 1615, available here: "Galileo Galilei: Letter to the Grand Duchess Christina of Tuscany, 1615," Internet History Sourcebooks Project, accessed April 7, 2021, https://sourcebooks.fordham.edu/mod/galileo-tuscany.asp. It should also be noted that this quote does *not* mean Galileo (or any of the Christian scientists who followed him) believed that the Bible had *nothing* to say about the nature of the real world as revealed by science. In fact, many scientific truths are affirmed in the Christian Scriptures, well before these truths were inferred from scientific discoveries. For example, the book of Job accurately describes important constellations (J. Warner Wallace, "Is the Astronomy in the Book of Job Scientifically Consistent?," Cold-Case Christianity, August 17, 2018, https://coldcasechristianity.com/writings/is-the-astronomy-in-the-book-of-job-scientifically-consistent/); Genesis accurately describes the standard cosmological model of a universe that came into being from nothing (J. Warner Wallace, "Is God Real? Science Agrees with the Bible: The Universe Began to Exist," Cold-Case Christianity, November 23, 2018, https://coldcasechristianity.com/writings/science-agrees-with-the-bible-the-universe-began-to-exist/); and numerous biblical passages correctly describe features of our world and the universe (J. Warner Wallace, "Scientific Consistency in the Bible Is More Important than Scientific Revelation," Cold-Case Christianity, April 20, 2018, https://coldcasechristianity.com/writings/scientific-consistency-in-the-bible-is-more-important-than-scientific-revelation/).

12. Galileo Galilei, *Discoveries and Opinions of Galileo*, ed. Stillman Drake (New York: Doubleday, 1957), 128.

13. This chart is clearly not to scale and was formed with "tip of the iceberg" statistics.

We gathered information from online resources for the most significant scientific developments and the most important scientists from all of history (including Christian and non-Christian scientists). If you're interested in replicating the chart, you might simply begin by searching for the most significant scientific discoveries or the most significant scientists in each century. This won't reveal *every* piece of data that could be used in a chart such as this, but it will reveal enough to create a proportional chart.

14. For more on this precipitous decline in Muslim scientific achievement, refer to Robert R. Reilly, *The Closing of the Muslim Mind: How Intellectual Suicide Created the Modern Islamist Crisis* (Wilmington, DE: Intercollegiate Studies Institute, 2010). Reilly argues that a theological battle took place within Islam between the Muʻtazilites (who were advocates of reason) and their opponents, the Ashʻarites (ultimately represented by al-Ghazali). As the theology of al-Ghazali and the Ashʻarites prevailed, the role of philosophy, reason, and scientific investigation suffered. According to Reilly, the Ashʻarites proposed a notion of God that allowed for Allah to change our world at any moment for motivations known only to Allah. If this is true, our ability—as humans—to understand causal relationships within the natural realm would be nullified, given that we cannot understand the unknown motivations of Allah. "The fatal disconnect," Reilly says, "between the Creator and the mind of his creature is the source of Sunni Islam's most profound woes. This bifurcation, located not in the Quran but in early Islamic theology, ultimately led to the closing of the Muslim mind." Reilly, *The Closing of the Muslim Mind*, 4.

15. Diogenes Allen, *Christian Belief in a Postmodern World: The Full Wealth of Conviction* (Louisville: Westminster John Knox, 1989), 23.

16. This illustration is from Hans Rottenhammer's 1602 CE painting, *Götterfest, Hochzeit von Bacchus und Ariadne* (*Festival of the gods, wedding of Bacchus and Ariadne*). It is typical of how the Greek and Roman gods have been depicted and reflects their nature. I've purposely clothed many of the gods in the illustration as most of them are naked in the original painting.

17. Alfred North Whitehead (1861–1947), a British mathematician and philosopher, wrote that the origin of science required Christianity's "insistence on the rationality of God." Alfred North Whitehead, *Science and the Modern World* (New York: Macmillan, 1925; New York: Free Press, 1997), 18. Citation refers to the Free Press edition.

18. *New World Encyclopedia*, s.v. "Johannes Kepler," accessed September 25, 2020, https://www.newworldencyclopedia.org/entry/Johannes_Kepler.

19. Galileo, "Letter to the Grand Duchess Christina."

20. Refer again to Psalm 19:1–2 and Romans 1:20.

21. Wernher von Braun, "Religious Implications of Space Exploration: A Personal View," November 22, 1971, Belmont Abbey College, North Carolina. Cited here: "Dr. Wernher von Braun at Wheaton College," ReCollections, Wheaton College, September 28, 2011, https://recollections.wheaton.edu/2011/09/dr-wernher-von-braun-at-wheaton-college/.

22. With very few exceptions. For example, Archimedes (c. 287–c. 212 BCE) built a water screw and a device to study geometry, and Galen (c. 129–c. 210 CE) dissected animals and some human cadavers.

23. Oxford Reference, s.v. "miracle," accessed March 12, 2021, https://www.oxfordreference.com/view/10.1093/oi/authority.20110803100200612#:~:text=A%20surprising%20and%20welcome%20event,%2C%20from%20mirus%20'wonderful'.

24. For more, refer to Lynn White, "The Significance of Medieval Christianity," in *The Vitality of the Christian Tradition*, ed. George F. Thomas (New York: Harper, 1945), 93.

25. For larger, more readable images, please visit https://coldcasechristianity.com/selected -images-from-person-of-interest/. To review a list of ancient Christians who contributed to the development of the sciences, refer to our comprehensive Case Note PDF file, downloadable here: https://coldcasechristianity.com/case-notes-for-person-of-interest/.

26. The kalam cosmological argument is based on the notion of a "prime mover." William Lane Craig has popularized the argument with the following syllogism:

    1. Whatever begins to exist has a cause.
    2. The universe began to exist.
    3. Therefore, the universe has a cause.

    Accordingly, if the universe has a cause, then an uncaused, personal Creator of the universe exists:

    > Transcending the entire universe there exists a cause which brought the universe into being ex nihilo . . . our whole universe was caused to exist by something beyond it and greater than it. For it is no secret that one of the most important conceptions of what theists mean by 'God' is Creator of heaven and earth. (William Lane Craig and J. P. Moreland, eds., *The Blackwell Companion to Natural Theology* [New York: Wiley, 2009], 149.)

27. To review a list of Christians who contributed to the development of the sciences in the Early Middle Ages, refer to our comprehensive Case Note PDF file, downloadable here: https://coldcasechristianity.com/case-notes-for-person-of-interest/.

28. For larger, more readable images, please visit https://coldcasechristianity.com/selected -images-from-person-of-interest/.

29. According to Gary Ferngren, Ph.D. (an expert on the early formation of hospitals), "The hospital was, in origin and conception, a distinctively Christian institution, rooted in Christian concepts of charity and philanthropy. There were no pre-Christian institutions in the ancient world that served the purpose that Christian hospitals were created to serve. . . . None of the provisions for health care in classical times . . . resembled hospitals as they developed in the late fourth century" Gary B. Ferngren, *Medicine and Health Care in Early Christianity* (Baltimore: Johns Hopkins University Press, 2016), 124. A more robust chronicle of the role Christianity played in the formation of early modern hospitals can be found here: Chris R. Armstrong, ed., "Healthcare and Hospitals in the Mission of the Church," *Christian History* no. 101 (2011), accessed February 24, 2021, https://christianhistoryinstitute.org/magazine/issue /healthcare-and-hospitals-in-the-mission-of-the-church.

30. Wikipedia, s.v. "Catholic Church and health care," accessed February 24, 2021, https:// en.wikipedia.org/wiki/Catholic_Church_and_health_care.

31. To review a list of Christians who contributed to the development of the sciences in the Middle Ages, refer to our comprehensive Case Note PDF file, downloadable here: https:// coldcasechristianity.com/case-notes-for-person-of-interest/.

32. To review a list of Christians who contributed to the development of the sciences in the early Renaissance period, refer to our comprehensive Case Note PDF file, downloadable here: https://coldcasechristianity.com/case-notes-for-person-of-interest/.

33. To review a list of Christians who contributed to the development of the sciences in the scientific revolution, refer to our comprehensive Case Note PDF file, downloadable here: https://coldcasechristianity.com/case-notes-for-person-of-interest/.

34. For larger, more readable images, please visit https://coldcasechristianity.com/selected -images-from-person-of-interest/.

35. The Accademia dei Lincei (founded in Rome in 1603), the Accademia del Cimento (founded in Florence in 1657), the Royal Society of London (founded in England in 1660), and the Royal Academy of Sciences (founded in Paris in 1666) were all founded by Christians or had Christians as their majority membership.

36. For larger, more readable images, please visit https://coldcasechristianity.com/selected -images-from-person-of-interest/.

37. Richard Dawkins, *The Blind Watchmaker: Why the Evidence of Evolution Reveals a Universe without Design* (New York: Norton, 1986), 6.

38. To review a list of Christians who contributed to the development of the sciences in the late modern period, refer to our comprehensive Case Note PDF file, downloadable here: https://coldcasechristianity.com/case-notes-for-person-of-interest/.

39. For larger, more readable images, please visit https://coldcasechristianity.com/selected -images-from-person-of-interest/. To review a list of Christian scientists who were instrumental in advocating or interacting with the theory of evolution, refer to our comprehensive Case Note PDF file, downloadable here: https://coldcasechristianity.com /case-notes-for-person-of-interest/.

40. To review a list of living Christian scientists who are still active in their disciplines, refer to our comprehensive Case Note PDF file, downloadable here: https://coldcase christianity.com/case-notes-for-person-of-interest/.

41. *New World Encyclopedia*, s.v. "Johannes Kepler."

42. For the names related to each "science father," refer to the Case Notes related to each group of contributors.

43. To review a list institutions, societies, academies, associations, and universities that have given awards to Christian scientists, refer to our comprehensive Case Note PDF file, downloadable here: https://coldcasechristianity.com/case-notes-for-person-of -interest/.

44. This diagram was constructed from research found in Baruch Aba Shalev, *100 Years of Nobel Prizes* (New Delhi, India: Atlantic, 2003).

45. For more on this, refer to Shalev, *100 Years of Nobel Prizes* and "Religion of Nobel Prize Winners," Wikimedia Commons, last modified February 2, 2021, https://commons.wiki media.org/wiki/File:Religion_of_Nobel_Prize_winners.png.

46. Refer to Lee Rainie, Scott Keeter, and Andrew Perrin, "Trust and Distrust in America," Pew Research Center, July 22, 2019, https://www.pewresearch.org/politics/2019/07/22 /trust-and-distrust-in-america/.

47. For larger, more readable images, please visit https://coldcasechristianity.com/selected -images-from-person-of-interest/. To review a summary of the claims historic (and contemporary) scientists have made about the nature of Jesus and his followers, refer to our comprehensive Case Note PDF file, downloadable here: https://coldcasechristianity .com/case-notes-for-person-of-interest/.

48. Henry F. Schaefer III, *Science and Christianity: Conflict or Coherence?* (Athens, GA: University of Georgia, 2003), 71.

Chapter 10: Jesus, the One and Only?

1. Indra (the god we described in chapter 3) is an ancient deity in the Hindu religion.
2. For more information on sadhus, refer to Encyclopedia.com, s.v. "Sadhu," last updated February 27, 2021, https://www.encyclopedia.com/philosophy-and-religion/eastern -religions/hinduism/sadhu.
3. For an excellent description of how one Hindu perceives saint Ishu, read Shaunaka Rishi Das, "Jesus in Hinduism," BBC, last modified March 24, 2009, https://www.bbc.co .uk/religion/religions/hinduism/beliefs/jesus_1.shtml.
4. For more on this, refer to "Digest 224A: Srila Prabhupada as Acharya," Ask Romapada Swami, accessed March 12, 2021, https://askromapadaswami.com/digest-00224a-srila -prabhupada-as-acharya-by-romapadaswami.
5. More on this also at Das, "Jesus in Hinduism."
6. Some Hindus see Jesus as a symbol of what humans can attain, rather than as a true historical person.
7. Huston Smith describes it similarly: "Many Hindus acknowledge Christ as a God-man, while believing that there have been others, such as Rama, Krishna, and the Buddha." Huston Smith, *The World's Religions: Our Great Wisdom Traditions* (New York: HarperOne, 1991), 36. For many Hindus, Jesus is divine in his modeling, if not in his nature, and he is not the only such model. Jesus is simply one of many "ishtas" (forms of the divine) in the history of humankind.
8. Gandhi once said the Sermon on the Mount in the New Testament "went straight to my heart." M. K. Gandhi, *An Autobiography or The Story of My Experiments with Truth* (Ahmedabad: Navajivan, 1927), 49. He also said, "What does Jesus mean to me? To me, he was one of the greatest teachers humanity has ever had." M. S. Deshpande, ed., *Light of India: Message of the Mahatmaji* (Mumbai: Wilco Publishing House, 1958), 66.
9. Gandhi said, "Jesus lived and died in vain if He did not teach us to regulate the whole of life by the eternal law of love." M. K. Gandhi, *Non-Violence in Peace and War, Volume I* (Ahmedabad: Navajivan, 1948), 181; and "Jesus was the most active resister known perhaps to history. His was non-violence par excellence." Gandhi, *Non-Violence in Peace and War*, 1:16. From Gandhi again: "Jesus expressed as no other could the spirit and will of God. It is in this sense that I see him and recognize as the Son of God. And because the life of Jesus has the significance and the transcendence to which I have alluded, I believe that he belongs not solely to Christianity but to the entire world, to all races and people. It matters little under what flag, name or doctrine they may work, profess a faith or worship a God inherited from their ancestors." M. K. Gandhi, *My Religion*, ed. Bharatan Kumarappa (Ahmedabad: Navajivan, 1955), 25.
10. This map was reconstructed with data from Pew Research: "Percentage of Hindus by Country, According to the Pew Research Center," *Wikipedia*, June 29, 2014, https://en .wikipedia.org/wiki/Hinduism_by_country#/media/File:Hinduism_percent_population _in_each_nation_World_Map_Hindu_data_by_Pew_Research.svg.
11. For more information on Pausanias, refer to "Pausanias, Description of Greece, Book 1.1–16," Theoi Project, accessed April 8, 2021, https://www.theoi.com/Text/Pausanias 1A.html. This site includes a translation of his work: Pausanias, *Description of Greece*, trans. W. H. S. Jones and H. A. Ormerod, Loeb Classical Library Volumes (Cambridge, MA: Harvard University Press; London: William Heinemann, 1918). According to Jan Bremmer, "Apparently, things started to change in the second century CE when

Pausanias (7.17.12) relates that his body would not see corruption. Arnobius' mention of the moving little finger probably has to be assigned to the same period." Jan N. Bremmer, "Attis: A Greek God in Anatolian Pessinous and Catullan Rome," *Mnemosyne* 57, no. 5 (2004): 534–73, www.jstor.org/stable/4433594. See Pausanias, *Description of Greece* 7.17.12, available online here: "Pausanias, Description of Greece, Book 7.17–27," Theoi Project, accessed April 8, 2021, https://www.theoi.com/Text/Pausanias7B.html.

12. According to George C. Ring, "The likelihood is that the propagandists of the Cybele and Attis cult acquired an imperfect knowledge of rebirth in Christ, borrowed the term renatus and attached it clumsily to a pagan purification rite." George C. Ring, "Christ's Resurrection and the Dying and Rising Gods," *The Catholic Biblical Quarterly* 6, no. 2 (April 1944): 224, www.jstor.org/stable/43719772. In addition, Duncan Fishwick states, "One would think the addition of an earlier stage to the cycle of Attis' life coincided with the new importance Attis assumed in the second half of the second century when he first became a god of resurrection and the rival of Dionysus and Osiris." Duncan Fishwick, "The Cannophori and the March Festival of Magna Mater," *Transactions and Proceedings of the American Philological Association* 97 (1966): 198, https://www.jstor .org/stable/2936006. In addition, Fishwick states, "The final stage of development saw the growth of the Hilaria into the high point of a festival that by the third and fourth centuries A. D. celebrated the death and resurrection of Attis. When exactly the joyful rites of this day (their nature is uncertain) first found their place in the cult is not clear. The earliest possible mention is a passage in the Historia Augusta from the life of Alexander Severus (37.6); all other texts belong to the late third and fourth centuries." Fishwick, "The Cannophori and the March Festival," 202. Fishwick demonstrates that stories of Attis's resurrection and divinity (and the creation of rebirth ceremonies for followers) came well after the appearance of Christianity.

13. G. Sfameni Gasparro agrees: "The Attis cult evolved in response to Christianity." G. Sfameni Gasparro, *Soteriology and Mystic Aspects in the Cult of Cybele and Attis: Education and Society in the Middle Ages and Renaissance* (Leiden: Brill Academic, 1997), 106.

14. "Also, in philosophical circles, especially among Stoics and Cynics, and thanks to an allegorical interpretation of his legend, Hercules had then become a paragon of the wise man and the incarnation of all virtues. Concurrently, philosophical thought endowed with him a cosmic significance. The Stoic Cornutus, giving an allegorical exegesis of mythology in his treatise Theologiae Graecae Compendium, shows Hercules as 'the Logos infused in all things, which gives nature both its power and its cohesion.'" Marcel Simon, "Early Christianity and Pagan Thought: Confluences and Conflicts," *Religious Studies* 9, no. 4 (December 1973): 396, https://www.jstor.org/stable/20005092.

15. Simon, "Early Christianity and Pagan Thought," 396.

16. John described Jesus as the Logos (the "Word") in John 1:1 and John 1:14.

17. In Colossians 1:17, Paul describes Jesus as "before all things, and in him all things hold together."

18. "The Christian influence appears even more indisputable in the case of Julian the Apostate. There is hardly a doubt that here transposition and plagiarism were deliberate. In his eyes, Hercules was the model both of a wise man and of a sovereign. To the traditional feats which Hercules was credited with by mythology, Julian added others: Hercules crossed the sea dry-shod, an obvious transposition of the episode in

the Gospel when Jesus walks on the waters. His interpretation of Hercules' character was directly inspired by Christianity. It is to make him the saviour of the universe that Jupiter begot his son: which he did through the agency of Athene Pronoia, who played a part very closely comparable to—and described in the same terms as—that which the Christian symbols of faith attribute to the Holy Ghost. So that the divine triad thus sketched out closely resembles a Trinity." Simon, "Early Christianity and Pagan Thought," 398. For further confirmation of Julian's influence and beliefs related to Heracles, refer to David Neal Greenwood, "Crafting Divine Personae in Julian's *Oration 7*," *Classical Philology* 109, no. 2 (2014): 140–49, https://doi.org/10.1086/675618.

19. Simon, "Early Christianity and Pagan Thought," 398.

20. Justin Martyr describes several adaptations of mythology to incorporate elements of the Jesus story:

> "Be well assured, then, Trypho," I continued, "that I am established in the knowledge of and faith in the Scriptures by those counterfeits which he who is called the devil is said to have performed among the Greeks; just as some were wrought by the Magi in Egypt, and others by the false prophets in Elijah's days. For when they tell that Bacchus, son of Jupiter, was begotten by [Jupiter's] intercourse with Semele, and that he was the discoverer of the vine; and when they relate, that being torn in pieces, and having died, he rose again, and ascended to heaven; and when they introduce wine into his mysteries, do I not perceive that [the devil] has imitated the prophecy announced by the patriarch Jacob, and recorded by Moses? And when they tell that Hercules was strong, and travelled over all the world, and was begotten by Jove of Alcmene, and ascended to heaven when he died, do I not perceive that the Scripture which speaks of Christ, 'strong as a giant to run his race,' has been in like manner imitated? And when he [the devil] brings forward sculapius as the raiser of the dead and healer of all diseases, may I not say that in this matter likewise he has imitated the prophecies about Christ?" (Justin Martyr, *Dialogue with Trypho* 69. Available online here: "Roberts-Donaldson English Translation: *Dialogue with Trypho*," Early Christian Writings, accessed April 8, 2021, http://www.earlychristianwritings.com/text/justinmartyr-dialoguetrypho.html.)

21. "The German writer, Weber, held that Krishnaism was indebted to Christianity on the grounds that the worship of Krishna as the sole deity was a post-Christian phase in Hinduism, and the legend of his birth and the celebration of his birthdays, the honour paid to his mother Devika, and his life as a herdsman, all showed Christian influence (XI p. 131) . . . Summing up the data Hopkins says, 'Considering how late are these Krishna legends in India, there can be no doubt that the Hindus borrowed the tales, but not in name.'" Benjamin Walker, *The Hindu World: An Encyclopedic Survey of Hinduism, in Two Volumes, vol. 1* (New York: Praeger, 1968), 240.

22. Dr. Edwin Bryant, professor of Hinduism at Rutgers University, observes that parallels such as this one come from two Hindu scriptures, the Bhagavata Purana and the Harivamsa. Bryant believes the Bhagavata Purana "to be prior to the 7th century CE (although many scholars have hitherto considered it to be 11 century CE)." Mike Licona, "A Refutation of Acharaya S's Book, The Christ Conspiracy," Risen Jesus, July 8, 2015, https://www.risenjesus.com/a-refutation-of-acharya-ss-book-the-christ-conspiracy. Most

sources place the composition of the Harivamsa between the fourth and sixth centuries CE. Both scriptures appear hundreds of years after the gospel accounts had been written and circulated.

23. Scholar Richard Garbe states,

> The celebration of Krishna's birthday, however, is an imitation of the Christian festival. . . . We have proof that the first Nestorian mission into central north India took place in the year 639; and since there is no doubt that the Christmas festival and other Christian elements had been brought by the Nestorians into that region, that is, into the home of Krishnaism, the time (the first half of the seventh century) agrees very well with the age of the Puranas which are our earliest sources for the observance of Krishna's birthday . . . Christian influence upon the Krishna festival is further very distinctly betrayed by the fact that in it the scene of the ancient Krishna legend—according to which Krishna was born in prison under circumstances of poverty and danger and was made away with in great haste and rescued by his father—appears in a completely altered form. The place of Krishna's birth has become a peaceful cattle stall (*gokula*) in which form for the festive purpose a confinement home (*sûtikâgriha*) is set up and is fitted out with a picture of the mother lying upon a bed with the divine child at her breast, and also with paintings or sculptured representations of Krishna's father, of shepherds and shepherdesses, cattle, asses, etc., including all sorts of deities and demigods in the air. Hence exactly the same as the scene among the shepherds after the birth of the Saviour is represented in Christianity for purposes of edification . . . The result of the whole festival is that the Christian stories of the birth of Jesus are widely known in their Indian garb among the Hindus down to the present day, even if otherwise they know nothing of Christianity. (Richard Garbe, "Christian Elements in Later Krishnaism and in Other Hinduistic Sects," *The Monist* 24, no. 1 (January 1914): 36–41, https://www.jstor.org/stable/27900474.)

In addition, "Some scholars believe that, except for the name, the Krishna cycle of stories has borrowed extensively from Christian sources, especially in relation to the birth, childhood and divinity of Jesus. The Great orientalist, Sir William Jones, held that the spurious Gospels which abounded in the first years of Christianity found their way to India and were known to the Hindus." Walker, *The Hindu World*, 240.

24. "The German writer, [Albrecht] Weber, held that Krishnaism was indebted to Christianity on the grounds that the worship of Krishna as the sole deity was a post-Christian phase in Hinduism, and the legend of his birth and the celebration of his birthdays, the honour paid to his mother Devika, and his life as a herdsman, all showed Christian influence (XI p. 131). . . . Summing up the data [Edward Washburn] Hopkins says, 'Considering how late are these Krishna legends in India, there can be no doubt that the Hindus borrowed the tales, but not in name.'" Walker, *The Hindu World*, 240.

25. "According to others, Krishna's victory over Kaliya is a travestied version of Christ's victory over Satan, the Serpent." Walker, *The Hindu World*, 240.

26. "The legend there given of the raising of the dead son of Duhshalâ by Krishna must be referred to Christian influence, because the older form of the story of Duhshalâ as it appears in the *Mahâbhârata*, XIV, 2275–2297, knows nothing of the awakening of the son." Garbe, "Christian Elements in Later Krishnaism," 42.

27. "Krishna Consciousness (Bhakti-Yoga)," Krishna.com, accessed October 3, 2020, http://www.krishna.com/info/krishna-consciousness-bhakti-yoga.

28. "God also has unlimited representatives—His devotees—who work on His behalf to give knowledge and love of God to everyone in the material world. Jesus was the perfect guru, showing by example how to love and serve God. For us to be able to love God, we have to learn about Him from someone who knows—God's trusted representative—and to have as much faith in his representative as we have in God Himself." "If Jesus Is the Only Way, Is Krishna Consciousness Invalid?," Krishna.com, accessed October 3, 2020, http://www.krishna.com/if-jesus-only-way-krishna-consciousness-invalid.

29. "We accept Christ as the Son of God, as God's empowered representative on earth, but not as the sole representative who has ever come or will ever come. The Supreme Person visits this world in many ways. Sometimes God sends His son, like Christ, but sometimes He comes Himself, as Krishna or Rama." "Jesus, Christianity, and Hell," Krishna.com, accessed October 3, 2020, http://www.krishna.com/jesus-christianity-and-hell.

30. Srila Prabhupada once said,

> Such a great personality, the son of God. He wanted to deliver God consciousness. And in return, he was crucified. We don't take Jesus Christ as insignificant. We give him all honor. He is a pure representative of God. Of course, he directed his preaching according to time, place, and circumstance, the era and region and people's mentality. In any case, he is a pure representative of God. . . . Unless Christ is God's representative, how can he be so enduringly famous? That we know—Christ represents God. In Melbourne, when a priest asked me, "What is your idea of Jesus Christ?" I told them, "He's our guru." This they very much appreciated. Christ is preaching consciousness of God. So he is our guru, our spiritual master. That's a fact. Don't take him otherwise. He's our guru. ("Christ Is Our Guru," Krishna.com, accessed October 3, 2020, http://www.krishna.com/christ-our-guru.)

In addition, Srila Prabhupada repeatedly refers to Jesus as "Lord Jesus" in interviews such as the ones found here: "The Reading Room," Krishna.com, accessed April 8, 2021, http://www.krishna.com/taxonomy/term/76/contact?page=2.

31. As an example, the dialogue quoted at "Christ is Our Guru," Krishna.com, demonstrates the degree to which Hare Krishna believers accept what is written in the New Testament (even as they make different inferences from the biblical data).

32. J. P. Arendzen wrote, "The origin of the cult of Mithra dates from the time that the Hindus and Persians still formed one people, for the god Mithra occurs in the religion and the sacred books of both races, i.e. in the Vedas and in the Avesta. In Vedic hymns he is frequently mentioned and is nearly always coupled with Varuna, but beyond the bare occurrence of his name, little is known of him." J. P. Arendzen, "Mithraism," *The Catholic Encyclopedia*, vol. 10 (New York: Appleton, 1911). Available online here: "Mithraism," New Advent, accessed October 3, 2020, http://www.newadvent.org/cathen/10402a.htm. In addition, Bruce Metzger, the Princeton biblical scholar, suggested this idea of rebirth was likely an example of Christianity influencing Mithraism. See Lee Strobel, *The Case for the Real Jesus: A Journalist Investigates Current Attacks on the Identity of Christ* (Grand Rapids: Zondervan, 2007), 175.

33. "The form of the cult most familiar to us, the initiatory cult, does not seem to derive from Persia at all. It is found first in the west, has no significant resemblance to its supposed Persian 'origins', and seems largely to be a western construct." Mary Beard, John S. North, and Simon Price, *Religions of Rome: Volume 1, A History* (New York: Cambridge University Press, 1998), 279.

34. "The idea of a rebirth through the instrumentality of the taurobolium only emerges in isolated instances towards the end of the fourth century A.D.; it is not originally associated with this blood-bath." Gunter Wagner, *Pauline Baptism and the Pagan Mysteries: The Problem of the Pauline Doctrine of Baptism in Romans VI.1–11, in the Light of its Religio-Historical "Parallels,"* (Edinburgh: Oliver & Boyd, 1967), 266.

35. The earliest dating for this liturgy is somewhere between the mid-second century and the fourth century. Refer to Marvin Meyer, "The Mithras Liturgy," in *The Historical Jesus in Context*, eds. A. J. Levine, Dale C. Allison Jr., and John Dominic Crossan (Princeton: Princeton University Press, 2006), 182. This is well after the earliest Christian document establishes a similar meal (Paul's description of the Lord's Supper in 1 Corinthians 11, dated as early as 55 CE). In addition, Justin Martyr described this borrowing from Christianity in *First Apology*, chapter 66 (written between 155 and 157 CE): "For the apostles, in the memoirs composed by them, which are called Gospels, have thus delivered unto us what was enjoined upon them; that Jesus took bread, and when He had given thanks, said, 'This do ye in remembrance of Me, this is My body,' and that, after the same manner, having taken the cup and given thanks, He said, 'This is My blood,' and gave it to them alone. Which the wicked devils have imitated in the mysteries of Mithras, commanding the same thing to be done. For, that bread and a cup of water are placed with certain incantations in the mystic rites of one who is being initiated, you either know or can learn." Available online here: "Saint Justin Martyr (110–165), *First Apology*, Chapter 66," Logos Virtual Library, accessed March 12, 2021, https://www.logoslibrary.org/justin/apology1/66.html.

36. Nyogen Senzaki, "Not Far from Buddhahood," in *101 Zen Stories* (London: Rider, 1919).

37. According to the Dalai Lama, "Jesus Christ also lived previous lives. So, you see, he reached a high state, either as a *Bodhisattva*, or an enlightened person, through Buddhist practice or something like that." James A. Beverley, *Nelson's Illustrated Guide to Religions: A Comprehensive Introduction to the Religions of the World* (Nashville: Thomas Nelson, 2009), 68.

38. His Holiness the Dalai Lama, *The Good Heart: A Buddhist Perspective on the Teachings of Jesus* (Somerville, MA: Wisdom, 1996), 83. Also discussed here: John B. Cobb Jr., review of *A Good Heart: A Buddhist Perspective on the Teachings of Jesus*, by His Holiness the Dalai Lama, *Journal of Ecumenical Studies* 34, no. 4 (Fall 1997): 580, http://ccbs.ntu.edu.tw/FULLTEXT/JR-EPT/cobb.htm.

39. For example, when talking about the Sermon on the Mount, the Dalai Lama, said, "About the sermon on the mount: The practice of tolerance and patience that is being advocated in these passages is extremely similar to the practice of tolerance and patience that is advocated in Buddhism in general." His Holiness the Dalai Lama, *The Good Heart*, 46.

40. "And so, in the Christian tradition, we see that one does not read the Gospels merely to learn about the facts of the life of Jesus or the answers to catechism questions. It is an awakening of the mystical intelligence. One could say that reading the Gospels in this

way is the strengthening of buddhi, spiritual intelligence." Laurence Freeman in His Holiness the Dalai Lama, *The Good Heart*, 26.

41. Buddhists accept this miracle of Jesus in addition to many others, although "magical acts" such as these are not seen as exceptional: "Magic as such is theologically neutral for Buddhists. Most, and perhaps all, of the extraordinary feats Jesus performed Buddhists would classify as "common accomplishments" (*thun mongs ba'I dngos grub*): common because they are feats that can be accomplished by Buddhists and non-Buddhists alike, requiring a certain degree of meditative competence, but no real degree of permanent spiritual maturity. This being said, the fact that Jesus performed these various actions for the benefit of others does point to an important fact: namely, that he was operating from an altruistic motivation, and this perhaps is the more important point for Buddhists: not that Jesus was a magician, but that he was a loving one." José Ignacio Cabezón, "Jesus through a Buddhist's Eyes," *Buddhist-Christian Studies* 19 (1999): 54, https://www.jstor.org/stable/1390519.

42. These passages are described specifically in His Holiness the Dalai Lama, *The Good Heart*. While the Dalai Lama may interpret the passages differently than Christians, he accepts the teaching of the New Testament as a reliable account of the teaching and actions of Jesus.

43. This map was reconstructed with data from Pew Research: "Percentage of Buddhists by Country, According to Pew Research Center," Wikipedia, June 29, 2014, https://en .wikipedia.org/wiki/Buddhism_by_country#/media/File:Buddhism_percent_population _in_each_nation_World_Map_Buddhist_data_by_Pew_Research.svg.

44. "She said, 'Indeed, I seek refuge in the Most Merciful from you, [so leave me], if you should be fearing of Allah.' He said, 'I am only the messenger of your Lord to give you [news of] a pure boy.' She said, 'How can I have a boy while no man has touched me and I have not been unchaste?' He said, 'Thus [it will be]; your Lord says, "It is easy for Me, and We will make him a sign to the people and a mercy from Us. And it is a matter [already] decreed.'" So she conceived him, and she withdrew with him to a remote place," (Qur'an 19:18–22). Both Muslims and Christians believe that Jesus was miraculously born without a human biological father by the will of God and that his mother, Mary (Maryam in Arabic), is among the most saintly, pious, chaste, and virtuous women ever. See John Esposito, *What Everyone Needs to Know About Islam* (New York: Oxford University Press, 2002), 31.

45. From the Qur'an 19:19: "He responded, 'I am only a messenger from your Lord, sent to bless you with a pure son.'" And from the Qur'an 3:36: "When she delivered, she said, 'My Lord! I have given birth to a girl,'—and Allah fully knew what she had delivered—'and the male is not like the female. I have named her Mary, and I seek Your protection for her and her offspring from Satan, the accursed.'" The Islamic Hadith (a collection of Muslim literature said to contain the words and actions of the prophet Muhammad) also affirms that Allah uniquely prevented Satan from touching Jesus in any way. "Abu Huraira said, 'I heard Allah's Apostle saying, "There is none born among the off-spring of Adam, but Satan touches it. A child therefore, cries loudly at the time of birth because of the touch of Satan, except Mary and her child.'"" *Sahih al-Bukhari (The Authentic Collection)* 4.55.641, https://www.sahih-bukhari.com/Pages /Bukhari_4_55.php. "Abu Huraira reported Allah's Messenger (may peace be upon him) as saying: The satan touches every son of Adam on the day when his mother gives

birth to him with the exception of Mary and her son," *Sahih Muslim* 30.5838, http://www.hadithcollection.com/sahihmuslim/Sahih%20Muslim%20Book%2030.%20The%20Excellent%20Qualities%20Of%20The%20Holy%20Prophet%20(PBUH)%20And%20His%20Companions/sahih-muslim-book-030-hadith-number-5838.html.

46. "Then We sent following their footsteps Our messengers and followed [them] with Jesus, the son of Mary, and gave him the Gospel. And We placed in the hearts of those who followed him compassion and mercy," (Qur'an 57:27); "O you who have believed, be supporters of Allah, as when Jesus, the son of Mary, said to the disciples, 'Who are my supporters for Allah?' The disciples said, 'We are supporters of Allah.' And a faction of the Children of Israel believed and a faction disbelieved. So We supported those who believed against their enemy, and they became dominant" (Qur'an 61:14).

47. "And We did certainly give Moses the Torah and followed up after him with messengers. And We gave Jesus, the son of Mary, clear proofs and supported him with the Pure Spirit. But is it [not] that every time a messenger came to you, [O Children of Israel], with what your souls did not desire, you were arrogant? And a party [of messengers] you denied and another party you killed" (Qur'an 2:87). The Qur'an specifies that Jesus was able to perform miracles—though only by the will of God—including being able to raise the dead, restore sight to the blind, and cure lepers. See Diane Morgan, *Essential Islam: A Comprehensive Guide to Belief and Practice* (Santa Barbara, CA: ABC-Clio, 2010), 45–46. One miracle attributed to Jesus in the Qur'an but not in the New Testament is his being able to speak at only a few days old, to defend his mother from accusations of adultery (Qur'an 19:27–33). "I cure the blind and the leper, and I give life to the dead—by permission of Allah. And I inform you of what you eat and what you store in your houses. Indeed in that is a sign for you, if you are believers" (Qur'an 3:49).

48. "[Mention] when Allah said, 'O Jesus, indeed I will take you and raise you to Myself and purify you from those who disbelieve and make those who follow you [in submission to Allah alone] superior to those who disbelieve until the Day of Resurrection. Then to Me is your return, and I will judge between you concerning that in which you used to differ'" (Qur'an 3:55).

49. While Muhammad is described as the final prophet from God, he listed the previous prophets and included Jesus in that list. Muslims believe Jesus was a prophet, but they deny that he is God: "The Messiah, son of Mary, was not but a messenger; [other] messengers have passed on before him. And his mother was a supporter of truth. They both used to eat food. Look how We make clear to them the signs; then look how they are deluded" (Qur'an 5:75). The Qur'an mentions Jesus by name twenty-five times—more often than Muhammad. See Youssef H. Aboul-Enein, *Militant Islamist Ideology: Understanding the Global Threat* (Annapolis, MD: Naval Institute, 2010), 20. Islam emphasizes that Jesus was a mortal human who, like all other prophets, had been divinely chosen to spread God's message. See Darrell J. Fasching and Dell deChant, *Comparative Religious Ethics: A Narrative Approach* (New York: Wiley & Sons, 2001), 241, 274–75. Unlike Christian writings, the Qur'an does not describe Jesus as the Son of God but as one of four major human messengers (out of many prophets) sent by God throughout history to guide humankind. See Annemarie Schimmel, *Mystical Dimensions of Islam* (Chapel Hill: University of North Carolina Press, 1975), 202. "And Zechariah and John and Jesus and Elias—and all were of the righteous" (Qur'an 6:85).

50. "When the apostle prayed the noon prayer on the day of the conquest he ordered that all the idols which were round the Ka'ba should be collected and burned with fire and broken up. . . . Quraysh had put pictures in the Ka'ba including two of Jesus son of Mary and Mary (on both of whom be peace!). . . . The apostle ordered that the pictures should be erased except those of Jesus and Mary." A. Guillaume, *The Life of Muhammad: A Translation of Ishaq's "Sirat Rasul Allah"* (Oxford: Oxford University Press, 1955), 552.

51. While Muslims believe Jesus was to be revered as a prophet and apostle of God, they do not believe he was more than this: "O People of the Scripture, do not commit excess in your religion or say about Allah except the truth. The Messiah, Jesus, the son of Mary, was but a messenger of Allah and His word which He directed to Mary and a soul [created at a command] from Him. So believe in Allah and His messengers. And do not say, 'Three'; desist—it is better for you. Indeed, Allah is but one God. Exalted is He above having a son. To Him belongs whatever is in the heavens and whatever is on the earth. And sufficient is Allah as Disposer of affairs" (Qur'an 4:171).

52. And [make him] a messenger to the Children of Israel, [who will say], "Indeed I have come to you with a sign from your Lord in that I design for you from clay [that which is] like the form of a bird, then I breathe into it and it becomes a bird by permission of Allah. And I cure the blind and the leper, and I give life to the dead—by permission of Allah. And I inform you of what you eat and what you store in your houses. Indeed in that is a sign for you, if you are believers. And [I have come] confirming what was before me of the Torah and to make lawful for you some of what was forbidden to you. And I have come to you with a sign from your Lord, so fear Allah and obey me. Indeed, Allah is my Lord and your Lord, so worship Him. That is the straight path." (Qur'an 3:49–51)

    For more on this, see Cyril Glassé, *The New Encyclopedia of Islam, 3rd ed.* (Lanham, MD: Rowman & Littlefield, 2008), 270–71, and John L. Esposito, ed., *The Oxford Dictionary of Islam* (Oxford: Oxford University Press, 2003), 158. Muslims also believe that Jesus received a gospel from God, called the Injil. However, Muslims hold that Jesus's original message was lost or altered and that the Christian New Testament does not accurately represent God's original message to humankind. See James C. Paget, "Quests for the Historical Jesus," in *The Cambridge Companion to Jesus*, ed. Markus Bockmuehl (Cambridge: Cambridge University Press, 2001), 83.

53. "And there is none from the People of the Scripture but that he will surely believe in Jesus before his death. And on the Day of Resurrection he will be against them a witness" (Qur'an 4:159). While Muslims acknowledge the ascension, they either deny that Jesus was crucified or that he died on the cross. Most simply believe Jesus's death was an illusion (and some even believe that Judas Iscariot was mistaken for Jesus on the cross): "And [for] their saying, 'Indeed, we have killed the Messiah, Jesus, the son of Mary, the messenger of Allah.' And they did not kill him, nor did they crucify him; but [another] was made to resemble him to them. And indeed, those who differ over it are in doubt about it. They have no knowledge of it except the following of assumption. And they did not kill him, for certain" (Qur'an 4:157).

54. While Muslims acknowledge the second coming, they maintain that Jesus will return as a Muslim ("Ummati") and as a follower of Muhammad, returning to earth to revive Islam.

55. This map was reconstructed with data from Pew Research: "Percentage of Muslims by Country, According to Pew Research Center," *Wikipedia*, June 29, 2014, https://en.wikipedia.org/wiki/Muslim_world#/media/File:Islam_percent_population_in_each_nation_World_Map_Muslim_data_by_Pew_Research.svg.

56. "As to the position of Christianity, let it be stated without any hesitation or equivocation that its divine origin is unconditionally acknowledged, that the Sonship and Divinity of Jesus Christ are fearlessly asserted, that the divine inspiration of the Gospel is fully recognized, that the reality of the mystery of the Immaculacy of the Virgin Mary is confessed." Shoghi Effendi, *The Promised Day Is Come, rev. ed.* (Wilmette, IL: Bahá'í, 1980), 109–10. "Reflect upon the state and condition of Mary. So deep was the perplexity of that most beauteous countenance, so grievous her case, that she bitterly regretted she had ever been born." Bahá'u'lláh, *The Kitáb-i-Íqán: The Book of Certitude*, trans. Shoghi Effendi Rabbani (Wilmette, IL: Bahá'í, 1970), 56–57. "The Founder of the Christian Faith is designated by Bahá'u'lláh as the 'Spirit of God,' is proclaimed as the One Who 'appeared out of the breath of the Holy Ghost,' and is even extolled as the 'Essence of the Spirit.' His mother is described as 'that veiled and immortal, that most beauteous, countenance,' and the station of her Son eulogized as a 'station which hath been exalted above the imaginings of all that dwell on earth.'" Effendi, *The Promised Day Is Come*, 109–10.

57. Bahá'u'lláh cited the star and argued that every "manifestation" of God was announced by celestial phenomena and human precursors. Refer to Bahá'u'lláh, *The Kitáb-i-Íqán: The Book of Certitude*, 64.

58. "As to the sign in the invisible heaven—the heaven of divine knowledge and understanding—it was Yahya [John], son of Zechariah, who gave unto the people the tidings of the Manifestation of Jesus." Bahá'u'lláh, *The Kitáb-i-Íqán: The Book of Certitude*, 64. Bahá'u'lláh also wrote that John the Baptist came to prepare the people for his successor. See Bahá'u'lláh, *Iqtidarat va Chand Lawh-i Digar* (Bombay, 1892), 95–96.

59. Refer to `Abdu'l-Hamid Ishraq-Khavari, ed., *Ma'idih-'i Asmani*, vol. 7 (Tehran: Bahá'í, 1980), 228–29.

60. Islamic Sufi mystics considered Jesus the perfect ascetic and also embraced several noncanonical legends that describe Jesus in this way. See James Roy King, "Jesus and Joseph in Rumi's *Mathnawi*," *The Muslim World 80*, no. 2 (April 1990): 81–95, https://doi.org/10.1111/j.1478-1913.1990.tb03487.x. Bahá'u'lláh occasionally quoted these sources in addition to the gospel accounts. Refer to Ishraq-Khavari, *Ma'idih-'i Asmani*, vol. 8 (Tehran: Bahá'í, 1971–3), 128; Javad Nurbakhsh, *Jesus in the Eyes of the Sufis*, trans. Terry Graham, Leonard Lewisohn, and Hamid Mashkuri (London: Khaniqah-i Ni`matu'llahi, 1983), 98–100; and Bahá'u'lláh, *The Kitáb-i-Íqán: The Book of Certitude*, 130–31.

61. "As to the position of Christianity, let it be stated without any hesitation or equivocation that its divine origin is unconditionally acknowledged, that the Sonship and Divinity of Jesus Christ are fearlessly asserted." Effendi, *The Promised Day Is Come*, 109–10.

62. Bahá'u'lláh believed that Jesus possessed spiritual sovereignty. Despite his references to miracle stories, Bahá'u'lláh rejected a purely literal interpretation of them in the Gospels and in the Qur'an. He was more interested in what he thought the scriptures were trying to communicate on a spiritual level, interpreting Jesus's miracles as a symbol of his spiritual impact. "We testify that when He came into the world, He shed the splendor of His glory upon all created things. Through Him the leper recovered

from the leprosy of perversity and ignorance. Through Him, the unchaste and wayward were healed. Through His power, born of Almighty God, the eyes of the blind were opened, and the soul of the sinner sanctified." Bahá'u'lláh, *Gleanings from the Writings of Bahá'u'lláh*, trans. Shoghi Effendi Rabbani (Wilmette, IL: Bahá'í, 1976), 85.

63. According to Bahá'u'lláh, this story has been cited so the reader "will comprehend the inner meaning of sovereignty and the like, spoken of in the traditions and scriptures." Bahá'u'lláh, *The Kitáb-i-Íqán: The Book of Certitude*, 133–35.

64. "Leprosy may be interpreted as any veil that interveneth between man and the recognition of the Lord, his God. Whoso alloweth himself to be shut out from Him is indeed a leper, who shall not be remembered in the Kingdom of God, the Mighty, the All-Praised. We bear witness that through the power of the Word of God every leper was cleansed, every sickness was healed, every human infirmity was banished. He it is Who purified the world. Blessed is the man who, with a face beaming with light, hath turned towards Him." Bahá'u'lláh, *Gleanings from the Writings of Bahá'u'lláh*, 86.

65. Bahá'u'lláh also quoted the apostle Paul's letter to the Romans (13:1–2): "Let every soul be subject to the higher powers." Bahá'u'lláh, *Epistle to the Son of the Wolf*, trans. Shoghi Effendi Rabbani (Wilmette, IL: Bahá'í, 1976), 89–91.

66. "The primacy of Peter, the Prince of the Apostles, is upheld and defended. . . . Peter is recognized as one whom God has caused "the mysteries of wisdom and of utterance to flow out of his mouth." Effendi, *The Promised Day Is Come*, 109–10.

67. Bahá'u'lláh quoted John 16:5–7, describing the Counselor or Comforter (Gr. *paraclete*) who would come once Jesus departed. Bahá'u'lláh, *Athar-i Qalam-i A`la*, vol. 4 (Tehra: Bahá'í, 1968), 11–12.

68. "He Who was Thy Spirit (Jesus), O my God, withdrew all alone in the darkness of the night preceding His last day on earth, and falling on His face to the ground besought Thee saying, 'If it be Thy will, O my Lord, my Well-Beloved, let this cup, through thy grace and bounty, pass from Me.' By Thy bounty, O Thou Who art the Lord of all names and the Creator of the heavens! I can smell the fragrance of the words which, in His love for Thee, His lips uttered." Bahá'u'lláh, *Prayers and Meditations*, trans. Shoghi Effendi Rabbani (Wilmette, IL: Bahá'í, 1971), 192–93.

69. "Similarly, call thou to mind the day when the Jews, who had surrounded Jesus, Son of Mary, were pressing Him to confess His claim of being the Messiah and Prophet of God, so that they might declare Him an infidel and sentence Him to death. Then, they led Him away, He Who was the Day-star of the heaven of divine Revelation, unto Pilate and Caiaphas, who was the leading divine (a`zam-i `ulama) of that age. The chief priests were all assembled in the palace, also a multitude of people who had gathered to witness His sufferings, to deride and injure Him." Bahá'u'lláh, *The Kitáb-i-Íqán: The Book of Certitude*, 132–33. Bahá'u'lláh acknowledged that Jesus responded to his accusers in the following manner: "Beholdest thou not the Son of Man sitting on the right hand of power and might?" (summarizing Mark 14:62). Bahá'u'lláh, *The Kitáb-i-Íqán: The Book of Certitude*, 133.

70. Bahá'u'lláh affirmed that God's will permitted the crucifixion. Bahá'u'lláh, *Gleanings from the Writings of Bahá'u'lláh*, 89, and Bahá'u'lláh, *Athar-i Qalam-i A`la*, 4:9. In the *Book of Certitude*, Bahá'u'lláh writes that Jesus was "persecuted and killed" (*idha' va qatl*). Bahá'u'lláh, *The Kitáb-i-Íqán*, 103. Bahá'u'lláh also stated, "Know thou that when the Son of Man yielded up His breath to God, the whole creation wept with a great

weeping. By sacrificing Himself, however, a fresh capacity was infused into all created things. Its evidences, as witnessed in all the peoples of the earth, are now manifest before thee. The deepest wisdom which the sages have uttered, the profoundest learning which any mind hath unfolded, the arts which the ablest hands have produced, the influence exerted by the most potent of rulers, are but manifestations of the quickening power released by His transcendent, His all-pervasive, and resplendent Spirit" Bahá'u'lláh, *Gleanings from the Writings of Bahá'u'lláh*, 85.

71. Bahá'u'lláh took God's command to Abraham to sacrifice his first-born, "to sacrifice him as a ransom [*fida'i*] for the sins and iniquities [`isyan va khataha*] of all the peoples of the earth." Bahá'u'lláh, *Gleanings from the Writings of Bahá'u'lláh*, 76, and Ishraq-Khavari, *Ma'idih-'i Asmani,* 7:77. Then he compared this act to Jesus: "This same honor [*maqam*], Jesus, the Son of Mary, besought the one true God . . . to confer upon Him." Bahá'u'lláh, *Gleanings from the Writings of Bahá'u'lláh*, 76, and Ishraq-Khavari, *Ma'idih-'i Asmani,* 7:77. Bahá'í rejects the idea of original sin, so the redemption offered is not based on the sin of Adam, but rather on the historical guilt of having tortured and killed the messengers of God.

72. Bahá'u'lláh took a figurative approach to interpretation and considered the idea of the kingdom of God as a present reality rather than a future idea. In his view, the "resurrection" of the "dead" involves infusing spiritual faith and life into deadened souls. Bahá'u'lláh, *The Kitáb-i-Íqán: The Book of Certitude*, 118; and Nurbakhsh, *Jesus in the Eyes of the Sufis*, 84. Consistent with his symbolic approach to Jesus's miracles, he considered resurrection narratives in Matthew and Luke to be spiritual events in the lives of the disciples rather than a physical reality. Bahá'u'lláh, *Munajat (Rio de Janeiro: Editora Bahá'í-Brasil, 1981)*, 103–5; and `Abdu'l-Bahá, *An-Nur al-Abha fi Mufawadat `Abdi'l-Bahá* (New Delhi: Bahá'í, 1983), 76–78.

73. According to Bahá'u'lláh, Jesus severs himself from this world when on the cross and "ascends" into the divine presence. `Abdu'l-Hamid Ishraq-Khavari, ed., *Ganj-i Shayigan* (Tehran: Bahá'í, 1967), 193–94. He appears to consider it symbolically: "They at last heaped on His blessed Person such woes that He took His flight unto the fourth heaven." Bahá'u'lláh, *The Kitáb-i-Íqán: The Book of Certitude*, 133.

74. See Juan Cole, "The Concept of Manifestation in the Bahá'í Writings," *The Journal of Bahá'í Studies* 9 (1982): 1–38; Peter Smith, "Progressive Revelation," *A Concise Encyclopedia of the Bahá'í Faith* (Oxford: Oneworld, 2000), 276–77; and "The Bahá'í Faith and Christianity," Bahá'ís of the United States, accessed October 1, 2020, https://www.bahai.us/christianity/.

75. "The deepest wisdom which the sages have uttered, the profoundest learning which any mind hath unfolded, the arts which the ablest hands have produced, the influence exerted by the most potent of rulers, are but manifestations of the quickening power released by His transcendent, His all-pervasive, and resplendent Spirit." Bahá'u'lláh, *Gleanings from the Writings of Bahá'u'lláh*, 85.

76. This map reconstructed from "Bahá'í Houses of Worship," Wikipedia, February 15, 2007, https://en.wikipedia.org/wiki/Bah%C3%A1%CA%BC%C3%AD_House_of_Worship#/media/File:Bahai-house-worship-locations.png.

77. For more information, refer to Hadrat Mirza Ghulam Ahmad, *Jesus in India*, trans. Qazi Abdul Hamid and Chaudhry Muhammad Ali (Qadian: Islam International Publications, 2003), https://www.alislam.org/library/books/Jesus-in-India.pdf.

78. Refer to the Ahmadi Muslim website for this section: "Jesus, a Humble Prophet of God," Al Islam, accessed October 6, 2020, https://www.alislam.org/jesus/.

79. "It is not unreasonable to conclude, that the Biblical usage of the term 'Son of God' does not necessarily connote a literal 'sonship to God' but a metaphorical one instead." "Jesus, a Humble Prophet of God," Al Islam accessed October 6, 2020, https://www.alislam.org/jesus/.

80. Mirza Ghulam Ahmad wrote that Jesus lost consciousness on the cross and only appeared dead; he described this condition in a manner similar to Jonah's condition in the belly of the fish. According to Ahmad, Jesus was removed from the cross and his injuries were treated with *Marham-e-Issa* ("Ointment of Jesus"). He appeared to his disciples, then traveled to Afghanistan and Kashmir, where he continued to teach, preach, and heal the sick. He eventually died at the age of 120 in India and was supposedly buried in Srinaga. "Jesus, a Humble Prophet of God," Al Islam, accessed October 6, 2020, https://www.alislam.org/jesus/.

81. This map was reconstructed with data from Pew Research: "World Ahmadi Muslim Population," Wikipedia, September 26, 2016, https://en.wikipedia.org/wiki/Ahmadiyya_by_country#/media/File:Ahmadiyya_population_map.svg.

82. Wouter Hanegraaff, *New Age Religion and Western Culture: Esotericism in the Mirror of Secular Thought* (Leiden: Brill, 1996), 189–90.

83. J. Gordon Melton, "New Thought and the New Age," in *Perspectives on the New Age*, eds. James R. Lewis and J. Gordon Melton (Albany, NY: State University of New York Press, 1992), 22; Chopra: "I want to offer the possibility that Jesus was truly, as he proclaimed, a savior . . . Not the savior, not the one and only Son of God. Rather Jesus embodied the highest level of enlightenment. He spent his brief adult life describing it, teaching it, and passing it on to future generations. . . . Jesus intended to save the world by showing others the path to God-consciousness." Deepak Chopra in Michelle Nichols, "Who Is Jesus? He's Three People, says Deepak Chopra," *Reuters*, February 21, 2008, https://www.reuters.com/article/us-religion-chopra/who-is-jesus-hes-three-people-says-deepak-chopra-idUSN1918295720080221.

84. They typically highlight those areas of Jesus's teaching that align with the principles of Eastern mysticism, and they often distort the words of Jesus to accomplish this. They also typically ignore Jesus's teaching about his own identity. Many revere Jesus's moral teaching, and some argue that the ethics of Jesus are not those of the Christians who follow him.

85. This, even though they reject the idea that salvation can be found through Jesus. See Fritz Ridenour, *So What's the Difference? A Look at 20 Worldviews, Faiths, and Religions and How They Compare to Christianity* (Ventura, CA: Gospel Light, 2001), 151.

86. Chopra in Nichols, "Who Is Jesus? He's Three People, says Deepak Chopra."

87. To review a summary of what we can learn about Jesus from the scriptures and statements of competing religious systems, refer to our comprehensive Case Note PDF file, downloadable here: https://coldcasechristianity.com/case-notes-for-person-of-interest/.

88. In this chapter, I purposely omitted several unorthodox, pseudo-Christian movements, including Mormonism, Christian Science, Jehovah's Witnesses, The Way International, and the Unification Church. These historically late corruptions of Christianity include the New Testament in their sacred texts, so the entire story of Jesus can easily be reconstructed (although each religion makes its own theological conclusions). If every

New Testament manuscript were destroyed, these religions would lose their scripture, just like Christianity. For this reason, I focused on non-Christian religions that use something other than the New Testament as their holy text.

89. For larger, more readable images, please visit https://coldcasechristianity.com/selected-images-from-person-of-interest/.

90. "Religious Composition by Country, 2010–2050," Pew Research Center, April 2, 2015, https://www.pewforum.org/2015/04/02/religious-projection-table/2020/number/all.

Postscript: The Unlikeliest of Suspects

1. Judicial Council of California, *Judicial Council of California Criminal Jury Instructions* (New York: Matthew Bender, 2021), CALCRIM No. 103, https://www.courts.ca.gov/partners/documents/calcrim-2021.pdf.

2. This section was inspired by a sermon called "Arise Sir Knight!" by Dr. James Allan Francis from *The Real Jesus and Other Sermons* (Philadelphia: Judson, 1926), 123–24. The text of the original sermon is available online: "One Solitary Life," Anointed Christian Links, accessed April 9, 2021, http://www.anointedlinks.com/one_solitary_life_original.html.

3. For more information about the reliability of the New Testament gospels, please read J. Warner Wallace, *Cold-Case Christianity: A Homicide Detective Investigates the Claims of the Gospels* (Colorado Springs: Cook Publishers, 2013).

4. Here are a few more examples:

> Therefore, this is what the Lord, the LORD Almighty, says:
>
>> "My people who live in Zion,
>>> do not be afraid of the Assyrians,
>> who beat you with a rod
>>> and lift up a club against you, as Egypt did." (Isaiah 10:24)

> This is what the Sovereign LORD says: This is Jerusalem, which I have set in the center of the nations, with countries all around her. (Ezekiel 5:5)

> This is what the LORD says:
>
>> "For three sins of Israel,
>>> even for four, I will not relent.
>> They sell the innocent for silver,
>>> and the needy for a pair of sandals." (Amos 2:6)

> This is what the Sovereign LORD says about Edom—
>
>> We have heard a message from the LORD:
>>> An envoy was sent to the nations to say,
>> "Rise, let us go against her for battle." (Obadiah 1:1)

> This is what the LORD says:
>
>> "As for the prophets
>>> who lead my people astray,

> they proclaim 'peace'
> > if they have something to eat,
> but prepare to wage war against anyone
> > who refuses to feed them." (Micah 3:5)

This is what the LORD says:

> "Although they have allies and are numerous,
> > they will be destroyed and pass away.
> Although I have afflicted you, Judah,
> > I will afflict you no more." (Nahum 1:12)

This is what the LORD Almighty says: "These people say, 'The time has not yet come to rebuild the LORD's house.'" (Haggai 1:2)

This is what the LORD says: "I will return to Jerusalem with mercy, and there my house will be rebuilt. And the measuring line will be stretched out over Jerusalem." (Zechariah 1:16)

5. Additional examples:

Truly I tell you, until heaven and earth disappear, not the smallest letter, not the least stroke of a pen, will by any means disappear from the Law until everything is accomplished. (Matthew 5:18)

Truly I tell you, among those born of women there has not risen anyone greater than John the Baptist; yet whoever is least in the kingdom of heaven is greater than he. (Matthew 11:11)

Truly I tell you, if anyone says to this mountain, "Go, throw yourself into the sea," and does not doubt in their heart but believes that what they say will happen, it will be done for them. (Mark 11:23)

Truly I tell you, wherever the gospel is preached throughout the world, what she has done will also be told, in memory of her. (Mark 14:9)

Very truly I tell you, a time is coming and has now come when the dead will hear the voice of the Son of God and those who hear will live. (John 5:25)

Very truly I tell you Pharisees, anyone who does not enter the sheep pen by the gate, but climbs in by some other way, is a thief and a robber. (John 10:1)

6. Later, when addressing Pontius Pilate's questions about Jesus's position as the "King of the Jews," Jesus said,

"My kingdom is not of this world. If it were, my servants would fight to prevent my arrest by the Jewish leaders. But now my kingdom is from another place."

"You are a king, then!" said Pilate.

Jesus answered, "You say that I am a king. In fact, the reason I was born and came into the world is to testify to the truth. Everyone on the side of truth listens to me." (John 18:36–37)

Jesus repeatedly told his listeners that he was not of human origin and that he and God the Father came from the same spiritual kingdom.

7. In other places in the Gospels, the "angels of God" and the "kingdom of God" were described as belonging to God the Father, not Jesus:

> I tell you, whoever publicly acknowledges me before others, the Son of Man will also acknowledge before the angels of God. But whoever disowns me before others will be disowned before the angels of God. (Luke 12:8–9)

To claim that God's angels are, in fact, *his* angels (as in Matthew 13:41) would be highly inappropriate unless Jesus and God are one in the same. Jesus also made several comments about his relationship with God the Father that would be difficult to understand if Jesus did not consider himself equal in essence with God:

> Jesus answered, "I am the way and the truth and the life. No one comes to the Father except through me. If you really know me, you will know my Father as well. From now on, you do know him and have seen him."
>
> Philip said, "Lord, show us the Father and that will be enough for us."
>
> Jesus answered: "Don't you know me, Philip, even after I have been among you such a long time? Anyone who has seen me has seen the Father." (John 14:6–9)

> Anyone who loves me will obey my teaching. My Father will love them, and we will come to them and make our home with them. (John 14:23)

These statements make sense if we hear them in the way Jesus intended them to be heard. He appeared to be saying he and the Father are one. Other statements confirm this as well.

8. Speaking again to nonbelievers, Jesus made the argument that his miracles alone should have been enough to demonstrate his deity. These miracles were proof that he was, in fact, God:

> Jesus answered, "I did tell you, but you do not believe. The works I do in my Father's name testify about me, but you do not believe because you are not my sheep. My sheep listen to my voice; I know them, and they follow me. I give them eternal life, and they shall never perish; no one will snatch them out of my hand. My Father, who has given them to me, is greater than all; no one can snatch them out of my Father's hand. I and the Father are one." (John 10:25–30)

The Jewish leaders knew what Jesus said here; they knew Jesus claimed equality with God. That's why they sought to stone him for blasphemy:

> His Jewish opponents picked up stones to stone him, but Jesus said to them, "I have shown you many good works from the Father. For which of these do you stone me?"
>
> "We are not stoning you for any good work," they replied, "but for blasphemy, because you, a mere man, claim to be God." (John 10:31–33)

9. When God first appeared to Moses in the burning bush, Moses was adept enough to ask God for his name. And God gave Moses an interesting reply:

God said to Moses, "I AM WHO I AM. This is what you are to say to the Israelites: 'I AM has sent me to you.'" (Exodus 3:14)

For generations after this interaction between God and Moses, the Israelites revered the name of God ("I AM") as a precious title that was not to be slandered or given to anyone or anything other than God himself. Then along came Jesus. The gospel of John tells us that on a day when the Pharisees were questioning Jesus's power, authority, and teaching, they accused him of being demon possessed. Look at how he responded:

"I am not possessed by a demon," said Jesus, "but I honor my Father and you dishonor me. I am not seeking glory for myself; but there is one who seeks it, and he is the judge. Very truly I tell you, whoever obeys my word will never see death."

At this they exclaimed, "Now we know that you are demon-possessed! Abraham died and so did the prophets, yet you say that whoever obeys your word will never taste death. Are you greater than our father Abraham? He died, and so did the prophets. Who do you think you are?"

Jesus replied, "If I glorify myself, my glory means nothing. My Father, whom you claim as your God, is the one who glorifies me. Though you do not know him, I know him. If I said I did not, I would be a liar like you, but I do know him and obey his word. Your father Abraham rejoiced at the thought of seeing my day; he saw it and was glad."

"You are not yet fifty years old," they said to him, "and you have seen Abraham!"

"Very truly I tell you," Jesus answered, "before Abraham was born, I am!" (John 8:49–58)

Jesus made two remarkable statements. First, he claimed to be eternal and to have existed before Abraham! But more importantly, Jesus called himself by the ancient title ascribed only to God himself, "I AM." The Pharisees knew exactly what Jesus meant by this. From their perspective, Jesus said specifically, "I am God." How do we know this was their interpretation of his words? We know it from their reaction. They responded by attempting to stone Jesus for claiming to be God (an act of blasphemy they considered worthy of death): "At this, they picked up stones to stone him, but Jesus hid himself, slipping away from the temple grounds" (John 8:59).

When Jesus took on God's holy title as his own, he was stating the modern equivalent of "I am God." He did this repeatedly over the course of his ministry (see Mark 14:62; John 18:5–6; John 8:24; and John 8:28).

10. Jesus's disciples were raised in a first-century Jewish culture and faith system, so they understood the universally accepted notion that God alone is worthy of our worship. This concept was central to the Ten Commandments (see Exodus 20:3–6) and was repeatedly taught throughout the Jewish scripture (see Deuteronomy 4:35; 6:4; 6:13–16; 32:39; 2 Samuel 7:22; and Isaiah 8:13; 43:10–11). The Old Testament was clear about this truth; Yahweh was the only God the Jews were to love, fear, worship, and revere. The authors of the New Testament often repeated this message. Jesus frequently quoted the Jewish scriptures, proclaiming the existence of one God we are to serve and worship (see Matthew 4:10). The New Testament provides us with a number of

examples of people trying to worship something or someone other than God, and then being instructed to worship God alone (take a look at Revelation 22:8–9; Acts 10:25–26 and 14:11–15). The disciples, like other first-century Jewish believers, understood that God alone was to be worshiped. To worship something or someone other than God was to be an idolater, and this violated the first commandment of God.

11. Matthew 2:10–12; 8:2; 9:18–19; 14:32–33; 20:20–21; 28:8–10 and John 9:35–38. From his first days on earth to his last, Jesus was worshiped as God. Those who were in a position to see his power, hear his teaching, and witness his resurrection were convinced by what they saw. Jesus claimed to be God and then demonstrated the power and authority that belong to God alone. The disciples responded in worship, even though their Jewish upbringing taught them the danger of worshiping anything or anyone other than God. The disciples worshiped Jesus without fear because they knew they were not breaking the commands of God. They knew they were still worshiping the only true God.

12. The writers of Scripture described Jesus as more than simply our Savior. According to the Bible, Jesus is also our creator:

> Through him all things were made; without him nothing was made that has been made. (John 1:3)

> In him all things were created: things in heaven and on earth, visible and invisible, whether thrones or powers or rulers or authorities; all things have been created through him and for him. (Colossians 1:16)

Jesus also repeatedly demonstrated his divine authority to forgive sin:

> Jesus stepped into a boat, crossed over and came to his own town. Some men brought to him a paralyzed man, lying on a mat. When Jesus saw their faith, he said to the man, "Take heart, son; your sins are forgiven."
>
> At this, some of the teachers of the law said to themselves, "This fellow is blaspheming!"
>
> Knowing their thoughts, Jesus said, "Why do you entertain evil thoughts in your hearts? Which is easier: to say, 'Your sins are forgiven,' or to say, 'Get up and walk'? But I want you to know that the Son of Man has authority on earth to forgive sins." So he said to the paralyzed man, "Get up, take your mat and go home." Then the man got up and went home. When the crowd saw this, they were filled with awe. (Matthew 9:1–8)

As the creator of life, Jesus also demonstrated the ability to give of eternal life:

> I give them eternal life, and they shall never perish; no one will snatch them out of my hand. (John 10:28)

> I am the resurrection and the life. The one who believes in me will live, even though they die; and whoever lives by believing in me will never die. (John 11:25–26)

As the author of our lives, Jesus proclaimed the right to evaluate how we have lived as his creation:

> When the Son of Man comes in his glory, and all the angels with him, he will sit on his glorious throne. All the nations will be gathered before him, and he will separate the people one from another as a shepherd separates the sheep from the goats. He will put the sheep on his right and the goats on his left. (Matthew 25:31–33)

13. For more information about the evidence for Jesus's resurrection, read Wallace, *Cold-Case Christianity*, and also J. Warner Wallace, "A Brief Review of Explanations Offered for the Resurrection," Cold-Case Christianity, May 4, 2018, https://coldcasechristianity.com/writings/a-brief-review-of-explanations-offered-for-the-resurrection-free-bible-insert/.

14. Romans 6:23 says, "For the wages of sin is death, but the gift of God is eternal life in Christ Jesus our Lord."

15. 2 Corinthians 5:21: "God made him who had no sin to be sin for us, so that in him we might become the righteousness of God."

16. Here are a few promises for those of us who are willing to trust Jesus:

> If you declare with your mouth, "Jesus is Lord," and believe in your heart that God raised him from the dead, you will be saved. (Romans 10:9)

> For God so loved the world that he gave his one and only Son, that whoever believes in him shall not perish but have eternal life. For God did not send his Son into the world to condemn the world, but to save the world through him. Whoever believes in him is not condemned, but whoever does not believe stands condemned already because they have not believed in the name of God's one and only Son. (John 3:16–18)

> Very truly I tell you, whoever hears my word and believes him who sent me has eternal life and will not be judged but has crossed over from death to life. (John 5:24)

17. If God is all-powerful, do humans really have the ability to decide and embrace claims supported by the evidence? I address this apparent tension between God's sovereignty and human freedom in *Forensic Faith: A Homicide Detective Makes the Case for a More Reasonable, Evidential Christian Faith* (Colorado Springs: Cook, 2017), and in this brief article: "Why Make the Case for Christianity, If God Is in Control?," Cold-Case Christianity, July 31, 2017, https://coldcasechristianity.com/writings/why-make-the-case-for-christianity-if-god-is-in-control/.

Person of Interest Video Study

Why Jesus Still Matters in a World that Rejects the Bible

13 Sessions on 2 DVDs

J. Warner Wallace

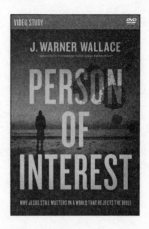

Imagine investigating a murder in which there was no crime scene, no physical evidence, and no victim's body. How would you identify a person of interest in such a case?

Dateline-featured cold-case detective and bestselling author J. Warner Wallace has investigated a number of these no-body homicide cases and has successfully identified and convicted the killers, even without the victim's body or evidence from the crime scene.

Can the historicity of Jesus be investigated in the same way? Can the truth about Jesus be uncovered even without a body or a crime scene? In *Person of Interest*, Wallace describes his own personal investigative journey from atheism to Christianity, as he employs a unique investigative strategy to confirm the historicity and deity of Jesus—*without relying on the New Testament manuscripts.*

Person of Interest Video Study will:

- Invite viewers into the life of a cold-case detective as he uncovers the truth about Jesus using the same approach he also employs to solve a real murder case
- Teach viewers how to become good detectives, using an innovative and unique "fuse and fallout" investigative strategy they can also use to examine other claims of history
- Help viewers explore common objections to Christianity

Concrete and compelling in its approach, *Person of Interest Video Study* will strengthen the faith of believers and engage those curious about Jesus with evidence for his one-of-a-kind, world-altering significance.

Available in stores and online!